Generation '68:
The Elite Revolution and Its Legacy

Kerry R. Bolton

GENERATION '68

The Elite Revolution and Its Legacy

ANTELOPE HILL PUBLISHING

Cover art by Swifty.
Edited by Harlan Wallace and Christopher Jolliffe.
Layout by Margaret Bauer.

Antelope Hill Publishing | antelopehillpublishing.com

Paperback ISBN-13: 979-8-89252-001-0
EPUB ISBN-13: 979-8-89252-002-7

CONTENTS

INTRODUCTION

Not only do the new social movements have nothing in common; their only coherent demand aims at inclusion in the dominant structures rather than at a revolutionary transformation of social relations.

– Christopher Lasch

Capitalism is the great equalizer, leveler, and obliterator of all those organic distinctions, cultivated over millennia, that have traditionally defined what it is to be human beyond the basest level of existence. Today, and indeed for generations within the Western epoch of decay,[1] the dominant conception of life is that it is determined by the forces of social production.

Martin Heidegger, a rightist whom the New Left nevertheless attempted to appropriate, saw this epoch as "the darkening of the world," "the disempowering of the spirit," the "flight of the gods, the destruction of the earth," and "the presence of the mediocre," a literal "demonism . . . in the sense of the destructively evil."[2]

When ideologues of the New Left started talking about "authenticity," they did so by adopting Heideggerian terminology stripped of its essence. The left *at root* is in revolt against authenticity, a feature

---

[1] For more, see my previous book, *Decline and Fall of Civilisations*.
[2] Heidegger, *Introduction to Metaphysics*, 47.

1

it shares with its supposed antithesis, capitalism. Before the shallow intelligentsia of the left scoff, consider that one of the most eminent minds on the left, Christopher Lasch, came to the same conclusion. In the wake of the New Left, with anarchy reigning in the streets and on the quads, Lasch perceptively noted that the deconstruction of traditional society was a product of the "revolt of the elites":

> When Ortega y Gasset published *The Revolt of the Masses* in 1930, he could not have foreseen a time when it would be more appropriate to speak of a revolt of the elites. Writing in the era of the Bolshevik revolution and the rise of fascism, in the aftermath of a cataclysmic war that had torn Europe apart, Ortega attributed the crisis of Western culture to the "political domination of the masses." In our time, however, the chief threat seems to come not from the masses but from those at the top of the social hierarchy, the elites who control the international flow of money and information, preside over philanthropic foundations and institutions of higher learning, manage the instruments of cultural production, and thus set the terms of public debate. Members of the elite have lost faith in the values, or what remains of them, of the West. For many people, the very term "Western civilization" now calls to mind an organized system of domination designed to enforce conformity to bourgeois values and to keep the victims of patriarchal oppression—women, children, homosexuals, people of color—in a permanent state of subjection. In a remarkable turn of events that confounds our expectations about the course of history, something that Ortega never dreamed of has occurred—the revolt of the elites.[3]

Lasch realized the bogus character of the "new social movements," accurately diagnosing the New Left as something inextricably bound *to* elite consensus—by no means was the counterculture the product of any grassroots, "mass" movement.

> Not only do the new social movements—feminism, gay rights, welfare rights, agitation against racial discrimination—have nothing in common; their only coherent demand aims at *inclusion in the*

---

[3] Lasch, "Revolt of the Elites."

dominant structures rather than at a revolutionary transformation of social relations.[4]

"Inclusion" is the key word to understand the nexus between the elites and the left, for the first demands an "inclusive economy," the second an "inclusive society," and both arrive at the same destination. Lasch concludes:

> The revolt of the masses that Ortega feared is no longer a plausible threat. But the revolt of the elites against time-honored traditions of locality, obligation, and restraint may yet unleash a war of all against all.[5]

These "time-honored traditions" against which the oligarchs and their managerial elite rebel are the "primary ties" disdained as intrinsically "fascist" by all the major ideologues of the New Left, from Fromm to Marcuse.

Heidegger foresaw the destruction of authenticity as the inevitable result of technocracy, a key ideological tenet among the elite in both the liberal-democratic Anglosphere and the communistic Eastern Bloc. This "demonism," this attack on the human spirit, was a feature of utilitarian productivism in both the US and the USSR.[6] Between capitalism and Marxism there is only disagreement over who controls the forces of production, a disagreement over whether the reigns of global industry are held by the bourgeoisie or the proletariat. As the historian and philosopher Oswald Spengler observed a century ago: "There is no proletarian, not even a Communist, movement that has not operated in the interests of money."[7] Spengler observed that "the concepts of Liberalism and Socialism are set in effective motion only by money."[8] Heidegger foresaw globalization, with capitalism and communism representing "the same hopeless

---

4 Ibid., 40. Emphasis added.
5 Ibid., 49.
6 Heidegger, *Introduction to Metaphysics*, 40.
7 Spengler, *Decline of the West*, vol. 2, 402.
8 Ibid.

frenzy of unchained technology and of the rootless organization of the average man."[9]

Spengler also observed that, over the course of centuries, oligarchs often used social revolts to pursue their agendas in the name of "the people." His earliest example of this is the Gracchi revolt in Rome (133 BC):

> It was the *Equites*, the big-money party, which made Tiberius Gracchus's popular movement possible at all: and as soon as that part of the reforms that was advantageous to themselves had been successfully legalized, they withdrew, and the movement collapsed.[10]

Gracchus took power through the manipulation of the *plebeian* vote.

Oliver Cromwell, whose grandfather and great-grandfather had profited by the confiscation of church lands under Henry VIII, had married Elizabeth, daughter of the City merchant Sir James Bourchier. During the Puritan Revolution, King Charles I and the Cavaliers were obliged to beg and borrow, while the revolutionists received funding from "The City," the famous financial sector of London. The financiers were described as "the most disloyal City of London":

> During the English Civil War 1641–46 both sides were surprised that the King was able to maintain an army in the field against Parliament. King Charles was "robbed of his revenues, arms, ships and magazines, and above all of the love of his people," while Parliament was "supplied not only with the money, plate and other contributions of the most disloyal City of London, and the rest of their faction throughout the Kingdom; with the money raised for suppressing the rebellion in Ireland, the twentieth part of all men's estates, the excise on all commodities, and lastly with the sequestration of the estates and plundering of all in their power."[11]

The following century, in France, financial speculators profited from the confiscation of the lands of the Church and nobility by the

---

[9] Heidegger, *Introduction to Metaphysics*, 40.
[10] Spengler, *Decline of the West*, vol. 2, 402.
[11] Engburg, "Royalist Finances."

French Revolution, a revolution carried out "in the name of the people," as Edmund Burke observed:

> The confiscators have indeed made some allowance to their victims from the scraps and fragments of their own tables from which they have been so harshly driven, tables that have been so bountifully spread for a feast to the greedy predators of usury.[12]

The French revolutionists were settling debts to financiers by selling the confiscated land to speculators. Edmund Burke regarded the sanctity of private property as above the claims of speculative finance. He observed the alliance between speculative capital and revolution in France:

> These professors of the rights of men are so busy teaching others that they have no spare time in which to learn anything themselves; otherwise they would have known that the first and original faith of civil society is pledged to the property of the citizen, and not to the demands of the creditor of the state. The claim of the citizen is prior in time, paramount in title, superior in equity. The fortunes of individuals, whether possessed by acquisition or by descent or in virtue of a participation in the goods of some community, were not—explicitly or implicitly—any part of the creditor's security.[13]

Burke identified the actual dichotomy behind the social revolts: it is that of "old nobility versus new money." The "oppressed" become cannon fodder for the rising class. Burke continued:

> Through the vast debt of France a great moneyed interest had gradually grown up, and with it a great power. . . .
> In this state of real (though not always perceived) warfare between the noble ancient landed interest and the new moneyed interest, the latter was stronger because its power . . . was easier to deploy. The moneyed interest is in its nature more ready for any adventure, and its possessors are more disposed to new enterprises of any kind. Being of recent acquisition, it goes along more

---

[12] Burke, *Reflections on the Revolution*, 59.
[13] Ibid., 60.

naturally with any novelties. So it is the kind of wealth that will be resorted to by all who wish for change.[14]

This demand for "change" and "novelty" against tradition is the calling card of the moneyed interests that subsidize the left, now as ever.

One hundred and thirty years after Burke, Spengler would describe this same alliance as a pact between money and revolution against tradition—what Spengler called the "conflict between money and blood"—explaining:

> The *private* powers of the economy want free paths for their acquisition of great resources. No legislation must stand in their way. They want to make the laws for themselves, and their interests, and to that end they make use of the tool they have made for themselves, democracy, the subsidized party.[15]

In France, the bourgeois revolutionists aligned with the moneyed interests against the crown and the Church, as they had done in England under Cromwell. Burke continues:

> Along with the moneyed interest, a new description of men had grown up with whom the moneyed interest soon formed a close and marked union—I mean the political men of letters.[16]

Burke described a situation that closely resembles what is taking place now, as the influence of "men of letters" in the media gradually increased, in concert with money:

> And as controversial zeal soon turns its thoughts on force, they began to insinuate themselves into a correspondence with foreign princes, hoping that through their authority, which at first they flattered, they might bring about the changes they had in view. They didn't care whether these changes were to be accomplished by the thunderbolt of despotism or the earthquake of popular commotion. For that same purpose they conspicuously cultivated the

---

[14] Ibid., 61.
[15] Spengler, *Decline of The West*, vol. 2, 506.
[16] Burke, *Reflections on the Revolution*, 62.

moneyed interest of France; and partly through the means provided by those whose offices gave them the most extensive and certain means of communication, they carefully occupied all the avenues to opinion.

Writers, especially when they act in a body and with one direction, have great influence on the public mind; so the alliance of these writers with the moneyed interest had a big effect in removing the popular odium and envy evoked by that sort of wealth. These writers, like the propagators of all novelties, claimed to have a great zeal for the poor and the lower orders, while in their satires they used every exaggeration to make horrible the faults of courts, of nobility, and of priesthood. They became sort of demagogues. They served as a link to unite obnoxious wealth with restless and desperate poverty, all in the service of one objective.[17]

Why do we see the financial oligarchy assume such alliances with revolutionists to depose "old wealth"? The answer is that "old wealth," represented by Throne, *Aristos*, and Altar, stands between speculative capital and the masses, while new money's loyal "men of letters," whether in press or academia, divert attention away from the real exploiters. Spengler stated that "law needs, in order to resist this onslaught, a high tradition and an ambition of strong families that finds its satisfaction not in the heaping up of riches, but in the task of true rulership, above and beyond all money-advantage."[18]

It was the annihilation of "high tradition" and the vestiges of nobility that was undertaken in France. The "hatred of the owner has long enlisted itself in the service of the bourse,"[19] explained Spengler, in describing the role of the left. Entrepreneurs who have a direct relationship with their property are attacked by the revolutionists as "capitalist exploiters," while the faceless oligarchs of financial capital are left undisturbed. The business owner is dispossessed, even butchered, while the international bankers provide subsidies even for

---

[17] Ibid., 62–3.
[18] Spengler, *Decline of The West*, vol. 2, 506.
[19] See Bolton, *Decline and Fall of Civilisations*.

Bolshevism, and the most revolutionary of states continued to borrow from international finance.[20]

In 1905 Jacob Schiff of Kuhn, Loeb & Co., a Wall Street investment bank, funded the establishment of revolutionary cadres among Russian POWs from the Russo-Japanese War, which culminated in the 1917 revolutions, also funded by Schiff, along with other businessmen and financiers, in the name of "Russian freedom."[21]

Today the same process is undertaken in the name of "human rights," whether in the form of a color revolution that "spontaneously" overthrows a "rogue state" that refuses to submit to the "international community," or by NATO, US, or UN military action.[22] The Afrikaners were dispossessed in the name of "humans rights" because their own system of self-preservation was an obstacle to the vision of Harry Oppenheimer and other oligarchs[23] of what is now called among the global corporations an "inclusive economy."[24]

Of particular significance has been manipulation of what is often called "youthful idealism," which might less charitably be called infantilism in a prolonged Oedipal tantrum against the state as substitute parents.[25] This generation, whose "youthful radicalism" culminated in the worldwide outbreak of riots in 1968, has been the curtain-raiser for the color revolutions that have continued to reshape the political, moral, cultural, and social premises of Western civilization—and eventually the entire world—in the name of "globalization." The generation of 1968, although failing to unseat a single government, ushered in fundamental changes that go deeper than politics, having a lasting impact even on those who would consider

---

[20] For example, in 1922 the USSR formed Ruskombank to secure loans for foreign trade, with Olof Aschberg of the Nye Banken, Sweden, as head. The chief deputy in charge of foreign transactions was Max May, formerly with the Guaranty Trust Company, Wall Street (J.P. Morgan). See McMeekin, *History's Greatest Heist*, 224.
[21] This funding is documented definitively in Spence, *Wall Street and the Russian Revolution.*
[22] Bolton, *Tyranny of Human Rights*, 1–2.
[23] For the forces at work behind the anti-apartheid rhetoric, see Oppenheimer, "Portrait of a Millionaire," 7–16.
[24] Bolton, *Tyranny of Human Rights*, 186–9.
[25] The Oedipal aspect of New Left revolt, particularly among Jewish youths, is examined by Stanley Rothman and S. Robert Lichter in *Roots of Radicalism: Jews, Christians and the New Left.*

themselves "conservative." This generation's ethos has become the "new normality," making great gains in the name of "progress" for attitudes and behaviors that were hitherto seen as aberrant.[26]

The '68ers were mobilized to change societies according to the requirements of the establishment, against which these alleged radicals imagined they were revolting. As for their "revolt," nothing could be further from actuality: they were the useful idiots of the system that they decried. Their purpose was dialectical: their aims were so nihilistic that the establishment was able to push its left-wing agenda in the name of "reform," "progress" and "modernization," which seemed moderate, even conservative, by comparison.

The same strategies proceed today. The outer enemy of globalization remains the same: Russia. Color revolutions that shattered the Soviet bloc and detached Russia from her allies were, like the New Left of the West, youth-based, and these movements, like their Western counterparts, appealed vaguely to "freedom." What this "freedom" amounts to is the freedom of *plutocracy* to establish a new world order on the ruins of all authentic, organic attachments—family, faith, *ethnos*, and homeland—the "primary ties" that left-wing Critical Theorists claim oppress the individual. These Critical Theorists, sponsored by the Rockefeller Foundation and entrenched in US academia, synthesized Marxism with psychoanalysis, providing an ideological framework for the New Left. The doctrine remains the same, but now social media is used to mobilize youth at an instant, in uprisings that appear to be popular and spontaneous, but which follow tactics formulated within globalist think tanks like the National Endowment for Democracy and the Open Society Foundation.

As with today's color revolutions, the pseudo-revolt of the '68ers, arising during the Cold War, served geopolitical purposes. Far from being part of a "communist conspiracy" orchestrated by Moscow, as many conservatives alleged, the New Left emerged from the CIA's sponsorship of the National Student Association and the American delegations to the World Youth Festivals. Like the Congress for Cultural Freedom, which promoted anti-Sovietism and American liberalism among the intelligentsia, recruiting leftists who had a

---

[26] See Bolton, *Perversion of Normality*.

grievance against the USSR, the New Left served as a CIA tactic to attract youth away from the USSR and toward the "freedom" offered by American liberalism, interpreted by academics like the sexologist Alfred Kinsey, and Critical Theorists such as Erich Fromm, Theodor Adorno, and Herbert Marcuse.

Perhaps the "idealism" of this generation was most cogently— albeit fatuously—expressed in the lyrics of John Lennon's "Imagine," a song that contains all the platitudes of the time. Tom Wolfe called the co-producer of the song, Phil Spector, "the first tycoon of teen"— a title indicative of the interests that profited from the "youth rebellion."[27]

Generation Identity: A Genuine Revolt

Now that the pseudo-radicalism of yesteryear is the new normal, a genuine youth revolt has arisen to question the status quo of global consumerism and the inane character of "freedom" given to us by liberalism under American auspices and, where necessary, enforced with NATO bombs. This new generation, in contrast to the '68ers, does not receive funding from oligarchic foundations, is not acclaimed by mass media scriptwriters, and does not get its books issued by major publishers and reviewed in *The New York Times*. To the contrary, such genuine dissidents must establish their own publishing houses on the fringe. They are never portrayed by the media as anything other than pariahs. They are deplatformed by Amazon, Google, Facebook, Twitter, YouTube, and PayPal; their academic mentors, unlike Herbert Marcuse, are—at best—given "early retirement,"[28] and those heirs to the '68ers are too mentally stupefied to ask why this is so. Why is it that leftists are accorded such different treatment than the dissident right, if it is the left who are the genuine "radicals"?

The subversion of the West that the '68ers have wrought has resulted in a reaction from a new generation, *Generation Identity*; a "revolt against the modern world," to paraphrase Julius Evola. Among

---

[27] Wolfe, "Phil Spector."
[28] Bolton, *Tyranny of Human Rights*, 365–81.

the leaders of Generation Identity, Joakim Andresen issued a declaration of war against the pseudo-values of the '68ers, who enslaved us to the marketplace and called this "freedom."[29]

The befuddled youth of the left today regurgitate the same slogans of their counterculture forebears and congratulate themselves on their philosophical depth and revolutionary commitment. They are, like the pseudo-rebels before them, stupefied by their egos in a soma-like delusion, indoctrinated and mentally numbed by the entertainment industry, prattling allegedly radical slogans that emanate from the boardrooms of the managerial elite.

For example, what is one to make of the fact that Movements.org, an organization whose mission is to coordinate young "activists" through social media, was founded in 2008 by the CEOs of Google and Howcast Media, in conjunction with the US State Department and USAID? Part of its network was supposedly non-conformist media such as *The Huffington Post*. The original name was the Alliance of Youth Movements. Again, the focus is on the manipulation of youth for supposedly idealistic purposes. As the '68ers showed, gullibility and self-deception are difficult to shift. If the knee-jerk reaction is to dismiss as a "conspiracy theory" the contention that the New Left was manipulated by the establishment, the fact of Movements.org's provenance stands as a present-day example of how this strategy continues to operate. Such is the paradigm shift toward the left, that what was once part of a covert deep-state strategy is now able to operate openly in what might now be called, to borrow a term from H. G. Wells, an "open conspiracy."[30] The manipulation of the "youth revolt" played a primary role in what has brought us to the modern predicament.

---

[29] See Andersen, *Rising from the Ruins*.
[30] See Wells, *The Open Conspiracy*.

I

BUILDING THE LIBERAL INTERNATIONAL ORDER

The character of the Open Conspiracy will now be plainly displayed. It will have become a great world movement as wide-spread and evident as socialism or communism. It will have taken the place of these movements very largely. It will be more than they were, it will be frankly a world religion. This large, loose assimilatory mass of movements, groups, and societies will be definitely and obviously attempting to swallow up the entire population of the world and become the new human community.

– H. G. Wells, *The Open Conspiracy*, XV

Our "inclusive economy" does not have room for authentic, organic diversity, but requires the individual to be constantly reinvented, made "fluid," according to the needs of the market. "Identity" becomes an economic unit, something packaged and sold to *homo economicus*, whose fluidity assures an expanding market. We see this alliance between manufactured identity and the rulers of the world quite clearly in the following excerpt, from the Rockefeller Foundation:

> June marked LGBT Pride Month, and a key question emerged for the Diversity & Inclusion Ambassador Group here at The Rockefeller Foundation as we reflected on LGBT issues *alongside our goal of advancing inclusive economies*: Has the recent increase in attention

to LGBT issues both within the U.S. and lower-income countries catalyzed greater investment in addressing the barriers that LGBT people face in developing secure livelihoods?[31]

Jennifer Bilek, the outspoken feminist and environmentalist who woke up to an agenda at work, succinctly described a situation that can be applied to the range of agendas promoted as "progressive":

> It's hard to imagine a civil rights movement so indelibly tied to the capitalist marketplace that it could be used to sell fashion, makeup, hormones, surgery, cosmetology services, movies, TV series, mental health treatment, and women's underwear, while concurrently being invested in by billionaire philanthropists, the technology and pharmaceutical industries, major corporations, and banks. . . .
>
> Transgenderism, a purported civil rights movement, now intersects at every juncture of the global marketplace. It is hard to remember it came out of the medical industrial complex as a term for the most intense body dysphoria. . . .
>
> Transgenderism is looking more and more like Transgenderism™, when we look at the markets opening and its insidious presence in Hollywood. Whoopi Goldberg has started her own trans modeling company on Oprah's Oxygen network, with trans models reported as the future of modeling. Supernatural Extraterrestrial and Co, a high-fashion clothing line, promotes their willingness to embrace a future of male pregnancy. A look at their new clothing line for 2019 has men strutting fashion runways in pregnancy prosthesis. . . .
>
> TomBoyX is a woman's undergarment company. It uses the term "tomboy" in its company name to denote a girl who enjoys so-called stereotypical boy activities like running and climbing trees to sell boxer shorts and comfortable underwear to women. Their message is of empowerment, not being hemmed in by feminine attire, but able to run and feel free "like a boy," by donning clothes like his, but made for a woman's body. In a recent ad they chose an attractive young woman with double mastectomy scars donning their boxers under a caption that reads: "This canvas was given to you but you made it your own. You crafted your own story. Share it with the world. #moretome."

---

[31] Korberg and Garris, "Inclusive Economies."

This message is a clear glorification of chosen body disfigurement posing as self-actualization and liberation, sickness as wellness, self-hatred made into empowerment, and cutting and maiming female flesh for public consumption via uber-marketing. George Orwell must be turning over in his grave with the language of doublespeak as prime-time advertisement. . . .

It is not just the pharmaceutical giants, the IT industry, fashion houses, Hollywood, and artists melding themselves to everything trans. Banks and investment houses are sending millions of dollars to transgender organizations all over the globe.

Men at the highest echelons of society—such as billionaire philanthropist Jennifer Pritzker and the creator of SiriusXM Satellite Radio, Martine Rothblatt—are claiming not just a transgender identity, but for Rothblatt, that of a transhumanist as well. Rothblatt believes "transgenderism is the onramp to transhumanism," the precursor to superhumans. . . .[32]

Although transgenderism is positioned under the LGB civil rights banner, it appears to have a much closer relationship to commerce and global powerbrokers who have a penchant for technological megalomania. There is plenty of money flowing to transgender organizations, but even more going to normalizing transgender ideology in the culture, in language, through media, marketing, and commerce, and by billionaires' philanthropic funding of nonprofits and other institutions.

One has to wonder if the LGB civil rights banner has not just been strategic positioning for transgenderism to claim civil rights, currying popular sympathies already well cultivated for the LGB community, as a pretext to insert itself into the global marketplace, our schools, universities, courts, and medical establishments for more nefarious purposes.[33]

While Bilek writes that it is "hard to imagine a civil rights movement so indelibly tied to the capitalist marketplace," the left has long been beholden to the interests of financial capital, from the Black civil rights movement, to opposition to apartheid, to feminism and

---

[32] For more on transhumanism and posthumanism, see Bolton, *Perversion of Normality*, 493–510.
[33] Bilek, "Transgenderism is Just Big Business."

abortion liberalization.[34] Already in 1928, advertiser Edward Bernays, working for the tobacco industry, developed an ad campaign portraying cigarettes as the "freedom torches" of the "liberated," "progressive" woman. Suffice to say, none of this is new.

The New Left demanded an *inclusive society*, while the oligarchy requires an *inclusive economy*. Both converge against tradition and organic, authentic identities. Leslie Gelb, president of the Council on Foreign Relations (CFR), founded in 1921 as a nexus between academia and oligarchy, described the globalist ideology as "American internationalism based on American interests."[35] The '68 generation was imbued with this ideology, which was spawned by Cold War strategies.

The Crucial Role of Foundations

Alarmed by the rise of *populism*, especially during the Trump interregnum, Darren Walker, president of the Ford Foundation, wrote in the CFR magazine *Foreign Affairs*:

> The world is experiencing a realignment unlike any other since the end of World War II. Nationalism and populism are surging in the United States and Europe, at the expense of liberal internationalism and democratic values. This poses a challenge to a wide range of institutions, including philanthropies committed to international development and social justice. *Such foundations played a crucial role in building the liberal international order that has come under assault in recent years*, and that the United States seems less willing to defend than ever before.
>
> *During much of the last century, philanthropic foundations based in the United States exported American ideals about democracy, market economies, and civil society. That mission was made possible by ideological support from and alignment with the U.S. government, which, in turn, imbued foundations with prestige and*

---

[34] 1960s feminism, with its establishment origins, diverged from the patriotic and authoritarian suffragettes of a prior era. Many notable early feminists, such as Norah Dacre-Fox, Mary Richardson, Mary Allen, Christabel Pankhurst, and Adele Pankhurst, turned sharply to the right after World War I.

[35] Gelb, president of the CFR, in his foreword to Grose, *Continuing the Inquiry*, xiv.

influence as they operated around the world. American philanthropies such as the Ford Foundation can no longer count on such support. Nor can they be sure that the goals of increased equality, the advancement of human rights, and the promotion of democracy will find backing in Washington.[36]

As U.S. leadership of the global order falters, American foundations must blaze a new path.[37]

Trump Presidency a Temporary Setback

An alliance of oligarchs and leftists played a major role in the defeat of Donald Trump's presidential re-election, the sneering ridicule of "conspiracy theories" notwithstanding.[38] One might think that the left, with its inane talk of "world peace" and "Yankee imperialism," would have been encouraged by Trump's efforts to reduce congressional spending on the National Endowment for Democracy,[39] as well as his statement that the US should no longer be considered the "world's policeman."[40] But when it came down to it, the left maintained its historic position as servant of the globalist oligarchy, while Trump was excoriated by the establishment media as a crypto-fascist for a foreign policy that closely aligned with that outlined in George Washington's farewell address.

With Joe Biden's ascension to the presidency, the US resumed the destructive world-mission that the globalist oligarchy feared had been lost. The new New Left, represented by networks such as Antifa, kept up a riotous agitation in the streets throughout the Trump administration, seeking—in tandem with pressure from oligarchic think tanks and the mass media—to make the US ungovernable.

---

[36] While President Trump undertook efforts to align the US on the non-interventionist course urged by George Washington in his "Farewell Address," internationalist foreign policy was resumed with his ouster.

[37] Walker, "Old Money, New Order." Emphasis added.

[38] Ball, "Secret History."

[39] Ballesteros, "Trump State Department Accused."

[40] Holland, "Trump to West Point Grads."

2

Freudian PR

The conscious and intelligent manipulation of the organized habits and opinions of the masses is an important element in democratic society.

– Edward Bernays, *Propaganda* (1928)

How do the international oligarchy, the managerial elite, and the US ruling class sell ideas such as plundering the wealth of South Africa, turning women from mothers into factory fodder, opening borders for mass migrant labor, and globalizing the minerals of Kosovo with slogans like "human rights," "majority rule," and "gender equity"? These techniques were perfected decades ago. Edward Bernays, the father of public relations, explained in his book *Propaganda*:

> *The conscious and intelligent manipulation of the organized habits and opinions of the masses is an important element in democratic society. Those who manipulate this unseen mechanism of society constitute an invisible government which is the true ruling power of our country.... We are governed, our minds are molded, our tastes formed, our ideas suggested, largely by men we have never heard of. This is a logical result of the way in which our democratic society is organized. Vast numbers of human beings must cooperate in this manner if they are to live together as a smoothly functioning*

society. . . . In almost every act of our daily lives, whether in the sphere of politics or business, in our social conduct or our ethical thinking, we are dominated by the relatively small number of persons . . . who understand the mental processes and social patterns of the masses. It is they who pull the wires which control the public mind.[41]

Bernays wrote of how the public mind is molded by an "invisible government" in matters ranging from how one lives to the issue of immigration:

Who are the men, who, without our realizing it, give us our ideas, tell us whom to admire and whom to despise, what to believe about the ownership of public utilities . . . about immigration; who tell us how our houses should be designed, what furniture we should put into them, what menus we should serve at our table, what kind of shirts we must wear, what sports we should indulge in, what plays we should see, what charities we should support, what pictures we should admire, what slang we should affect, what jokes we should laugh at?[42]

Note that Bernays states that this social and mental manipulation is an essential part of our much-vaunted *democracy*. Anyone else making such claims would be called a right-wing conspiracy theorist.

Bernays was hired by sundry enterprises to radically change public perceptions on a number of issues, particularly personal morality. He applied the theories of his uncle, Sigmund Freud, to marketing. The Critical Theorists combined Freud with Marx and spawned the New Left.

The techniques of mass marketing are the same as those used for selling social and political agendas. In discussing Bernays' pervasive influence, Dr. Erik M. Gregory, founder of the Media Psychology Research Center, remarks that Bernays, by using Freud's theories, made social acceptance a major part of marketing.[43] The same techniques that were used to make bacon a staple of the American diet, boost

---

[41] Bernays, *Propaganda*, 37. Emphasis added.
[42] Ibid., 59.
[43] Gregory, "Edward Bernays, Uncle Freud, and Betty Crocker."

the popularity of instant cake mix, and make cigarettes fashionable among women have been used to make left-liberal political ideas the criteria for what is socially acceptable thinking, leading those who reject them to become social pariahs—"racists," "fascists," "misogynists," "bigots," "rednecks," "neo-Nazis," "White supremacists."

Freudianism was used in selling products and ideology. Erik Gregory remarks: "Bernays also began the insidious practice of selling products by playing to our needs for social acceptance and our fears of rejection." Here might be traced the origins of what became the counterculture of the 1960s, and how it was mainstreamed. In an earlier example of shifting the moral paradigm, Bernays produced the performances of Vaslav Nijinsky in the US, writing:

> The whole country was discussing the ballet. The ballet liberated American dance and, through it, the American spirit. It fostered a more tolerant view toward sex; it changed our music and our appreciation of it. . . . The ballet scenarios made modern art more palatable; color assumed new importance. It was a turning point in the appreciation of the arts in the United States.[44]

The now-familiar appeal to relativistic freedom and "change" for its own sake, leading to radical changes in moral and aesthetic outlooks in the 1960s, is already evident here. Maxim Boon, a theater critic, enthused that:

> Nijinsky's dance inhabited this hinterland between the innovative and the insane. It comprehensively rejected the formality and discipline of classical ballet. The familiar positions, the arabesques, the pirouettes, the *grand jetés: every semblance of traditional aesthetic was thrown out. In its place was a language of movement that drew its power from somewhere deeply visceral, where lust, ugliness and violence trumped saccharine beauty.*
>
> As the choreographer Marie Rambert observed, "Everything he invented was opposite to everything he had learned." Hunched backs and hammering feet; blade-like hands carving through the air; knock-kneed, angular contortions; Nijinsky's ballets were explosively divisive, between those who saw his work as thrilling and

---

44 Quoted in Boon, "Vaslav Nijinsky."

courageous and those who thought it to be artistic sacrilege. Stra-
vinsky's primal score for *The Rite of Spring* is often credited with
causing the riot at its premiere at the Théâtre des Champs-Élysées
in 1913, but it was at least equally incited by Nijinsky's choreogra-
phy. A year earlier, Nijinsky's setting of Debussy's *L'après-midi d'un
Faune* was so sexually explicit that Diaghilev was forced to censor
it, demanding one particularly erotic *pas des trois*, originally intended for three male dancers, be changed to two female dancers
and just a single male.[45]

During the 1920s, Bernays managed publicity for the National Association for the Advancement of Colored People (NAACP). The
NAACP has always been a recipient of oligarchic funding, as the leading organization aiming to integrate Blacks into the "inclusive economy" in the name of "freedom." The NAACP was conceived by an
eminent banker of the time, Jacob H. Schiff (referred to previously as
a significant patron of the communist movement in Russia), at a
meeting of the Henry Street Settlement, a socialist Jewish aid project.[46] Another leading patron at the founding of the NAACP was
Herbert H. Lehman, of Lehman Brothers. Later serving as governor
and senator for the state of New York, Lehman's most notable
achievement was the role he played in the Senate censure of Joseph
McCarthy, whose most dangerous enemies were not in the Communist Party but on Wall Street.[47]

Woman's Liberation via American Tobacco

In 1928 Bernays was employed by the American Tobacco Company. He hired a group of young women to march in the New York
City Easter Parade, stating to the press that a group of "women's
rights marchers" would light "Torches of Freedom." On his signal,
the models lit Lucky Strike cigarettes in front of photographers. Under the guise of "freedom," the consumer market for cigarettes was

---

[45] Ibid. Emphasis added.
[46] Bolton, *Babel Inc.*, 135–37.
[47] Bolton, *Revolution from Above*, 40–41. See also Bolton, "Joe McCarthy's Real
Enemies."

massively extended.[48] This melding of economic interests to the women's movement would define much of what became known as "women's liberation."

Bernays: A Cold War Enigma

The origins of the New Left, so far from being a Soviet plot, are rooted in the Cold War strategy of the US. This will be examined in detail. Edward Bernays, for his part, contributed to Cold War strategy and had a relationship with the anti-Stalinist left, a group that would prove to be significant in the CIA's Cold War meddling.

In 1985 Christopher Hitchens wrote an article in *The Nation*, in which he quoted from a book on the CIA-sponsored coup in Guatemala in 1954. As is now well-known, one of the primary factors in this coup was the United Fruit Company, for which Bernays was a lobbyist. What is relevant for us here is that, according to Stephen Schlesinger and Stephen Kinzer in *Bitter Fruit:*

> [Bernays] had an especially close relationship with *The New Leader*, a vigorously anti-Communist liberal weekly. Bernays persuaded the Fruit Company to sponsor public service advertisements on behalf of the Red Cross and U.S. Savings Bonds in the magazine for $1,000 a page, far above the going rate.[49]

When such leftist projects as *The New Leader* are referred to as "anti-Communist," it should be kept in mind that these were Marxists, socialists, and social democrats who despised how Bolshevism had developed in the USSR, particularly under Stalin. CIA and State Department anti-Soviet programs had nothing to do with opposing communism as an ideology. While the US opposed Soviet influence around the world, domestic anti-communism, such as that led by Senator Joseph McCarthy, was regarded with alarm by the establishment, who feared it would become a nationalist-populist mass

---

48 Lee, "Big Tobacco's Spin."
49 Quoted in Hitchens, "Minority Report."

movement.[50] When Senator Barry Goldwater challenged the establishment on a populist platform, the New Left "revolutionaries" harkened to the establishment drum to support the opposition. Trump found himself in the same situation.

As for *The New Leader*, it was more than simply "liberal." The magazine had been edited by Sidney Hook, one of the foremost American Marxist academics. Hook, with John Dewey, the father of "progressive education," had established a committee to exonerate Leon Trotsky from the charges that the USSR had leveled against him.[51] Dewey was also a founder of the League for Industrial Democracy, a social democratic organization whose youth wing birthed the Students for a Democratic Society (SDS). In 1948 Hook established Americans for Intellectual Freedom, which in 1951 became the Congress for Cultural Freedom, one of the most important CIA front organizations during the Cold War. Chaired by Hook, the Congress for Cultural Freedom had the purpose of co-opting intellectuals and artists to the anti-Soviet side of the Cold War. At the same time the CIA was similarly using the National Student Association to co-opt youth, leading directly to the New Left. A "Soviet conspiracy" it was not.

The executive editor of *The New Leader* from 1937 to 1961 was a Jewish immigrant from Russia, Sol Levitas, who had been Menshevik mayor of Vladivostok, and who had worked with Bolshevik leaders Trotsky and Bukharin.[52] *The New Leader* was an important part of the Cold War propaganda arsenal. Funds were provided via CIA operative Tom Braden.[53]

Bernays was eager to assist the US in its ideological offensive against the USSR. He sought to advise the CIA and headed an

---

[50] That even the moderate, middle-class anti-communist John Birch Society was regarded as extremist by the Establishment, at a time when the US was supposedly the leader of the West in opposing communism, is instructive, as indicated by the amount of time the FBI spent surveilling the JBS.

[51] The Preliminary Commission of Inquiry into the Charges Made Against Leon Trotsky (Dewey Commission) was formed in 1937. On this and the Moscow Trials, see Bolton, *Stalin*, 55–92.

[52] Saunders, *Cultural Cold War*, 163.

[53] Ibid. On the Congress for Cultural Freedom, see Bolton, *Revolution from Above*, 138–41.

obscure organization, the National Committee for an Adequate Overseas U.S. Information Program. Toward this end, in 1958 he sent CIA director Allen Dulles a treatise, *What the British Think of Us*, which was circulated within the agency.[54]

In 1969 Bernays was described as the "main moving force" behind a meeting of "one hundred communicators, professors and public relations personnel," convened in New York to discuss the America's Cold War propaganda offensive throughout the world.[55]

---

[54] CIA Executive Officer to Edward Bernays, April 2, 1958.
[55] Snow, "World Image of U.S."

3

ENTER STAGE LEFT: THE CRITICAL THEORISTS

A charismatic teacher, Marcuse's students began to gain influential academic positions and to promote his ideas, making him a major force in US intellectual life.

– Douglas Kellner, "Marcuse,"
The American National Bibliography

A primary factor in laying the groundwork for a paradigm shift in Western consciousness was the seminal study of American moral attitudes, *The Authoritarian Personality*. This work, promoted in the aftermath of World War II as an attempt to understand from a psychological perspective why "fascist" attitudes emerge, found that the roots of "fascism" are imbedded in the traditional family and the authority of parents. This Freudo-Marxian offensive was translated within a few decades into the Oedipal revolt of the New Left. The '68ers were acting on the redefinition of morality that had been hatched by the Frankfurt School of Critical Theory. The Critical Theorists were transplanted from Germany to the US courtesy of the Rockefeller Foundation and the US State Department. They quickly came to dominate the social sciences and became the incubators of the New Left.[56]

---

[56] For the use of the social sciences in politics and US foreign policy, see Bolton, *Perversion of Normality*.

The Critical Theorists synthesized Freudian psychoanalysis with Marxism to create a new offensive against the remnants of traditional Western culture. Critical Theory, together with the sexology studies of Alfred Kinsey (also a recipient of Rockefeller and other such funding), laid the ideological foundations for the New Left. Sexual liberation from "hypocrisy" and "repression," expressed as a libertine rejection of any form of authority, whether from one's parents or the state, was a primary aim. It was an *Oedipal* rebellion, supplanting the class war of classical Marxism by introducing elements of Freudian psychology. Critical Theorists such as Erich Fromm and New Left guru Herbert Marcuse taught that traditional bonds such as family, home, ethnicity, and homeland were the "primary ties" that repress individual freedom and give rise to "fascism." These must be destroyed if the individual is to "self-actualize," a phrase that came into vogue during the period. Marcuse in particular articulated a new strategy for the left: agitate the youth, minority ethnic groups, and the *lumpenproletariat*, the latter being the vagabond element of the working class that had been regarded with disdain by Marx and Engels.[57]

Critical Theory's view of the family as the incubator of "fascism" was summarized by Mirra Komarovsky: "Even a partial breakdown of parental authority in the family might tend to increase the readiness of a coming generation to accept social change."[58]

The statement is intended to convey an impression of change via youthful rebellion. However, what the oligarchs sought in funding the social sciences, including Critical Theory and Kinseyan sexology, was to create social change by manipulating the next generation, offering an interpretation of "freedom" that was as narrow and false as that used by Bernays to sell tobacco to women. That is to say, the "youth revolt" that began in the 1960s and continues to this day has been little more than a big sales gimmick.

---

[57] Marx and Engles, *Communist Manifesto*, 20. For a reassessment of the revolutionary role of the *lumpenproletariat* in the New Left, see Franklin, "Lumpenproletariat and the Revolutionary."

[58] Komarovsky, *Unemployed Man and His Family*, 3.

Herbert Marcuse

Among the most influential Critical Theorists was Herbert Marcuse. In *Eros and Civilization*, he argued that instincts should not be repressed, and that such repression is inherent in Western civilization. Marcuse became an idol of the New Left. His name was chanted by the '68ers on the streets of the US, France, and Germany, in tandem with Ho Chi Minh, Mao, and Che. Marcuse argued that capitalism represses the libido of the proletariat.[59] He echoed the "sex-pol" doctrines of Wilhelm Reich, another exile from Germany, whose efforts to synthesize Marxism with psychoanalysis had been repudiated by the German Communist Party and the USSR.[60] It is notable that Wilhelm Reich and the Critical Theorists fled to the US rather than the USSR, where their theories were always anathema.

Marcuse pursued an eminent career, courtesy of the establishment. This was noted by the Soviet press at the time. Martin Duberman, a leading left-wing theorist and gay activist, stated: "The philosopher Herbert Marcuse predicted that the new 'sexual liberation movements' would become a powerful force, THE agency for producing significant social transformation."[61] Marcuse biographer Douglas Kellner writes:

> During the 1960s, Marcuse achieved world renown as "the guru of the New Left" . . . his work was often discussed in the mass media. A charismatic teacher, Marcuse's students began to gain influential academic positions and to promote his ideas, making him a major force in US intellectual life. After working for the US Government for almost ten years Marcuse returned to university life. He received a Rockefeller Foundation grant to study Soviet Marxism, lecturing on the topic at Columbia University during 1952–53, and Harvard from 1954–55.[62]

---

59 Marcuse, *Eros and Civilization*.
60 Bolton, *Perversion of Normality*, 287–93.
61 Duberman, *Left Out*, 347.
62 Kellner, "Marcuse, Herbert."

Serving in the Office of Strategic Services (the predecessor of the CIA) during World War II, and working in the US State Department until 1951, Marcuse became part of the cultural Cold War against the USSR.[63]

In 1964 Marcuse published his *One-Dimensional Man*, of which Kellner writes: "In contrast to orthodox Marxism, Marcuse championed non-integrated forces like minorities, outsiders and radical intelligentsia, attempting to nourish oppositional thought through promoting radical thinking and opposition."[64] This is the root of identity politics, which has since become mainstream, leading to a society that is fractured on the ruins of traditional bonds. Both *Eros and Civilization* and *One-Dimensional Man* received Rockefeller Foundation funding.[65]

Like Adorno's *Authoritarian Personality*, Alfred Kinsey's *Sexual Behavior in the Male* and *Sexual Behavior in the Female*, funded by the Rockefeller Foundation, have had a seminal impact on attitudes and laws. Dr. John Bancroft, former director of the Kinsey Institute, called "sexual nonconformity" a "vehicle for dissent."[66] This sexology came to define the meaning of what is "modern," "progressive," and "liberated," and was a means for undermining traditional morality. This "liberation from repression" via "sexual revolution" became a mainstay of the New Left.

Ann Snitow, a cofounder of New York Radical Feminists who was said to be "at the heart of the feminist movement during the 1960s and '70s,"[67] regarded the New Left as having challenged the sexual conservatism of the Old Left, including the USSR:

> The generation of radicals that came of age in the 1960s tried to divest itself of the Old Left's sexual restraint. The New Left—especially its men—plunged into a second "sexual revolution," facilitated by cheap, accessible birth control. Student radicals identified sex as potentially revolutionary, a way to break out of the deadening psychological structures of U.S. middle-class life. Multiple and

---

[63] Ibid. See also Laudani, *Secret Reports on Nazi Germany*.
[64] Ibid.
[65] Marcuse, *One Dimensional Man*, "Acknowledgements."
[66] Bolton, *Perversion of Normality*. See also "Kinsey Institute Exposed."
[67] Tanenbaum, "Ann Snitow (1943–2019)."

varied sexual relationships came to be associated with cultural liberation.[68]

Any form of "restraint" is anathema to the post-1945 liberal international order, which requires fluidity in all things, starting with a global market that is bound to nothing other than profit maximization, production, and consumption. This is why, when the Critical Theorists and their New Left spawn spoke of "human authenticity" and expressed concern at the "commodification" of culture and human values, they were merely engaging in cant. The notion of authenticity had seeped through to the left from Martin Heidegger via former students like Herbert Marcuse.[69] It was a concept that was distorted into the antithesis of what Heidegger intended. Heidegger sought human authenticity through the restoration of organic—authentic—bonds; whereas the left seeks the obliteration of these same bonds in the name of "freedom."[70]

---

[68] Snitow, "Sex and Socialism."
[69] Backman, "Radical Conservatism and the Heideggerian Right."
[70] Fromm, *Escape from Freedom*.

4

THE SIGNIFICANCE OF '68

1968 has become a universal symbol that is invoked to talk about our present situation.

– Aleida Assman, The Kyiv International

That the ideology of the '68 generation has become mainstream is widely accepted. The accounts as to why vary. New Leftists themselves, as well as their allies, engage in self-flattery, chalking up their victory to the fact that they were vanguards for some inevitable progress. On the other hand, their conservative critics give them a begrudging recognition for the astuteness of their tactics. In this latter regard there are allusions to the dictum ascribed to the Italian Marxist theorist Antonio Gramsci, who is widely credited with having formulated a new strategy of cultural revolution via the march through the institutions. One must change a culture and its consciousness to lay the foundations for deep, long-term change. Mundane politics is just one part of the process, and not even the most important. In the US this tactic was advocated by Herbert Marcuse, and by Saul Alinsky, both leaders of the New Left, and both sponsored by the establishment they professed to oppose.

This march through the institutions is analogous to the aims of the Fabian Society in Britain. The Fabians sought influence among the intelligentsia, as opposed to the failed Marxist formula of agitating the proletariat. The Fabians' primary agency has been the

London School of Economics and Political Science (LSE), established with funding from the Rothschilds, Sir Julius Wernher and Sir Ernest Cassel, and, beginning in 1923, the Rockefellers.[71] The LSE has educated policymakers and executives throughout the world, playing a leading role in the creation of our rootless managerial and intellectual global bureaucracy.

Socialist Students and the Managerial Elite

In 1968, LSE students rioted like their counterparts in the US and Europe. In 2003, *The Guardian*, reporting on a reunion of those students, quoted Martin Shaw, professor of international relations and global politics at the University of Sussex, who was one of the '68ers at LSE. Shaw remarked:

> 1968 led a generation of young intellectuals away from traditional social democracy, out of the Labour party and (in many cases) into what proved to be the dead-end of far-left groups, although many of them eventually returned to Labour and (ironically) played a part in the development of New Labour in the 1990s. Many of us moved on to different kinds of political position in later life.[72]

There was nothing "ironic" about the influence of this generation on New Labour, which became in Britain, as in New Zealand under finance minister Roger Douglas, the harbinger for the revival of free-market dogma. The left was again playing its role as the lackey of capitalism, in a script written years before by their patrons in the boardrooms of Europe and the US. Why else is it to be supposed that the oligarchy had been funding the "socialist" LSE for over a century? What the LSE students became, as the *Guardian* article indicates, is what they were intended to be: establishment intelligentsia,

---

[71] This funding is documented in my book *Revolution from Above*, 99–100. The information on the funding of the LSE that was readily accessible on the LSE website in 2011 now seems elusive. Instead, the focus is on the Will of Derby lawyer Henry Hutchinson, who bequeathed the Fabian Society his estate in 1894. Donnelly, "Funding the Vision."

[72] Mair, "Agitators."

managers, and functionaries, having postured as "revolutionaries," going nowhere, and vehemently debating—in Trotskyite manner—whether the USSR is a "deformed workers' state" or "a capitalist one." Note that these bourgeois radicals were identified by one of their own as having set the Labour Party (that is, New Labour) on a course favorable to global capitalism, as did many other erstwhile "social-ists" throughout the world. Specifically, several of the old comrades were quoted by *The Guardian*:

> "In a curious way, it is neo-liberalism and capitalism that have made the main gains," says Crouch. "There has been a shift from authority as such toward the use of market forces as the means through which power is exercised." "We helped to make a lot of changes that later generations take for granted," adds Shaw. For Tomkinson, the heady days of 1968 are a period that remain unsur-passed. "Future generations have been and are openly envious of those who lived through these 'happenings.'"[73]

"Market forces" became the basis of the international utopia, and the socialists helped to reanimate the nineteenth-century corpse of free trade that Marx had welcomed as a step in the dialectical process of world transformation.[74] Colin Crouch, one of the LSE '68ers, who be-came head of the department of social and political science at the European Institute in Florence, pointed out approvingly that these market forces had deposed what vestiges remained of traditional au-thority. As Spengler had observed, in the conflict between money and tradition, the left serves money.

1968—A Universal Symbol

Of the influence of the '68ers on the present, Aleida Assman, an authority on "cultural memory," in a lecture commemorating the surge of 1968 revolts across Europe and the US, stated in a lec-ture to the Kyiv International:

---

73 Ibid.
74 Marx and Engles, *Communist Manifesto*, 25.

There is so much that we admire and ascribe today to the '68 generation: they have transformed our lifestyle, they have democratized the society, they have reformed the institutions, and they have broken with the Nazi past. This is quite a workload for young people aged between 18 and 28. After 50 years, we are no longer dealing with the history of this generation but with the myth that has been created around it. 1968 has become a universal symbol that is invoked to talk about our present situation. It synthesizes many revolts, political movements and social changes of the late sixties. In its most general sense, 1968 today stands for a shift in the Cold War era from a traditional to a modern society, emphasizing the liberation from repressive bourgeois traditions, the fight for political equality, the celebration of pop culture including Beat and Jazz, Hippie and Flower Power movements, a new concept of the gendered body and drugs, gender emancipation, postcolonial politics, peace movements and ecological awareness—all of this framed by new mass media such as records, radio, films, and (colour) television programs. Before the '68 generation decided to liberate itself and the world, it had already been liberated to a large extent.[75]

The Kyiv International is itself an organization inspired by the '68 legacy, stating of the epoch in its celebratory program:

The Kyiv International edition of May 2018 will explore the political and cultural heritage of the revolt and struggle of 1968, considering the antinomies of this moment for the West and East of Europe fifty years onward. The legacy of May 1968 remains a symbol of liberation and rebellion against entrenched power structures, and a cultural and artistic benchmark for Western Europe. The commemoration of the 50th anniversary of the Prague Spring and Soviet military invasion of Czechoslovakia—most immediate in Eastern Europe—continue to define political and cultural divides across the continent. By overlapping the contrasting dimensions of this event, which is the starting point of contemporaneity, *The Kyiv International -'68 NOW* contributes to the development of a united

---

[75] From the Visual Culture Research Center's page on The Kyiv International, '68 NOW.

European subjectivity grounded in democratic internationalism, based on the principles of solidarity and inclusivity.[76]

The Kyiv International is a globalist institution organized by the Visual Culture Research Center. The purpose of this NGO is to promote the incorporation of Ukraine into a "united Europe" based on "democratic internationalism," and to encourage the creation of what is called "a new International."[77] The organization collaborates with the National Endowment for Democracy, European Endowment for Democracy, International Renaissance Foundation (established as part of the Soros globalist network),[78] and the Open Ukraine Foundation, which is sponsored by NATO and the US State Department.[79] Therefore, when "revolts against entrenched authority" are mentioned, what this means is the color revolutions that have toppled those regimes that have hindered globalization. How apt that this new generation of pseudo-revolutionaries should emulate and eulogize the '68ers: the strings are being pulled by the same groups both then and now.

Assman ascribed to the work of '68 generation a "shift" from what remnants there were of "traditional society" to "modern society." Her reference to what remained of traditional morals and culture as "repressive bourgeois traditions," what the Frankfurt Institute condemned as the repressive primary ties, shows how Critical Theory has become the dominant paradigm in politics, morals, and culture. In all of this, Assman ascribes a crucial role to the '68 generation.

How far could the '68ers have gone in the mainstreaming of "their" ideas, in their march through the institutions, if the ground had not been prepared by the establishment?

---

76 Ibid.
77 From the Visual Culture Research Center's homepage.
78 From the International Renaissance Foundation's "About Us" page, which no longer mentions George Soros. The original page may be found on Internet Archive: https://tinyurl.com/43dhftjj.
79 The "Partners" page on their website is no longer available but is archived: https://archive.ph/hx9t2.

Have the various globalist foundations and NGOs funded the "new concept of the gendered body and drugs, gender emancipation, postcolonial politics, peace movements and ecological awareness" because their minds were "liberated" by the '68ers, or because the '68ers served as their dupes? We are now widely familiar with the way the color revolutions are sponsored in states targeted for regime change. Ukraine was one such state that was targeted in 2014 by a revolution that has placed that country in the globalist camp, positioned against Russia. There is no longer any excuse for ignorance as to how certain revolts are used by globalists and American strategists, with youth again acting as mere pawns. The '68 generation, as Assman unwittingly reminds us, were precursors of this process.

5

New Left Origins

The non-Soviet ideologies of the Left are something quite different, no matter whether they are personified by communists like Tito, Mao, and Dubček, or Western writers like Jean-Paul Sartre or Herbert Marcuse. These the Kremlin has taken to be genuine rivals diverting the Left-wing stream into their own channels to the detriment of the Moscow orientated Communist parties.

– Klaus Mehnert, 1974

The New Left was a product of the Cold War. Much of the conservative right and Middle America worried that it was a communist plot. Instead, it was a liberal plot with oligarchic and establishment sponsorship that ended up making the USSR seem like a paragon of conservative values. At the earliest stage of the Cold War the CIA recruited disaffected leftists with an anti-Soviet program. This included recruiting leftist intelligentsia and artists via the Congress for Cultural Freedom, and student delegates who could counter Soviet propaganda with American liberalism at the World Youth Festivals.

A feature in *Encounter*, one of the primary magazines sponsored by the CIA (then under the editorship of Melvin J. Lasky, a prominent figure in this Cold War program), stated that what the Soviet leadership feared was neither liberal nor conservative ideologies, but the "non-Soviet ideologies of the Left." The author, Klaus Mehnert, a political scientist, Kremlinologist, and government adviser, cited the examples of Tito (Yugoslavia), Mao Zedong (China), Dubček (Czech-oslovakia), and New Left intellectual icons Jean-Paul Sartre and Hebert Marcuse. After the revolt against Moscow by Tito, Mao, and the German Social Democrats, "Marcuse and his 'werewolves'" finally arrived ("werewolves" being an allusion to the term used by Soviet analysts to describe Marcuse's influence on the world student up-heavals). Mehnert stated that what appeared as a communist revolt by youths in the Western capitals was an "anarchist" and "anti-Soviet trend." It was not directed or inspired by Moscow. Mehnert stated that the New Left "contributed a further degree of fragmentation to an already fragmented communist world." Mehnert lauded what he considered the emergence of Trotskyites who were, he claimed, more prominent in the 1960s than during the Stalinist purges. Mehnert foresaw that these New Left youths would eventually contribute to "the overall trend—the decline of Kremlin authority." Soviet analysts regarded the New Left as being potentially a "dangerous infection."[80]

Consensus Between American Executive and Youth Leaders

Joel Kotek of the Free University of Brussels commented on the era: "It is not going too far to speak of an alliance—at this particular period, to be sure—between the CIA and the left." The World Youth Assembly (WYA) was created to rival the Soviet-sponsored youth fes-tivals and the International Union of Students, which were under Eastern Bloc control. The WYA followed the anti-colonial and anti-Soviet doctrines of the CIA. Kotek writes:

> Despite the Atlantic Alliance the American government was not enamoured of British and French colonialism. During this period, it systematically undermined the positions of Britain and France in North Africa, the Middle East, and Far East. The American youth and student leaders looked upon their government as a champion of colonial emancipation. . . . There was a real consensus between the American executive and the youth leaders of the time.[81]

---

[80] Mehnert, "Moscow & the New Left." For all.
[81] Kotek, *Students and the Cold War*, 220.

Were the student leaders so superficial in their thinking that they assumed US foreign policy against the European colonial powers was motivated by concern for the colonial subjects, rather than as a tactic to take over those territories when Britain, France, and Portugal scuttled their empires? Some, such as National Student Association president Bill Dentzer, who later disclosed his acceptance of CIA funding,[82] and Avrea Ingram, NSA international affairs vice president, were not under any such illusions: they later joined the CIA.[83]

National Student Association

The National Student Association (NSA) was one of the primary elements in the emergence of the New Left. The NSA was at an early period funded by the CIA as part of the Cold War strategy to recruit leftist and liberal youth in opposition to the authoritarianism of the USSR.

Tom Hayden, a future leader of the SDS, encountered the CIA presence among student organizations prior to the emergence of the New Left, but he denied knowing that the CIA was funding and manipulating them. However, in his memoirs he alluded to this being widely suspected among the lower echelons of the NSA. Hayden, commenting that he underwent his final initiation into student politics when attending an NSA congress at the University of Minnesota in 1960, claimed that he "did not know it at the time, but the NSA . . . was funded primarily by the CIA and State Department" for the purpose of combatting the USSR.[84] Hayden commented that the older leadership of the NSA, "despite their ties to U.S. government agencies, tended to be quite liberal, a response to the revolutions of rising expectations they saw everywhere in the world."[85]

These "revolutions of rising expectations" had been promoted by the US foreign policy establishment since Woodrow Wilson's Fourteen Points for postwar reconstruction, and were reiterated in

---

[82] Ibid., 207.
[83] Ibid., 221.
[84] Hayden, *Reunion*, 36.
[85] Ibid.

Roosevelt's Atlantic Charter.[86] Only the US and the USSR could fill the void of the scuttled European colonial powers, and US agencies such as the CIA-funded Africa-America Institute were far more insidious than any Soviet plotters.[87] The senior NSA leaders, who "felt a need to keep control of their organization and shroud its sources of money," were also encouraged by the student involvement in the mounting turmoil in the South,[88] where many got their start in student radicalism with the Freedom Rides.

Hayden stated that when he first approached the NSA it was the "only national forum for students," and "took strong stands" on most of the issues that aroused him. It was "almost an apprenticeship for future American political leaders."[89]

When Hayden first joined the NSA it was led by Allard Lowenstein, a future president of the left-liberal lobby, Americans for Democratic Action (ADA). Lowenstein claimed not to have known of the CIA funding of the NSA. A CIA report in 1951, referring to NSA funding by the Rockefeller Foundation for international projects and seminars, stated that CIA funds would be indirectly given for specific projects and discussed Lowenstein's strong stance against the Soviet bloc. To ensure Lowenstein's continuing control of the NSA, the CIA memorandum stated that his draft into the army would be deferred, although he would not be aware of the CIA involvement. The CIA memorandum also referred to the "penetration" that the agency had made into the NSA, and that Lowenstein's anti-Soviet stance had the backing of the majority of the NSA National Executive.[90]

Origins of NSA

The NSA was founded in 1947 and remained the primary student organization in the US until its CIA links were exposed in 1967.

---

[86] Bolton, *Babel Inc.*, 44–77.
[87] Ibid., 59–63.
[88] Hayden, *Reunion*, 36.
[89] Ibid., 37.
[90] Buffington to CSP, "U.S. National Student Association," in Schwartz, *American Students Organize*, 569.

The origins of the NSA are analogous to the Congress for Cultural Freedom (CCF). As with the CCF among the intelligentsia and artists, the establishment wanted an organization that could be used to counter Soviet influence among youth worldwide. In 1946, two dozen American students were selected by the CIA to attend the Soviet-sponsored Prague World Youth Congress, from which the International Union of Students (IUS) emerged. The intention was to take over the Prague meeting and portray the US as the leader of the post-war world, with American liberalism as the ideology of the future. The International Union of Students that came out of the Prague congress included Russian and American vice presidents, and a Czech president. The communist coup in Czechoslovakia in 1948 resulted in the resignation of the NSA officials from the IUS, which they charged had done nothing to oppose the communists.[91] Hayden alluded to this when citing a CIA memorandum to the FBI on the American delegation to the Eighth World Youth Festival, where the focus would be on cultivating "key delegates from the developing areas."[92]

In December 1946 the students who had composed the US delegation to Prague held a conference to prepare for a constitutional convention for the organization of the NSA. Race issues dominated the congress. William Ellis and Joyce Roberts, delegates to the Prague congress, reported to the National Intercollegiate Christian Council that the US delegation "strongly supported the United Nations and advocated a strong atomic control commission which should be exempt from the veto of the Security Council." An anti-colonial policy was also advocated.[93] These were also the primary aims of the US foreign policy establishment for the postwar world. The embryonic student left was from the start a tool of US foreign policy, advocating "world federalism" and countering the USSR with

---

[91] Berlin, "American Society and American," in Schwartz, *American Students Organize*, 6–12.

[92] Hayden, *Reunion*, 37–8.

[93] Ellis and Roberts, "Learning the Art of Cold War Politics," in Schwartz, *American Students Organize*, 107.

left-liberal ideology. The Soviet rejection of such "world federalism" is what sparked the Cold War.[94]

Although most of the US delegation to the Prague congress (whom William Ellis and Joyce Roberts described as all being "left-wing") endorsed US policies, three did not. Two of those were described as communists.[95] It is apparent that the issue of contention was the promotion of the UN as a world government,[96] and the UN control of atomic energy, which the USSR regarded as de facto US control.[97]

John Simons, treasurer of the National Continuation Committee (1946–1947),[98] writing in the August 23rd, 1947, issue of the student newspaper *New Leader*, reflected on the gulf existing between the Soviet-aligned American Youth for Democracy and the Council of Student Clubs of the Communist Party on the one side and the World Federalists, Students for Democratic Action, et al. on the other. Simons was strident in warning against infiltration by student affiliates of the Communist Party USA.[99] He became the NSA's executive director of the Foundation of Youth and Student Affairs, "which served as a major conduit of U.S. Government funding of NSA's international programs from the 1950s through 1967."[100]

In 1948 the NSA held its first congress, with more than seven hundred delegates. Ted Harris, a Black man, was elected president.[101]

In December 1950, Lowenstein went to Stockholm to meet with delegates from twenty other student organizations to establish the International Student Conference. The focus was to be on contacting students in "developing nations." In 1952 a Coordinating Secretariat

---

94 Bolton, *Stalin*, 125–9.

95 Ellis and Roberts, "Learning the Art of Cold War Politics," in Schwartz, *American Students Organize*, 107.

96 This is confirmed by the Soviet foreign minister of the time, Andrei Gromyko, in his autobiography, *Memories*, 116–7.

97 Ibid., 137–40.

98 Established to create a national student organization out of the American student experience at Prague.

99 "John Simons: An Eloquent Advocate," in Schwartz, *American Students Organize*, 125.

100 Ibid., 124.

101 "The World Student Congress, Prague, 1946" in Schwartz, *American Students Organize*, 81.

was established in Leiden. It was to serve as an anti-Soviet alternative to the Soviet–dominated International Union of Students.[102]

Under NSA president William Dentzer, the CIA began to fund NSA international programs in 1951. That year, Dentzer was approached by the CIA to consult on project funding.[103]

An Arm of US Foreign Policy

NSA provided me, as it did others, with fundamental education on the issues of our generation.
            – Janet Welsh Brown (NSA Vice President, 1952–1953)

Sol Stern's famous exposé of the NSA's connections with the CIA showed how the NSA was pursuing a two-pronged policy of domestic leftism and international anti-Sovietism:

> NSA has always shown two faces. Its domestic programs, its Congresses and its regional meetings have always been open and spontaneous. If NSA national leaders were occasionally over-cautious, they still moved with the liberal current of opinion among American students. In the '50s, NSA took an even more liberal stand, than the prevailing apathy among students might have suggested. And in the '60s, NSA responded to the new militant protest mood on the campuses. It supported students against the draft, opposed the war in Vietnam, and participated in civil rights struggles. It played a crucial role in the formation of the Student Nonviolent Coordinating Committee and was one of its staunchest supporters, a position which cost it the affiliation of many schools in 1961.
> Yet NSA's overseas image has been very different. Despite its liberal rhetoric, NSA-ers abroad seemed more like professional diplomats than students; there was something tough and secretive about them that was out of keeping with their openness and spontaneity back home.

---

[102] Dentzer, "From Minneapolis to Bloomington," in Schwartz, *American Students Organize*, 299.
[103] Ibid., 302.

In the light of all this, it is not surprising that a number of NSA's critics have pointed a suspicious finger at its international operations. Nor is it a shock to discover that some people in the left wing of the NSA, like Paul Potter, who was elected national affairs vice president in 1961 and went on to become president of Students for a Democratic Society, revealed that they had always suspected NSA's international operations of being tightly tied in with the State Department. Very few ever seriously raised the more sinister specter of CIA involvement.[104]

This included the era of so-called McCarthyism, and although the NSA was part of the foreign policy establishment's anti-Soviet offensive, this anti-Sovietism had to proceed on strictly establishment terms, lest it develop into a populist mass movement that would turn against the establishment.[105]

Carroll Quigley, a historian at Georgetown who was part of the foreign policy establishment, on his own account being "close to many of its instruments" for most of his life,[106] stated in his magnum opus *Tragedy and Hope* that the establishment's liberalism was often confused with communism: "It is this power structure," referring to a Wall Street network, "which the Radical Right in the United States has been attacking for years in the belief that they were attacking the Communists."[107]

"McCarthyism" Danger to the Establishment

Senator Joseph McCarthy was even coming close to the actual source, with his intention to investigate the CIA and the tax-exempt foundations. Dentzer, when president of the NSA, wrote of the "Challenge and Test of McCarthyism." McCarthyism was to be combatted as vigorously as the USSR. Dentzer equated Sovietism, "flag-

---

[104] Stern, "Short Account of International Student Politics."

[105] The Trump presidency and the MAGA movement, despite their inadequacies, allowed us to witness the frenzy with which the Establishment reacts to any such challenge, and the way the left is still utilized to cause chaos at street level.

[106] Quigley, *Tragedy and Hope*, 950.

[107] Ibid., 956.

waving Americanism," McCarthyism, and fascism as all of a piece in threatening the US as citadel of liberal-democratic international-ism.[108] The whole premise of Cold War strategy was to outflank the USSR from the left in showing the world, especially the decolonized developing nations, that liberal internationalism under US auspices could provide more freedom, equality, and consumer trinkets than the USSR.

Dentzer, like many others of his milieu, became part of the Kennedy and Johnson administrations. He was involved in the creation of USAID in 1961,[109] a government agency that would come to play an important part in the US foreign policy apparatus. As president of the NSA, Dentzer stated that organizations like the NSA could often do more to serve US interests overseas than official government agencies. "Student activity in the underdeveloped areas is especially important," he said, remarking that "international relationships" could be initiated by "international student relations." He explicitly stated that "plain persons who honestly are interested in peace, liberty and democracy," such as NSA delegates, can avoid the suspicion of being "an agent of the State Department."[110]

The International Coordinating Secretariat was of particular importance in this program. Regional student seminars were organized by the NSA in Latin America, Asia, and Europe.[111] It is no real mystery, as Tom Hayden had said of it in his memoirs twenty years later, how and why the 1968 student riots quickly spread from the US to Europe and into the Soviet bloc. A liberal-democratic internationale of students had been rigorously planned and funded for twenty years. It was no more a mystery, and no more spontaneous, than the color revolutions across Africa, Asia, and Eastern Europe, organized and funded by the same interests.[112]

---

[108] Dentzer, "Challenge and Test of McCarthyism," in Schwartz, *American Students Organize*, 310.

[109] Ibid., 303. Dentzer was appointed New York superintendent of banks in 1970 by Governor Nelson Rockefeller.

[110] Dentzer, "Student Programs for International Understanding," in Schwartz, *American Students Organize*, 315-6.

[111] Ibid.

[112] Bolton, *Revolution from Above*, 213-44.

CIA versus FBI

Since the NSA was under FBI surveillance and was regarded with suspicion by the House Un-American Activities Committee, there was a naive assumption that it was regarded by the establishment as a threat. Reminiscing decades later, Janet Welsh Brown, an NSA vice president, remarked that "the FBI onslaught was largely responsible for my not recognizing at the time the soon obvious source of money flowing to NSA international programs. . . . It was inconceivable to me that one federal agency [the CIA] might be funding NSA while another [the FBI] was harassing it." When traveling through Asia on a Fulbright scholarship, Brown learned of the programs the CIA funded and the "agents through whom they worked (including student/youth organizations such as the World Assembly of Youth)." When she learned of these CIA fronts, she realized how the NSA had been used. Brown nonetheless acknowledged that the NSA provided her with her political apprenticeship when she became a New Leftist during her time teaching at Howard University and the University of the District of Columbia. "NSA provided me, as it did others, with fundamental education on the issues of our generation."[113]

Ms. Brown's recollections lead us to several notable points:

1. The left claims martyr status when under FBI surveillance, but being the subject of this does not give leftists any unique anti-establishment credentials. Tom Hayden cited FBI documents on him throughout his memoirs. While the FBI ran the COINTELPRO operation to disrupt both the extreme left and the extreme right, it also kept moderate conservative organizations—the John Birch Society in particular—under surveillance, indicating that the left has no special status to martyrdom.

2. The NSA provided the training and ideology for the emergence of the New Left.

3. The CIA had sponsored a network of left-liberal student organizations throughout the world to counter Soviet influence. An

---

[113] Brown, "Student Rights, Academic Freedom," in Schwartz, *American Students Organize*, 386.

important element of this was to propagandize the students of decolonized nations, who would become the future leaders of their countries.

Ms. Brown commented in a footnote to her article on the NSA that:

> One of the NSA colleagues I interviewed while working on this piece, a man who subsequently worked for the CIA, mused about the differences between the FBI and the CIA during the 1950s. His explanation of the Federal schizophrenia with respect to NSA was that the FBI was anticommunist, conservative and antidemocratic, whereas the CIA was anticommunist, liberal and prodemocracy.[114]

NSA and CIA

Barry Farber, NSA delegate to the 1951 Zagreb peace conference and to the Rio Inter-American Conference in 1952, stated in 1968 that the CIA was to be congratulated for recognizing the usefulness of the NSA in rivalling Moscow's work among students.[115]

In 1951 the CIA decided that the best approach would be to fund specific NSA projects, especially student seminars in Europe, Southeast Asia, and the Middle East. Such projects were already being funded by the Rockefeller Foundation, which was to grant $60,000 for the establishment of the International Student Information Service and for student seminars overseas.[116]

Stern wrote in *Ramparts* of the CIA use of foundations and other fronts to channel funds into the NSA:

---

[114] Ibid., 387, note 49.
[115] Farber, "Remembering Avrea Ingram," in Schwartz, *American Students Organize*, 575.
[116] Buffington to CSP, "Memorandum for CSP," "United States National Student Association," in Schwartz, *American Students Organize*, 569. Lt. Col. Buffington was Tom Braden's assistant in the CIA's International Organizations Division, responsible for sponsoring the anti-Soviet left, including the Congress for Cultural Freedom, via the various tax-exempt foundations.

It is widely known that the CIA has a number of foundations which serve as direct fronts or as secret "conduits" that channel money from the CIA to preferred organizations. An intimation of the scope of this financial web was afforded the public on August 31, 1964, when Texas Congressman Wright Patman, in the course of an investigation into the use of foundations for tax dodges, announced that the J. M. Kaplan Fund of New York was serving as a secret conduit for CIA funds. As soon as Patman made his announcement, representatives of the CIA and Internal Revenue came scurrying to his office for a hasty conference. Patman apparently was satisfied with the results. Without retracting his allegations about the Kaplan Fund, he announced: "The CIA does not belong in this foundation investigation."

Before bringing down the curtain of secrecy, he did, at least, reveal one fact of substance. It turned out that a number of other foundations had contributed to the Kaplan Fund during the crucial years of 1961-63 when the Fund had been serving the CIA. Five of these foundations were not even on the Internal Revenue Service's list of tax-exempt foundations. They were the Borden Trust, the Price Fund, the Edsel Fund, the Beacon Fund, and the Kentfield Fund. The implication was clear that some or all of these were the channel through which the CIA money passed into the Kaplan foundation coffers.[117]

After discussing the role of foundations such as the J. Frederick Brown Foundation, the Independence Foundation, and the Sidney and Esther Rabb Charitable Foundation, Stern discussed the role of the CIA-run Foundation for Youth and Student Affairs:

As far back as anyone can remember, the mainstay of NSA's overseas operations has been the Foundation for Youth and Student Affairs of New York City, founded in 1952. In contrast to the likes of Independence and San Jacinto [foundations], FYSA has a for-real office, a full-time staff and an imminently respectable board of directors.

In recent years, FYSA annually pumped hundreds of thousands of dollars per year into NSA's treasury. The figure for October 1965 to October 1966 was $292,753.60. It provided a general

---

[117] Stern, "A Short Account of International."

administrative grant of up to $120,000 per year and funded projects such as NSA's magazine, *The American Student*, foreign student participation at NSA congresses, technical assistance projects; and its fund paid NSA's dues to the ISC. In addition, FYSA could be relied upon to pick up any operating deficit that NSA incurred during the year, and FYSA gives "scholarships" to ex-NSA officers for overseas study.

FYSA has also been the chief U.S. source for channeling money overseas to national unions of students favored by the NSA leadership. And FYSA has been practically the only external source of support, except for the mysterious San Jacinto Foundation, of the programs of the ISC. Between 1962–1964, ISC records show that these two foundations provided over 90 per cent of ISC's program budget (most of it from FYSA)—a gargantuan total of $1,826,000 in grants completed or in progress. The ISC would be literally impotent as an international organization without the support of FYSA, having been unable to establish sizable alternative sources of funding.

The executive secretary of FYSA is Harry Lunn, a tall, ruddy-faced, balding man in his middle thirties, himself a past president of NSA, who used to make applications for grants to the foundation which he now directs. Lunn vehemently denied the suggestion that his foundation might be channeling CIA money for NSA, although he would not release a financial statement to this magazine.
After his presidency of NSA (1954–55) had terminated, Lunn became a member of an ISC delegation to Southeast Asia. Then, following a short stint in the Army, he went to the Department of Defense as a research analyst. From there he went on up the ladder to the political desk of the American embassy in Paris and then on up to the Agency for International Development, where he worked on the Alliance for Progress. It was from this last position that Lunn came to FYSA in 1965. Lunn also took part in the activities of the militantly anti-communist Independent Research Service at the Vienna Youth Festival in 1959, while he was attached to the Department of Defense.

Lunn's career is a case study in the intimate relationship between NSA, international student politics and the Cold War.

Stern wrote that "so intimately was the CIA involved in NSA's international program, that it treated NSA as an arm of U.S. foreign policy."

In 1957 Ray Farabee was elected NSA president. Farabee secured support for the NSA's Southern Student Human Relations Project (SSHRP) from the Marshall Field Foundation. Constance Curry, director of the SSHRP, was elected adult advisor to the Student Nonviolent Coordinating Committee (SNCC) and was able to provide funding from the SSHRP, and "through the NSA's national office, built support for the civil rights movement on northern campuses." In 1960, at an SSHRP seminar, Constance Curry recruited Tom Hayden's wife, Sandra Cason, "and a Cason speech on the necessity of civil disobedience galvanized the NSA Congress that year." Black American law student Timothy Jenkins was elected NSA vice president, and "he went on to play a significant leadership role in the SNCC's early development."[118] The SNCC became a pivotal element in the emergence of the New Left, where Tom Hayden and many others served their political apprenticeship.

Having become ineffectual for Cold War purposes after its exposure by *Ramparts* in 1967, in 1978 the NSA merged with the National Student Lobby to become the US Student Association (USSA). The USSA, while maintaining a New Left stance on domestic and foreign policy issues, worked closely with the American government via the Department of Education, while resuming the role of the NSA in "observing" the Soviet-backed International Union of Students and the World Federation of Democratic Youth and attending the world youth festivals sponsored by the Soviet bloc. USSA president Frank X. Viggiano, when asked about the association's connections with the Soviet-backed organizations, said that this gave the USSA the opportunity to "discuss issues" at the world youth festivals. The conservative magazine *Human Events* aptly called the USSA "the return of the NSA," but saw this as a Soviet rather than a US maneuver.[119]

---

[118] Mjagkij, *Organizing Black America*, 421. For all.
[119] "Return of the National Student Association," 5.

6

STUDENT WORLD FEDERALISTS

World Federation often serves only to conceal the aspirations of several great powers to a role of domination over the entire world.

– Opinion from Moscow, 1946

Among the preparatory committee for the American delegation to the 1946 Prague student congress was a representative from the Student World Federalists (SWF).[120] The SWF was established as the student division of the United World Federalists (UWF) in 1947. The UWF was an amalgam of several internationalist associations. It continues to function. The SWF was at the vanguard of student activism at this early date and was engaged in broader issues such as racial integration, assisting the National Association for the Advancement of Colored People (NAACP) on campuses. The SWF was yet another piece of the US foreign policy establishment's Cold War strategy.

The SWF was involved in the founding of the National Student Association. The SWF was "urged" to participate in the US delegation to the 1947 World Youth Festival in Prague, "with the suggestion that the 300 American delegates would help to provide a democratic (and even federalist) balance to the event."[121] It was for this initial propose

---

[120] "American Preparatory Committee," in Schwartz, *American Students Organize*, 103.

[121] Jonas, *One Shining Moment*, 50.

that the NSA was brought into the CIA fold. It was also at this time that the USSR rejected the US proposal to turn the UN General Assembly into a world parliament, along with the Baruch Plan, which would give the UN "the power to control atomic power and weapons."[122] This was the type of coercive global authority that the World Federalists wanted vested with the UN. The situation was summarized by *Newsweek*:

> The Communist fellow-traveling fringe, with one or two lonely exceptions, has kept aloof, obviously, because the official Communist party line frowns on the idea of world government as a "reactionary Utopia." It insists, in accordance with current Soviet policy, on the inviolability of national sovereignty. This means that for the time being, at least, the world-government movement is one of the few political currents of our time in which liberals can participate without getting tangled up in Communist party intrigues and "front" maneuvers.[123]

Note that, contrary to what many American conservatives assumed, it was the USSR that was resisting what *Newsweek* overtly called "world government" and insisting on "the inviolability of national sovereignty."

Director of the U.S. Office of Public Affairs Francis H. Russell, speaking in 1950 to a UWF meeting in Washington, D.C., lambasted the USSR as being the obstacle in the way of "one world" government. He alluded to this being the primary reason for the advent of the Cold War. He stated:

> For if there is one thing that is clear, it is that the Soviet Union does not have, and has never had, the slightest intention of joining in any plan of world federation in any sense that would be acceptable to any believer in democracy. In fact, it is precisely because the Soviet Union has its own unbending ideas of how the entire world should be organized that the tensions exist today.[124]

---

[122] Ibid.
[123] "World Government Visions in U.S.," 45.
[124] Russell, "Toward a Stronger World Organization," 220–2.

As for the USSR, the Soviets cogently exposed the actual aims of the "world federalists" in a cable sent from Moscow to the leading Mexican newspaper *El Nacional*:

> World Federation often serves only to conceal the aspirations of several great powers to a role of domination over the entire world. It is significant that exhortations to perfect the United Nations Charter may be reduced basically to the demand for annulling the principle, established in the Charter, of the unanimity of the Great Powers, permanent members of the Security Council. Once again this principle of unanimity, called by its opponents the Right of Veto, is being attacked.[125]

With an allusion to the Baruch Plan for the UN control of atomic energy, the Soviet memo referred to the atomic bomb as "the principal argument for World Federalism."

Among the youth organizations aligned with the SWF were the Student League for Industrial Democracy (which would later become the SDS), the Youth Division of the NAACP, B'nai B'rith Youth Organization, Students for Democratic Action, and the NSA.[126]

In 1949 the SWF played a major role alongside the NSA in forming the World Assembly of Youth, created to rival the Soviet-controlled World Federation of Democratic Youth.[127] Al Lowenstein, president of the NSA, also served as national field secretary of the Collegiate Council for the United Nations (CCUN), the youth branch of the American Association of the United Nations, cofounded by Eleanor Roosevelt. Constance Curry, Southern Regional Chair of the NSA, assumed the CCUN position in 1957, using her NSA network to establish CCUN branches on campuses, and countering widespread anti-UN sentiments among conservative Americans.[128]

In 1966 the Student World Federalists aligned themselves with the New Left and the Negotiate Now movement for US withdrawal

---

[125] "Opinion from Moscow," a cable translated and reprinted in *The Student Federalist*.
[126] Jonas, *One Shining Moment*, 66.
[127] Ibid., 74.
[128] Curry, "NSA's Southern Civil Rights Initiative," in Schwartz, *American Students Organize*, 445.

from Vietnam. The SWF subsequently invited New Left notables such as Dr. Benjamin Spock, Joan Baez, David Harris,[129] and Herbert Marcuse as featured speakers to their conventions.[130]

Immanuel Wallerstein

From the start, a notable presence was Immanuel Wallerstein, who was on the United World Federalists executive committee. Wallerstein became a primary intellectual influence on the New Left a decade later, being on the faculty of Columbia University during the 1968 riots.

In 1949 Wallerstein urged the UWF to adopt an anti-colonialist revolutionary agenda, alluding to "world revolution," while urging that pro-Soviet elements be "deposed from this movement for freedom," and that ultimately there must be a UN "world federal government." This "world federal government" must have recourse to force due to the "limitations of negotiations in a lawless world," and must be subjected to "fundamental principles."[131] Rather than the UWF parent body, it was the SWF who were influenced by the Wallerstein manifesto.

Wallerstein's path to becoming an iconic figure of the leftist intelligentsia in the US was paved by CIA operative David Davis, from 1952 to 1961 executive director of the Foundation for Youth & Student Affairs, the main CIA conduit for funds to the NSA. Davis had attended the 1951 World Assembly of Youth (WAY) representing the American Association for the United Nations, "but who was, to the knowledge of us all, a government figure (who most of us believed to be connected to the State Department but who, in retrospect, was probably with the CIA.)"[132]

---

[129] Harris was founder of The Resistance, an organization advocating draft evasion. He was married to protest singer Joan Baez.

[130] Yoder, "United World Federalists."

[131] Jonas, "Student Federalist Movement," in Schwartz, *American Students Organize*, 770.

[132] "Student Voices Influencing the NSA," in Schwartz, *American Students Organize*, 772.

As a vice president of WAY, Wallerstein traveled widely in Africa, conveying information to the CIA on his assessment of African anti-colonialist leaders, whom the US foreign policy establishment could cultivate in their offensive against the colonial powers. His studies of West Africa were enabled by a Ford Foundation fellowship.[133]

The CIA utilized social scientists even of the most far-left persuasions to provide data on Africa and other areas marked by the US for "national liberation."[134]

The CIA took an active interest in the African Studies Association (ASA), Wallerstein having served as president.[135] Among the financial patrons of the ASA during the years of Wallerstein's presidency (1972–1973) was the Ford Foundation (at a time when Ford was presided over by establishment eminence and former National Security Advisor McGeorge Bundy), along with representatives from the Brookings Institute, Royal Dutch Petroleum, and the International Bank of Reconstruction & Development (then headed by former Secretary of State Robert McNamara, a chief architect of the Vietnam War).[136]

The primary venue for Wallerstein's political writings on "the struggles of the new African states during the 1960s" was the *New Leader*, which "subsisted on CIA funding."[137] This was one of the most important leftist magazines that the CIA was subsidizing as part of its world program of recruiting the anti-Soviet Left. "As one of WAY's international officers in the mid-1950s, Wallerstein may or may not have known of the CIA backing it received—though WAY's contest with the Soviet-backed WFDY [World Federation of Democratic Youth] was clear."[138]

---

[133] Plys, "Immanuel Wallerstein."
[134] Price, *Cold War Anthropology*. See also Bolton, *Perversion of Normality*, 143–9.
[135] Mills, *CIA Off Campus*, 37.
[136] Ford Foundation, *Annual Report 1972*, 68; Ford Foundation, *Annual Report 1974*, 49.
[137] Brick, et al., *Lineages of the Literary Left*, 32.
[138] Ibid.

7

WORLD ASSEMBLY OF YOUTH

The World Assembly of Youth (WAY) marked a major development in the left's response to the Cold War. WAY offered Wallerstein a more radical and active option than the UWF and SWF. It is in this milieu that his ideology germinated, thanks to the anti-imperialist position of WAY, which reflected the position of the US foreign policy establishment.

A "secret report" by the US State Department's Office of Intelligence stated that WAY was formed in 1949 in Brussels, with affiliated organizations in fifty states. It was described as the only youth organization offering opposition to the Soviet-controlled World Federation of Democratic Youth. WAY "grew out of two international preparatory conferences" held in London in 1947 and 1948, which had been sponsored by the British Labour government through the National Council of Social Service and the Foreign Office.[139]

It is notable that the US State Department assessment placed emphasis on WAY's potential in working with Third World youth "to formulate a program of action that will inspire and stimulate the enthusiastic support of non-Communist youth, particularly, those in the colonial and underdeveloped areas," and "championing the rights of youth and particularly colonial youth."[140]

---

[139] *World Assembly of Youth.*
[140] Ibid.

In 1949, a three-point program for WAY's first year included the following: "To sponsor and spread information on international travel and exchange, particularly in Africa, Asia and South America."[141] The program continues, committing WAY to "bring to the attention of appropriate agencies the real needs of young people and those of dependent countries, urging them to take action, help and support them, in all possible ways."[142] The program was intended to sell the superiority of American liberalism to young people, which had its counterpart in the Congress for Cultural Freedom.

A program was formulated in 1951 that included: the development of youth movements and their co-ordination in all countries; establishing an information and documentation center; establishing travel and exchange programs; education reforms; the representation of youth in trades unions and workers' organizations; youth control of their own affairs, and a commitment to work for peace by "overcoming prejudice and injustice."[143]

Again, the focus was on conditions in colonial territories. Interestingly, it was the Scandinavian delegates who threatened to leave the congress if resolutions were passed interfering in the affairs of colonial powers, and the anti-colonial resolutions were shelved.[144]

What this does say, however, is that the intention of the foreign policy establishment was to use WAY in the anti-colonial offensive, the aim of which was for the US to supplant Europe in the scuttled former imperial territories.[145]

Despite the protest of the Scandinavian delegates, the *raison d'etre* of WAY was to interfere in the internal affairs of sovereign nations, particularly the European colonies, in accordance with the aims of US foreign policy. An indication of the anti-imperialist doctrine was the equal voting rights that delegates from colonial territories were given at WAY congresses. While this might seem commendably "progressive" today, it was meant as a belligerent and subversive policy against the imperial powers that were supposedly U.S.

---

[141] Ibid., 12–3.
[142] Ibid.
[143] Ibid., 7.
[144] Ibid., 8.
[145] Bolton, *Babel Inc.*, 41–77.

allies. The Atlantic Charter, imposed by Roosevelt on Churchill during World War II, demanded the dismantling of the European colonial empires after the war. The American-backed youth organizations played an important role in cultivating youth leaders as part of the "anti-imperialist" strategy of the US.

At the time the US State Department reported that WAY, along with its US affiliate, the Young Adult Council (YAC), was perpetually short of funds, and that YAC itself, chronically underfunded, had not contributed financially to WAY. If this was correct in 1950, funding was soon forthcoming. Toward the end of the State Department report there is a summation of YAC's potential as a servant of US foreign policy, which would become a sales pitch for funding.[146] In particular, the report stated that WAY had developed a "social reform program" designed to appeal to the youth of "underdeveloped and colonial areas," those same territories that the US aimed to detach from Britain and Europe. WAY's information outlets would also provide a more vigorous counter to those of the USSR.[147] Its use in Cold War operations would also be significant in forming youth organizations in "such sensitive areas as the Near, Middle and Far East, Africa and Latin America." WAY had established a better foothold among the young in those regions than the WFDY "by championing the fight of colonial youth for 'national liberation.'"[148] All that was required was "a sound financial basis nationally and internationally."[149]

In 1950, YAC assisted the US occupation authorities with a summer camp seminar for German students, organized by US High Commissioner John J. McCloy, who provided funding (30,000 Deutschmarks), as did the Rockefeller Foundation ($10,000). CIA funding subsequently reached WAY.[150] YAC provided most of WAY's funding via the Foundation for Youth and Student Affairs, the organization through which the CIA channeled funding. All told, YAC contributed $301,000 to WAY through the foundation.[151]

---

[146] Ibid., 25.
[147] Ibid., 27.
[148] Ibid., 28.
[149] Ibid., 29.
[150] Paget, "From Stockholm to Leiden," in Scott-Smith and Krabbendam, *Cultural Cold War*, 141.
[151] Maunders, "Controlling Youth for Democracy."

SDS Affiliation

At the height of its strength during the late 1960s, the US Youth Council (USYC) comprised thirty-seven organizational affiliates, including the College Democrats of America, the National Student Association, Students for a Democratic Society, and the Youth Division of the NAACP.[152]

The fact that SDS, one of the most radical factions of the New Left, was a member organization in the USYC was cited in a list of affiliated organizations included in a Senate Armed Services Committee report. Other affiliates included: Campus Americans for Democratic Action, Student World Federalists, Workmen's Circle (a New York Yiddish socialist group), and the Young People's Socialist League (the youth division of the Socialist Party of America).[153] The *Vietnam News Service* commented that the organizations listed were identified as beneficiaries of CIA funds or had received a major part of their funding from CIA conduit foundations. It does not appear that the *Vietnam News Service* or any other leftist organization asked: for what purpose? Such a question might have necessitated introspection.

Note that the SDS was affiliated with the US Youth Council at a time when the council was receiving funds from the CIA and the Rockefeller Foundation.

In 1967, *The New York Times* revealed that the CIA had provided 90 percent of YAC's funds and was defining its agenda. As with the NSA, YAC/USYC presidents and vice presidents knew of the CIA funding. They received top-secret security clearances from the CIA and were required to sign a twenty-year confidentiality agreement to keep the agency's involvement secret.[154] After 1967, funding of the USYC was assumed by the US State Department, and later by the US Information Agency, until the organization ceased operations in 1986.

---

[152] Reed, "Youth Council to Investigate."
[153] *Additional Procurement of M-16 Rifles*.
[154] Reed, "Youth Council to Investigate." See also Sheehan, "Foundations Linked to C.I.A."

Gloria Steinem

Feminist icon Gloria Steinem got her start as founding director of the above-cited Independent Research Service. At the 1959 Vienna Youth Festival she ran the IRS press bureau.

Like the *Ramparts* exposé, the exposé of Steinem was also undertaken by a New Left journal, *Redstockings*.[155] Steinem's explanation in later years was that she regarded the CIA as a "progressive," "liberal" organization, laudable for its opposition to Senator Joseph McCarthy, although she also threatened a lawsuit against those who raised the matter of her employment by a CIA front.[156]

Steinem stated to *The Washington Post* in 1968, regarding revelations about the CIA and NSA, that the CIA "was the only one with enough guts and foresight to see that youth and student affairs were important."[157]

The radical-feminist journal *oob*, reporting on the *Redstockings*–Steinem controversy, pointed out that she was still listed as a member of the IRS Board of Directors during 1968–1969, according to her entry in *Who's Who in America*. *oob* asked how it was that Steinem rose to the leadership of "women's liberation" so quickly, despite having been hitherto unknown to any movement or cause. *oob* pointed out that it was Steinem's followers around *Ms.* magazine that had "all the money and power" within the women's movement. *oob* regarded *Ms.* as "a capitalist commercial enterprise," and wondered whether *Ms.* owed its existence to money from corporations, or whether it was a CIA front.[158] With some detachment, *oob* could have questioned whether the women's movement *per se* had been a front ever since Margaret Sanger received funds from the Rockefeller Foundation for her Birth Control League in 1924, on the personal request of John D. Rockefeller Jr.[159]

---

[155] "Redstockings' Statement," 8.
[156] Lofton, "Ms. Steinem's CIA Connection."
[157] "Redstockings' Statement," 8.
[158] Ibid.
[159] Raymond Fosdick to John D. Rockefeller, Jr., June 13, 1924.

As for *Ms.*, it was launched in 1971 with support from Katherine Graham, publisher of *The Washington Post* (the establishment standard-bearer in journalism), the Ford Foundation, the Rockefeller Trust, and Warner Communications, which invested $1 million.[160] Eighty-five thousand copies of the first issue were inserted as a *gratis* promotion into *New York* magazine, where Steinem had been employed as a columnist by the magazine's editor, Clay Felker, who had worked with Steinem in the IRS at the 1962 Helsinki World Youth Festival.[161] *Ms.* was saved from bankruptcy in 1979 with a $200,000 grant from *The New York Post*, and a matching grant from the Ford Foundation. A total of $1.4 million was given by real estate developer Mortimer Zuckerman, owner of the *US News & World Report*, among others.[162]

Feminism became an important, albeit disruptive, component of the New Left. Feminists expressed their angst, viewing their male counterparts in the New Left males as being as much part of "White patriarchy" as any other men. Bernadine Dohrn, the leader of the most extreme faction of the Weather Underground (an extremist outgrowth of SDS), praised the Manson Family with laudatory declarations on the stabbing of the pregnant Sharon Tate, concluding that "white babies were pigs."[163] In 1970, three of the four members of the Weather Underground, wanted by the FBI for "interstate flight, mob action, riot, and conspiracy," were women: Kathy Boudin, Judith Clark, and Bernadine Dohrn, described as having a "dangerous . . . propensity for violence."[164]

When the New Left adopted the "struggle session" self-criticism techniques used by Maoists to impose collective conformity, it became a means by which the feminists could assume dominance. Tom Hayden recalled of the group he joined at Berkeley, the Red Family, that "discussions took the form of self-criticism, a group psychotherapy in which it was assumed that anything said in one's own self-defense—whether about washing dishes, exhibiting macho

---

[160] Snodgrass, *Encyclopedia of Feminist Literature*, "Ms."
[161] Marcello, *Gloria Steinem*, 73.
[162] Conkling, *Ms. Gloria Steinem*, 26.
[163] Hayden, *Reunion*, 472.
[164] From an FBI poster. The fourth individual was Dohrn's partner, Bill Ayers.

attitudes, or being attracted to a woman—was probably a self-serving defensive alibi. I found these meetings to be torture sessions."[165] Hayden was purged from the feminist-dominated collective, written off as "an oppressive male chauvinist." Soon after his expulsion, the Red Family "self-destructed, its members scattering everywhere. The appetite for splits and purges was uncontrollable."[166]

Feminism steamrollered its way through the New Left. It had been enabled when New Left intellectuals like Herbert Marcuse had declared women to be among a select group of the "oppressed" that would replace the proletariat as the revolutionary class. On March 7th, 1974, Marcuse delivered a lecture at Stanford University entitled "Marxism and Feminism," beginning: "I believe the Women's Liberation Movement today is perhaps the most important and potentially the most radical movement that we have, even if the consciousness of this fact has not yet penetrated the Movement as a whole."[167] In the New Left manner that caused old-line Marxists in Moscow to look not only askance but with suspicion, Marcuse stated that the feminist issue cut across "class lines."

Marcuse referred to the definition of "female" and "feminine" as being "socially conditioned," which does not stop even under "socialism."[168] Here we have the beginnings of the now-flourishing LGBT movement that has, ironically, caused deep rifts within the feminist movement, with old-line feminists now finding accord with conservatives in rejecting transgenderism as an affront to women. Again, at odds with classical Marxism, Marcuse stated that women can never be fully liberated within any "class society." A society "beyond equality" is required where the premise is "a different Reality Principle," "where the established dichotomy between masculine and feminine is overcome in the social and individual relationships between human beings." Hence the feminist movement requires a "change in consciousness" to fulfill its "most radical, subversive potential."[169] Marcuse sees the heretical twelfth and thirteenth century sects, the

---

[165] Hayden, *Reunion*, 421.
[166] Ibid., 425.
[167] Marcuse, "Marxism and Feminism."
[168] Ibid., 280.
[169] Ibid., 281.

Cathars and Albigensians, as precursors to the progressive movement, as their repudiation of childbearing meant that women became "liberated" from the exploitative character of motherhood.[170] The ultimate aim, according to Marcuse, is a "synthesis" of the "masculine–feminine antithesis" toward "the legendary idea of *androgynism.*"[171]

Androgynism was presented by Marcuse as the ultimate aim of the New Left revolt. Here we see the actual aim to be the "liberation of women" from the family and from childrearing; the obliteration of all genders, and the creation of one nebulous mass—in the name of "identity." So far from being the most "radical and subversive revolt" against capitalism, this has been part of the general trend of capitalism for several generations, first with transhumanism, as championed by UNESCO's Julian Huxley,[172] and now under the guise of posthumanism, with feminism transforming into postgenderism and cyberfeminism. In all cases, the aim is clear: to enable the elimination of all familial and procreative functions by technology, leading to control by a global technocracy.[173] In phraseology analogous to that of Marcuse, we now have well-placed and well-funded scientists (not fringe cranks or cultists) affirming: "Postgenderism is an extrapolation of ways that technology is eroding the biological, psychological and social role of gender, and an argument for why the erosion of binary gender will be liberatory."[174]

170 Ibid., 283.
171 Ibid., 287.
172 Bolton, *Perversion of Normality*, 493–9.
173 Ibid., 501–10.
174 Dvorsky and Hughes, "Postgenderism."

8

INTERNATIONAL STUDENT CONFERENCE

In 1952 the International Student Conference (ISC) was founded in Edinburgh, Scotland. Twenty-five student unions were represented.[175] A secretariat was established in Leiden. Funding from the CIA was channeled via the Foundation for Youth and Student Affairs.[176] The intention was to rival the Soviet-dominated International Union of Students (IUS).

Like WAY and YAC, the ISC "took strong and consistent stands against colonialism and imperialism," of both European and Soviet varieties.[177] The issues discussed at ISC congresses were standard New Left fare: racism, colonialism, the role of students in independent Asia, the role of student unions in national life, and so on.[178] *The Student*, the main ISC organ, ran from 1956 to 1968, with around twenty-five thousand copies distributed *gratis* to student unions, published in English, French, Spanish, and occasionally Arabic. Additionally, there was the ISC *Information Bulletin*.[179]

In 1967, *Democratic Education* was founded, featuring articles on education reform.[180] It is notable that this was produced at a time

---

[175] Altbach, "The Student Internationals."
[176] Ibid., 36.
[177] Ibid., 39.
[178] Ibid., 43.
[179] Ibid., 47.
[180] Ibid., 48.

when the New Left was demanding the "democratization" of education, and the Ford Foundation was purveying similar ideas, culminating in the worldwide student riots the following year. The ISC, like WAY, YAC, and the NSA, served the interests of US foreign policy in assisting student unions in the developing world, which was then contested between the West and the Eastern Bloc:

> The ISC stimulated several of its member unions, such as the German National Union of Students, to engage in overseas technical assistance programs in developing countries. These projects were, not surprisingly, linked to the political positions of the international student groups. A good example of this is the fact that the ISC gave substantial aid to the anti-Communist National Council of University Students of India (NCUSI), an ISC member, while the IUS provided similar assistance to its Indian affiliate, the All-India Students' Federation. In other countries as well the student internationals gave aid to those unions which supported their policies. For the most part, a typewriter or mimeograph machine could not substantially alter the direction or the program of a specific national union, but in at least one case, foreign assistance did make a difference in the development of the organization. The Indian NCUSI was never a very popular or highly representative organization and it is clear that it could not have built itself into a recognized national student organization without outside support, in this case from the ISC and from the U.S. National Student Association. Much of the office equipment of the NCUSI was donated from the outside and funds for publishing the NCUSI's newspaper and for issuing the Asian Press Bulletin were provided by outside sources. In addition, funds to aid in several student conferences in India were supplied by foreign sources. The USNSA even supplied a telephone for the NCUSI. While most student unions were not influenced by foreign sources as much as the NCUSI was, even the gift of a typewriter was important for a student union that had little domestic financial resources.[181]

Student scholarships for study abroad were arranged through the International University Exchange Fund (IUEF). Of particular

---

[181] Ibid., 51.

significance, funds were provided to sponsor leftist students who were operating against the colonial states targeted by the US:

> The IUEF not only arranged for interchanges between student leaders from various countries, but also provided scholarships for students forced to flee their countries for political reasons. Refugee students from South Africa, Angola, and Algeria received valuable support from the IUEF.[182]

Altbach placed this aid in a Cold War context: "It is clear that even in the context of Cold War politics and within highly partisan international student organizations active programs designed at least in part to serve the world student community were conducted."[183]

At times student leaders received support from both the CIA-sponsored ISC and the Soviet-sponsored IUS. This should not be surprising, given that both the US and the USSR were in accord in aiming for the destruction of the old European colonial empires: "Both organizations served, in part, the same constituency—the student unions of the Third World, and indeed some individual student leaders participated in programs sponsored by the two groups at different times."[184]

The social democratic parties had a youth international, the International Union of Socialist Youth (IUSY), headquartered in Vienna, which also received CIA funding through US tax-exempt foundations.[185]

> The "service" programs carried out by the international student organizations do not obscure the fact that the organizations were (and in the case of the IUS, still are) a part of the Cold War. Their basic *raison d'etre* in the eyes of those who control them and supply the all-important financial resources has been and still is political.[186]

---

[182] Ibid.
[183] Ibid., 53.
[184] Ibid.
[185] Ibid., 91.
[186] Ibid., 55.

The NSA constituted the controlling element within the ISC:

> It is estimated that between 85 and 90 per cent of the ISC's annual
> budgets between approximately 1953 and 1967 were contributed
> through various channels by the U.S. government. In addition, at
> least one American was on the senior staff of the Coordinating Sec-
> retariat of the ISC at all times between 1953 and 1967, and these
> individuals were without exception former officers or officials of
> the U.S. National Student Association. Thus, it is very likely that
> these individuals constituted a link between the American funding
> agencies and the ISC secretariat.[187]

The NSA influence ensured that the ISC focused on issues that were
of importance to the US foreign policy establishment:

> It is significant that the U.S. National Student Association (US-
> NSA), while a member of the dominant European group of student
> unions within the ISC, emphasized that the ISC should take strong
> positions on issues important in the struggle with the IUS, such as
> colonialism and imperialism. In view of the connection between
> USNSA officials and the CIA, this position is not surprising since
> the NSA wanted to maintain its influence in the Third World. A
> final part of the ISC political equation was the impact of student
> unions from the developing countries. . . .[188]

At the 1956 congress the question of imperialism was debated regarding Algeria, with the NSA taking a strong anti-imperialist position:

> The question of Algerian independence received substantial atten-
> tion and aroused a good deal of debate. The dispute came close to
> precipitating a crisis in the ISC with the more conservative Euro-
> pean unions arguing that these political questions were not a

---

[187] Ibid., 59.

[188] Ibid., 70. Altbach remarked that the student unions of the developing states
increased in influence until they held a balance of power. Whether their ideological
positions were any different from those that served the long-term objectives of the
US foreign policy establishment is, however, unlikely. The priority for both was to
push for imperial scuttle. The way in which the NSA was a tool of US foreign policy
is indicated by its adamant *opposition* to Puerto Rican independence, while insisting
on its anti-imperialist doctrine against the European imperial powers.

legitimate concern. But, in the end, Algerian independence was supported—the American USNSA taking a strong position in favor of the Algerians—and the ISC did survive.[189]

By 1968, the ISC had collapsed, like the NSA and the Congress for Cultural Freedom, embarrassed by the revelation of CIA subsidies.

The US government-commissioned report concludes that the NSA was particularly important within the ISC. An anti-colonialist agenda was a focus, reflecting postwar US doctrine.

> The role of the NSA in the ISC was particularly important. Not only did the NSA provide almost one-half of the ISC's budget which was collected directly from its affiliates, but the ISC's funds from the Foundation for Youth and Student Affairs inevitably came through ex-NSA staff members on the ISC secretariat, and ex-NSA staff members serving as FYSA officials. As one participant put it, "NSA played a role at ISC far out of proportion to its single vote." NSA delegations also played important roles at ISC meetings and other events. They were among the best informed on international student affairs and, because of the extensive traveling by NSA staff members, many contacts among student leaders had been developed. It is significant that the NSA had especially cordial relations with student unions from developing countries, and often sided with these groups in the ISC. There was at least one former NSA official on the ISC at all times from the beginning to the end of the organization, with the exception of the final year after the NSA-CIA disclosures, and often several Americans were stationed in Leiden. For a long period, the editor of the *Student* was an ex-NSA official. It is clear that the USNSA was the key to the ISC's existence in the crucial financial area, and that American NSA officers were of the utmost importance in ISC's affairs. The NSA's international programs were critically important for the non-Communist international student organizations. Its direct activities, such as the Foreign Student Leadership Project, technical assistance to foreign student unions, scholarship programs for Angolan and Algerian refugee students, the publications of the international commission, and other activities were quite vital, but perhaps of even more importance were indirect aspects of NSA's international work—its key

---

[189] Ibid., 72.

role in financing the ISC and its activities at ISC meetings and other international student events.[190]

---

[190] Ibid., 107–108.

9

STUDENTS FOR DEMOCRATIC ACTION

Precursor of the Revolution

Students for Democratic Action (SDA) was formed as the youth affiliate of the Americans for Democratic Action (ADA), which had been founded to carry on the legacy of New Deal establishment-socialism in the aftermath of FDR's death. The SDA was launched at the 1947 convention of the ADA, the same year as the founding of the NSA.

The ADA/SDA "included an aggressive foreign policy that recognized the emerging Soviet threat," and supported the Marshall Plan and the Truman Doctrine, which were integral parts of the Cold War strategy for extending US influence and containing the USSR.[191] The SDA also opposed Southern segregation, urged the purging from liberal organizations of Soviet influence, supported the UN, and advocated an "aggressive response to a spreading national pattern of loyalty oaths and what became known as McCarthyism."[192]

Each of these primary aims of the SDA, like the emerging postwar student activist movement generally, reflected establishment Cold War policies. Here we see the type of left-wing anti-Sovietism that

---

[191] Reisin, "The SDA–NSA Connection: A Post-War Major Force and Source of Leadership," in Schwartz, *American Students Organize*, 781–2.
[192] Ibid., 782.

vigorously repudiated any action against communism *domestically* ("McCarthyism" and "loyalty oaths") that might develop into a mass populist reaction that could sweep away not only communism but the liberalism of Wall Street. The USSR and its agents could only be opposed insofar as they thwarted US foreign policy aims for world governance. Hence the vehement opposition to Joseph McCarthy from the CIA, Wall Street, and the Council on Foreign Relations.[193] From 1950 to 1952, NSA presidents Dick Murphy, Allard Lowenstein, and Bill Dentzer were vociferous opponents of "McCarthyism" and "loyalty oaths."[194]

There was close interaction between the SDA, the NSA, and the Student World Federalists. Reisin states that these organizations were a "precursor of the revolution that did not emerge until the 1960s."[195] Among those who emerged from SDA leadership were Allard Lowenstein, president of the NSA and later chairman of the ADA; Marvin Rich, organizer of the Congress for Racial Equality; Dick Murphy, another NSA president, and Evelyn Jones Rich, executive director of the Rubin Foundation. Many others became notable as politicians and academics.[196]

---

[193] CFR historian Peter Grose wrote of the establishment's horror at McCarthyism: "The nation was in danger of succumbing to a red-baiting frenzy, marked by the rise into the headlines of Senator Joseph R. McCarthy. Not surprisingly, the Council's membership seemed solidly united in contempt for the Wisconsin demagogue; under his provocative rhetoric, after all, was a *thinly veiled attack on the entire East Coast foreign policy establishment,* [emphasis added] whose members gathered regularly in the closed conference rooms of the Harold Pratt House." Grose, *Continuing the Inquiry.* See also Bolton, "Joe McCarthy and the Establishment Bolsheviks."

[194] Reisin, "The SDA-NSA Connection," 783.

[195] Ibid. 782.

[196] Ibid. The Samuel Rubin Foundation has funded sundry leftist organizations, including the Institute for Policy Studies (IPS), influential in training New Left activists and formulating New Left ideology.

10

STUDENTS FOR A DEMOCRATIC SOCIETY

SDS and the Student League for Industrial Democracy

Tom Hayden observed the infiltration of the Shachtmanites. These ex-Trotskyites were named after Max Shachtman, who had been Leon Trotsky's personal secretary in New York. This faction was especially successful in entering the AFL–CIO, the country's largest federation of labor unions. Hayden wrote: "In a curious twist of history, Shachtmanite anti-Stalinism converged with the Cold War interests of the CIA, which covertly funded many AFL–CIO programs aboard." Hayden observed that the Shachtmanites infiltrated the Democratic Party, changing the party's direction by purging it of "Southern racists." Their youth group, the Young People's Socialist League (YPSL), was at the founding of the SDS. The YPSL was an affiliate of the World Assembly of Youth (WAY).

Tom Kahn and Rachelle Horowitz from the YPSL were officials of the League for Industrial Democracy (LID), from which the SDS emerged.[197] Michael Harrington, also from LID and YPSL, was the LID liaison at the SDS organizational conference at Port Huron. He insisted on a vigorous anti-Stalinist line, and support for the *status*

---

[197] Tom Kahn founded the National Endowment for Democracy in 1983. NED, established with congressional funding, has been a primary organization for propagating American liberal internationalism, fomenting color revolutions in conjunction with tax-exempt foundations, think tanks, and government agencies. See Bolton, *Revolution from Above*, 218–21.

quo in the CIA-backed labor movement, the AFL–CIO. These anti-Stalinist Marxists gained increasing influence in the labor movement.[198]

The Cold War agendas of the US establishment and disaffected Marxists converged in their opposition to the USSR, in supporting decolonization, and increasingly in domestic policies such as opposition to Southern segregation. Hayden was dismayed that the AFL–CIO organizers and Shachtmanites even supported US involvement in the Vietnam War. The phenomenon was not new. In 1951, Natalia Sedova, Trotsky's widow, resigned from the Fourth International, called the USSR the primary obstacle to the "world revolution," and supported American forces fighting the "Stalinists" in Korea.[199]

The Student League for Industrial Democracy (SLID) was the youth affiliate of LID, the latter having been founded in 1905 as the Intercollegiate Socialist Society. Changing its name to LID in 1921, its aims had been to educate students on socialism and the labor movement. Succumbing to a preoccupation with anti-Stalinism in the aftermath of World War II, LID led the anti-Soviet campaign among the labor movement.

The SDS was in fact the new name for SLID. The name change was urged by Aryeh Neier, who had been SLID president, and then executive director of LID. Neier went on to serve as president of George Soros' Open Society Foundations from 1993 to 2012. In 1978 he cofounded and directed Helsinki Watch, designed to monitor the USSR, which broadened into the Human Rights Watch, which plays an important role in demonizing states marked for regime change by the US.

The purpose of renaming SLID to SDS was to reinvigorate a stagnating organization. Kirkpatrick Sale, in his history of the SDS, writes:

> It was a measure of the new restlessness on the campuses that the members of SLID decided early in 1960 that the time had come to change its name. . . . An October meeting of the SLID leaders had

---

[198] Hayden, *Reunion*, 86–92.
[199] Natalia Sedova Trotsky to the Fourth International and the Socialist Workers Party, May 9, 1951.

debated "National Student Forum" without being able to engender much enthusiasm, but a month later a new choice, "Students for a Democratic Society," emerged as the clear favorite. . . . In January 1960, with some trepidation as to how the elders in LID would take it, the young leaders of SLID made the switch.[200]

The SDS founding document, the Port Huron Statement, drafted by Tom Hayden, included a strong rejection of the USSR that had been insisted upon by socialist eminence Michael Harrington, key LID liaison with the SDS, and Dick Flacks of LID, who had inserted into the Port Huron Statement an anti-Soviet[201] position, reading:

> As democrats we are in basic opposition to the communist system. The Soviet Union, as a system, rests on the total suppression of organized opposition. . . . The Communist Party has equated falsely the "triumph of socialism" with centralized bureaucracy. The Soviet state lacks independent labor organizations and other liberties we consider basic. . . . Communist parties throughout the rest of the world are generally undemocratic in internal structure and mode of action. . . . The communist movement has failed, in every sense, to achieve its stated intentions of leading a worldwide movement for human emancipation.[202]

Harrington had gained fame as a socialist for his book *The Other America*. He became part of Lyndon Johnson's taskforce on poverty. He had been a Shachtmanite, leading the youth wing of the Socialist Party into the Young Socialist League, the youth wing of Max Shachtman's Independent Socialist League, in 1953. Shachtman had broken with Leon Trotsky in 1940 and formed the ISL. Shachtman's hatred of the USSR was so pronounced that he did not believe that the Soviet Union should be assisted in the war against Germany. Jim Creegan, who had been Penn State chairman of the SDS during the 1960s, wrote of Shachtman:

---

[200] Sale, *SDS*, 8.
[201] Hayden, *Reunion*, 92.
[202] Hayden et al., *The Port Huron Statement*, 31

By the early 60s, he had decided that Stalinism was a greater obstacle to socialism and human progress than capitalism. He reasoned that, if capitalism and Stalinism were both class societies that exploited workers, workers in Western democracies at least enjoyed political freedoms that they were denied in the USSR. Shachtman's belief in Western capitalism as the lesser evil eventually led him to support America's worldwide anti-communist crusade, including the 1962 US Bay of Pigs invasion of Cuba, and—at first only privately—the Vietnam war. Domestically, Shachtman came to see the Democratic Party as the political arena in which socialists should work, and within the Democratic Party, he viewed the AFL-CIO bureaucracy—first in the person of United Auto Workers chief Walter Reuther, then in the federation's president, George Meany—as representing the true interests of the American working class.[203]

Alan Haber (first president of the SDS) and Tom Hayden were, at the urging of Harrington, called before an inquisitional board of LID to account for their lack of enthusiasm for the Cold War. LID softened its initial outrage, however, and LID's break with the SDS did not take place until 1965.

In 1982 Harrington formed the Democratic Socialists of America, at present the largest and most influential left-wing group in America. Despite their calls for "class struggle," DSA strongly supports US global hegemony. Jim Creegan, writing of Harrington's career, stated of the left at this time:

Political circumstances had greatly altered by the time DSOC [Democratic Socialist Organizing Committee] merged with the New American Movement (NAM) to form the Democratic Socialists of America (DSA) in 1982. The election of Ronald Reagan to the presidency in 1980, and the subsequent right-wing onslaught, made Harrington's socialist brand appear considerably more radical than it had looked fifteen years earlier. Moreover, many of the now older New Leftists and SDSers who comprised the core of NAM had gone on to raise families, acquire professional careers and adopt a commensurably more moderate politics.[204]

---

[203] Creegan, "The Left Wing of the Permissible."
[204] Ibid.

NSA and SDS

The NSA was a primary source from which Al Haber recruited the first members of the SDS. The initial recruits were drawn from the 1961 NSA congress, at a time when the NSA was still being subsidized by the CIA and tax-exempt foundations. Haber formed a front called the Liberal Study Group for the purpose. A paper on SDS recruiting and communications stated:

> SDS sent contingents to the conferences of such groups as the National Student Association (NSA), and the Student Peace Union (SPU).[205] At these meetings, SDS members circulated and participated in panels and debates. They located people who seemed sympathetic to SDS's message, or such persons located them after hearing them speak in public, and they obtained the names and addresses of these individuals for future contacts. The most important blitzing was done at the NSA. In 1961, Al Haber, then President of SDS, proposed a "Liberal Study Group" as a source of position papers on liberal points of view within the NSA. At the time, NSA was under pressure from right-wing students, especially those influenced by William Buckley and his National Review, as being too left-wing in the positions it adopted. The Liberal Study Group was approved, perhaps in part because it was viewed as a counter-balance to organized forces on the right wing of the organization. The approved Liberal Study Group published papers and bibliographies, and it conducted seminars and presented displays at NSA conventions and conferences. The group became the focus for left-wing activity within the NSA. As such, it became a fecund source of recruits for SDS. . . .
>
> SDS walked a delicate balance between exploiting NSA and remaining an asset to that organization. SDS recruiters in the Liberal Study Group attracted attention in many ways. They used seminars

---

[205] The Student Peace Union, founded in 1959, was a significant precursor to the New Left. From the start, the Shachtmanite-dominated Young People's Socialist League sought to infiltrate the SPU. Wracked by the usual Trotskyist factionalism introduced into its ranks by the Shachtmanites, the SPU dissolved in 1964, but was soon reorganized. The second incarnation merged with the Campus Americans for Democratic Action in 1967, forming the Independent Student's Union.

and displays to attract potential recruits at conventions, spoke publicly during workshops and plenary sessions, and spent their evenings assembling and distributing a newsletter which continued each day's discussions or introduced issues which SDS believed might be of interest to the NSA. The speeches and newsletters led many conventioneers to contact SDS members individually to continue a discussion, seek information about an issue, or seek information about SDS. SDS organizers also buttonholed conventioneers whose comments had indicated that they might be sympathetic with SDS.[206]

Tom Hayden was prompted to join the New Left by the presence of twenty-five delegates from the Student Nonviolent Coordinating Committee (SNCC) "gathered for a *foundation-funded* retreat" that "paralleled" the NSA congress.[207] Hayden did not seem perturbed by the sponsorship of the SNCC by tax-exempt foundations, nor by the rumors among rank-and-file members of the NSA that their association was controlled by an older cabal that had long been working with the CIA. It was also at this NSA congress that Hayden met his first wife, Sandra Cason,[208] who was among the most vocal radicals at the congress.

Dr. Angus Johnston, a former member of the US Student Association, writes of the association between the NSA and SDS:

NSA played a vital role in the wave of student activism that rose in the early 1960s, doing much to advance a student-centered vision for the American university. Many founders of Students for a Democratic Society (SDS) met and became involved in national activism through NSA, and thousands of students got their first glimpse of the civil rights and anti-war movements through NSA events. Although SNCC and SDS were often critical of NSA's national leadership's moderation, they relied on the association for volunteers, publicity, and national communication.

By the mid-sixties, many of NSA's incoming officers were perturbed by the group's CIA ties, and the association began taking steps to disentangle itself from the agency. By late 1966 CIA funding

---

206 Robert, "Rhetoric of Social Movements."
207 Hayden, *Reunion*, 39. Emphasis added.
208 Ibid., 40.

had slowed to a trickle. The relationship was on the verge of disintegration when *Ramparts* magazine broke the story in February 1967, exposing not only NSA's CIA ties but the agency's support to a long list of supposedly independent organizations as well.[209]

Angus Johnston, in his history of the US Student Association, writes that after the 1967 *Ramparts* revelations about the NSA's long-time association with the CIA, the organization recalibrated. One of the first campaigns of the reformed NSA was initiated by Allard Lowenstein, a former NSA president. As we have seen, Lowenstein had the support of the CIA, and it is implausible that Lowenstein was unaware of the CIA connections with the NSA. Lowenstein instigated the NSA "Dump Johnson" campaign in support of Robert Kennedy and Eugene McCarthy's candidacies for the Democratic presidential nomination in 1968. It was this issue that was the central focus of the New Left that year, culminating in riots at the Democratic National Convention in Chicago. Sensing the displeasure with his administration from the New Left, Johnson withdrew from the race early in 1968, designating his vice president, Hubert Humphrey, as his chosen successor. After the assassination of Robert Kennedy, Eugene McCarthy became the New Left choice. As will be seen, McCarthy was also the Wall Street choice for the presidential nomination.

The Ford Foundation started giving grants to the NSA in 1955.[210] One commentator, Randall Holcombe, professor of economics at Florida State University, remarked, "through the NSA, the Ford Foundation financed the campus rebellion that was a visible part of the 1960s social activism."[211] David R. Jones, executive director of the conservative organization Young Americans for Freedom, speaking before the House Committee on Tax Reform, stated that the NSA had been funded by the Ford Foundation, the Fund for the Republic (a Ford Foundation initiative), the Catherwood Foundation, and the General Mills Foundation.[212] The congressional committee further cited the following foundations as having provided grants to the

---

209 Johnston, "Brief History."
210 Johnston, "United States National Student Association," 29.
211 Holcombe, *Writing Off Ideas*, 94–5.
212 Jones, "Tax Reform," 864.

NSA: the Clara Buttenweiser Unger Memorial Foundation, Asia Foundation of San Francisco, Edward W. Hazen Foundation, Edward John Nobel Foundation, and a number of 'foundations' which subsequently turned out to be tax-exempt fronts formed and controlled by the U.S. Central Intelligence Agency. The NSA seems to have been granted its tax-exempt status by the Internal Revenue Service at the urging of the CIA. The tax-exempt NSA Educational Travel Inc. also received hundreds of thousands of dollars from tax-exempt foundations and the CIA.[213]

Of the above foundations, in 1967 the Catherwood Foundation was among those referred to as "CIA co-operators" in the channeling of CIA funds in the *Congressional Quarterly*.[214] The Asia Foundation was formed in 1954 as an oligarchic think tank, whose founders included T. S. Peterson, CEO of Standard Oil; Paul G. Hoffman, first administrator of the Marshall Plan; Paul C. Smith, president, Crowell-Collier Publishing, and Grayson Kirk, president of Columbia University. The Hazen Foundation was established in 1925 to fund the organizing of Black youth.

Jones referred to the NSA National Supervisory Board as having issued a statement in February 1967, after *Rampart*'s widely reported revelations, that the CIA had for the past fifteen years provided "as much as 80% of the NSA budget," channeled through a CIA front, the Foundation for Youth and Student Affairs.[215]

Angus Johnston states that the NSA "now reached out to constituencies it had slighted in the past. The 1969 Congress featured workshops on gay rights and a new pledge of support to activists of color, and in 1971 the association elected its first woman president, Marge Tabankin."[216] The NSA became more extreme as the SDS and other elements of the New Left fractured. In 1972, Tabankin went to North Vietnam to seek out evidence of US atrocities. After itself fracturing in 1971, the NSA and a breakaway organization, the National Student Lobby, reunited to form the United States Student Association in 1978. The organization turned to identity politics under the influence

---

[213] Ibid., 868.
[214] "Foundations, Private Organizations Linked to CIA," 2.
[215] Jones, "Tax Reform," 868.
[216] Johnston, "Brief History."

of the National Third World Student Coalition (now called the National People of Color Student Coalition). In 1989 a racial quota of 50 percent was mandated for the seats of the USSA board of directors to go to people of color, followed by a similar embrace of LGBT.

Funding for the USSA is channeled through the USSA Foundation. As in the days of the USSA's predecessor, the NSA, funding continues from the Ford Foundation and other oligarchic sources.[217] In 2022 Sarita Gupta assumed the role of vice president of US programs for the Ford Foundation. Ms. Gupta sits on the boards of the Institute for Policy Studies (a think tank that played a seminal role in the emergence of the New Left), and the USSA Foundation, among others. In 2005, Ford gave $150,000 to the USSAF.[218]

---

[217] Although not so easy to determine, Soros funds have reached the USSA and other left-wing youth organizations via the Youth Engagement Fund. See Vandenberg, "Raising New Voices." In 2001 the Bill and Melinda Gates Foundation gave $40,000 to the USSAF. Bill and Melinda Gates Foundation, "Grantee, October 2001." In 2004 the Andrew W. Mellon Foundation, along with other foundations, helped fund a USSA book on the NSA.

[218] Ford Foundation, *Annual Report 2005*, 96. Ford's records show grants to the ASSU Foundation since 2008, for the purposes of "training" and "organizing" on campuses, with annual donations up to $400,000. See the "Grants Database" on their website.

II

ESTABLISHMENT AGENDA: THE PORT HURON STATEMENT

What you Radicals and we who hold opposing views differ about, is not so much the ends as the means, not so much what should be brought about as how it should and can be brought about.
— Otto Kahn, Wall Street banker, 1925

The Port Huron Statement, drafted by Tom Hayden and ratified by the SDS in 1962, became the definitive statement of the New Left's ascent to domestic prominence. The statement, far from challenging the establishment at its core, reflects what one could read in the annual reports and position papers of the major oligarchic foundations. The manifesto retained the most important Cold War premises that had been advocated by the NSA, World Federalists, and SDA, such as the empowering of the UN to impose "international law," stating:

It will involve the simultaneous creation of international rulemaking and enforcement machinery beginning under the United Nations, and the gradual transfer of sovereignties—such as national armies and national determination of "international" law—to such machinery. It will involve the initiation of an explicitly political— as opposed to military—foreign policy on the part of the two major superstates. Neither has formulated the political terms in which they would conduct their behavior in a disarming or disarmed world. Neither dares to disarm until such an understanding is reached.[219]

Here we see national armies subsumed by an international authority, operating under "international law" that can impose its will on any reticent state. US and Soviet world hegemony were assumed as a partnership. This was the policy that the US had advocated immediately after World War II, which the USSR had rejected. Hayden sought to place the plan back on the globalist agenda, again using the "world federalist" threat of a nuclear holocaust if such a world order did not ensue. This would be policed by "world or at least regional enforcement agencies, an international civil service and inspection service, and other supranational groups [that] must come into reality under the United Nations."[220]

With the drain that military spending and the Vietnam War was having on the US economy, Wall Street was as avid for America's economic redirection and "disengagement" from overseas conflicts as the SDS and IPS. The Port Huron Statement is in accord with the foreign policy establishment in seeing such redirection as "especially crucial . . . while America is entering into favorable trade relations with the European Economic Community: such a gesture, combining economic ambition with less dependence on the military, would demonstrate the kind of competitive 'co-existence' America intends to conduct with the communist-bloc nations."[221]

The SDS urged military disengagement so that Wall Street would have a competitive edge in trade relations. Richard Barnet of the IPS alluded in *Global Reach* to the attitude of the "global corporate managers" toward the Vietnam War as follows: "a military policy that leads to economic weakness needs changing."[222] The foreign policy urged by the SDS reflected that of the US foreign policy establishment in the aftermath of World War II.

---

[219] Hayden et al., *The Port Huron Statement*, (2) 3.
[220] Ibid., (4).
[221] Ibid.
[222] Barnet and Müller, *Global Reach*, 97.

World Industrialization

The SDS urged "industrialization of the world." The Port Huron Statement said of this:

> Many Americans are prone to think of the industrialization of the newly developed countries as a modern form of American *noblesse*, undertaken sacrificially for the benefit of others. On the contrary, the task of world industrialization, of eliminating the disparity between have and have-not nations, is as important as any issue facing America. The colonial revolution signals the end of an era for the old Western powers and a time of new beginnings for most of the people of the earth. In the course of these upheavals, many problems will emerge: American policies must be revised or accelerated in several ways.[223]

That had been the aim of the democratic internationalism of Woodrow Wilson's Fourteen Points and Roosevelt's Atlantic Charter proclaimed by the US after each world war, with the aim of shaping a world order under American auspices. Both demanded the dismantling of the European empires, and the opening of the former colonies to free trade: neo-colonialism in everything but name. Here too, decolonization had been the program of the CIA-backed student organizations, as well as the US State Department and the Council on Foreign Relations. Today this is called "globalization." As the "industrialization of the world" proceeds via transnational corporations, NGOs, and color revolutions, when reticent states require regime change, the result is universal standardization caused by the internationalization of the modes of production and consumption, to paraphrase Karl Marx in *The Communist Manifesto*.[224]

This globalization was justified in precisely the terms used by the Ford, Rockefeller, and Carnegie foundations: "The United States' principal goal should be creating a world where hunger, poverty, disease, ignorance, violence, and exploitation are replaced as central

---

[223] Hayden et al., *Port Huron Statement*, 38.
[224] Marx and Engels, *Communist Manifesto*, 25.

features by abundance, reason, love, and international cooperation."[225]

For this utopia to be achieved, the globalists must have the power
to control states through groups like the World Bank, the International Monetary Fund, UNESCO. When Slobodan Milošević in Yugoslavia, Saddam Hussein in Iraq, and Muammar Gaddafi in Libya
objected to this globalization, they were obliterated by international
authority under international law. In the name of "abundance, reason, love, and international cooperation," their countries were
sacked and hundreds of thousands of their peoples killed. President
George H. W. Bush used the same rhetoric when justifying the destruction of a sovereign Iraq during the Persian Gulf War:

> Out of these troubled times, our fifth objective—a new world or-
> der—can emerge: A new era—freer from the threat of terror,
> stronger in the pursuit of justice and more secure in the quest for
> peace. An era in which the nations of the world, east and west,
> north and south, can prosper and live in harmony.[226]

Hayden and his coauthors even advocated US leadership for "the industrialization of the world," and placed this in a Cold War context:

> We should undertake here and now a fifty-year effort to prepare for
> all nations the conditions of industrialization. Even with far more
> capital and skill than we now import to emerging areas, serious
> prophets expect that two generations will pass before accelerating
> industrialism is a worldwide act. The needs are numerous: every
> nation must build an adequate infrastructure (transportation, com-
> munication, land resources, waterways) for future industrial
> growth; there must be industries suited to the rapid development
> of differing raw materials and other resources; education must
> begin on a continuing basis for everyone in the society, especially
> including engineering and technical training; technical assistance
> from outside sources must be adequate to meet present and long-
> term needs; atomic power plants must spring up to make electrical
> energy available. With America's idle productive capacity, it is

---

[225] Hayden et al., *Port Huron Statement*, 38.
[226] Bush, "Out of these Troubled Times."

possible to begin this process immediately without changing our military allocations. This might catalyze a "peace race" since it would demand a response of such magnitude from the Soviet Union that arms spending and "coexistence" spending would become strenuous, perhaps impossible, for the Soviets to carry on simultaneously.[227]

These aims were the same as the overseas development programs of USAID, the Peace Corps, the Rockefeller Foundation, the Ford Foundation, and many others. The aim was clear: to extend US geopolitical and financial interests.

The "industrialization of the world" should be undertaken through the UN, according to the SDS. This would "enhance the importance of the United Nations itself, as the disarming process would enhance the UN as a rule-enforcement agency."[228] The UN would be empowered by its control of global resource and development allocations, just as it would have the ultimate sanction for destroying rebel states through its control of atomic weapons. This was the same agenda that had been rejected by the USSR, which regarded the proposals as a means of advancing US global hegemony behind a democratic and humanitarian façade. Andrei Gromyko, Soviet foreign minister, had explained the USSR's position:

> The US position in fact allowed the UN to be turned into an instrument for imposing the will of one group of states upon another, above all upon the Soviet Union. The states which had a majority within the Security Council might therefore be tempted to use force, rather than seek mutually acceptable solution.[229]

The "force" advocated by the US foreign policy establishment was intended to be UN control of atomic energy—the "Baruch Plan," named after the senior Wall Street eminence, Bernard M. Baruch, a perennial presidential adviser, who was the US representative at the

---

[227] Hayden et al., *Port Huron Statement*, 38
[228] Ibid., 40.
[229] Gromyko, *Memories*, 116.

UN Atomic Energy Commission. Again, the USSR saw through this, with Gromyko stating of the plan that it

> boiled down to making sure that the US retained the monopoly on nuclear weapons. The intention was that the USSR and the rest of the world should to a significant extent place their security in Washington's hands. The USSR found this unacceptable. The actual intention was to be camouflaged by the creation of an international body to monitor the use of nuclear energy. However, Washington did not even attempt to hide the fact that they intended to take the leading part in this body, to keep in its own hands everything to do with the production and storage of fissionable material, and, under the guise of the need for international inspection, to interfere in the internal affairs of sovereign nations.[230]

This repudiation of the UN by the USSR was the primary catalyst for the Cold War. The US plans (or more accurately the CFR plans) for the postwar world became the program of the student organizations that were sponsored by the CIA and the oligarchic foundations in the immediate postwar period: the Student World Federalists, Students for Democratic Action, and the NSA. These, examined previously, morphed into the New Left. The SDS was advocating for the reintroduction of the Baruch Plan.

Internationalizing Education

The SDS program called for the "internationalization" of education:

> Education is too vital a public problem to be completely entrusted to the province of the various states and local units. In fact, there is no good reason why America should not progress now toward internationalizing rather than localizing, its educational system— children and young adults studying everywhere in the world,

---

[230] Ibid., 138.

through a United Nations program, would go far to create mutual understanding.[231]

The Port Huron Statement called for "experiments in decentralization, based on the vision of man as master of his machines and his society."[232] Yet the SDS also demanded "internationalization" via UN bureaucrats, and an education system that would not only be taken away from communities but would be brought under international control and serve as an indoctrination process for a new generation of global citizens. The internationalization of education was part of the establishment agenda. A Ford-funded 2003 report on the internationalization of US education states that "Internationalization has been high on the agenda of the American Council on Education (ACE) since the 1950s."[233]

One can be specific in tracing the origins of "education internationalization" to the think tanks of the establishment. A doctoral dissertation on the subject stated:

> Education and World Affairs (EWA) was established in 1962 as a private non-profit organization to encourage and guide the international endeavors of American institutions of higher education. The Ford Foundation facilitated the creation of the organization and provided funding as did the Carnegie Corporation of New York. During this time, the late 1950s through the mid-1960s, there was great interest by the major foundations and the federal government in international education and in strengthening the involvement of colleges and universities in world affairs.[234]

This was during the Cold War, and "it was imperative that Americans become knowledgeable about other countries, languages, and cultures" as part of the response to the USSR. "Private philanthropy funded many of these new initiatives,"[235] including the "Henry Luce Foundation, the Carnegie Endowment for International Peace, [and]

---

[231] Hayden, et al., *Port Huron Statement*, 47.
[232] Ibid.
[233] Siaya and Hayward, *Mapping Internationalization*, vii.
[234] Hertko, "Internationalization of American," vi.
[235] Ibid., 3.

the Danforth Foundation."[236] Funding for the EWA from the Federal Government came from "the United States Agency for International Development [USAID], the United States Department of State, Bureau of Educational and Cultural Affairs, the Department of Health, Education and Welfare, and the Office of Education," and EWA "became involved in various efforts which supported the internationalization of American higher education."[237] The EWA helped to extend US influence to the newly decolonized countries: "In addition to supporting international education activities in the United States, EWA was active in providing guidance to colleges and universities in developing countries."[238]

Harold Taylor and the New Left

The importance of the "internationalization of education" can be discerned by a 1968 US government-sponsored report.[239] In 1965 former Sarah Lawrence College president Harold Taylor, of the American Association of Colleges for Teacher Education, was commissioned by the U.S. Department of Health, Education, and Welfare (HEW) to write a book on the training of teachers for their role in "world affairs."[240]

The book was published in 1968, a particularly riotous year for the New Left, when Taylor was enthusing about the SDS on campus. Taylor referred to the connections that had been formed between US government agencies, UN organs, and the oligarchic foundations:

> Liaison has been established with the major foundations, private organizations, and government agencies with an interest in international education, including the U.S. Commission for UNESCO, the U.S. Committee for UNICEF, the Peace Corps, Education and

---

[236] Ibid., 4.

[237] Ibid.

[238] Ibid., 5.

[239] Smiley, *Fifth Annual Report.*

[240] Taylor is acclaimed as a progressive educationalist. He founded the Peace Research Institute, which was incorporated into the Institute for Policy Studies at an early stage. Rarick, "Institute for Policy Studies," 37418.

World Affairs, the Ford Foundation, the Carnegie Corporation, and the Asia Society, which has developed valuable guidelines and materials for the use of Asian studies in the education of teachers.[241]

Here, the role of US education is described as "linking the need for internationalism in the spirit and practices of American education with the position of the United States as a world power."[242] In this the New Left had a role, and Taylor specifically referred to the SDS:

> to make reform possible, it is necessary to use every possible part of the system as a whole from the Peace Corps and the Office of Education to the United Nations Association and the Students for a Democratic Society.[243]

Taylor described the role of the US as a power with a world-revolutionary mission: The US, as "the world's most powerful economic, social, military, and political force," possesses "a vast and latent power for taking initiatives in cultural and educational change on a world scale." He called the US, with its mass media, science, technology, cultural and educational institutions, mass transport, and urban problems, "the forerunner of what mass societies will some day [sic] be" on a global scale. The US was the "middle of the world," the world leader, serving as "a point of linkage among the thousands of elements which make up the cultural and social fabric of world society," which could be a "meeting ground and laboratory in social change," to which students and teachers from around the world could gravitate in finding solutions, if only the US itself underwent revolutionary change.[244]

Taylor was proposing that the US become what the original Bolsheviks had envisioned for the Soviet Union prior to Stalin's having determined a different course: the center of world-revolution. But the doctrine would be that of US liberal-democratic internationalism.

---

[241] Taylor, *World and the American Teacher*, 6.
[242] Ibid., 7.
[243] Ibid., 12.
[244] Ibid., 20.

Like John D. Rockefeller III and Jerry Rubin, Taylor saw the mass news and entertainment media, especially television, as crucial in reshaping the minds of young Americans:

> [W]ho are sensitive to social questions ranging from the cultural habits of the hippy movement to the mistreatment of the Negro, and for the increased sophistication of a growing minority of college students and young political activists to the issues of domestic politics, war and peace, and world affairs in general. The formation of a youth culture with its own interests and values, separate from the older generation yet with influence on it, can be traced to some of the cultural effects of the television medium and the opening up of questions, ideas, and examples of human conduct which in former years were unavailable to the young because the medium did not then exist.[245]

On the other hand, Taylor expressed his dissatisfaction at vestiges of traditional normality extant in the media.

Taylor lauded the rise of campus radicalism as the wave of the future, which would change the US, should "wise government" prevail. He alluded to the break between the NSA and the CIA, after widescale exposure of the links, coming to the extraordinary conclusion that NSA policy had changed into something genuinely dissident, although there was no change in its core doctrines. He saw the greatest potential being in the "new constituency" of six million student radicals and 450,000 faculty, so long as it is not diverted into "established channels."[246] Paradoxically, while he lauded the belated "independence" of the NSA from the CIA, he welcomed funding for an NSA project from the Office of Economic Opportunity.[247] Although Taylor warned of the diversion of this youthful idealism, largely imbibed from television, "into established channels," he commended foreign and domestic programs *initiated or run* by "established channels" such as USAID, VISTA, the Peace Corps, EWA,[248]

---

[245] Ibid., 22.
[246] Ibid., 41.
[247] Ibid., 93.
[248] Ibid., 55, 56, 60, 62, 72, 93.

and the Asia Society.[249] Taylor also referred to "important work" being undertaken in promoting the concepts of multicultural curricula "through UNESCO, educational organizations, foundations, [and] government."[250]

Taylor was encouraged by student unrest, seeing it as a positive sign of interest in social and political issues, including undergraduate students "who while intending to build their careers on the campus are also seriously interested in effecting social and political change through their work as teachers and research scholars."[251] It is here that the SDS received fulsome praise for preparing these undergraduates to become part of academia. In this federally funded two-year study, Taylor castigated those college administrators who had resisted the demands of the New Left rioters:

> Many of them have been associated as undergraduates with the National Student Association and with Students for a Democratic Society (SDS), an organization which has provoked a great deal of negative comment and alarmed action from administrators on some campuses but which is one of the most intellectually alive and socially aware organizations in contemporary politics. SDS students have been militant in their protests against the war in Vietnam, as they have in their protests and action programs against the draft and against many other government policies. . . .
> Not only do SDS chapters usually provide interesting political controversies and militant intellectual leadership within the student body, but they also often are the only source of such campus leadership.[252]

Taylor advocated the creation of a "World College," with a "UN Teacher Corps."[253] He referred to US examples of what could be carried out in internationalizing education, supported "by foundation grants . . . developed and administered programs for [US]AID, the

---

[249] Ibid., 65–66. The Asia Society was founded as a globalist think tank by John D. Rockefeller III in 1956.
[250] Taylor, *World and the American Teacher*, 89.
[251] Ibid., 95.
[252] Ibid.
[253] Ibid., 154.

Department of State, the Department of Agriculture, the Institute of International Education, and other organizations."[254] How Taylor defined "established channels" is unclear.

In Taylor's view, American foreign policy should be extended by cultural and educational means, with the use of military and economic coercion as a last resort. After a large part of the world had succumbed to liberal globalism through "the interlocking use of economic, moral, and cultural power for the development of a world order," states that stepped outside the world order would be subjected to reaction from both within and without. The extent of "cultural power as a factor in American foreign affairs" would have so imbued the masses with a sense of conformity to global authority that there would be a "negative response" against dissent.[255]

So much for the New Left posturing about "American cultural imperialism."

Taylor called for a vastly extended US program for educational and cultural initiatives around the world, referring specifically to the decolonized African states. He referred to education as "a factor in the international power structure."[256] Taylor listed Indonesia as an example of a country where the US was able to exert influence through its aid programs, while the remnants of European colonialism had failed:

> American cultural, political, and economic influence, exercised in an enlightened way through the preceding years mainly by the Ford Foundation and the American program of foreign aid (a fair proportion of which had to do with teacher education), was able to operate without the handicap of military intervention. The result was that after the change in political leadership, achieved not without violence and bloodshed, Indonesia created a new and viable political situation of very great consequence for the stability of the whole of Asia.[257]

---

[254] Ibid., 173.
[255] Ibid., 248.
[256] Ibid., 251.
[257] Ibid., 252.

It is notable that Taylor referred to Ford Foundation programs in conjunction with American aid as the means by which the US could operate against European colonialism, replacing the old empires with an international power structure under UN auspices via "international, political, and educational instruments."[258] This should be buttressed by "an American philosophy of education,"[259] and "developing new cultural policies designed to develop an international context for American ideas [that] can be extended radically in the future."[260] These "American ideas" should not however be based on a concept of an "American nationalism," but that of liberal-democratic internationalism,[261] in forming an "international community."[262]

> What is needed as the basis for a wider policy is the conception of the United States as an international culture, along with the idea that the American point of view is not "American," but international, where the US is a meeting ground for the people of the world, a place where we can pool the world's resources, . . . a lively democratic culture.[263]

If Taylor's doctrine on internationalizing education under the auspices of the UN seems to be reflected in the Port Huron Statement, it is probably due to his having been at the founding conference of the SDS at Port Huron as a representative from the League for Industrial Democracy. He had been an "important influence" on Tom Hayden since Hayden's days as a student editor.[264]

To what extent was Harold Taylor co-opted into "established channels"? From 1959 to 1960 he studied political, social, and cultural development among students, teachers, and intelligentsia in Asia and Russia, supported by a Ford Foundation Grant. During 1964 and 1965 he lectured on philosophy, education, and the arts in Greece, Turkey, and Iran, operating for the US State Department. At the time

---

[258] Ibid.
[259] Ibid., 255.
[260] Ibid., 259.
[261] Ibid., 260.
[262] Ibid., 261.
[263] Ibid., 266, 278.
[264] Hayden, *Reunion*, 86.

he was also a consultant to the Eleanor Roosevelt Memorial Fund, a congressionally funded program established by John F. Kennedy to pursue the left-wing objectives of the federal government.[265] Among other presidential trustees appointed at the time were the globally influential plutocrat Armand Hammer (of Occidental Petroleum);[266] Mrs. Herbert H. Lehman, widow of the New York senator and banking scion;[267] and Jacob Blaustein, founder of the American Oil Company, a wire-puller for the Kennedy and Johnson administrations, and an important partisan for Israel in US, UN, and global politics.[268]

Heirs of New Deal Liberalism

The New Left were the children of New Deal liberalism. The founder of the SDS, Al Haber, was the son of William Haber, an academic who was prominent in the Democratic Party during the New Deal era. Hayden wrote that Al Haber wanted to pick up "the threads of his father's political past [and] weave them into a new fabric for the students of his time."[269] Haber called the preliminary organization for the SDS the Liberal Study Group.[270] A New Deal for the postwar era was the aim of Americans for Democratic Action, whose youth affiliate, Students for Democratic Action, as seen above, was a precursor of the New Left and part of the CIA's Cold War strategy.[271]

---

[265] Watts, "Taylor Fascinates Audience." The ERMF, uniting with the Franklin D. Roosevelt Foundation in 1987, operates as the Roosevelt Institute, directed toward mobilizing youth.

[266] Weinberg, *Armand Hammer*, 147.

[267] "Mrs. Lehman Named Foundation Trustee."

[268] "Johnson Names Blaustein."

[269] Hayden, *Reunion*, 30.

[270] Ibid., 38.

[271] The ADA, cofounded in 1947 by Eleanor Roosevelt, states of itself that it is "the nation's most experienced organization committed to liberal politics, liberal policies, and a liberal future. . . . Our goal then? To keep the New Deal dream of a fair and prosperous America for all alive for generations to come." Among the ADA patrons were Senator Herbert Lehman, the international banker. Among ADA's presidents was Allard Lowenstein, who, as we have seen, headed the NSA during the time that it was part of the CIA's Cold War network.

Roosevelt's New Deal, so far from challenging Wall Street, brought Wall Street into the White House. The oligarchs wanted state intervention that would allow them to prosper from state contracts. Roosevelt's primary adviser was Wall Street broker Bernard M. Baruch. The Secretary of the Treasury, Henry Morgenthau Jr., although not having had experience with economics, was married to a Lehman. James Warburg was Roosevelt's representative at the 1933 London Economic Conference. The New Deal represented the type of state regulation that was desired by Wall Street. For example, of the Glass-Steagall Act for bank regulation, Nomi Prins, author of *All the Presidents' Bankers: The Hidden Alliances that Drive American Power*, who had worked as a senior manager for Goldman Sachs and for Bear Stearns, writes:

> From the correspondence between FDR and two of his friends, bankers James Perkins, chairman of National City Bank (now Citigroup) and Winthrop Aldrich, chairman of Chase (now JP Morgan Chase), I began to understand how FDR became known as a bank reformer and that it wasn't really the will of the population that pressed FDR to reform banking as he did; it was the will of these men. They had more in common with FDR—from status to money to yachts—than any of them had in common with farmers, or shopkeepers, or factory workers.
>
> More than any other Washington insider or progressive, it was Wall Street financier Winthrop Aldrich who helped FDR reform banking. Blue-blooded, Republican, and pedigreed, Winthrop's father Senator Nelson Aldrich had organized the select group of bankers that drafted the first Federal Reserve Bill at Jekyll Island in 1910. His nephew, Nelson Rockefeller, would become New York Governor and Vice President of the US, while his other nephew, David Rockefeller, would become a future chairman of Chase. I discovered that it was Aldrich who pressed for a more rigid set of regulations than even the banking-reform bill's sponsor, Carter Glass, envisioned.[272]

The Federal Reserve Bank Act was heralded as a great step toward state regulation of banking and currency that would ensure

---

[272] Prins, "Bankers Behind FDR."

economic stability. However, so far from striking at the power of the bankers, the primary architect was Paul Warburg, whose son James became a primary ideologue and financial patron of the Institute for Policy Studies.

The alliance between the left and the international financial class is longstanding. In 1924 Otto Kahn, of Kuhn, Loeb & Co., accepted an invitation to speak before the League for Industrial Democracy. Kahn stated that "reaction had done the world more harm than radicalism."[273] Kahn was not a socialist. But he, like many other oligarchs, saw that socialism could be used to reorder society. He remarked to LID:

> What you Radicals and we who hold opposing views differ about, is not so much the ends as the means, not so much what should be brought about as how it should and can be brought about, believing as we do that running after the Utopian not only is fruitless and ineffectual, but gets in the way of, and retards, progress toward attainable improvement.[274]

---

[273] Matz, *Many Lives of Otto Kahn*, 232.
[274] Kahn, *Of Many Things*, 175.

12

Sponsoring Campus Tumult

"Democratization" of the campuses and curricula was a key demand of the New Left. It was also on the agenda of the Ford Foundation. In supporting the turmoil on the campuses, the oligarchy aimed to deconstruct what remained of the traditional basis of Western education. The Ford Foundation financed the New Left revolt on campus. At a time when campuses were being convulsed by riots, sit-ins, teach-ins, vandalism, and violence, the Ford Foundation declared its support for the New Left's demands, referring approvingly to the "current acceleration of social change" that was "making increasing and often conflicting demands upon America's traditional institutions," mentioning "intense debate and widening experimentation" in educational institutions, "from the primary to the graduate level."[275] Ford specifically endorsed the demands that were made by the New Left, stating that "in this situation the Foundation has sought to assist in the incubation and testing of ideas for the modernization of the governing structures of education."[276]

Ford made it clear that these changes included "combining student concerns with social and community problems" with academic studies.[277]

---

[275] Ford Foundation, *Annual Report 1970*, 31.
[276] Ibid.
[277] Ibid., 37.

Stanford Workshops

An example of the programs Ford supported was the Stanford Workshops on Social and Political Issues established by the Associated Students of Stanford University.[278] That these "workshops" were of an explicitly New Left character is seen by the description provided by the university:

> Beginning in the 1960s, students also advocated for a more inclusive curriculum, faculty diversity, and development of community structures to support their academic and personal growth. Founded in 1969, and inspired in part by the teach-ins of the civil rights and Vietnam War resistance movements, the student-initiated, action-oriented Stanford Workshops on Political and Social Issues (SWOPSI) offered courses on emerging issues not addressed in the standard curriculum. Many of the issues germane to the modification and expansion of Stanford's academic programs were initially explored in SWOPSI workshops, which were discontinued in the early 1990s.[279]

Center for Education Reform (NSA)

The Center for Education Reform (CER) was established in 1969 at the University of California, Berkeley (the center of New Left activity),[280] as the tax-exempt branch of the National Student Association, with a grant of $315,000 from the Ford Foundation.[281] In 1970 its national conference was addressed by SDS Chicago Seven defendants Tom Hayden and Rennie Davis. David Ifshin, elected NSA president, stated to the conference that he did *not* eschew violence and urged

---

[278] Ibid.

[279] "Stanford Workshops on Political."

[280] It was at Berkeley that the Free Speech Movement was riotously established in 1964. The FSM was a foundational element of the New Left.

[281] *Tax Reform 1969*, 865.

support for Davis' motion for a "massive" May Day mobilization.[282] The CER was headed by Larry Magid, student coordinator for the Center for Participant Education, and organizer of a course taught by Black Panther Party officer Eldridge Cleaver.

Julie A. Reuben, professor of the history of education at Harvard University, stated:

> In 1968 a Berkeley student, Larry Magid, invited Eldridge Cleaver to teach a course at UC Berkeley. Magid, a member of a student organization called the Center for Participant Education (CPE), had attended a meeting at which a number of black students complained about the dearth of classes dealing with their experiences and political struggles. The CPE had been created to offer the kind of education many Berkeley students perceived they needed but were not getting, so Magid decided that the group should do something to address the students' complaints. Cleaver at the time was a notorious figure. Many activists viewed Cleaver, minister of public information for the Black Panther Party, presidential nominee for the California branch of the Peace and Freedom Party, and author of the best-selling book *Soul on Ice*, as an articulate new spokesman for black liberation. But others saw Cleaver, a convicted rapist, then under indictment for assault with a deadly weapon, as a dangerous advocate of violence and racial hatred. To Magid, Cleaver offered a perspective not present on the Berkeley faculty and therefore seemed to be the perfect choice for a course on race.[283]

The conservative Church League of America commented at the time:

> Magid, a recent graduate of Berkeley, was the organizer of the Eldridge Cleaver-taught course that caused a round of disturbances and riots. . . . Now, with Ford money, Magid is able to print a newsletter for 3,500 subscribers and, with a bus, to tour the country informing college students of "radical educational reform."[284]

---

[282] Church League of America. *The National Laymen's Digest*. The Church League of America, an anti-Communist organization, maintained documentation on the left said to be second only to the FBI's.
[283] Reuben, "The Limits of Freedom: Student Activists and Educational Reform at Berkeley in the 1960s," in Cohen and Zelnik, *The Free Speech Movement*, 485–510.
[284] Church League of America. *The National Laymen's Digest*.

Magid, described by *The Los Angeles Times* as "one of the prominent revolutionaries of our time,"[285] recounted nearly half a century later:

> In 1967 I had the privilege of being one of the student coordinators of Berkeley's Center for Participant Education, a student-initiated course program that was born out of Berkeley's Free Speech Movement. CPE, like other "free universities" and "alternative schools" that popped up around the world in the '60s and '70s, promoted student-centered learning by giving students the power to initiate and help direct their own learning, using resources from local faculty, the community and subject matter experts, including some without traditional academic credentials. By getting faculty sponsors, we were able to offer academic credit for non-traditional learning. . . .
>
> In 1969, I moved to Washington, D.C., to run the Center for Educational Reform, a Ford Foundation project of the now-defunct National Student Association, that helped bring this concept to universities and secondary schools around the country. Another nonprofit, New Schools Exchange, published a newsletter that supported hundreds of student-centered "free schools," where even young children were able to help shape their own learning environment.[286]

The Ford Foundation funded the dismantling of American education at all levels, utilizing the tumult of the New Left on campus to push an agenda which, as can be seen by the statements in the Foundation's annual reports and by the ideology of New Leftists, were the same.

It should be kept in mind that while the Ford Foundation was funding these New Left projects, its trustees were drawn from the establishment, and they took a hands-on approach to grants. At the time the Ford Foundation was funding what it called "the incubation and testing of ideas for the modernization of the governing structures of education."[287] Ford's president was McGeorge Bundy, US National Security Adviser during the Kennedy and Johnson administrations. The chairman of the board was Julius A. Stratton, a trustee of the RAND Corporation. Other board members included Stephen D.

---

[285] Seidenbaum, "Portrait of a Young Man," 7.
[286] Magid, "Magid: Back to the Future."
[287] Ford Foundation, *Annual Report 1970*, 31.

Bechtel of the Bechtel Corporation, Kermit Gordon, president of the Brookings Institute, Roy E. Larsen, chairman of Time, Inc., John H. Loudon, chairman of the Royal Dutch Petroleum Company, and Robert S. McNamara, chairman of the International Bank for Reconstruction & Development and former US Secretary of State.[288]

---

[288] Ford Foundation, *Annual Report 1969*.

13

FUND FOR THE REPUBLIC

The Fund for the Republic was established in 1951 by the Ford Foundation with a grant of $1 million and a further grant totaling $14 million in 1953.[289]

In his testimony before the Reece Committee of the US Congress, investigating the grant-making of the tax-exempt foundations in 1954, H. Rowan Gaither Jr., then president of the Ford Foundation, emphasized that the trustees "are responsible for determining policy to guide the foundation in contributing to these objectives and for approving and authorizing the specific actions undertaken in pursuit of them."[290] Gaither stated that the Ford Foundation often conferred grants through "intermediary" organizations. When these do not exist, Ford might create them. He stated that the Fund for the Republic was one such organization.[291]

Gaither remarked that one of the primary reasons that foundation trustees initiated the Fund for the Republic was because "some of the measures taken to deal with the threat of communism in themselves pose grave problems concerning traditional American freedoms."[292] The fear of the elite was that investigations into the threat of communism would expand into a populist revolt. Senator

---

[289] FBI, "FOIA: FBI Monograph Fund," 3.
[290] *Tax-Exempt Foundations, Before*, 1022.
[291] Ibid., 1027.
[292] Ibid., 1050.

Joseph McCarthy in particular was seen as a greater threat to their definition of "American traditions" than communism, particularly when McCarthy announced that he would turn his attention on the activities of CIA operative Cord Meyer and establishment luminary John J. McCloy.[293]

Gaither had stated that the "intermediary organizations" initiated by the Ford Foundation, including the Fund for the Republic, were completely separate from Ford:

> Each of these organizations has its own independent board of directors, and its own staff. I make reference to these particular intermediaries at this point because it allows me to clear up a confusion reflected in the views of some witnesses in these proceedings. It is often assumed that the staff members of these organizations are employees of the Ford Foundation, which they are not; or that their detailed administration is my responsibility or that of the foundation's trustees, which it is not. The trustees are fully acquainted with their proposed programs, but these intermediary organizations are responsible for the selection of projects to carry out those programs. They are not subsidiaries or divisions of the Ford Foundation.[294]

This was supposed to enable Ford to deny responsibility for controversial funding by the Fund for the Republic and other "intermediaries" that might come under scrutiny from renegade politicians like Congressman Carroll Reece or Senator Joseph McCarthy. Yet in the same testimony that he had given to the Reece Committee, Gaither listed "James F. Brownlee, partner of the New York investment firm of J. H. Whitney & Co." as a trustee of the Ford Foundation and as a director of the Fund for the Republic.[295] Moreover, Gaither stated that "each of the directors of the fund had been approved by each of the trustees of the foundation."[296]

The impressive line-up of establishment figures on the board of directors of the Ford Foundation, when founding the Fund for the

[293] Bolton, "Joe McCarthy's Real Enemies."
[294] *Tax-Exempt Foundations, Before*, 1027.
[295] Ibid., 1021.
[296] Ibid., 1051.

Republic, and the other impressive establishment line-up on the board of the Fund itself, were supposed to reassure the American public and the congressional committee that the Fund for the Republic could not be anything other than a paragon of American virtues. Gaither testified that Ford Foundation directors had a hands-on approach to the way money was used and were fully informed as to the character of "intermediary" organizations such as the Fund for the Republic. In the name of "national security," the Fund for the Republic undertook to lavish money on left-wing projects and protect well-placed left-wingers from investigation. Gaither testified that the Fund was set up to espouse liberal internationalism while fighting the emerging tendency toward populist nationalism during the McCarthy era:

> The Ford Foundation hopes to strengthen democratic institutions and processes because they are fundamental to the advancement of human welfare. In considering how to work toward this vitally important objective, the trustees and their advisers have had to assess the stresses and strains put upon American democracy by the upheavals of the first half of this century and especially by the internal and external threats of communism. In this connection the trustees decided after many months of careful staff work and consultation to establish the Fund for the Republic, Inc. This new, independent, nonpartisan organization, devoted to the problem of achieving security with freedom and justice, has received $15 million from the foundation.[297]

More specifically, Gaither referred to the actual danger posed to the establishment, noting "that some of the measures taken to deal with the threat of communism in themselves pose grave problems concerning traditional American freedoms."[298] Section C of the objectives of the Fund for the Republic, accepted by the Ford trustees in October 1951, stated that the Fund would "take into account . . . the danger to the national security arising from fear and mutual suspicion fomented by short-sighted or irresponsible attempts to combat

---

[297] Ibid., 1031.
[298] Ibid., 1050.

Communism through methods which impair the true sources of our strength."[299]

In a report assessing the hearings of the congressional committee, some of the countering arguments submitted by Paul G. Hoffman,[300] who had headed at different times the Ford Foundation and the Fund for the Republic, were addressed. The size of the grant to initiate the Fund was noted:

> The aggregate donation of The Ford Foundation to its offspring, created for the purpose, was $15,000,000. This is a rather large sum of money, even for the gigantic Ford Foundation. After all, that foundation's principal assets are in stock of the Ford Company. Its cash resources are pretty much limited to its income of something over $31,000,000 per year. Thus about half a year's gross income of earnings of the Ford Motor Company was allotted to The Fund for the Republic. While the Fund for the Republic is presumably under independent management, its Chairman is Mr. Paul Hoffman, who was formerly Chairman of The Ford Foundation and who was appointed to head the Fund upon his resignation from The Ford Foundation.[301]

The Reece Committee's assessment, Ford testimony to the contrary, was that the Fund had been primarily established to undermine congressional investigations into communism. The committee pointed to a Fund grant to the American Bar Association to investigate congressional investigations.[302] The Reece Committee concluded:

---

[299] Ibid., 1051.

[300] Hoffman, an establishment eminence, was chairman of the board of the Studebaker–Packard Corporation. In February 1949, while he was administrator of the Economic Cooperation Administration, Hoffman, according to the FBI report on the Fund, "urged Congress to eliminate provisions in the Government's loyalty program which required certification that no ECA employees had formerly been members of any organizations cited by the Attorney General. Hoffman termed such certification 'silly' and 'unsound'—as it barred employment of 'very good people.' The Senate Foreign Relations Committee, however, declined to relax the loyalty requirements in the operation of the European Recovery Program." FBI, "FOIA: FBI Monograph Fund," 11.

[301] *Tax-Exempt Foundations, Report*, 111.

[302] Ibid., 112.

The Fund for the Republic was created for the purpose, among others, of investigating Congressional investigations. Whether this is a proper field for the private expenditure of public trust funds is a question we submit to Congress and the people. We conclude that it was the intention of those who were responsible for the creation of the Fund for the Republic to use it, in part, to launch an attack upon Congressional investigations. This strikes us as a wholly unjustifiable use of the public's money.[303]

Senator Joseph McCarthy was censured by the US Senate in 1954, the year that the Reece Committee's report was published. A primary threat to the establishment had been silenced.

Center for the Study of Democratic Institutions (CSDI)

The Fund for the Republic was incorporated into the Center for the Study of Democratic Institutions (CSDI) in 1979, the CSDI having been established by the Fund in 1959. The CSDI became a worldwide think tank under the presidency of Robert M. Hutchins, former president of the University of Chicago, who became chief executive of the Fund for the Republic in 1954.[304] The Fund acted as the Center's "corporate entity." The CSDI claimed to be "non-partisan," and claimed that because the original $15 million of Ford money had been spent it was not beholden to anyone except the members who paid subscription fees.[305] However, its publications and sponsorships can be easily seen as entirely within the parameters of Ford's liberal internationalism. From this there could be no dissent. In 1988, the center merged with the Los Angeles-based Institute for National Strategy.[306]

---

[303] Ibid., 113.
[304] Redmon, "Center for the Study."
[305] "Dialogue."
[306] Redmon, "Center for the Study."

National Conference for New Politics (NCNP)

The CSDI played a direct role in the formation of the New Left. In 1965 the CSDI co-sponsored the New Left School in Los Angeles, via CSDI Fellows Harvey Wheeler, Richard Lichtman, and Irving Laucks (of Laucks Laboratories Inc. and Laucks Chemical Company). New Left and associated organizations involved included the SDS, CORE, and SNCC. The Old Left was also represented by the Communist Party USA, Socialist Workers Party (Trotskyite), the American Civil Liberties Union (ACLU), and the Socialist Party.[307]

Of particular importance, the CSDI hosted and helped to fund the National Conference for New Politics (NCNP) in August 1965, a meeting of leftist radicals in Santa Barbara. The working paper for the conference was prepared by Arthur Waskow (a trustee of the Institute for Policy Studies), David T. Bazelon (visiting scholar at the IPS), and Stanley L. Newman (an IPS Fellow and legislative aide to left-liberal New York Congressman William Fitts Ryan). The original concept had been called National Coalition for a New Congress (NCNC) and was intended to bring people and resources together to create a leftist-dominated US Congress with a leftist president. A 1964 preliminary paper by Waskow called this a "politer local revolution" than that of the Bolsheviks. The NCNP worked closely with CORE and SNCC.[308]

Organizations represented at the 1965 NCNP included the SDS, SNCC, the World Federalists, the Mississippi Freedom Democratic Party, the Industrial Union Department of the AFL–CIO, the Oregon teach-in movement, and many others.[309]

The NCNP national board consisted of Stokely Carmichael of SNCC, Dr. Benjamin Spock (who achieved iconic status for his theories on permissive child-rearing), Paul Booth of the SDS, Paul Albert and Michael Schneider of the California Democratic Council, Josiah Beeman III of the California Federation of Young Democrats, Warren Hinkle (executive editor of *Ramparts*), and Hallock Hoffman

---

[307] "New Left School," 1–2.
[308] Thurmond, "Elizabeth Osth's Commentaries," 34959.
[309] Ibid., 34960.

(secretary-treasurer of the Center for the Study of Democratic Institutions).[310]

The immediate task of the NCNP was to support "liberal" candidates for public office, by "building a skilled cadre of campaign workers to move in where they are needed," according to national co-chairman Simon Casady.[311] Such a cadre could quickly be converted into street rioters. The "Community for New Politics" was organized for this purpose. At Berkeley it was called the Campus Community for New Politics, where it collaborated with the SDS.[312]

Senator James O. Eastland, chairman of the Senate Internal Security Subcommittee, traced the development of the NCNP through the Center for the Study of Democratic Institutions and the IPS. Strom Thurmond, speaking in Congress, commented on the subsidization of these organizations by the tax-exempt foundations:

> Until these free-flowing funds supporting rebellion leading to outright revolution, are dried up we will continue to see increasing tactics of disruption and new phases of insurrection among what Waskow and others involved call "movement people."[313]

Eastland stated that his committee had accumulated a great deal of documentation on the National Conference for New Politics, and that it had been "spawned by the New Left, with a little midwifery by the Center for the Study of Democratic Institutions, that liberal-left stepchild of the Ford Foundation, out of the Fund for the Republic."[314]

Reporting on the 1967 convention of the NCNP, *The Southern Courier* (a left-wing newspaper) described the scene of "3,500 people who gathered in the elegant ballroom of Chicago's Palmer House hotel."[315] Mostly middle class, they represented 350 organizations, including the SDS, the Communist Party, American Atheists, and various hippie groups and communes. However, after three days of pre-

---

[310] California Legislature, *Fourteenth Report*, 100.
[311] Ibid., 104.
[312] Ibid., 107.
[313] Thurmond, "Elizabeth Osth's Commentaries," 34959.
[314] Eastland, "National Conference for New Politics."
[315] Diamante, "Black Power in Action?" 4.

convention meetings, where committees were formed, Black delegates alleged that they had not been given equal opportunity for decision-making, and that insufficient concern was given to "Black liberation" on the agenda. They formed a "Black caucus," walking out
of the convention and holding their own convention, from which
Whites were excluded. "So the convention began with a group of
white people debating how much representation to give to black
people."[316] On the last day of the convention, the delegates voted to
give the Black caucus 50 percent of the votes. Following this, the
Blacks returned.

The importance of the NCNP can be gauged by its central role in
organizing the iconic New Left riots at the Democratic National Convention in Chicago in 1968. A congressional investigation into the
riots determined that the New Left mobilization had been organized
at a meeting of the NCNP held at Columbia University on October
17th, 1967. The meeting was run by John J. Abt, a national committee
member of the NCNP. Speakers referred to the aim of a "real show-
down" at Chicago. Abt stated that tactics would be discussed at further meetings of the NCNP.[317]

Despite the extremism of the NCNP, like many New Left organizations, it enjoyed tax-exempt status, while moderate conservative
organizations such as Christian Crusade and the Committee of Christian Laymen, Inc., were rejected for tax exemption. The NCNP was
integrally connected with the Center for the Study of Democratic Institutions, which had assumed the role of its parent body, the Fund
for the Republic. Two members of the CSDI—the previously cited
Hallock Hoffman and CSDI's vice-president, Wilbur H. Ferry, who
had first suggested the establishment of the Fund for the Republic to
the Ford Foundation—were on the national council of the NCNP.[318]

Given the origin of the CSDI through the Fund for the Republic
(and ultimately the Ford Foundation), it is notable that Ferry's public
relations firm, ENCO, was hired by both the Ford Foundation and
the Ford Motor Company, for which he became public relations director, and personal PR man to Henry Ford II. Having previously

---

[316] Ibid.
[317] *Subversive Involvement in Disruption*, 2269–70.
[318] "Double Standard on Tax Exemption," 1–3.

worked for the labor movement, Ferry's experience was useful in Ford's disputes with the United Auto Workers.[319] Ferry departed from the CSDI in 1969 as the result of an internal dispute. In 1973 Ferry married Carol Underwood Bernstein, widow of stockbroker Daniel Bernstein, who had established the DJB Foundation in 1948. Ferry and his wife lavished DJB Foundation money on the left.[320]

Radical Education Project (SDS)

Among the four board members of the DJB Foundation was Robert S. Browne, who in 1966 became a sponsor of the Ann Arbor-based Radical Education Project (REP). This was a front for the SDS at the University of Michigan. By 1968 REP had sufficient funds to maintain a seven-room headquarters and a paid staff of five.

Dr. Harold Taylor, a REP sponsor,[321] in his government-funded study on internationalizing education, recommended the REP as a student initiative, and again praised the SDS:

> At present, a group of graduate and undergraduate students at Michigan, following in the tradition of ACWR and SDS on the campus, have formed the Radical Education Project to carry out an "independent education, research, and publication program . . . devoted to the cause of democratic radicalism and aspiring to the creation of a new left in America." Over the past year, the Project has produced a series of student research papers on foreign and domestic policy, power politics, labor, community schools, the universities, and other topics (which are used by student and faculty groups on campuses in the Midwest), along with a series of study guides for students of political and social science. These have been used by faculty members to reorganize their own courses and by students to teach each other and to conduct their own seminars. Among the topics, on which the Project will be working during the coming year are the university and the military, college and university teaching as a profession, youth, the social sciences and social

---

[319] Cutlip, *Unseen Power*, 711.
[320] See the People Pill entry for "Wilbur Hugh Ferry."
[321] Ibid.

problems, disaffection in the United States, and contemporary educational theory and practice. Their work, related in varying degrees to direct political action, is matched in comparable form by other students on other campuses, both inside and outside the SDS organization.[322]

It is notable that these SDS position papers were utilized by faculty as a basis for courses. REP and the SDS were, according to Taylor, intended to be a basis around which educational reform could proceed.

The association between the "New Politics" movement that had been funded and initiated by the CSDI and REP/SDS goes much further. For example, the REP's *Radicals in Professions* was edited by Ted Steege, who is cited as having been "active with Voice-SDS at the University of Michigan and on the Ann Arbor Committee for New Politics."[323] The REP was described as "an independent education, research and publication program initiated by the Students for a Democratic Society . . . devoted to the cause of democratic radicalism."[324] The series of articles based on the "First Radical Professionals Conference," held in July 1967, dealt with the position of students after graduation, and how they could work toward SDS aims from within the professions:

> The great majority of student radicals have been trained, however, in skills which are relevant to mainstream institutions, and they usually enter the recognized professional slots which are provided by the society. It is within this setting that they must find ways to maintain their radicalism.[325]
>
> The conference was attended by about 250 people, including members from the professions of journalism, city planning, law, social work, ministry, education—primary, secondary, and university teachers and administrators—and health.[326]

---

[322] Taylor, *World and the American Teacher*, 97.
[323] Steege, *Radicals in Professions*, 3.
[324] Ibid.
[325] Ibid., 4.
[326] Ibid., 5.

Among the contributors were Barbara and Al Haber, cofounders of the SDS, who at the time of the conference were affiliated with the Institute for Policy Studies.[327]

[327] Ibid., 44.

14

FUNDING THE SDS

The shrewdest elements of the ruling class devise schemes to co-opt incipient revolutionary movements by channeling their energies into harmless paths.

– Progressive Labor, 1969

The Students for a Democratic Society withdrew from its alliance with the Student Nonviolent Coordinating Committee (SNCC) because of the latter's funding by the tax-exempt oligarchic foundations. Yet oligarchic money still found its way into the SDS treasury. A Senate hearing held in 1969 quoted FBI director J. Edgar Hoover:

> Although the majority of gifts are in the $10 to $50 range, wealthy benefactors who have acquired their fortunes in the United States, have contributed substantial amounts in support of the New Left movement and in support of the SDS in particular.[328]

Hoover's examples included a Cleveland industrialist, the wife of a millionaire Chicago attorney, a New England heiress married to a New Left activist in academia, and a wealthy New York academic and writer. Hoover stated that these individuals had contributed more

---

[328] "Extent of Subversion," 653–4.

than $100,000 to the New Left. More significantly, however, Hoover said:

> The New Left has also received money from several foundations. A very prominent foundation in New York for example, has contributed more than a quarter of a million dollars from 1961 to 1968, to various individuals and groups, most of which have been identified as either past or present sympathizers of the Communist Party– USA or the New Left movement.[329]

The Senate hearing focused on three foundations: The Institute for Policy Studies, the Louis M. Rabinowitz Inc. Foundation, and the Cambridge Iron and Steel Company of Massachusetts.

Institute for Policy Studies

In most histories of the sixties, the Institute for Policy Studies (IPS) gets short shrift. It deserves much more attention, especially in the case of an intellectual history of the New Left.

– Kevin Mattson[330]

The IPS was a primary element in the emergence of the New Left. The IPS always had the support of wealthy patrons. Money from establishment wealth would be channeled to IPS and, from there, passed on to leftist radical groups.

After the Chicago riots of October 8th through October 11th, 1969, iconic in New Left history as the so-called Days of Rage, IPS director Arthur Waskow sent $500 to Neil Burnbaum, SDS coordinator of funds, for bail bonds and legal fees to assist 248 persons arrested during the riots.[331] Among the IPS grants to individuals for the fiscal year ending September 30th, 1968, SDS members who were recipients included Mark Spiegel ($50), SDS committee member, and former national secretary, arrested during the Chicago riots;

---

[329] Ibid., 654.
[330] Mattson, *Intellectuals in Action*, 122.
[331] "Extent of Subversion," 660.

Charlotte ($850) and James Weeks ($900), Charlotte being the SDS women's organizer at Ohio State University; John McAuliff ($1,000), involved with the selection of SDS volunteers (Venceremos Brigade) to cut sugar cane in Cuba; and Christopher Jencks ($5,500), involved in another iconic New Left riot in Chicago in 1968, at the Democratic National Convention.[332]

IPS also provided courses for New Left notables, including Charles Sherrod of SNCC, Jeremy Brecher of SDS, and future feminist organizer and ideologue Charlotte Bunch-Weeks, noted above as a recipient of IPS money in 1968.[333]

Ramparts magazine was also the recipient of an IPS grant at this time ($2,200). According to the Senate report, *Ramparts* also received funding from Stewart Mott ($50,000), son of General Motors executive Charles Mott, and from Massachusetts businessman Richard Russell who, with Harvard assistant professor Martin Peretz, gave $400,000.[334]

The commission hearing noted that the IPS is "financed in part by the Edgar Stern Foundation and the Seth Glickenhaus Fund."[335]

The IPS, founded in 1963 by Richard Barnet and Marc Raskin, both former aides in the Kennedy administration, continues to be a notable factor in sustaining the heirs of the New Left. *The Nation*, whose publisher and later editor Katrina vanden Heuvel is a member of the Council on Foreign Relations and a board member of the IPS, eulogized the IPS on its fiftieth anniversary, stating of its founding:

> *The Nation* has enjoyed a long and deep relationship with IPS and its fellows. Raskin and Wilkins have served for many years on our editorial board, helping to guide our reporting, with Ehrenreich joining more recently. Katrina vanden Heuvel, *The Nation's* publisher and editor, is a member of the IPS board, and IPS fellows and associates have been frequent contributors to *The Nation*. In 2008 IPS collaborated with us to produce a prescient and award-winning special issue on "The New Inequality." We are proud to join in celebrating this vital institution.

---

[332] Ibid.
[333] Mueller, "Think Tank on the Left," 64.
[334] "Extent of Subversion," 661-2.
[335] Ibid., 663.

IPS was formed just as New Frontier idealism was beginning to curdle into Vietnam War disillusion. It was the brainchild of Raskin and Barnet, then brilliant young officials in the Kennedy administration. The legend is that they met when John McCloy, the dean of the establishment, opened a meeting on arms control attended by Pentagon officials, national security mandarins and military contractors by saying, "If this group cannot achieve disarmament, no one can." Marc and Dick, the only two who laughed at the absurdity of the statement, bonded—and went on to create the institute. Its start-up funding came from Sears heir Philip Stern, banking heir James Warburg and Fabergé cosmetics founder Samuel Rubin, later supplemented by a generous endowment from Wall Street whiz Daniel Bernstein. IPS refused to take money from the government, to be free to "speak truth to power."[336]

It is nonsense to claim that the IPS refused money from the government to ensure that it would be independent. For example, in keeping with the largesse meted out by federal agencies to New Left projects, the US Office of Economic Opportunity gave a $193,393 grant to the Center for the Study of Public Policy, an offshoot of the IPS, according to a report in *The Chicago Tribune* cited by the Senate commission investigation.[337]

However one obfuscates the funding from federal agencies, funds from private sources is notable. In 1964 the Ford Foundation gave an initial grant, and has continued to do so.[338] IPS funder Philip Stern was described in a eulogy in *The Washington Post* as "a man of the highest Establishment credentials, and independently wealthy," who gave his money to left-wing causes.[339] He had overseen his grandfather's Rosenwald Fund, and then the Stern Family Fund. Daniel Bernstein, named as an IPS sponsor in the *Nation* article quoted above, made his fortune at Loeb, Rhoades & Co., a Wall Street investment firm.

The previously mentioned James Warburg and Philip Stern served on the founding IPS board of trustees. Several universities,

---

[336] *Nation* Editors, "Happy Fiftieth Anniversary, IPS!"
[337] "Extent of Subversion," 662.
[338] Ford Foundation, *Annual Report 1964*, 134.
[339] Barnes, "Philip M. Stern Dies, 66."

including Cornell, Northwestern, and Rutgers, paid for salaries and administrative costs to have faculty join IPS as visiting fellows.[340] Mueller wrote in his dissertation on the IPS:

> Through March 1964, IPS received funds totaling $167,577.74, which included large grants from the Stern Family Fund, the Ford Foundation, the EDO Foundation and James Warburg. Three years later, Warburg donated $400,000 to IPS. The next largest donation in 1967, $25,000, came from the Samuel Rubin Foundation, followed by smaller contributions from Philip Stern and Irving Laucks of the Center for the Study of Democratic Institutions. The largest contributions in 1968 came from Philip Stern, who gave IPS just over $91,000, in addition to another $11,000 from the Stern Family Fund. $30,000 came from the Samuel Rubin Foundation. The D.J. Bernstein Foundation contributed $50,000; donations of $17,000 came from the Carnegie Corporation; and the Field Foundation provided IPS with funds totaling $15,000.33.[341]

Far from eschewing the establishment as the enemy, the purpose of the IPS in setting up in Washington was "to play an educative role for government officials. Besides providing research to policymakers, IPS used seminars for congressional assistants . . . as an educational forum." IPS held seminars for congressional assistants because, according to a proposal for a seminar on "Defense and Disarmament" in January 1964, "in almost all Congressional offices the legislative assistant is the person whose role it is to be the first to absorb new ideas, cope with new policy problems, and develop new legislative approaches."[342] Twenty-three congressional assistants were enrolled in the IPS program in 1965. During its first years, the IPS also held six seminars for congressmen. These, according to Raskin, focused on education and foreign policy.[343]

Ford's initial grant was given when John J. McCloy was chairman of the board of trustees (1958–1965). Richard Barnet served as an aide to McCloy in the US Arms Control & Disarmament Agency. Barnet

---

[340] Mueller, "Think Tank on the Left," 49.
[341] Ibid., 50.
[342] Ibid., 53.
[343] Ibid., 54.

was a member of the CFR when McCloy was CFR chairman (1954–1970).[344] At the same time, McCloy was a trustee of the Rockefeller Foundation.[345] It is odd that Barnet, co-author of the excellent book *Global Reach*, a critique of transnational corporations and what he called "the World Managers," was a member of the CFR, the longest running and most influential think-tank of the oligarchy.

IPS continues to rely on Ford Foundation grants for 68 percent of their budget.[346] A *Washington Post* article on the IPS, alluding to its influence with the establishment and its funding, states:

> [During] the halcyon days before the Vietnam war, IPS became a regular part of the policy-making culture, where officials and scholars mingled daily. (Assistant Secretary of Labor Daniel Patrick Moynihan, for example, was an active participant in education seminars). Individual donors and foundations provide the bulk of the funding. Among the former are Smith Bagley, an R.J. Reynolds Inc. heir; Robert Potter, former general counsel of *The Wall Street Journal*, and Max Palevsky, a high-tech entrepreneur. Foundation support this year includes grants from MacArthur ($200,000) and Ford ($50,000). The Rubin Foundation, whose endowment comes from the Faberge' perfume fortune, has given millions over the years.[347]

McCloy was, as the *Nation* article mentions, "dean of the establishment." Before the war he was a Wall Street lawyer. During World War II he was appointed Assistant Secretary for War, and after the war he served as president of the World Bank, US High Commissioner for Germany, and Chairman of the Rockefeller Chase Manhattan Bank.

Frances Stonor Saunders, in her study of the CIA and its use of the left in the "world of arts and letters," mentions McCloy as part of "the elite which ran American foreign policy," the "internationalist

---

[344] Barnet was elected to CFR membership in 1969. Grose, *Continuing the Inquiry*, 46.

[345] Parmar, *Foundations of the American Century*, 55.

[346] According to their annual report, total IPS income for 2017 was $4,806,524. 68 percent was raised from Foundations, 28 percent from individuals, and 4 percent from other sources.

[347] Blumenthal, "Left Stuff."

paladins of democracy" who sought to bring their system to the world.

> Through think tanks, to foundations, directorates to membership of gentlemen's clubs, these mandarins were interlocked by their institutional affiliations and a shared belief in their own superiority. Their job was to establish and then to justify the post-war *pax Americana*. And they were staunch supporters of the CIA, which was fast being staffed by their friends from school or the 'old show' of OSS.[348]

During his presidency of the Ford Foundation, McCloy established a unit to deal specifically with the CIA.[349] Hence it was during McCloy's presidency that Ford acted as a conduit for funds to the CIA's Congress for Cultural.

Present funders of IPS include the Ford Foundation, the Open Society Foundations, the Rockefeller Brothers Fund, the Moriah Fund Inc., the NoVo Fund (Warren Buffett), the Samuel Rubin Foundation, and the Stewart R. Mott Foundation.[350] IPS's total income in 2018 (the latest available figures) was $4,556,000, of which 59 percent was raised from foundations, and 36 percent from individuals.[351]

IPS Seminars for New Left

The importance of the IPS in helping to launch the New Left is indicated by its having established in 1964 a training program for field organizers of the Student Nonviolent Coordinating Council, organized by IPS fellow Bob Moses. IPS also had an important role in feminism and in the anti-apartheid campaign:

> In these early years, IPS was also at the forefront of the feminist movement. Fellow Charlotte Bunch organized a historic women's liberation conference in 1966 and later launched two feminist

---

[348] Saunders, *Cultural Cold War*, 37–8.
[349] Ibid., 141.
[350] IPS, *Annual Report 2018*.
[351] Ibid.

periodicals, *Quest* and *Off Our Backs*.[352] Rita Mae Brown wrote and published her path-breaking lesbian coming-of-age novel *Rubyfruit Jungle* while on the staff in the 1970s. In the early 1980s, Barbara Ehrenreich . . . led the Institute's Women in the Economy Project. Isabel Letelier brought three dozen "Third World women" to the United States for educational tours across the country. IPS was also on the cutting edge of the anti-apartheid movement. In 1977, it began a South Africa project that produced a series of studies and books on the subject. In 1985, Fellow Roger Wilkins helped found the Free South Africa Movement, which organized a year-long series of demonstrations that led to the imposition of U.S. sanctions.[353]

The IPS seminars attracted not only Congressional aides, but the New Left, including the SDS. Brian Mueller referred to the IPS relationship with the New Left during the 1960s as "close."[354] In his dissertation on the IPS, he writes:

> Inquiring about the possibility of joining IPS for the fall of 1964, Tom Hayden confessed that he knew little about the Institute except the writings of certain fellows, but nonetheless liked "that it creates a new role opportunity for intellectuals to become involved in the process of social change while maintaining critical independence."[355]

SDS president Todd Gitlin wrote to Raskin in 1964 requesting a recent article on the Vietnam War by the IPS co-director, stating that this would have wide coverage since "we [SDS] have better access to the campus than almost all other student organizations, maybe all." Gitlin's successor as SDS president, Paul Potter, suggested to Waskow in 1965 that IPS and SDS jointly sponsor a summer seminar for SDS members that "should be exactly the kind of thing that IPS would like to be involved in." In March 1966, Lee Webb, former SDS National Secretary, wrote to Waskow that he "would very much like"

---

[352] Note that *Off Our Backs* (oob) was the radical feminist journal that condemned Gloria Steinem for her association with the CIA at the World Youth Festivals.
[353] From the IPS website's "Our History" page.
[354] Mueller, "A Think Tank on the Left," 112.
[355] Ibid.

to enroll in the upcoming IPS student program that fall. Activists involved with the civil rights movement in the South also frequented IPS. Waskow recounted one seminar led by the Student Nonviolent Coordinating Committee's Charles Sherrod:

> And we got in good touch very soon with the SNCC people. So Bob Moses, Charles Sherrod, other folks, [like] Marion Berry, who became the mayor of Washington D.C.; those folks came to IPS almost as a place to catch their breath from the incredible intensity of what was happening in the South. So they came, we set up seminars for them. I remember an amazing, amazing moment when Charles Sherrod, who was a young minister, or acting like a minister, in Southwest Georgia, came and spent a month or two at IPS, and we arranged a seminar in the evening for members of Congress to meet him and to hear what the civil rights movement really was, because they had not a clue. A bunch of them came, maybe even a dozen members of Congress, and Sherrod began in a fairly conventional seminar way to describe what they were doing in Georgia, Mississippi, and so on. And then, about 10-15 minutes into his talk, he kind of modulated into being a minister giving a freedom sermon at his congregation in Albany, Georgia. So none of them had ever heard anything like it. In fact, the IPS fellows, me, Marcus, etc., had never heard anything like it, it just mulled us over, absolutely, it was incredible. I think it was really important, for us for sure, but, I think for the members of Congress too, to actually have that experience, which was different from just hearing an academic seminar about the civil rights movement. Suddenly they found themselves in one of those churches that was doing the civil rights movement.[356]
>
> New Left support for IPS swelled, for the most part, due to the latter's stance on American foreign policy and Cold War liberalism.[357]

Mueller stated that James P. Warburg, a scion of the famous banking dynasty, besides being a major funder of the IPS, was also a primary intellectual influence. He was in particular a proponent of "world federalism" via the UN. This type of "global governance," which was

---

[356] Ibid., footnote 54.
[357] Ibid., 107–108.

the aim of postwar US foreign policy, was, for the most part, supported by the IPS insofar as they "supported multilateral solutions to
the world's problems through an alliance of nations from both the
East and West acting under the direction of the UN."[358]

So influential was Warburg that Raskin considered renaming the
IPS the "James Warburg Institute." Mueller writes that Raskin also
had an ulterior motive for considering a name change. He thought
that it could increase funding. This is the noble institution that eschewed state funding (supposedly) so that it could maintain its independence. Mueller writes:

> While Raskin saw the new name as a way to honor Warburg's ef-
> forts at securing peace, he also recognized that using Warburg's
> name offered certain financial incentives. Raskin confided to Bar-
> net that "my commercial and *Talmudic* guess is that the Warburg
> name could be used as an instrument to get money for an endow-
> ment from the Warburgs themselves as well as such people as Land,
> McCloy, Stevenson, etc. Putting aside the monetary value IPS
> placed on Warburg's name, intellectuals associated with the Insti-
> tute, especially the co-directors, owed much of their thinking to the
> ideas put forth by Warburg in the decades preceding IPS.[359]

Did Richard Barnet co-author the excellent *Global Reach* as a warning about the influence of transnational corporations and their innate tendency to level ethnicities and cultures into Wendell Willkie's
vision of "one world"? Or did he write the book to uphold the transnational corporations as the hope of the future? Barnet's assessment
of US involvement in Vietnam in 1971 and how it could be changed
by the influence of the transnational corporations and non-military
bureaucracies like the Peace Corps seems to indicate an apology for,
rather than a critique of, globalization. Mueller writes:

> Barnet predicted that the influence of "nondefense bureaucracies,"
> which included transnational corporations and the Peace Corps,
> would grow as the national security bureaucracies committed one
> misstep after another. Nondefense bureaucracies, according to

---

[358] Ibid., 139.
[359] Ibid, 109.

Barnet, saw "their own interests served by the development of co-operative transnational relationships rather than by the manipulation of violence." No doubt, Barnet considered IPS one of these nondefense bureaucracies working to change, through education and other means, the American mindset regarding threats, security, and peace.[360]

So far from seeking the dissipation of US global influence, the IPS directors saw the best outcome for the US in Vietnam being negotiation with the National Liberation Front. The IPS directors considered that an NLF and North Vietnamese takeover of the South could result in a new leadership of Vietnam, after the death of Ho Chi Minh, pursuing US rather than Russian or Chinese collaboration. Barnet referred to the prospect of an "Asian Tito" who "would in all likelihood court the friendship of the United States as counterweight to the nearby communist giants."[361] The assumption that the military–industrial complex supported the Vietnam War as a profitable enterprise is erroneous. The war was having a distorting impact on the US economy, and Wall Street wanted the US out. Here again the oligarchy and the left were in accord.

Hence, according to the IPS scenario, US foreign policy could be changed by an alliance of agencies, NGOs, and global corporations, what is today called "civil society." Certainly, it is a scenario that has been fulfilled, and it explains the close relationship maintained between leftist organizations and the oligarchy via think tanks and tax-exempt foundations.

The IPS held seminars for government bureaucrats and New Left radicals, constituting the thesis and antithesis of a dialectic. The same process operates today relatively openly in the color revolutions orchestrated by a combination of nondefense bureaucracies and global corporations, such as the US State Department, USAID, the National Endowment for Democracy, and Open Society, while on the ground there are the same types of befuddled, rioting dupes that comprised the New Left of the 1960s and 1970s.

---

[360] Mueller, 162.
[361] Ibid., 172.

Cambridge Iron and Steel Company

The Cambridge Iron and Steel Company (CIS) was a paper front used to channel funds to the SDS. Michael Sterns Ansara, fundraiser for the SDS, was vice president of the company. The company treasurer was David Landau, counselor for the Boston Draft Resistance Group. The 1969 report of the Senate commission on campus disorders detailed that from February to November 1969, Cambridge Iron and Steel contributed thousands of dollars to the SDS, to the biweekly radical newspaper *Old Mole*, to the Liberation News Service, a "news service for approximately 300 underground newspapers" throughout the USA, and to other New Left individuals and projects.[362]

Kirkpatrick Sale said of this:

> CIS opened its bank account in February and during the next few months is known to have given $400 to the New York SDS office, $2,000 to Liberation News Service, $3,000 to the *Old Mole*, $5,000 to the *Guardian*, and a few hundred dollars each to SDSers Linda Gordon, Beverly Kane, Sue Parker, and Ansara himself.[363]

The idea of the dummy corporation had been suggested by Ralph P. Hoagland III, a thirty-five-year-old millionaire. Hoagland made his fortune with the creation of a cosmetics and pharmaceutical chain store (Consumer Value Stores, now known as CVS, America's largest pharmacy chain). *The Boston Globe* ran an informative feature when the SDS was condemned by the Progressive Labor (PL) faction for its involvement with the company, pointing out that despite the current building boom, the company had not been involved in a single enterprise: "the name has absolutely nothing to do with its avowed purpose."[364] The firm figured prominently in the factional dispute between the Maoist PL and the SDS in Boston, the Maoists charging

---

[362] "Extent of Subversion," 664–5.
[363] Sale, *SDS*, 365.
[364] Connolly, "Businessman, Dummy Firm, Fund Boston SDS," 12.

that the SDS was "selling out to the bourgeoisie." *The Boston Globe* quoted the PL position:

> Cambridge Iron and Steel (CIS) is an example of how the shrewdest elements of the ruling class devise schemes to co-opt incipient revolutionary movements by channeling their energies into harmless paths, according to the PL faction.[365]

PL had produced a lengthy critique on the SDS and Cambridge Iron and Steel, called *An Expose!*, for distribution within the SDS, over which the PL was attempting to usurp leadership. The statement continued: "To support CIS is to collaborate with the enemy. Therefore it is necessary to oppose CIS to attack the ruling class."[366]

The CIS-connected Boston Draft Resistance Group (BDRG) had among its cadres Abby Rockefeller, daughter of David Rockefeller. Because of a perceived patriarchy running the BDRG, Abby was among the women who left in 1968 to form Cell 16, "one of the first radical feminist groups in the country."[367]

Alongside Ansara on the CIS board was his wife Amy, granddaughter of Charles E. Merrill, founder of Merrill Lynch, one of America's largest investment banks.[368]

While the SDS's corporate executives at CIS countered that the PL misunderstood revolutionary doctrine, *Boston Globe* columnist Richard Connolly noted that Hoagland, "the financial angel behind the controversial enterprise, doesn't appear in the corporate records. He described himself as an investor in Cambridge Iron and Steel. The firm says he promised it $100,000, $25,000 of which has been received."[369]

The PL's *Expose!* stated that Hoagland is "a sharp and highly influential political agent of the ruling class," with "brilliant business expertise." Ansara and the CIS coterie replied that all movement money is "dirty," and that the CIS money is no more and no less dirty

---

[365] Ibid.
[366] Ibid.
[367] McMillian and Buhle, *New Left Revisited*, 185.
[368] Connolly, "Businessman, Dummy Firm, Fund Boston SDS," 12.
[369] Ibid.

than the money PL uses "from Georgia Land and Texas Oil."[370] The allusion to Texas Oil was to Albert Maher, millionaire son of the owner John F. Maher. Albert helped to organize the 1963 and 1964 youth delegations to Cuba, which included members of PL, in defiance of the State Department travel ban.

In 1968, Hoagland formed the Fund for Urban Negro Development (FUND) to solicit money from Boston's oligarchy for the most radical of the Black groups in the wake of MLK's assassination. What emerged was an effort to channel Black revolt into the development of "Black capitalism." When the Boston Black radicals were not compliant, funding dried up. One might conclude that Hoagland had similar motives for funding the SDS.

Louis M. Rabinowitz Foundation Inc.

The Louis M. Rabinowitz Foundation Inc. was presided over by Victor Rabinowitz, who was also president of the National Lawyers Guild (NLG), "founded in 1937 as an association of progressive lawyers and jurists." The NLG, although a paragon of anti-establishment resistance in the courts, was chosen by the US Government for special roles, as the NLG states on the "History" page on its website:

> The Guild was one of the nongovernmental organizations selected by the U.S. government to officially represent the American people at the founding of the United Nations in 1945. Members helped draft the Universal Declaration of Human Rights and founded one of the first UN-accredited human rights NGOs in 1948, the International Association of Democratic Lawyers (IADL).

Speaking of its activities in the 1960s, the Guild itself states on the same page:

> Guild members represented Vietnam War draft resisters, antiwar activists, and the Chicago 7 after the 1968 Chicago Democratic Convention. Guild offices in Asia represented GIs who opposed the war.

---

[370] Ibid.

In 1967, the Rabinowitz Foundation gave a $4,000 grant to Nancy and Todd Gitlin of the Chicago SDS,[371] Todd being a key member of the SDS National Office.[372]

Other Contributors

By the time of the 1969 Senate investigation into campus disorders, the Senate report referred to the dwindling finances caused by the fracturing of the SDS. Funding came through the "exorbitant speaking fees" charged by SDS leaders such as Tom Hayden ("as much as $1000").[373]

Of particular interest, the social elite sustained the coffers of the New Left, with the Senate inquiry stating:

> Leaders of groups such as the SDS, the Black Panthers and the Youth International Party are frequently invited to the homes and apartments of various wealthy members of the community. They are often paid for their attendance. Their presence is used to enhance the "chic" astrosphere of the parties. On occasion parties are used as fund-raiding gatherings. Of late it has become fashionable to invited members of the Black Panthers to such assemblages in suburban homes.[374]

One such contributor is mentioned by Kirkpatrick Sale in his history of the SDS:

> In neither money nor efficiency was the NO notable.[375] It seemed that no matter how much came in by way of contributions the organization always found a way to spend it and be on the lookout for more. This fall, for example, Mike Spiegel[376] inveigled a handsome $12,000[377] gift from an anonymous figure—it was, he agreed,

---

[371] "Extent of Subversion," 668.
[372] Ibid., 669.
[373] Ibid., 681. $1,000 in 1969 is the equivalent of $8,000 in 2023.
[374] Ibid.
[375] NO is the SDS National Office.
[376] SDS National Secretary.
[377] The equivalent of $99,000 in 2023.

"a charitable handout from the middle class which likes our libertarian ideas"[378]—but a month later the coffers were virtually empty.[379]

Anne Farnsworth, a jazz musician, gave $25,000 to SDS in the fall of 1964 and $10,000 in the summer of 1965. Farnsworth's husband, Harvard assistant professor Martin Peretz (who bought the influential *New Republic* in 1974), also donated and helped with fundraising among the wealthy liberal elite.[380] Sale referred to the Boston SDS chapter as being the largest contributor to National Office funds, conjecturing that this would have been thanks to wealthy individuals such as "Anne Peretz, Abby Rockefeller (heir to part of the family's wealth, a radical, and a resident of New England at the time), perhaps John Maher, and certain unidentifiable scions of American wealth found in such profusion at Harvard."[381]

In 1964 the J.M. Kaplan Fund (later named as one of the conduits for CIA funds), the Stern Family Fund, and New York lawyer Victor Rabinowitz (of the Louis M. Rabinowitz Foundation) provided money for the Economic Research and Action Project (ERAP), formed by the SDS in 1963 as a "community organizing project," when it was low on funds, after appeals from Rennie Davis.[382]

While the Senate hearing admired the manner by which the SDS was seemingly able to function on a shoe-string budget in its final phase, Sale's opinion above gives a contrary picture. As a political investment, it was a spent force, fractured by the Weathermen and the Maoist (Progressive Labor) factions.

It is also notable that "the Commission could establish no evidence that funds are being contributed by foreign or Communist governments to militant activists in Illinois."[383] Most on the American right had it wrong: this was no Moscow plot, but rather something emanating from within the USA.

---

[378] Sale, *SDS*, footnote 18.
[379] Ibid., 260.
[380] Ibid., 116.
[381] Ibid.
[382] Ibid., 71.
[383] "Extent of Subversion," 681.

Given the association between the SDS front, the Radical Education Project (REP), and the Center for the Study of Democratic Institutions (the successor to the Fund for the Republic), it seems plausible that the SDS was the recipient of Ford money through this avenue.

James Kunen and *The Strawberry Statement*

James Kunen participated in SDS sit-ins at Columbia University in 1968. He subsequently had a successful career as a public defender and author. In 1968, Random House published his memoir as a student radical, *The Strawberry Statement*. Here he described how oligarchic interests, acting through the "Business International Roundtables," sought to subsidize the New Left for dialectical purposes. These oligarchic interests wanted the New Left to "act up" so that their preferred candidate for the presidency, Senator Eugene McCarthy, would look like a moderate option.

Kunen described how he went to an SDS "strategy meeting" where "a kid" reported on "an SDS convention":

There was some chagrin expressed at the convention that Columbia SDS had on its own piddling initiative called the First International Students' Conference, to be held at C.U. in the fall.

"New York is looked on as a real insane place," the kid said. "People are always surprised if they like someone from New York.

"Also at the convention, men from Business International Roundtables—the meetings sponsored by *Business International* for their client groups and heads of government—tried to buy up a few radicals. These men are the world's leading industrialists, and they convene to decide how our lives are going to go. These are the guys who wrote the Alliance for Progress. They're the left wing of the ruling class.

"They agreed with us on black control and student control. They were for kicking out Kirk.[384] Only thing they disagreed with us on was imperialism. They figure we've got the technology the world needs and we ought to have some control over where it goes and for what.

---

[384] Grayson Kirk, president of Columbia University, and a focus of New Left wrath.

"They wanted McCarthy in.[385] They see fascism as the threat; see it coming from Wallace.[386] The only way McCarthy could win is if the crazies and young radicals act up and make Gene look more reasonable. They offered to finance our demonstrations in Chicago.

"We were also offered Esso (Rockefeller) money. They want us to make a lot of radical commotion so they can look more in the center as they move to the left."[387]

The "Business International Roundtables" referred to by Kunen was the Business International Corporation, founded in 1953 as a research and consultancy firm for US corporations operating abroad. The reference to the oligarchy represented by the BIC as "the left wing of the ruling class" is reminiscent of the comment made by Carroll Quigley about the close-knit oligarchic network that often cooperates with the left, "the whole complicated network of tax-exempt foundations," representing "the power of the international financial coterie," which held sway over "these energetic left-wingers."[388]

As the annual reports of the Ford Foundation from the time show, these oligarchs and their functionaries did indeed support "reform" of the education system, and funded student and Black organizations for the purpose. There was not even fundamental contention over what is here termed "imperialism," despite all the anti-imperialist rhetoric of the left: As the Port Huron Statement indicates, the New Left advocated for technocratic and industrial development of the Third World under US and UN auspices—the type of Cold War neo-colonialism that the US foreign policy establishment was pursuing via USAID and the Peace Corps in the name of "humanitarianism" and "democracy."

---

[385] Senator Eugene McCarthy. His candidacy will be examined later.
[386] Governor George Wallace of Alabama. Wallace ran for the presidency in the 1968 election as the American Independent Party candidate. The Democratic Party nomination went to Hubert Humphrey, not Eugene McCarthy. In 1972, with a strong showing for the Democratic Party presidential nomination, Wallace was shot five times by Arthur Bremer, and was paralyzed below the waste, confined to a wheelchair for the rest of his life.
[387] Kunen, *Strawberry Statement*, 130–1.
[388] Quigley, *Tragedy and Hope*, 954–5.

Gerald Wayne Kirk

The radicals think they are fighting the forces of the superrich, like Rockefeller and Ford, and don't realize that it is precisely such forces which are behind their own revolution, financing it, and using it for their own purposes.

– Gerald Kirk, 1970

The sworn testimony of Gerald Kirk confirmed what was recorded by Kunen in *The Strawberry Statement*. Kirk, a Black man, was recruited into the SDS as a seventeen-year-old in 1965. The following year he joined the Communist Party USA youth front, the W.E.B. Du Bois Clubs, and then the Communist Party USA (CPUSA). He served as an FBI informant on both the Old Left and the New Left for the duration of his time at the University of Chicago (1965–1969). Kirk was subpoenaed to testify before the Senate hearing that was investigating the National Conference for New Politics (NCNP), held in Chicago in 1967, where the New Left riots at the 1968 Democratic National Convention were planned. Kirk was a member of the Black Caucus at the NCNP, Midwest director of the DuBois Clubs,[389] and a member of a CPUSA commission evaluating New Left organizations.[390]

Among the careful and detailed testimony by Gerald Kirk, it becomes evident that if a student was on bad terms with the left, the professors who controlled departments and courses would punish them with poor grades.[391] Many faculty were leftist, as indicated by the number of academics who sponsored the NCNP.

In concluding the first day of testimony Kirk was asked whether the SDS posed a real threat to the security of the United States. Kirk replied that the SDS was enabled by the image with which it had been portrayed by the establishment. Kirk stated that many Americans regarded the SDS as "just nice young Americans who may have some bad ideas but are basically good people and want only what is

---

[389] Kirk, Senate hearing, 6.
[390] Ibid., 23.
[391] Ibid., 113.

best for America." He stated that those who organized the demonstrations, sit-ins, and riots "are promoted in the sense of becoming
more influential in the student left," and that they are encouraged to
undertake increasingly destructive work.[392] Kirk explained:

> So what I am saying basically is that without the tacit consent of
> judges who let them off and [college] administrators who slap them
> on the wrist, and without the encouragement of a lot of organiza-
> tions of a lot of older people and without the sleepwalking of most
> Americans, they could not exist.
>
> But that is not the case, because they are encouraged, and all
> of those things do happen; because a lot of older people lend them
> aid, support and education.[393]

Kirk said of the New Left that "alone they couldn't last, but they are
not alone."[394] Here we might consider that the New Left did not
spontaneously emerge from the oppressed, repressed, and de-
pressed, any more than the color revolutions of today are "spontaneous." The New Left emerged from the bowels of the establishment
and from the Critical Theorists brought as a group to the US by the
Rockefeller Foundation and the State Department. The New Left was
nurtured by academia, romanticized by the news media and entertainment industry, marketed by the major publishers, subsidized by
the CIA and tax-exempt foundations, and employed by federal agencies such as USAID and the Peace Corps and by government-funded
"community projects."

Kirk gave, as an example of a "community project," the Woodlawn Organization (TWO), which had been established by the Rock-
efeller-subsidized professional revolutionist Saul Alinsky on Chicago's South Side. TWO was funded by the Office of Economic Opportunity and overseen by a Black gang, the Blackstone Rangers, that
aligned with the New Left.[395] TWO received funding from the Ford
Foundation, and in 1978 $1.2 million from the Department of Hous-
ing and Urban Development. In 1978 Ford stated it might stop its

[392] Ibid., 120.
[393] Ibid.
[394] Ibid.
[395] Ibid., 177–8.

funding because of TWO's financial ineptitude.[396] However, Ford's 1979 annual report shows that Ford had not only *not* stopped its funding but had redeemed TWO's $1.8 million debt, "accumulated when the organization was undergoing financial and management difficulties."[397]

Soon after Gerald Kirk ended his work for the FBI, he came to understand why the New Left received encouragement from oligarchic organizations and the well-to-do. The year that he testified before the Senate committee he remarked to author and journalist Gary Allen, an expert on the New Left:

> The radicals think they are fighting the forces of the superrich, like Rockefeller and Ford, and don't realize that it is precisely such forces which are behind their own revolution, financing it, and using it for their own purposes.[398]

Kirk commented that during his time on the New Left he never met anyone who understood the nature of the establishment. He had assumed that the wealthy and "respectable" men involved must be KGB agents, or else that they were being blackmailed by the Soviet apparatus.

> Until I began to catch on to the game I thought that if all the big people I had seen doing the work of the Communists were conscious of what they were doing, it was a matter of their being Soviet agents. That's all I could figure. I knew there were enormously important and wealthy people in the movement. I knew there were "respectable" men who were involved. But so far as I could see they had to be something like K.G.B. agents, or to have been blackmailed, or were on the make for power.[399]

---

396 Kneeland, "Chicago Group Faces Foundation Cutoff."
397 Ford Foundation, *Annual Report 1979*, 10.
398 Allen, "Who is Paying for the Student Revolutionary Movement?"
399 Ibid.

John D. Rockefeller III

Were the observations of Gerald Kirk and James Kunen on the use of the New Left by the oligarchy fanciful "conspiracy theories"? At most, was it a matter of leftists having taken over the tax-exempt foundations? The statements of Kirk and Kunen both concur that there were plutocratic interests seeking to use the New Left to push society in a leftward direction. But how does this reconcile with the principles of capitalism?

John D. Rockefeller III, at the time head of the Rockefeller Foundation, wrote a detailed article for the *Saturday Review* explaining why such oligarchs supported the New Left. Rockefeller indicated that the purpose the New Left served was to dialectically scare Middle America into a leftward direction. He reiterated what others had said, warning that more riots and urban guerrilla warfare would ensue if the "extremists" were not disarmed by the establishment's "moderate," compromise proposals—that is, the policies hatched by the tax-exempt foundations. That was the line taken, for example, by his brother Nelson Rockefeller in making his pitch for the Republican presidential nomination: unless Rockefeller liberalism was chosen the New Left and the Blacks would riot.

At the time of Rockefeller's article, the *Saturday Review* was edited by Norman Cousins, a noted internationalist and president of the World Federalists, where James Warburg and Cord Meyer had served. Cousins was also a member of the Council on Foreign Relations, long dominated by the Rockefeller family.

John Rockefeller explained, in an article adapted from a lecture given in October 1968, that his sympathies were entirely with the New Left "youth revolution," which he saw as the most hopeful sign of idealism. In his opening paragraph, he alluded to having spoken with New Leftists, perhaps something facilitated by his niece, New Left notable Abby Rockefeller:

> For some months, I have been engaged in the adventure of trying
> to understand a problem which, for want of a better term, has been
> called the "Youth Revolution." I found that young people will talk

to an older person—even though they may regard him as a member of the Establishment—but only if they feel he is genuinely interested in them.[400]

This is probably as close as one can get to an allusion to meetings between the oligarchy and the New Left by one of those involved. Rockefeller saw the "youth revolution" as much more than a generation gap—he saw an idealistic intensity of great promise for the future that he envisioned. He saw the "youth revolution" almost in Trotskyite terms as a *permanent revolution*. He welcomed this permanency of flux. One might wonder whether it is the means by which the "impulse for change" can be imposed according to whatever the establishment requires at the time:

> Every generation has had its gap. But it seems unmistakably clear to me that we are experiencing something much more than the age-old rebelliousness of youth. The ferment of today is deep and intense. Although the activists are a minority of young people, it is a larger and more vocal minority than ever before. The youth revolt is a world-wide phenomenon, occurring not only in the United States, but in a dozen other countries such as France, Mexico, Japan, and Czechoslovakia. There is a tenacity that was lacking in the past. Young people do not seem to be merely getting something out of their systems. Perhaps it is too early to tell, but I do not believe they will slip easily into the comforts of suburbia and the career, leaving behind their idealism and impulse for change.[401]

How does one explain this phenomenon in the United States? Rockefeller answered that this "youth revolt" was media driven. What youth assume to be their own highly rebellious mode of thought was really what they have imbibed from the mass media.

> Because of the influence of the mass media and the freedoms of our society, young people today learn faster and mature earlier. They become quickly aware—and deeply resentful—of the differences between what older people say and what they do. In short, the very

---

[400] Rockefeller, "In Praise of Young Revolutionaries," 18.
[401] Ibid.

accomplishments of our generation—in technology, communications, affluence—have served to focus the attention of the young on what we have failed to accomplish.[402]

Jerry Rubin, the Yippie leader, among the most outrageous of the New Leftists, confessed as much in his manifesto that he was "a child of Amerika," totally a part of it, with its corporate junk food, media, consumerism, Coke, Hollywood and rock music.[403] *That* is the type of revolution with which Rockefeller and his fellow oligarchs could work. This was not a transvaluation of values, not a transcendent rejection of capitalist society; it was just a nihilism that is born from it, one which Rockefeller could see as being of use. Rockefeller stated that he came to the question of the New Left with a bias, one that was *favorable*, a bias that only increased with time. His instincts as a plutocrat told him that the "youth revolt" was good.

> I want to confess frankly that when I started my inquiry I was biased. My instincts told me that very much of what young people are doing and saying today basically makes sense and is good. I found this to be even more true than I had thought.[404]

However, there is a dark side that might destroy society if the "reasonable" elements of the "youth revolt" (and the Black revolt) were not heeded:

> At the same time, I do not ignore the disturbing elements of the youth revolution. There are the far-left extremists who say that present society must be destroyed. Their challenge must be met. There are the truly alienated, the loners, and dropouts. They must be helped. There is the use of dangerous drugs. This must be stopped. Too often, while fighting for their beliefs, young people disregard the basic human values and rights which they are espousing. They frequently lack compassion. They are often contemptuous of those

---

[402] Ibid.
[403] Rubin, *Do It!*, 12.
[404] Rockefeller, "In Praise of Young Revolutionaries," 18.

who do not fully agree with them. While crying out to be heard, they will shout down a speaker.[405]

These alienated and doped-up youth could be co-opted as, ultimately, they too are really fighting for "the same basic human values and rights" as "moderates" such as, for example, the Rockefeller-funded Martin Luther King Jr.:

> There is much to irritate and disturb the older generation. But I submit that we have let ourselves be distracted by the colorful fringes to the point where we miss the central meaning of today's youthful protest. I am convinced that not only is there tremendous vitality here, but that there is also great potential for good if we can only understand and respond positively. I believe this becomes evident if we examine how the youth revolution is manifested in three of the basic institutions of our society.[406]

The rational element had proceeded through the prescribed channels such as joining the Peace Corps and supporting Eugene McCarthy for the presidency. Many of these young people were pursuing careers in law, for example, where they would focus on symptoms such as "how poor people and black people can get a better break before the law," rather than "trusts and estates and corporate law."[407]

But, as Rockefeller writes,

> it remains a fact that severe provocation and even violence have increased as forms of social protest. The protesters are fired by their sense of moral righteousness. They feel that they have learned from experience that it is necessary to be loud and demonstrative to get results. It is this behavior that compels attention and strikes fear for the very stability of American society.[408]

The US was at a crossroads and must establish a "dialogue" with the youth revolt, lest there was escalating violence, which the youth

---

[405] Ibid., 18–19.
[406] Ibid., 19.
[407] Ibid.
[408] Ibid.

revolt had found necessary in order to be heard. *Listen or suffer the consequences*, Rockefeller counsels. "The nature of our response is crucial, for it has everything to do with whether there will continue to be violence and whether violence will pay."[409]

> We must understand that social protest has an honorable history and has rightful channels of communication. We must have dialogue. If we do not—if we think the only answer is to suppress dissent, then the responsibility for violence hangs as heavily on us as it does on those who protest.[410]

Rockefeller was acting as a herald of the youth revolt, from moderates to extremists, giving an ultimatum to Middle America: *the youth revolt is honorable, the demands are just; submit or else.*

> If I am right that the ferment of youth is potentially of enormous benefit to society, then we might ask; Would we really rather have apathetic and obedient copies of ourselves? More importantly, we might take the criticisms of young people seriously and re-examine some of our basic assumptions.[411]

When Rockefeller referred to "we" while addressing Middle America it was a disarming way of pointing an accusing and threatening finger and declaring that the "youth ferment" was serving a vanguard role for the oligarchy, and Middle America, with its support for Barry Goldwater, must step aside. "Obedience and apathy" from Middle America were precisely what JDR and his colleagues desired. Within slumbering Middle America lay the possibility of authentic revolt, having already arisen through such "dangerous" figures as Joseph McCarthy, Barry Goldwater, and George Wallace, and, more recently, Donald Trump.

Rockefeller advised Middle America to accept the demands of the youth revolt. "Change can be very difficult and threatening, especially when the pressure comes from the young. The temptation is

---

[409] Ibid.
[410] Ibid.
[411] Ibid., 20.

to tune them out; it takes much more courage to listen."[412] What took *actual courage* was to challenge the youth revolt on campus and in the streets. Elements of the New Left such as the Weather Underground were prepared to use guns and explosives, while on campus they had a multitude of sympathizers and active backers on faculties. Their guru, Herbert Marcuse, had several years previously asserted that ideas dissenting from the left must not be tolerated.[413] As Gerald Kirk testified to the Senate committee, the New Left had the "tacit consent of judges" and the encouragement of influential organizations. They were portrayed as "nice young Americans," which was precisely the line taken by Rockefeller. Expulsions from campus were not upheld. New Leftists were glamorized in the mass entertainment industry. They had established their hegemony with the help of entrenched academicians; it was nonsense for Rockefeller to portray them as the underdogs.

Rockefeller warned Americans that if the youth revolt was suppressed:

> The only victors will be the small fringe of extremists who want to see our society destroyed. They are playing one of the oldest of political games, that of provocateurs. They want a backlash because they know that repression starts a vicious circle that inevitably leads to greater and greater explosions. If we are foolish enough to fall into this trap, then we will deserve what happens to us.[414]

It was JDR and his colleagues who were playing a "political game," using the threat of "the small fringe of extremists" to stampede Middle America into accepting a leftward direction in the name of *compromise* and *moderation*.

Nor should the youth revolt be ignored. Rather, for Rockefeller it was an opportunity to *accelerate* and *force through* the changes that the oligarchy required, even on a global scale:

---

[412] Ibid.
[413] Marcuse articulated this in his infamous essay, "Repressive Tolerance."
[414] Rockefeller, "In Praise," 20.

The greater tragedy will be the opportunity we will have lost. For we know all too well that time is running out on the great problems the world faces. It seems to me that we have a choice. By suppression or apathy, we can make the youth revolution into yet another problem—in which case the burden will become crushing. Or we can respond in positive ways so that the energy and idealism of youth can be a constructive force in helping to solve the world's great problems. The third possible response, then, is simply to be responsive—to trust our young people, to listen to them, to understand them, to let them know that we care deeply about them.[415]

Here this impending catastrophe is transposed onto the world stage. It can only be averted by adopting the solutions to "solve the world's great problems"— the stated purpose of the oligarchic foundations.

Rockefeller overtly urged the co-opting of the New Left as the great vanguard and reservoir of energy that can be used to reshape the world. The aim must be to "sustain the youth revolution," Rockefeller states, as the New Left is the "elite of our young people."

Instead of worrying about how to suppress the youth revolution, we of the older generation should be worrying about how to sustain it. The student activists are in many ways the elite of our young people. They perform a service in shaking us out of our complacency. We badly need their ability and fervor in these troubled and difficult times. The key to sustaining the energy and idealism of youth is more direct and effective action on the problems about which young people are concerned—the problems of our cities, of our environment, of racial injustice, of irrelevant and outmoded teachings, of overpopulation, of poverty, of war.[416]

Rockefeller called for revolutionary changes in society:

We must revitalize our existing institutions whether they be in education, government, religion, business, or politics. They must be made more relevant to today's problems and have a greater sense of mission. At the same time, in support of the initiative of the young, new programs and institutions must be developed which

---

[415] Ibid., 78.
[416] Ibid.

can be effective in areas of pressing social need. Fresh approaches to meeting today's problems are essential.[417]

Rockefeller concluded by calling for a nexus between the youth revolution and the oligarchy. With this combination the necessary changes can be made around the globe. Rockefeller and his ilk had the money and the organization necessary. Their experience provided the direction. He was clear enough: the majority in the middle must adapt or become passé.

> A unique opportunity is before us to bring together our age and experience and money and organization with the energy and idealism and social consciousness of the young. Working together, almost anything is possible. If we follow this course, each of us will be involved personally and positively in the great drama of our times, rather than feeling like weary and impotent victims of imponderable forces. The antidote to despair is to be involved, to be imbued with the same spirit that fires the imagination and the efforts of the young. There is a VISTA[418] slogan which captures this spirit: "If you're not part of the solution, you're part of the problem."[419]

As the Port Huron Statement shows, the New Left, full of alleged radicals, propounded views that were fundamentally in line with those of the establishment. The challenge was to Middle America

---

[417] Ibid.

[418] VISTA (Volunteers in Service to America) was established in 1965 by President Lyndon Johnson, having been conceived by John F. Kennedy as the domestic version of the Peace Corps. As with the Peace Corps, SDS members were employed as "advisers." Both PC and VISTA were among the federal programs in which New Leftists were employed or were given grants. Gary Allen gives as an example the Student Health Organization (SHO), which described itself as "a refuge for left-of-center health student activists." This received over $1 million in 1968–1969 from the Department of Health, Education, and Welfare, plus $85,000 from the Carnegie Foundation. The SHO's December 1969 newsletter was dedicated to the memory of Ho Chi Minh. An official SHO policy statement included support for the Vietcong and North Vietnam and the intention to work closely with the SDS. Among SHO organizers was Marsha Steinberg, a member of the Weathermen, and James Pinney, leader of the Revolutionary Youth Movement II, another SDS faction. See Allen, "Who is Paying for the Student Revolutionary Movement?"

[419] Rockefeller, "In Praise," 78.

and whatever few remnants of tradition that still held; the oligarchy was unscathed. New Left doctrine had long been formulated within tax-exempt foundations and their hirelings among the Critical Theorists in academia. The New Left, as Rockefeller indicated, was a means by which these doctrines could be imposed by threats of violence, while the establishment was enabled to present itself as the savior of peace and goodwill.

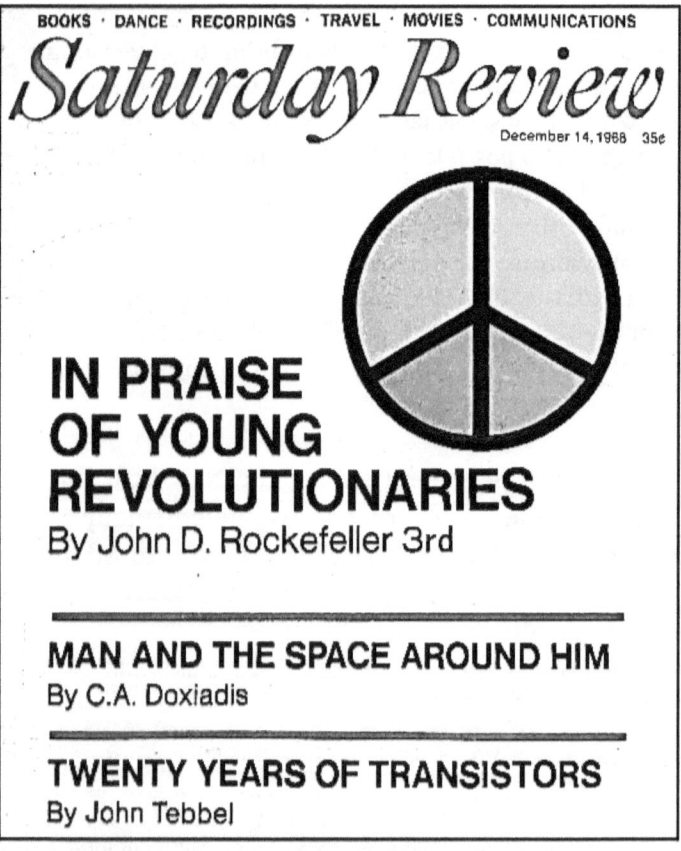

BOOKS · DANCE · RECORDINGS · TRAVEL · MOVIES · COMMUNICATIONS

Saturday Review

December 14, 1968   35¢

IN PRAISE OF YOUNG REVOLUTIONARIES
By John D. Rockefeller 3rd

MAN AND THE SPACE AROUND HIM
By C.A. Doxiadis

TWENTY YEARS OF TRANSISTORS
By John Tebbel

Issue of *Saturday Review* in which John D. Rockefeller III praised the New Left

15

PEACE CORPS

The establishment mobilization of youth manifested openly in the founding of the Peace Corps by the US government in 1960. Tom Hayden, as a student magazine editor listening to then-candidate John F. Kennedy's speech at the University of Michigan proposing the founding of the Peace Corps "to a cheering crowd of students," recalled that he was "swept up . . . on the occasion of a national leader calling on students to play an idealistic role [which] was clearly another turning point for our generation."[420] As Hayden commented, the University of Michigan was "the birthplace of the Students for a Democratic Society, the Peace Corps and the Vietnam teach-ins."[421] Kennedy was appealing to the same source that provided the recruits for the SDS. Hayden wrote that the idea originated when he gave a letter to Kennedy who presented the concept to the students at Michigan:

> University students, myself included, approached Sen. John F. Kennedy in October 1960 to request that he endorse international service as an alternative to the military draft. He read our letter and,

---

[420] Hayden, *Reunion*, 25. The other turning point was the integrationist invasion of the South and the formation of the SNCC.
[421] Ibid., 26.

over worries from his advisers, proposed the Peace Corps on the steps of the Michigan Union that night.[422]

Harold Taylor, in his HEW-sponsored study on the internationalization of education, wrote on the origins of the Peace Corps, under the heading "Student Initiatives in Internationalism":

> One of the student-faculty groups formed during this period at Michigan was called the Association for Commitment to World Responsibility (ACWR). Along with a careful, detailed, and imaginative research study of the rationale, design, and feasibility of a united nations university, the Association also furnished some working papers on the idea of a student peace corps for service abroad. John F. Kennedy spoke at Ann Arbor during his Presidential campaign and urged students to make their own contribution to American society by volunteering from one to three years of their lives to public service needed by their country. Alan E. Guskin, a graduate student in social psychology and a member of the Association, became the leader of a group of students who urged the then-Senator Kennedy to make good on his speech by committing himself to the formation of a government organization that would give American youth a chance to serve the world wherever they were needed. It is generally agreed that Mr. Guskin and his friends were thus responsible for the fact that Kennedy made his famous "Peace Corps" speech in San Francisco in November of 1960 and that the speech took the form that it did.
>
> When the Peace Corps began, Mr. Guskin and his wife, Judith Guskin, were among the first persons appointed to the staff in Washington.[423]

The Peace Corps had many links to the New Left. In 1965, Hayden, as a leader of the SDS, was invited by Frank Mankiewicz, head of the Peace Corps, to train Peace Corps volunteers in Latin America.[424] It could be assumed that the establishment was interested in using

---

[422] Hayden, "Personal Statement."
[423] Taylor, *World and the American Teacher*, "Student Initiatives in Internationalism."
[424] Hayden, *Reunion*, 132.

ultraleft ideology for propaganda purposes in Latin America, and the SDS ideology was in accord with establishment liberalism.

Already in 1961, a Peace Corps delegation aroused outrage among Nigerian students, who accused the organization of being "a scheme to foster neocolonialism."[425] Yet it was the same type of development aid that Hayden and the SDS urged in the Port Huron Statement as the premise of US foreign policy—this was that was being pursued as a means of US penetration into the decolonized states.

Taylor referred to the Peace Corps as

[A]n organization [with] a staff in Washington, supported by Congress and the executive branch with enough funds for educating approximately 7,000 teachers in world affairs each year. . . . Administrative connections with foreign educational institutions, governments, and individuals in 46 countries, in addition to connections with American government representatives in those countries. . . . Direct connections with students, teachers, and community workers around the world; connections with similar domestic and international programs abroad.[426]

It would be difficult to see the Peace Corps as anything other than another ideological and subversive weapon emerging from the Cold War. A paper in the *Journal of Pan African Studies* opined that

Kennedy . . . saw the Peace Corps as an ideological tool to inform the developing world about American ideals of liberty, equality, and democracy before the Soviets had a chance to take over because both countries were fighting for ideological favors in Africa. This is evident in the various speeches that Kennedy gave. . . .

Harris Wofford, one of the directors of the Peace Corps, agreed that the Peace Corps had ideological connotations when he recalled that Kennedy had remarked, "I want to demonstrate to Mr. Khrushchev and others that a new generation of Americans has taken over this country . . . young Americans who will serve the cause of

---

[425] "Rift on Peace Corps."
[426] Taylor, *World and the American Teacher*, 108.

freedom as servants around the world, working for freedom as the Communists work for their system."[427]

Like the NSA and the Congress for Cultural Freedom, the Peace Corps was part of the Cold War arsenal. Its ideology was an internationalized American liberalism. Whether one sees American liberalism as more desirable that Soviet rule is a matter of perspective. The doctrine was—and remains—as destructive of every form of tradition, faith, and sovereignty as communism, much of which was by then a mere shadow in the USSR.

Taylor, for all his professions of a youth-like radical idealism, stated the actual purpose of the Peace Corps in referring to "its relation to American foreign policy."[428] Specifically, Taylor writes:

> In the specific matter of education in world affairs, the establishment of the Peace Corps as *an instrument of American foreign policy and cultural diffusion* marks a turning point in both the theory and practice of teacher education.[429]

Taylor referred to the Peace Corps' role in creating an additional US foreign service, whose functionaries would serve a subversive role in those states that opened themselves to the embrace of American "aid."

> Through the appointment of country representatives to supervise the programs in the host country, the Peace Corps has developed a new breed of foreign service officer whose duties have in a large sense to do with education and social change, rather than with conventional diplomatic representation.[430]

It is notable that the new "cadres" being trained in the PC were intended to be as much agents of change in the US as they were overseas: "Over a period of five years it would thus be possible to build

---

[427] Bekoe, "The United States Peace Corps as a Facet of United States-Ghana Relations," 229.
[428] Taylor, *World and the American Teacher*, 108.
[429] Ibid., 109. Emphasis added.
[430] Ibid., 111.

up a sizable cadre of professional educators who are equally at home in the educational life of their own country and that of a foreign culture."[431] These cadres would be the means by which "we are to extend the international dimension of the curriculum and of teaching in the American schools and colleges."[432]

Taylor saw the Peace Corps as part of a network of organizations from which many radical teachers could be recruited to serve domestic programs. Other organizations included VISTA, the NSA, and the SDS. He estimated that, annually, 375,000 recruits could be had from such organizations to serve as cadres for revolutionizing US education.[433]

While Hayden turned down the invitation from Mankiewicz to head the Peace Corps' Latin American operations, he offered the use of personnel from the SDS front, the Newark Community Union Project (NCUP), to train the government's VISTA volunteers working in ghettos. Although there were further meetings to discuss the subject, the idea lapsed, but was revived in 1977 when Hayden formed the Campaign for Economic Democracy in California, which trained VISTA workers with a grant from the Carter administration.[434]

The Peace Corps had the additional purpose of helping to train the new elite that would govern the "developing" states in line with American interests, as the US vied with the USSR to fill the void left in the wake of decolonization. The establishment sought to mobilize New Left activism among American students, "to reorient the militancy of the youth from the civil rights and other social movements," to serve as "cadres of capitalism."[435]

Junald Ango assumed that the Peace Corps, in seeming to differ and even to oppose official US foreign policy, was acting on its own initiative, while maintaining "a respected position in the government bureaucracy so that it was able to preserve its autonomy in the State Department."[436] This assumption is naive. It assumes that the leftist

---

[431] Ibid.
[432] Ibid., 112.
[433] Ibid., 122.
[434] Hayden, *Reunion*, 132–3.
[435] Ango, "An Un-American Foreign Policy," 499.
[436] Ibid.

orientation of the Peace Corps was at odds with US foreign policy. The cultivation of leftists—from former Trotskyites to social democrats and liberals—carried out by the CIA, the oligarchic foundations, and the State Department, in promoting revolution and subversion, makes clear that the Peace Corps' "radicalism" was fundamentally in accord with the ends desired by those at the top of the ladder. Why would the establishment promote left-wing radicalism overseas unless it was part of a wider strategy? Certainly the US government was aware of this, as President Nixon sought to redirect the Peace Corps in 1971. Ango provides part of the answer to the seeming contradictions:

> After several years of operations, the Peace Corps had earned a respected reputation for its overseas assistance work. It was a reputation recognized as distinct and separate from the other United States overseas agencies so that some countries without diplomatic relations with the United States, but which did not want to establish or re-establish regular diplomatic relations or which had the relations strained, asked for the Peace Corps.[437]

The Peace Corps enabled the US to operate in states in which it could not be seen to officially assist, and to continue its various facades for public consumption. For example:

> Also, in September, 1963, President Juan Bosch of the Dominican Republic was overthrown. Following this revolution, the United States suspended diplomatic relations and all assistance to the country. The Peace Corps, however, continued with its activities under the supervision of the new government. Eventually, this new government was recognized by the United States, and diplomatic relations were re-established in that country. Less than two years later, another rebellion occurred in the Dominican Republic. During the civil war, the Peace Corps operations were allowed to go on by both sides. In rebel occupied areas, the volunteers carried on their assignments under the auspices of the rebel forces.[438]

---

[437] Ibid., 500.
[438] Ibid.

Revolutionary Cadres

Harold Taylor saw the Peace Corps as central to a revolutionizing process, both in the US and abroad. The Peace Corps acted as a training ground to internationalize teachers, a source for the new cadre of educators and bureaucrats, one that was funded by the federal government:

> By a kind of historical accident, including some of the political events preceding and following President Kennedy's election to office, the country has been presented with a national and international instrument for educating teachers, an idea which had not been contemplated by educators in the form of a Peace Corps, but which has now taken a place in the forefront of experiment and change in American higher education. In one great sweep, it has reformulated a philosophy of education whose roots lie deep within the history of American democratic thought, has linked it and American society to the going concerns of contemporary world society, and has developed workable methods backed by Congressional funds for putting the ideas into practice. In doing so, it has involved colleges, universities, and other components of the educational system in a national and international endeavor of high purpose and serious significance.[439]

The "roots [that] lie deep within the history of American democratic thought" were those of the American Jacobinism of Thomas Jefferson, Woodrow Wilson, Franklin D. Roosevelt, and the liberal-democratic internationalism that has for two centuries repudiated the America First doctrine of George Washington.[440] It is this liberal-democratic internationalism that has maintained the US as the actual center of a world revolution.[441]

Like their New Left counterparts in the US, Peace Corps volunteers overseas protested the Vietnam War. It is assumed that this was a rebellious act against their employers, the US government. There

---

[439] Taylor, *World and the American Teacher*, 107.
[440] Washington, "Farewell Address."
[441] Bolton, *Tyranny of Human Rights*, 7–11.

was never a coherent US policy on Vietnam. The only major political figure demanding a clear policy in Vietnam was Senator Barry Goldwater, who was decisively defeated in the presidential election of 1964 by Lyndon B. Johnson, whose campaign workers included SDS activists. Notable advisers and establishment figures in the Johnson administration including McGeorge Bundy, Cyrus Vance, and Robert McNamara, all of whom opposed any decisive military option. As will be seen, Wall Street was desperate for the US withdrawal from Vietnam. Senator Eugene McCarthy had the support of both Wall Street and the New Left in his bid for the Democratic nomination, while Senator Goldwater was opposed by both the New Left and Wall Street.

The Peace Corps was not only created to promote the US overseas, but to gain experiences as internationalists and return to the US with the objective of changing America, as Harold Taylor indicated. President Kennedy's brother-in-law, Sargent Shriver, the first director of the Peace Corps, frequently referred to the domestic mission of the returning volunteers:

> Shriver consistently emphasized the impact of the returned volunteer on American society. While the work that could be done abroad was crucial, to Shriver, the work to be done upon returning home was equally, if not more, important. His speeches, to the public, interest groups, and Congress, consistently returned to this point. "Probably the most important development of the future of the Peace Corps will be the impact of returning Volunteers on American society." At times, Shriver underscored this prediction with numbers—all the while, focusing on the knowledge production potential of the Peace Corps. "In succeeding years they will be coming back home at the rate of nearly 5,000 a year—coming home to take their places in American society, possessed with an intimate knowledge of the cultures and customs and languages of other people from all over the world, coming home with their skills and talents sharpened and developed."[442]

---

[442] Armentrout, "Politics of Experience," 21.

Shriver believed that Peace Corps volunteers would "return better able to assume the responsibilities of American citizenship and with greater understanding of our global responsibilities."[443] This was, it seems, intended to be the training of the new class of bureaucrats and policymakers, returning home to help implement America's leftward course after a decade of civil strife created by the New Left. The idea seems at least implicit to Armentrout when describing the aim in her dissertation:

> This conception of the Peace Corps volunteer as the crucial lynchpin to changing an insulated and under-informed American populace into a more cosmopolitan and well-informed American populace was very much related to the idea that the volunteer would be a distinct kind of one world traveler for whom knowledge was at the center of the experience abroad. "Service in the Peace Corps is not a tourist trip. . . . But it is a way . . . to bring together the virtues of the statesman with those of the scholar."[444] Thus, the Peace Corps volunteer was presented as a scholar of the world—and promised to produce knowledge relevant to American political discussions upon return to the United States.
>
> Senator Clifford Case of New Jersey noted the potential of the returning volunteers to improve both foreign policy and the function of national democracy. "I suspect also that their contribution will be a lifetime one which will just be beginning when they return to this country to participate in developing our foreign policy and in strengthening our practice of democracy at home."[445]

After being nominated to serve as Peace Corps director, Shriver stated to the Senate Foreign Relations Committee that the aim would be to see Peace Corps volunteers return to fill positions in the administrative state:

> I would hope that a substantial number of those people would like to pursue careers in Government upon their return. In that way, perhaps, this would give us a cadre of men and women more

---

443 Quoted in Ibid., 22. From Shriver's Commencement Address, Notre Dame, 1961.
444 Quoted in Ibid., 23-4.
445 Ibid., 22.

knowledgeable about some of the countries in the world than, perhaps, we have today.[446]

Here he alluded specifically to the training of a cadre of a decidedly
internationalist orientation. Armentrout stated the aim clearly:

> The Peace Corps was itself part of a new foreign policy—one that
> centered on sending Americans abroad, but it also promised to cre-
> ate a fundamental, long-term change in the way foreign policy was
> formulated in the future—through the incorporation of volunteers
> into foreign policymaking upon their return.[447]

In March 1965 the PC organized a conference about volunteers who
had returned to the USA. Armentrout commented: "High-level officials at the conference maintained their earlier optimism that returned volunteers had the potential to *infiltrate American institutions*."[448] Returning volunteers were expected to fill the roles of administration. A year after the formation of the Peace Corps, they
asked: "what part will returning volunteers play in American life?"
The answer was that "first indications are that they will play an ap-
preciable part in education and in the internal and foreign affairs of
the U.S. Government." In answer to a questionnaire, 34 percent of
returning volunteers replied that they wanted to work for the State
Department, USAID, or the US Information Service.[449] President
Kennedy issued an Executive Order simplifying the process by which
returning volunteers could enter federal employment.[450] To facilitate
this, the Ford Foundation provided grants for fifty graduate fellowships for the first year.[451]

The role of the returning volunteers was to provide the bureaucracy with those who could make a quiet social revolution in the US
of the type that had long been advocated by, for example, the recip-
ients of Ford Foundation grants. They were also welcomed in the employment of global corporations: DuPont, IBM, First National City

---

[446] Ibid., 24.
[447] Ibid.
[448] Ibid., 34. Emphasis added.
[449] Peace Corps, *2nd Annual Report*, 50.
[450] Ibid., 51.
[451] Ibid., 52.

Bank of New York, and International Minerals and Chemicals Corporation. The Carnegie Corporation funded the establishment of a Peace Corps Career Information Service.[452]

Amidst the applause of most of the news media, a small voice raised skepticism. *The World* of Monroe, Louisiana, commented that "Peace Corps members largely are propagating Kennedy's ideas of socialism and brotherhood of nations, which means one-worldism and the abandonment of American sovereignty."[453]

At the March 1965 Peace Corps convention, shortly after the United States began bombing North Vietnam, Harry Belafonte, Chief Justice Earl Warren, Secretary of Defense Robert McNamara, Secretary of State Dean Rusk,[454] Sargent Shriver, and Vice-President Hubert Humphrey linked arms and sang "We Shall Overcome."[455] Such was the fractured character of the US role in Vietnam.

Role of SDS

The political and social development of the country can only come through the infusion of a kind of revolutionary spirit such as the Peace Corps represents.

– Frank Mankiewicz,
Peace Corps Latin American regional director

What type of organization is it that is established by the US government for the purposes of "infiltrating" American society? While the word "infiltrate" is Armentrout's, the inference she draws is thoroughly documented. Armentrout showed that the incorporation of Peace Corps returnees into the State Department was not as initially successful as desired.[456] Nevertheless, these establishment-trained

---

[452] Ibid., 53.
[453] Ibid., 58.
[454] Rusk was another architect of the Vietnam War fiasco in the Kennedy and Johnson administrations and served as president of the Rockefeller Foundation.
[455] Geidel, *Peace Corps Fantasies*.
[456] Armentrout, "Politics of Experience," 36–46.

and sponsored volunteers augmented the presence of CORE, SDS, and SNCC on the streets.

In 1965 the Peace Corps began recruiting from the SDS, and SDS leaders spoke at Peace Corps training camps. Harold Taylor had seen the potential in his federally funded report. An article in the Berkeley student newspaper, the *California Aggie*, stated of Peace Corps recruiting among the SDS that when the PC fell short of its recruiting goal of five hundred the previous year and was perceived as becoming "somewhat square on campus," appealing to "political activists" was seen as a means of reinvigorating the organization:

> To get ideas on how to organize communities—and to recruit activists on the campuses Corps officials have met with Paul Booth and Carl Oglesby of S.D.S. S.D.S. runs community organization projects in city slums, and Peace Corps officials are considering having volunteers work in these projects as a part of their training. "S.D.S. community development projects require the political savvy and understanding we have developed," Mankiewicz said. "And the same thing that moves moral youth into political activity would be very useful to the Corps." Wiggins explains that whether a student approves of U. S. policy in the Dominican Republic and Vietnam is "irrelevant to the Corps." He is quick to warn that corpsmen will not be permitted to protest U. S. policy once abroad, but he tries to convince activists that although the Corps may be non-political it is involved in nation building. Perhaps the attitude of Peace Corps officials is indicative of a new feeling toward members of the "new left." After all, when it comes to work, a liberal S.D.S. member can sweat as well as anyone else.[457]

The establishment intended to use SDS "community projects" as a means of training Peace Corps volunteers for their sojourn in America's overseas development projects. This establishment outreach was seven months after the SDS, SNCC, and others mobilized up to twenty-five thousand for the March on Washington against US involvement in Vietnam. Frank Mankiewicz was at the time regional director of the Peace Corps for Latin America. In 1966 he became press secretary for Senator Robert Kennedy, who became the SDS

---

[457] Egerman, "'Students for a Democratic Society.'"

choice for the Democratic presidential nomination. In 1972 Mankie-wicz became campaign manager for George McGovern's presidential bid. He also served on the Pacific Southwest Regional Staff of the Anti-Defamation League for two years as Civil Rights Director.[458] As this last affiliation makes clear, this paragon of American liberalism served as a local director for one of the most suppressive, smear-mongering organizations in the United States, if not the world.

Revolutionary Spirit

Mankiewicz is quoted as stating: "The political and social development of the country can only come through the infusion of a kind of revolutionary spirit such as the Peace Corps represents."[459]

Mankiewicz was "generally regarded in the Peace Corps as a sort of resident revolutionary," wrote Professor Marshall Windmiller, who at the time assisted with training Peace Corps volunteers, lecturing to them on world affairs at San Francisco State College. Mankiewicz stated that "the things SDS has done in Newark are valuable for our volunteers to be exposed to. We want to take advantage of their experience." Windmiller commented that "this was before the Newark riots of July 1967." SDS national secretary Paul Booth stated that the SDS was "really open to this kind of move by the Peace Corps," should it not result in merely getting radicals off US streets and shipping them to Turkey.[460] The result was, rather, that Peace Corps recruits were radicalized. The Committee of Returned Volunteers (CRV), founded in 1966, increasingly saw itself as a component of 'the movement,' that loose amalgam of New Left forces ranging from the SDS to the Black Panthers. In the summer of 1969, the CRV sent two delegations to Cuba. Among them were former PC volunteers who had served in Latin America. The delegation returned to the US with laudatory reports on New Left idol Fidel Castro.[461]

---

[458] Peace Corps Worldwide, "Peru's First Peace Corps Staff."
[459] Bovard, "Forgotten Failures of the Peace Corps."
[460] Windmiller, *Peace Corps and Pax Americana*, 76.
[461] Ibid., 154.

Given that volunteers were sent overseas as missionaries of American liberalism to "change attitudes in the foreign cultures of Asia, Africa, and Latin America,"[462] as Windmiller put it, what else was to be expected when they returned home than that they would aim to reshape domestic attitudes? They were imbued with the liberal internationalism of the establishment. What they worked for overseas was indeed resulting in a "quiet social revolution," as the Peace Corps annual report for 1963 described the process.[463]

Pax Americana

Yet the members of the CRV were so inculcated with the fractured individualism of liberalism that they tended toward the anarchic, and as Windmiller commented, they could not agree on a common policy other than "doing one's own thing," which "had reached the status of dogma."[464] Windmiller, after two years of helping to instruct Peace Corps recruits, came to regard the corps as part of the Pax America that the CIA and other agencies were establishing throughout the world. The Peace Corps "was in fact one of its most effective instruments."[465]

Middle America stood bewildered and intimidated between the New Left's hammer of *noisy social revolution* and the establishment's anvil of *quiet social revolution*. This is again indicated by Armentrout's writing:

> Largely excluded from the State Department, Peace Corps volunteers—returned and abroad—found alternate ways of infiltrating national foreign policy discourse. Through demonstrations, petitions, published reports, and the formation of an ardently political organization of returned volunteers, volunteers finally fulfilled the early, hopeful expectations of Kennedy, Johnson and Shriver that

---

[462] Ibid., 143.
[463] Peace Corps, *2nd Annual Report*, 17.
[464] Windmiller, *Peace Corps and Pax Americana*, 143.
[465] Ibid., 10.

volunteers would "shake-up" the stale State Department with their new ideas and unique experiences.[466]

The Committee of Returned Volunteers adopted a radical position, joining the ranks of the New Left.

While President Johnson struggled to define a policy for US involvement in Vietnam, Wall Street converged with the New Left. The Peace Corps was still regarded as a cadre for the transformation of American society on the issue. William P. Rogers, in his keynote address when appointed Secretary of State, called for an increase in the participation of youth in the making of policy, naming the Peace Corps as a place from which to gather divergent views.[467] The fact that President Nixon was at the same time considering ways in which to curtail the Peace Corps by cutting funding and numbers indicates a dichotomy: that the establishment and elements of the US government, up to the presidency, are not necessarily synonymous. The existence of this deep state became undeniable during the Trump presidency.

Nonetheless, and as intended by the establishment, Peace Corps alumni *did* enter the State Department. "Over one thousand returned volunteers worked for the State Department in Washington and in foreign embassies by 1985."[468] In particular, USAID has been staffed by Peace Corps alumni. By 1985, 40 percent of USAID's intern staff, and 25 percent of USAID's professional staff, was made up of Peace Corps returnees.[469]

Ultimately, the Peace Corps served the purpose of the establishment in contributing toward what is euphemistically called "civil society," the vast globalist network of interlinked governmental agencies, NGOs, corporations, and foundations that topple states in the name of "the people" and declare wars against "rogue states" in the name of "peace." Armentrout lauded the Peace Corps' success in assisting this process:

---

[466] Armentrout, "Politics of Experience," 65.
[467] Grose, "Rogers Seeks Divergent Views."
[468] Rice, *Peace Corps in the 80's*, 46.
[469] Ibid.

Peace Corps experience propelled many volunteers into careers engaged with the rest of the world. With 80,000 returned volunteers
by 1980, and with the numbers of returned volunteers working in
internationally oriented fields, there is good reason to believe that
this influenced the global networks that characterized substantive
foreign policy changes in the 1970s. Many joined the *foreign policy
establishment* during the Carter administration. Some of them
filled central roles in a turn toward human rights such as Mark L.
Schneider who was a leading official in the administration's Bureau
of Human Rights and Humanitarian Affairs. But even those who
did not work in high profile positions helped make up what historian Akira Iriye has described as a vastly expanded *international
civil society*. While returned volunteers were certainly not the only
participants in this expansion, their continuing engagement in various types of international work converged with a shift in international politics. As Iriye explains, these groups grew "phenomenally"
in the 1970s and produced substantive changes: "Civil society was
asserting itself, willing to challenge the authority of the state and
to undertake tasks the latter was either unwilling or unable to perform." Active in this international civil society, returned volunteers
played a role in a changing apparatus of international affairs.[470]

SDS–Peace Corps Symbiosis

When Hayden died the Peace Corps eulogized him, alluding to
the New Left as a movement that sought to create "a more just society," confirming that Hayden was the inspiration for the creation of
the corps:

He also played a role in launching the Peace Corps. Harris Wofford
points out in his book, *Of Kennedys and Kings* how Tom Hayden,
editor of the *Michigan Daily*, was at the Student Union in Michigan
when Kennedy spoke to the crowd of students and Wofford writes:
"(Hayden) followed the development of the student organization
with amazement. It had been an era in which few young people had
been politically active, and in which graduate students were particularly known for their political apathy. That year Hayden's paper

---

[470] Armentrout, "Politics of Experience," 121. Emphases added.

won a journalism award for its "imaginative coverage and support of the Peace Corps movement."[471]

It is notable that the Peace Corps was founded at a time of "political apathy" among the youth. The Peace Corps served to mobilize youth from above while the embryonic New Left sought to agitate youth from below (at the street and ghetto level).

As for the SDS, it had an analogous role in training youth cadres domestically. This was recognized by an extreme faction within the SDS, a group in New York and Chicago that sought to replace the Port Huron Statement with a neo-Marxist manifesto, the Port Authority Statement. This was only partly published and in fragmented form in the SDS newsletter, *New Left Notes*. Therefore, the Port Huron Statement remained the SDS manifesto. The neo-Marxist faction split from the SDS and went with the Weather Underground and the Revolutionary Youth Movement. What is significant about the Port Authority Statement is the realization that the SDS was not a genuine revolutionary vanguard, but a front for the liberal internationalism of the establishment. The neo-Marxist faction saw how the New Left could be co-opted by the establishment by providing recruits for a new class of technocrats, citing SDS's endorsement of Robert Kennedy.[472] This neo-Marxist faction concluded:

> The potentiality for new developments in rationalizing American capitalism (economic planning, rationalization, greater equalization of income, full-employment practice–the Welfare State model) is directly tied to the potential of co-opting students, alienated by waste production and powerlessness, by enabling them to become the future rational technocrats. This role provides for a greater sense of power, specifically in dealing with the surface dislocations in American capitalism. Clark Kerr, one of the prime advocates of the new technocracy, was, after all, a member of the Student League for Industrial Democracy, the predecessor to SDS. Bobby Kennedy, the symbol of rational capitalism, has remarked that the

---

471 Peace Corps Worldwide, "A Small Peace Corps Connection."
472 Tom Hayden was to reminisce in 2008: "One of Bobby Kennedy's qualities, or perhaps it was a quality of the times, was an easy and growing familiarity with the New Left." Hayden, "Bobby and Barack."

SDS types will make the imaginative administrators for future governmental posts.[473]

What the ultra-Marxist faction described was the New Left as heir to the New Deal liberalism of their fathers: a collusion between the left and corporate America that had been eulogized by SDS patron Dr. Harold Taylor and his well-placed colleagues at the Eleanor Roosevelt Fund.

[473] Gilbert et al., "Toward a Theory of Social Change," 122.

16

THE GOLDWATER REVOLT

Prior to being asked to preside over the SDS in 1965, Carl Oglesby had been a technical editor for the defense contractor with secret security clearance at the Bendix Corporation. He was asked by his bosses to prepare a report on how their production was being used in the Vietnam War. After being invited by the University of Michigan (home of the SDS) student newspaper to publish his Bendix briefing, he was sought out by the SDS and elected to the presidency. A year later he was forced out by an extreme Marxist-Leninist faction, which included, among others, future Weather Underground leader Bernadine Dohrn. His heresy was that he sought an alliance between the New Left and the conservative right against the Vietnam War. He was not a Marxist, nor even a "socialist." He believed in the decentralization of political and economic power, ideas which converged with elements of the right.[474]

America First vs. Interventionism

The right had in prior decades been at the forefront of opposition to American interventionism overseas, while American liberalism under presidents Woodrow Wilson and Franklin Roosevelt had

---

[474] For a conservative eulogy for Oglesby, see Kauffman, "When the Left was Right."

brought the US into two world wars. Prior to Pearl Harbor, the mass anti-interventionist movement was led by the America First Committee, whose most notable spokesman was Charles Lindbergh, the star pilot known for his transatlantic flight. The establishment became jittery when President Trump began using the "America First" slogan, stating in his inaugural speech in 2017: "From this day forward a new vision will govern our land. From this day forward it is going to be only America first, America first."[475] It was the return of an old specter that brought fear to the foreign policy establishment.

SDS Founding President Becomes "Conspiracy Theorist"

After his ouster from the SDS, Carl Oglesby became a "conspiracy theorist." He had developed a theory that there were two conflicting factions within the power elite: the "Yankees" and the "Cowboys."[476] While the designations are not very satisfactory, the rivalry helps to explain, for example, why there was not a coherent policy in Vietnam. Oglesby was influenced by the eminent scholar from Harvard and Georgetown, Carroll Quigley, whose book *Tragedy and Hope* is extensively quoted by conservative "conspiracy theorists," albeit often incorrectly emphasizing the predominance of a British imperialist cabal.[477] The most quoted passage from Quigley, which Oglesby cites, states that there has existed for a generation a network that:

> [H]as no aversion to co-operating with Communists, or any other groups, and frequently does so. I know of the operations of this network because I have studied it for twenty years and was permitted for two years, in the early 1960s to examine its papers and secret records. I have no aversion to it or to most of its aims and have, for much of my life, been close to it and to many of its instruments. I have objected both in the past and recently to a few of its policies . . . but in general my chief difference of opinion is that it wishes to

---

475 See Goldberg, "'America first' isn't a Trump creation."
476 Oglesby, *Yankee and Cowboy War.*
477 Bolton, "Don't Blame the Brits."

remain unknown, and I believe its role in history is significant enough to be known.[478]

Quigley stated that "it is this power structure which the Radical Right in the United States has been attacking for years in the belief that they were attacking the Communists."[479] The Eastern liberal establishment, Wall Street, the CFR, and the oligarchic foundations pushed the US in a leftward direction. The "Radical Right," by which Quigley meant the moderate anti-big government conservatives who rallied around Barry Goldwater's presidential candidacy, thought the strings were being pulled by communists in the service of the USSR.

Vietnam Dilemma

The neo-imperialism of the global elite replaced the old imperialism of the European colonial powers that had been wounded by World War I and finally buried by World War II. The French withdrawal from Indochina was encouraged by US efforts against European colonialism. The OSS, predecessor to the CIA, had gotten along well with Ho Chi Minh, on the mistaken assumption that they were arming guerrillas to fight the Japanese—a mistake they had also made with Mao Zedong.[480] When Ho proclaimed Vietnam's independence in 1945, he quoted the American Declaration of Independence, and the OSS delegation saluted the raising of the Viet Minh flag.[481] Ho had been known to the power elite since 1919, when he was present at the Paris Peace Conference, the American delegation having been drawn from the Inquiry, the think tank that preceded the CFR.[482]

In 1953 the secretary of a CFR study group on Indochina, William Henderson, delivered a report stating:

---

[478] Quigley, *Tragedy and Hope*, 950.
[479] Ibid., 956.
[480] Hastings, *Vietnam*, 9. Hastings stated that the Vietminh staged "a few small showpiece actions" against the Japanese, while preparing to fight the French.
[481] Ibid., 10.
[482] Grose, *Continuing the Inquiry*, 40.

It was wrong to see Ho's Vietminh forces as simply a forward guard of world communism; nothing in Moscow's designs could explain the size and violence of the Vietnamese rebels. Marxism "has little to do with the current revolution;" rather, it was pent-up nationalism, pure and simple. With France discredited by its colonial past, the opportunity was opening for the United States to guide Ho's revolutionaries away from their irrelevant Marxist rhetoric.[483]

However, the foreign policy establishment never had a coherent policy on Indochina and became preoccupied with the internal "threat" from Joseph McCarthy,[484] whose naive anti-communism threatened to turn into a populist movement that might imperil the oligarchy.

Oglesby described the "Yankees" as the network referred to by Quigley, centered on the CFR and Wall Street, in alliance with the East Coast intelligentsia, Quigley among them.

The "Cowboys" in Oglesby's dichotomy were Southwestern and Western industrialists. The conflict over Vietnam within the establishment was between the "Yankees," who saw the war as sapping the US economy and wanted out, and the "Cowboys," who wanted a decisive military victory. This division became apparent in 1968, when corporate liberals joined forces with the street movement against the war. Oglesby duly notes the escalating costs of the war that were distressing Wall Street.[485]

Quigley also referred to the same dichotomy: the financial capital of the Eastern establishment and the industrial capital based on natural resources such as oil and gas. Although Oglesby saw the two factions as having similar influence, the Cowboys were hardly discernible as a power factor in comparison to Wall Street. However, it was enough to make the establishment nervous. Quigley referred to this industrial elite as the rise of the petty bourgeoisie, weakening the "economic influence of the Wall Street financial groups."[486] This was "the new wealth springing up outside the eastern cities, notably the southwest and far West."[487] This industrial wealth based on

---

483 Ibid.
484 Ibid.
485 Oglesby, *Yankee and Cowboy War*, 4.
486 Quigley, *Tragedy and Hope*, 1245.
487 Ibid.

petroleum, natural gas, natural resources, and aviation was "petty bourgeoisie rather than the semiaristocratic outlook that pervades the Eastern Establishment."[488] A cabal of usurers, stock market speculators, and descendants of market hagglers in old clothes with a collective messiah complex were portrayed by Quigley as "aristocrats" born to lead.

Revolt: Republican Populism

The petty bourgeoisie contended against the control of the parties by Wall Street. They had failed to nominate their presidential choices, conservatives such as Senators Knowland, Bricker, and Taft, at Republican conventions. The 1964 presidential election was a struggle between the civilized and cultured financial elite and the petty bourgeoisie upstarts. At issue was the meaning and future of America as a nation. For Quigley, the financial elite stood for the "Western traditions of diversity, tolerance, human rights and values, freedom, and the rest of it," whereas the petty bourgeoisie "stood for the narrow and fear-racked aims of petty-bourgeois insecurity and egocentricity."[489]

Quigley referred to this as partly a struggle between the isolationism or nationalism of the petty bourgeoisie and the internationalism of Wall Street. This conflict was replayed when Trump assumed the presidency, when once again the riotous left aligned with the establishment.

The Wall Street "aristocrats" wanted the US to withdraw from Vietnam because the war was, as we shall examine in a later chapter, bleeding American resources and causing volatility on the stock market. Wall Street has no problem with war if the stock market profits, or if war is required to eliminate a "rogue state." Vietnam was just the wrong type of war for Wall Street.

Barry Goldwater was aware of the internationalism of Wall Street, the CFR, and the Rockefeller dynasty. He later wrote of this:

---

[488] Ibid.
[489] Ibid., 1246.

The Trilateral Commission is a modern Praetorian Guard. David Rockefeller and Zbigniew Brzezinski found Jimmy Carter to be their ideal candidate. They helped him win the nomination and the presidency. To accomplish this purpose, they mobilized the money power of the Wall Street bankers, the intellectual influence of the academic community—which is subservient to the wealth of the great tax-free foundations—and the media controllers represented in the membership of the CFR and the Trilateral.[490]

Goldwater also knew that the mechanisms of money and credit creation were the basis of the power of international finance, writing of these issues in his autobiography.[491] Having been contracted to write the book, with an advance to Goldwater of $65,000 and an additional $135,000 on publication, the publisher reneged, stating the content was unsatisfactory, and attempted to get the advance payment returned. When the memoirs were later picked up and published by William Morrow and Company, the book became a bestseller.[492]

1964 Presidential Election:
New Left and Establishment Combine

Quigley referred to the decisive historical character of the 1964 presidential election, pitting incumbent Lyndon Johnson against Barry Goldwater.[493] The most forceful denunciation of Goldwater from within the Republican Party came from Nelson Rockefeller. In an obituary for Goldwater, *The Washington Post* stated that despite the landslide win for Johnson, Goldwater wrested "control of the GOP from the Eastern liberal wing that had dominated it for years."

---

[490] Goldwater, *With No Apologies*, 286.

[491] On the power of the international bankers, Goldwater wrote: "International bankers make money by extending credit to governments. The greater the debt of the political state, the larger the interest returned to the lenders. The national banks of Europe are actually owned and controlled by private interests." Ibid., 281.

[492] Lubasch, "Goldwater in Book Suit." Goldwater won the case, the judge stating that Harcourt Brace had failed to provide normal editorial assistance.

[493] Quigley, *Tragedy and Hope*, 1246.

During his 1964 presidential campaign, Mr. Goldwater was attacked by Democrats and opponents within his own party as a demagogue and a leader of right-wing extremists and racists who was likely to lead the United States into nuclear war, eliminate civil rights progress and destroy such social welfare programs as Social Security.[494]

Referring to the establishment, Goldwater said at a news conference in December 1961 that "sometimes I think this country would be better off if we could just see off the Eastern Seaboard and let it float out to sea." As Barnes would write in Goldwater's obituary, "in the Republican primaries, it was New York Gov. Nelson Rockefeller who stumped the country raising questions about what he called Mr. Goldwater's 'extremism.'" Rockefeller, the favorite to win the nomination, dropped out after being defeated by Goldwater in the California primaries. Referring in his autobiography *With No Apologies* to opposition from within his own party, he stated: "By the time the convention opened, I had been branded as a fascist, a racist, a trigger-happy warmonger, a nuclear madman and the candidate who couldn't win."[495] Barnes' *Washington Post* article continues:

> That convention, at the Cow Palace in San Francisco, was long remembered for the spectacle of Goldwater partisans drowning out Rockefeller with a chorus of boos and hoots when he addressed the delegates from the platform. It was also remembered for Mr. Goldwater's own acceptance speech, in which he declared that "extremism in the defense of liberty is no vice and . . . moderation in the pursuit of justice is no virtue."

Goldwater castigated the Johnson administration for what he and many others were calling the "no win war." Like Joe McCarthy, Goldwater was the crassest of personalities in the eyes of the establishment. Quigley, expressing the Eastern liberalism that Goldwater confronted, dropped the refined, cultivated, scholarly image and became frenetic in denouncing Goldwater and his supporters, although he was confident that "this struggle, which still goes on, is one in

---

[494] Barnes, "Barry Goldwater, GOP Hero, Dies."
[495] Ibid.

which civilized people can afford to be optimistic." Hence the title of his book, the "tragedy" being that the Wall Street aristocrats and their paid intelligentsia might lose out to the petty bourgeoisie. Fortunately for the financial elite, a consensus had formed among most Americans that regardless of Republican or Democratic parties, the middle-class outlook had become passé. No candidate of the ignorant petty bourgeoisie could ever be elected. Quigley bluntly stated that the two-party system was manipulated by the Eastern establishment from behind the scenes. The aim is that "the two parties should be almost identical," so that the American people can change parties "without leading to any profound or extensive shifts in policy."[496]

Quigley had shown that democracy is a farce, but he felt no unease about this. Indeed, maintaining the status quo was for him the hope of humanity. Unease came later, from what he said to the investigative journalist Robert Eringer, when *Tragedy and Hope* was suppressed and his position as a highly respected government consultant evaporated because he had said too much.[497]

Relentless Attack on the Middle-Class Family

One of Quigley's most prescient insights is his analysis of the destruction of what he calls the "middle-class outlook." He states that the middle-class outlook was not destroyed because it was abandoned by adult middle-class persons, but because of the inability of parents to pass their outlook on to their children. The education system no longer taught patriotism or nationalism, and was no longer turning out graduates with a middle-class outlook, especially at the higher levels.[498] While Quigley pointed to parental failure, he also stated that there was an external factor: the "relentless attack" on the middle-class family in contemporary literature. Whereas the literature of the nineteenth century often extolled the virtues of hearth and home, it is difficult to find even a single example of serious literary output in the twentieth century that is not mocking or critical

---

[496] Quigley, *Tragedy and Hope*, 1247–8.
[497] Eringer, *Global Manipulators*, 9.
[498] Quigley, *Tragedy and Hope*, 1250.

toward the family. This assault was an assault on self-discipline and future-oriented hope, which were replaced by immediate ego gratification. The latest attacks appeared in the existentialist novels and absurdist plays of Sartre and Samuel Beckett. Existentialism meant a "total rejection of time" and place.[499] The attack on self-discipline was rooted in an "oversimplified Freudianism" that "regarded all suppression of the human impulse as leading to frustration."[500] Self-indulgence, especially in sex, was the message. In education there came what Quigley called a:

> [W]holesale ending of discipline, both in the home and in school, and the advent of 'permissive education,' with all that it entailed. Children were encouraged to have opinions and to speak out on matters of which they were totally ignorant. . . . Every emphasis was placed on 'spontaneity.' . . . All this greatly weakened the disciplinary influence of the educational process, leaving the new generation much less disciplined, less organized, and less aware of time than their parents. . . . These influences in themselves would have contributed much to the weakening of the middle-class outlook among the rising generation.[501]

Quigley's description as one of the leading American academics at the time, who held the traditional moral, cultural, social, and ethical outlook in contempt, explained that this "assault on the middle-class family" came from the power system's opinion-molders, especially in education. It was out of the educational institutions that the New Left was spawned. It was from within the educational institutions that the revolt against tradition was inculcated among the youth. It was not a "revolt" against the establishment and its power structure, but a revolt against the petty bourgeoisie, whose values were regarded by the establishment as regressive.

---

[499] Martin Heidegger, the master philosopher and the progenitor of existential philosophy (though he himself disavowed the label), is inconvenient, because his philosophy is nothing if not one of time and place, despite efforts by his New Left admirers such as Herbert Marcuse to repackage his worldview as something unrecognizable, deracinated, and cosmopolitan.

[500] Quigley, *Tragedy and Hope*, 1251–2.

[501] Quigley, *Tragedy and Hope*, 1254.

The defeat of Goldwater (whom Quigley compared with Hitler) in the 1964 election, coupled with the "upsurge of nonbourgeoisie social groups and social pressures," moved the possibility of revolt "so far into the future that the steady change in social conditions makes it remote indeed."[502] The goalposts had been moved so far to the left that Quigley assumed there could be no further resistance from populists and conservatives such as Goldwater.

Wall Street Rallies to Senator

Nelson Rockefeller, one of the *Übermenschen* by Quigley's estimate, destined to rule the world by virtue of an inherent superiority over the petty bourgeoisie, was decisively rejected for the GOP presidential nomination by rank-and-file Republicans. There was a revolt within the Republican Party against the establishment. Like Trump, Goldwater was far from having the ideological background to lead a genuine counterrevolution. He was a constitutionalist, and was one of the few senators who had voted against the Civil Rights Act not because it would create racial turmoil, but because it was unconstitutional. Personally, Goldwater was an integrationist, and he supported liberalizing abortion laws on libertarian grounds. Nonetheless, like Senator Joseph McCarthy, Trump, and the Yellow Vests in France, any sign of populism makes the establishment nervous. Quigley had seen parallels to the rise of Hitler in Goldwater.

At that time, Phyllis Schlafly, a conservative columnist and author, was president of the Illinois Federation of Republican Women. She had been a delegate to three Republican National Conventions. She was an eyewitness to events within the Republican Party in 1964. Half a million copies of her book *A Choice, Not an Echo* had been distributed in California before the primary, which "was a major factor in bringing victory to Barry Goldwater against the terrific assault of the press, the pollsters and the paid political workers of the

---

[502] Ibid., 1252.

opposition," according to California Republican committeeman Gardiner Johnson.[503]

Schlafly stated that, "From 1936 through 1960 the Republican presidential nominee was selected by a small group of secret king-makers who are the most powerful opinion makers in the world."[504] Whatever quips and sneers might be made about "far-right conspiracy theories," this was precisely what Carroll Quigley himself said. As both Schlafly and Quigley note, the kingmakers had scuttled the nomination of Robert Taft in 1952, and Quigley considered the right flank of the Republican Party to be permanently eliminated as a decision-making factor.[505] As with Goldwater and Trump, the globalists within the Republican Party, with Eisenhower as their figurehead, were vehement in their hostility toward Senator Robert A. Taft, who knew the forces arraigned against him. Taft writes:

> First, it was the power of the New York financial interest and a large number of businessmen subject to New York influence. . . . Second, four-fifths of the influential newspapers in the country were opposed to me continuously and vociferously and many turned themselves into propaganda sheets for my opponent.[506]

In 1960, Goldwater had criticized Nixon during the Republican nomination process for "selling out to Rockefeller." Nixon had acceded to a change of the Republican Party platform to appease Nelson Rockefeller. Taft said that Nixon had gone to New York to "pay court to the Republican Left."[507] In return, Rockefeller nominated Nixon for the presidency. Goldwater opined that Nixon had lost the election to JFK because he was just another "me-too candidate."[508] When Nixon was elected to the presidency in 1969, with Rockefeller protégé Henry Kissinger as his closest advisor, the policy he pursued was a

---

[503] Schlafly, *Choice, Not an Echo.*
[504] Ibid., 6.
[505] Ibid., 56.
[506] Ibid., 63.
[507] Ibid., 75.
[508] Ibid., 77.

Rockefeller/CFR agenda, particularly in regard to opening China up to Western commerce and scaling back involvement in Vietnam.[509]

The kingmakers had chosen Wendell Willkie in 1940, Thomas Dewey in 1944, Dwight Eisenhower in 1952, and Nixon in 1960.[510] This was not just the opinion of a right-wing conspiracy theorist, albeit one observing first-hand, but had been stated unequivocally by a man as establishment in his credentials as Carroll Quigley. Conservative Republicans were beginning to organize a grassroots campaign in 1961 to have Goldwater nominated in 1964. Tom Wicker, Washington correspondent for *The New York Times*, was candid:

> The bitterest resistance to Senator Goldwater centers in the eastern, internationalist power structure that for two decades has dictated Republican nominations. The members of that elite will not lightly relinquish their party to Barry Goldwater.[511]

The rest of the establishment news media followed with an early start on smearing Goldwater, including *The New Yorker*, *Newsweek*, and *The Saturday Evening Post*.[512]

After Rockefeller lost the California primary to Goldwater, the oligarchy put up Governor William W. Scranton of Pennsylvania, who was a political unknown and had little political experience, having been elected governor merely a year prior. A series of luncheons promoting Scranton among the establishment in media and banking were organized by Thomas S. Gates (of the Morgan Guaranty Trust Co. and a former Secretary of Defense) and Thomas B. McCabe, former chairman of the Board of the Federal Reserve Bank and "public governor" of the New York Stock Exchange. Suddenly Scranton was promoted to celebrity status as the Republican favorite by *The New York Herald Tribune*, *The New York Times Magazine*, *Saturday Evening Post*, *Wall Street Journal*, *Newsweek*, *Look*, *Reader's Digest*, *Fortune*, and *Time*.[513]

---

[509] For the CFR's China policy see Bolton, *Revolution from Above*, 42–7. See also Peter Grose, *Continuing the Inquiry*, 42–3.

[510] Schlafly, *Choice, Not an Echo*, 86.

[511] Ibid., 87.

[512] Ibid., 87.

[513] Ibid., 94–5.

An anti-Goldwater journalist, William S. White, writing for an anti-Goldwater newspaper reported:

> An attack upon Goldwater of a ferocity never remotely approached in any of the eight national party conventions previously attended by this columnist was then opened. . . . They, the "moderns," loosed upon Goldwater a storm of accusation and innuendo that made their assaults upon the late Senator Robert A. Taft in 1952 look like warm endorsements. *Men of the stature of Nelson Rockefeller and Henry Cabot Lodge appeared before 40,000 Negro demonstrators in the streets in open incitation of them against the candidacy of the man about to be chosen to head their own party, Goldwater.* Scranton camp followers spread shocking tales suggesting that Goldwater was perhaps in league with neo-Nazis in Germany — and this about a man whose own father was Jewish. Scranton himself attacked Goldwater, in his challenge to a "debate," in tones plainly implying that Goldwater was not only wrong but actually evil.[514]

After a July 12th meeting with Nelson Rockefeller and Henry Cabot Lodge Jr.,[515] Scranton released a letter accusing Goldwater of having "bought, beaten and compromised" the delegates to secure the party nomination. Despite an intense smear campaign against Goldwater at the Republican National Convention, Scranton won only 19 of 100 votes at the RNC.[516]

Enter New Left

While establishment luncheons were being organized for Governor Scranton and the corporate news media was vilifying Goldwater, on the streets CORE organized the previously mentioned forty-

---

[514] Ibid, 97. Emphasis added.

[515] Ambassador to the United Nations under Eisenhower, and to South Vietnam under Kennedy and Johnson. He played a key role in working for Eisenhower to secure the Republican presidential nomination against Taft. He was also involved in the political destruction of Senator Joseph McCarthy. His grandfather, Henry Cabot Lodge Sr., was a nationalist who as a senator led the opposition to US membership in the League of Nations, stating in a speech against membership: "Internationalism, illustrated by the Bolshevik and by the men to whom all countries are alike . . . is to me repulsive."

[516] Schlafly, *Choice, Not an Echo*, 98.

thousand–member demonstration outside the Republican convention, trying to stop delegates from entering the hall. The chant went up: "Barry Goldwater must go." Signs read "Goldwater for Fuhrer, Freedom Is Dead, Hitler Was Sincere, Too," "Goldwater in '64, Bread and Water in '65, Hot Water in '66;" "Vote for Barry, stamp out peace;" "I'd rather have scurvy than Barry–Barry." One sign read "Barry go home," with a swastika in the 'o' of home.[517]

Nelson Rockefeller spoke to the Stop Goldwater demonstration. The Blacks however weren't in a mood to support any Republican, but it showed how desperate the establishment was to stop Goldwater, and how one of their inner circle had no qualms about trying to agitate the mob against his own party.

The SDS was in the forefront of the Stop Goldwater street campaign. They gave qualified support to Lyndon Johnson. On campus, SDS led the Stop Goldwater campaign. In a roundup of campus activities titled "The Elections—and After," the SDS special bulletin stated:

Boston University

The Students for a Democratic Society is now well-known on campus. We sponsored jointly with the Young Democrats a Citizens for Johnson-Humphery [sic] organization at B.U. and also set up an Anti-Goldwater Committee.

The BUSDS anti-Goldwater committee passed out 1,000 flyers publicizing the anti-Goldwater Vigil at Fenway Park. About forty members of the BUSDS conducted a separate Vigil at the entrance an hour before Boston Committee on Political Extremism (CAPE) arrived. Our SDS line grew to 140 people and we then joined onto the CAPE line as they passed us. It was quite impressive.

Chicago

CSA was very active in setting up the anti-Goldwater demonstration that SDS people held on October 16 in front of the Conrad Hilton (where Barry was speaking). The demonstration, initially planned by Chicago SANE, was picked up by Chicago SDS, and with minimal effort got about 125 people out. About 3000 leaflets were distributed.

Harvard

---

[517] Dickerson, "Never Goldwater."

Before the school year had begun, SDS groups had worked with the Massachusetts Freedom Movement to bring out 1200 people, mostly students, to a silent vigil around Fenway Park and Barry Goldwater. . . .

In the inter-campus sphere, plans for an anti-Goldwater march and rally on the Boston Commons originated here and has spread quickly; speakers will be Mark De Wolfe Howe, James Breeden of the Mass. Freedom Movement, Joseph Salerno, Int'l V.P. of Amalgamated Clothing Workers, and Richard Cotten, President of the Harvard Crimson. Aimed primarily at students, the march should bring together a few thousand.

Louisville

About 250 people signed our mailing list at registration, and about 35 signed the "work against Goldwater list." This latter list we sent to COPE, which will type it up and send us copies, thus saving us some clerical work.

We have made up a leaflet from "Goldwater A-Z" using his more militant statements. It's entitled "Barry and the Bomb." Literature we've received has been appreciated.

Three members picketed and leafleted in front of Goldwater headquarters downtown during lunch hour. In less than a half hour 450 copies of "Barry and the Bomb" were distributed. This disturbed the Goldwater people very much, and they came out and started distributing their own literature along side us, crying out "Goldwater Against Communism!"

Reed

Over 100 students demonstrated against Goldwater on his visit to Portland, with signs and a leaflet which pointed out vote by vote his opposition to the test ban treaty, medicare, civil rights bill, etc.

We did a certain amount of precinct work in a working-class white neighborhood in which there is absolutely no Democratic Party structure. Our objective was to organize anti-Goldwater committees of those who were interested in working against him. Even with the little work we did, we found a few people who were interested in working on some such committee, and who might have been potential members for some sort of continuing community-based political organization. Unfortunately we have not been able to follow through on the project as a result of other time demands.[518]

---

[518] Brecher, "Elections—and After."

A statement issued by the SDS Political Education Project before and after the 1964 election campaign backed Johnson, concluding with a very charitable evaluation of why such an opportunist should be supported:

> The Presidency does different things to different men. Lyndon Johnson, the astute politician from Texas, has been talking more like a statesman ever since he became Vice-President. Certainly we have every right to hope that, as President, he will retain the best qualities of the politician and continue to develop those of the statesman. The office of President is demanding, difficult, and a many-faced job; its holder needs all the support and good will possible.[519]

Using the ever-present specter of a post-Goldwater world in ruins, the SDS urged the vote for Johnson:

> We must back Lyndon Johnson in 1964 not only for what he could be, but because he is at least a responsive politician with a certain amount of freedom to move in a positive direction because of the broad nature of his coalition. We must oppose Goldwater not only because he counterposes the politics of the 1880's to the politics of the 1930's, as Mike Harrington has said, but because he wishes to vent the underbelly of frustration and greed in this nation in a final lunge of world nihilism. The choice is clear.[520]

We have taken an intensive detour through the Goldwater candidacy because it shows parallels with the recent Trump candidacy and presidency. The two illustrate how the left–establishment nexus works, and how easily the left, from middle-class liberals to Antifa sociopaths, is easily manipulated into operating for establishment ends. In 1964, SDS members went so far as to actively support Lyndon Johnson to stop Goldwater. Later the left in our own time backed Wall Street choice Hillary Clinton for the presidency, despite her record as a hawk when Secretary of State, in stark contrast to Trump's stated mission of withdrawing the US military from overseas commitments.

---

[519] Burlage, "Johnson—With Eyes Open," 8.
[520] Ibid., 3.

17

THE NEW RECONSTRUCTION

It will take extremism to create gradualism in the South.
— Tom Hayden, 1964

New Left Urged Federal Occupation of Dixie

The Port Huron Statement had among its first sentences references to the Southern states and how the issue of desegregation prompted many White bourgeois youth to become active in support of Black civil rights, becoming for them the first stage in their radicalization: "First the permeating and victimizing fact of human degradation, symbolized by the Southern struggle against racial bigotry, compelled most of us from silence to activism."[521] The invasion of the South by federal troops, FBI agents, and Black and student activists, and the growing opposition to the Dixiecrats by other factions within the Democratic Party, was the starting point for many in what became the New Left. The "shuttling of Southern Democrats [Dixiecrats] out of the Democratic Party" was a primary aim of the student-Black alliance that formed against the South.[522]

---

[521] Hayden et al., *The Port Huron Statement*, 3.
[522] Ibid., 13.

The Port Huron Statement accurately saw economic change as the primary driver for racial integration, calling this the result of "unavoidable changes in social structure." The establishment was seen as not doing enough to impose and enforce integration.[523] Instead of the SDS resisting this change, the SDS sought to accelerate the process.

The SDS was critical of Attorney General Robert Kennedy (later to become their choice of candidate for the Democratic presidential nomination) for not enforcing "the legal prerogative to keep Federal Marshals active in Southern areas before, during, and after any situation;" they were likewise critical of the FBI for not being more proactive in repressing signs of White discontent.[524]

The South was the final outpost of anti-establishment resistance, of agrarian values, and of local traditions. Like South Africa during apartheid, it was an anachronism in a rapidly globalizing world. The SDS disparaged what it called the South's "irrational regional mystique."[525] This mystique, this mythos of a unique agrarian culture, required obliterating before the US could complete the process of social disintegration and reintegration as a globalized entity.

The SDS demanded:

A full-scale public initiative for civil rights should be undertaken despite the clamor among conservatives (and liberals) about gradualism, property rights, and law and order. The executive and legislative branches of the Federal government should work by enforcement and enactment against any form of exploitation of minority groups. No Federal cooperation with racism is tolerable—from financing of schools, to the development of Federally-supported industry, to the social gatherings of the President. Laws backing school desegregation, voting rights, and economic protection for Negroes are needed right now. The moral force of the Executive Office should be exerted against the Dixiecrats specifically, and the national complacency about the race question generally.[526]

---

[523] Ibid., 35.
[524] Ibid., 35–36.
[525] Ibid., 49.
[526] Ibid., 47.

The Dixiecrats remained the true rebels. The SDS were the mindless foot soldiers of the establishment, the collaborators in subduing the South, just as Antifa, Black Lives Matter, and sundry others on the contemporary left are in our century.

The SDS had set itself up as an establishment ginger group whose riotous actions and rhetoric would make the same aims of the establishment seem a mild compromise. While this might now be dismissed as a "far-right conspiracy theory," it was the line being peddled by the establishment. David Riesman, echoing Howard Zinn in the *New Republic*, wrote that, while he feared that federal action against the South might drive Southern Democrats into supporting Goldwater's presidential bid, "unless white southerners show a little more flexibility, Mr. Zinn's approach might be the only alternative to anarchy. That this would be a catastrophe for the nation and would probably eliminate hope for civilizing the South in the foreseeable future, does not make it impossible."[527]

The Student Nonviolent Coordinating Committee, a precursor of the New Left where Hayden and many others served their radical apprenticeships, was the vanguard of the establishment repression of the South. They provided the "anarchy," and order could only be restored by integration. The New Left frenetically demanded that the US withdraw from Vietnam, while just as avidly demanding the federal occupation of the South.

Restructuring the South

Hayden wrote that while a "federal police force in the Deep South . . . is not a solution," it is "a beginning," and would "make rapid social change more possible."[528] Hayden outlined a program against the South, calling for an alliance between government, church, business, and labor unions; government and private material support (such as food and lawyers) for Negro resistance; purging the Dixiecrats from the Democratic Party; a march on Washington if a civil rights bill

---

[527] Hayden, *Liberal Analysis and Federal Power*, 3.
[528] Ibid., 6.

was not passed; and a technological transformation of society that would radically change human relationships. The aims included:

1. Agitation and street level organizing: the role of the New Left, referring to the role of the SNCC, SDS and Northern Student Movement.
2. Occupation by Federal police and military: "Federal power."
3. Southern capitulation.
4. Integration of the South into a technocracy.[529]

In his concluding sentence Hayden unequivocally described the dialectic at work: "It will take extremism to create gradualism in the South, and not until then will we be able to turn fully to these richer issues."[530]

'62 Revolt at Ole Miss

The month following the publication of the Port Huron Statement saw the start of a Southern rebellion. Students were in revolt on campus and others came to assist. It was a revolt against the establishment, a resistance against armed invasion, but the SDS was on the establishment side, and Attorney General Robert Kennedy was doing what the Port Huron Statement had urged the previous month: using armed troops to put down Southern resistance.

On September 26th, James Meredith, escorted by five hundred US marshals, sought to register as a student at the University of Mississippi in accordance with federal rulings on desegregation. Governor Ross Barnett refused to accede to federal impositions on his state, and personally prevented Meredith from entering. The result was an invasion of thirty thousand armed federal troops, marshals, and guardsmen to enforce the desegregation ruling. On September 30th, students and their allies confronted the armed force.

Tom Gregory, a staff writer for *The Meridian Star*, witnessing the events, stated that the use of tear gas on the students was unprovoked. Major General Edwin Walker, who had resigned from the

---

[529] Ibid.
[530] Ibid., 7.

Army in 1961 due to establishment opposition to his patriotic citizenship program for US troops stationed in Germany, arrived at the university to lead the resistance. In 1961 his role at Little Rock, Arkansas, had been very different, commanding the troops that imposed school integration on orders from President Eisenhower. At a time when the Kennedy administration was committing right-wing opponents to psychiatric institutions,[531] General Walker was arrested and placed under psychiatric observation at a Missouri prison, but was soon released because of his high-profile; other dissidents were less fortunate.[532]

General Walker had urged rebellion in a radio address: "Rise ... to a stand beside Governor Ross Barnett at Jackson, Mississippi! Now is the time to be heard! Thousands strong from every State in the Union! Rally to the cause of freedom!"[533] Governor Barnett was defiant: "We will not drink from the cup of genocide. . . . We must either submit to the unlawful dictates of the federal government or stand up like men and tell them never! . . . No school will be integrated in Mississippi while I am your Governor!"[534]

Three hundred were injured.[535] French journalist Paul Guihard was shot at close range and killed. He had met with White rebels before going to the campus and intended to write a sympathetic account. Ray Gunter, a jukebox repairman who had been watching the tumult, was also shot and killed. Dick Gentry, an editor of *The Daily Mississippian*, who witnessed the events, considered the two to have been shot by federal marshals.[536] Guihard, a correspondent for *Agence France Press*, had reported the initial scenes:

> The policemen are smiling. Newsmen—even those from the north—are received with open arms, and there's a feeling of relaxation in the crowd. [It is] difficult to believe that you are in the center of the most serious constitutional crisis ever experienced by the

531 Bolton, *Perversion of Normality*, 101–3, 111–6.
532 Ibid., 101–6. See Szasz, "Shame of Medicine." Szasz was the psychiatric adviser for Walker's defense, and an opponent of the politicization of psychiatry.
533 Walker's radio address, September 26, 1962.
534 Barnett, "Governor Barnett's Declaration."
535 Elliott, "Integrating Ole Miss."
536 Gentry, "Sad Story of the Journalist."

United States since the war of secession [and that] it is in these moments when you feel that there is the distance of a century between Washington and the irredentists of the South.[537]

In 1988, Hayden referred to these murderers as "the courageous federal marshals sent to Mississippi."[538]

Three years after the invasion of Mississippi, federal troops, FBI agents, and federalized guardsmen oversaw the invasion of Alabama by thousands of latter-day Northern Carpetbaggers and Blacks in the famous march from Selma to Montgomery to impose a new Reconstruction on the South. For this, they received the plaudits and acclaim of the embryonic New Left.

New Left Spawned from Student Nonviolent Coordinating Committee

The New Left was primarily the offspring of two factors: 1) The US student movement that was utilized by the CIA as part of their Cold War strategy against the USSR; and 2) The federal imposition of desegregation on the South.

The embryonic New Left was galvanized in the South amidst the conflict that had been caused by Supreme Court desegregation rulings. According to Hayden, Mississippi was "the heart of darkness, the underlying core of racist resistance, where even the bravest protesters suckled in fear with every breath."[539] Key figures in the New Left, including Abbie Hoffman and Tom Hayden, began their revolutionary careers in the Black civil rights movement. The primary organization for this apprenticeship was the Student Nonviolent Coordinating Committee.

Martin Luther King's Southern Christian Leadership Conference was founded in 1957. Ella Baker, who had been with the NAACP from 1938 to 1946 and again in 1952, organized the founding conference of the SNCC at North Carolina State University in 1960. The SNCC

---

[537] Doyle, *American Insurrection*, 162.
[538] Hayden, *Reunion*, 59.
[539] Ibid., 53.

conference was sponsored by the SCLC. Among the participants were representatives from the "Southern Project" of the National Student Association (Constance Curry and Donnah McGinty), CORE, and SCLC.[540] As previously stated, Constance Curry later became an adviser to SNCC.

In 1957 Baker had cofounded In Friendship, an organization which supported agitation in the South. The other cofounders were Bayard Rustin and Stanley Levison.[541] Stanley Levison was Martin Luther King's chief aide and speech writer. Levison combined his career as a realtor, lawyer, and financial coordinator of the Communist Party USA and the Manhattan branch of the American Jewish Congress. Levison saw the Selma to Montgomery march as epochal, writing to King: "For the first time, whites and Negroes from all over the nation physically joined the struggle in a pilgrimage to the deep south."[542] For Levison, Selma was a turning point in King's status as a leader: "It made you one of the most powerful figures in the country—a leader now not merely of Negroes, but of millions of whites."[543]

Levison arranged for financial patronage from the American Jewish Congress to King.[544] An FBI report on King a month prior to his death described Levison as a "shrewd, dedicated Communist," a principal aide, strategist, speech writer, and fundraiser. The book *Where do we go from here? Chaos or Community*, supposedly authored by King, was ghostwritten by Levison. Levison was cited as stating to Clarence Jones (King's other primary aide, legal counsel, and liaison with New York oligarchs) that King was such a "slow thinker" he should not be permitted to say anything without clearing it with them.[545] In 1961, Levison became a treasurer of the SCLC. Prior to that he was a covert fundraiser for the Communist Party USA.[546] In 1964,

---

540 "Present Status of SNCC."
541 See Stanford's MLK Encyclopedia for "Baker, Ella Josephine."
542 See Stanford's MLK Encyclopedia for "Levison, Stanley David."
543 Ibid.
544 See Stanford's MLK Encyclopedia for "American Jewish Congress."
545 FBI, *Martin Luther King Jr.*
546 Ibid., 5.

King asked Levison and Jones to submit speeches that he could use in accepting the Nobel Peace Prize.[547]

Maoz Brown, in a paper on the role of the foundations in funding US student movements, stated of the SNCC:

> Although individual rank and file donors appear to have been the backbone of SNCC's financial support, high-profile philanthropists also played a pivotal role in sustaining the organization and directing its operations. Foundation support clearly contributed to civil rights victories; grants funded bail and lawyer fees for jailed student activists, training and travel for new participants, and other pressing needs associated with protesting and voter registration.[548]

Initial funds for SNCC came from the National Student Association's Southern Student Human Relations Project (The Southern Project), funded by the Marshall Field Foundation,[549] via Constance Curry, director of the NSA Southern Project. The NSA also facilitated White student participation in SNCC.[550]

The aim was to break the Dixiecrats who dominated the Democratic Party in the South through a push to register the Black vote. Northern White students were recruited by Allard Lowenstein, the most famous of the National Student Association leaders from the 1950s, "who played a major role in the politics of the decade," according to Hayden.[551] "Lowenstein welcomed the civil rights movement in the South, as did most NSA leaders."[552] When Hayden first became involved with this activism, "the older NSA leaders . . . felt a need to keep control of their organization and shroud its sources of money."[553] In 1963, Lowenstein led one hundred Northern students

---

547 Ibid., 7.

548 Brown, *Philanthropy and the US*, 13.

549 Created in 1941 by Marshall Field III, a Chicago bond broker and publisher of *The Chicago Sun-Times*, Field is described by the Field Foundation's website as "a passionate integrationist" who "had a deep interest in matters of race and juvenile behavior."

550 Keller and Ruether, *Encyclopedia of Women and Religion*, vol. 1, 1086.

551 Hayden, *Reunion*, 36–7.

552 Ibid.

553 Ibid.

South. The following year, the number was a thousand.[554]

Several years before his death, Hayden wrote of the NSA connections with the CIA, including Lowenstein, who had been a key adviser to SNCC:

> Another figure I met at the turn of the 1960s was Allard Lowenstein, who had attended every NSA conference since the group's inception and had obscure but real connections to State Department and CIA powers behind the scenes. Lowenstein courageously helped smuggle black South Africans into the West, was an adviser to the Student Nonviolent Coordinating Committee during Mississippi Summer in 1964, led the national "Dump Johnson" campaign in 1967 and 1968, was elected to Congress in 1968, and eventually was murdered in 1980 by a disturbed protégé, Dennis Sweeney.[555]

Based on the research in Karen Paget's book *Patriotic Betrayal* (Yale University Press), as well as his talks with her, Hayden wrote that although Lowenstein was not an agent of the CIA, he knew about the CIA penetration, was an ardent anti-Soviet Cold War liberal, and

> Lowenstein went out of his way to block the *Ramparts* story from being published, joining a 1967 meeting of CIA and NSA officials considering how to manage the story if it was leaked.... Paget writes that "today none of the NSA officers who were present can explain Lowenstein's involvement." Lowenstein, she says, also went to the White House, where he was asked by Walt Rostow, Lyndon B. Johnson's national security adviser, to draft a reply to the *Ramparts* story if it came out.[556]

Black civil rights, the SCLC, and SNCC preceded the Vietnam War issue, and hence the efforts of the SNCC would become "the real catalyst to change."[557] The SNCC drive into Mississippi to register Black voters was the start not just of a movement, but a "revolution," according to Hayden.[558] As we have seen, the movement for voter

---

[554] McAdam, *Freedom Summer*, 37.
[555] Hayden, "CIA's Student Activism Phase."
[556] Ibid.
[557] Hayden, *Reunion*, 61.
[558] Ibid., 55.

registration was funded by Carnegie, Ford, Rockefeller, Field, and others via the Southern Regional Council.

However, when SNCC and the Congress of Racial Equality (CORE) adopted a Black nationalist ideology—that is to say, when they ditched integration for separatism—funding was redirected primarily to compliant Blacks in the Southern Regional Council, the NAACP, the NAACP Legal Defense and Education Fund (LDEF), and the National Urban League. After 1966, these organizations:

> [R]eceived increasingly greater shares of the movement's total outside funding. Not only did these three organizations suffer no financial backlash in the turbulent years of rioting and black nationalism, but their outside incomes rose more rapidly than ever before. The most moderate of the groups, the National Urban League, received a late-1960s windfall that was nothing less than astounding. Together the NUL, the LDEF, and the NAACP accounted for all the aggregate increases in combined movement income by the end of the 1960s. The radical organizations, on the other hand, received rapid increases in outside income during the early 1960s followed by equally rapid declines during the era of the new militancy.[559]

Role of the NSA

In 1957, Ray Farabee of the University of Texas was elected NSA president and sought to make the NSA the spearhead of integration in the South. He believed that Southern White students were sufficiently detached from their heritage to be manipulated into supporting the tides of social change.

In 1958, Farabee was given $10,000 (equivalent to $98,000 in 2023) by the Marshall Field Foundation to organize the Southern Student Human Relations Seminar. Eighteen Black and White college students from throughout the South were selected for a three-week intensive seminar led by various "experts." The students then attended the NSA national convention and regurgitated what they had been told. The Field Foundation then funded seminars in 1959

---

[559] Haines, "Black Radicalization," 40–1.

and 1960, to establish the NSA Southern Student Human Relations Project, also known as the Southern Project, with Constance Curry as its first director. Networks were organized across the South, drawn from students and faculty. The NSA Southern Project supported the sit-in movement, which spread like wildfire across the South, challenging segregated stores and diners.[560] Curry estimated that seventy thousand students were involved in what she described as "the first-time college students, mostly black, were involved in demonstrations . . . in direct action to bring about social change."[561]

The NSA was also helping to fund the Student Nonviolent Coordinating Committee. Curry remarked that Maxwell Hahn, director of the Field Foundation, "never questioned" the direction that the NSA Southern Project took. It was at the 1960 NSA convention that Casey Hayden, Tom's wife, instigated support for a SNCC resolution asking for NSA support for "civil disobedience."[562] Foundation money was given for the Voter Education Project in Atlanta, laying the groundwork for SNCC's future work, in which Casey Hayden was an advisor on the executive committee.

The funds for the Voter Registration Project were dispensed by the Southern Regional Council, which, unsurprisingly, "received large grants from the Ford, Rockefeller and Carnegie foundations."[563]

---

[560] Curry, "NSA's Southern Civil Rights," in Schwartz, *American Students Organize*, 446.
[561] Ibid.
[562] Ibid., 447–8.
[563] Roelofs, *Foundations and Public Policy*, 133.

18

RAMPARTS

Ramparts became the flagship organ of the New Left. Although started in 1962 as a Catholic lay magazine, initially material was included from all backgrounds. Opposition to American involvement in Vietnam was a primary issue. Like the radical feminist magazine *Redstockings* that exposed the role of Gloria Steinem in CIA Cold War operations, *Ramparts* is notable for having exposed the CIA funding of the National Student Association. Whereas today it is the so-called far-right that is accused of being purveyors of "conspiracy theories," "disinformation, and "misinformation," and the left are in the forefront of pointing their collective finger, it was a mere fifty years ago that *Ramparts* was, for example, featuring "conspiracy theories" on the assassination of John F. Kennedy[564] and Martin Luther King.[565]

In 1967, *Ramparts'* liberal Catholic founder, Edward Keating, was ousted. In financial trouble, significant backing was lost due to its support for Black power,[566] and for its condemnation of "Israeli imperialism" during the Six-Day War, with a high proportion of Jews in

---

[564] Welsh and Lifton, "Case for Three Assassins."
[565] Turner, "Some Disturbing Parallels."
[566] Eldridge Cleaver, information director of the Black Panthers, was a *Ramparts* senior editor. Some White and Jewish liberals got jittery about Black power racial nationalism, which was less tame than the Black movement of their house niggers such as Baynard Rustin and Martin Luther King.

the New Left being conflicted over their loyalty to Israel.[567] A *New York Times* article mentioned that *Ramparts* had veered from Catholic liberalism to left-liberalism in 1965 when two business consultants and subsequent stockholders, Howard Gossage and Dr. Gerald M. Feigen, suggested a change in direction, while Hinckle, whose first association with *Ramparts* was "as a public relations man," became editor.[568]

Warren Hinckle III, a businessman with a penchant for sensational journalism, found other contributors after taking over as editorial director. As of 1968 the stockholders of *Ramparts* were listed as Warren Hinckle III, Abigail Rockefeller, Stanley K. Sheinbaum (each with $25,000 of shares), and Nicholas Samstag ($5,000).[569] Stanley K. Sheinbaum was an economist at the CSDI. Nicholas Samstag was president of a communication consultancy, Nicholas Samstag Inc.[570] Abigail Rockefeller was spending her Rockefeller trust money on the ultraleft.

New Left luminaries on the *Ramparts* payroll included Michael Ansara, president of the SDS front Cambridge Iron and Steel (assistant editor); Carl Oglesby, SDS founder (consulting editor); Lee Webb, SDS committee member (consulting editor); IPS cofounder and trustee Marcus Raskin (consulting editor); and IPS trustee Arthur Waskow (contributing editor).

Underground, or Underworld?

Israel Schawartzberg, ombudsman editor of *Ramparts*, had been a "baseball fixer, swindler, bookmaker, and jailhouse lawyer," who had served a "small and light" sentence of eighteen months at Leavenworth Penitentiary for bribing a witness in a narcotics case.[571] Schawartzberg was a gangster who had previously served fourteen

---

567 O'Flynn, "Ramparts Magazine, Inc," 26.
568 "Ramparts: Gadfly to the Establishment," 1.
569 Ibid., 2.
570 Ibid., 15–6.
571 O'Flynn, "Ramparts Magazine, Inc.," 41.

years in jail.[572] Hinckle said that he had appointed Schawartzberg as *Rampart's* ombudsman "to hear complaints from the people about the Government."[573]

Schawartzberg served as go-between for Hinckle with Harold ("Kayo") Konigsberg, a freelance Jewish hitman for Mafia families. While in Springfield prison hospital, having been diagnosed as "insane," Konigsberg was allowed to be visited by Schawartzberg, in breach of standard regulations, so that a $1 million investment into *Ramparts* could be arranged. An article in *Life* quoted Hinckle as stating that when *Ramparts* was "about to go under," Izzy (Schawartzberg) told him that Kayo was "rich as hell." Konigsberg was considered by the FBI to have been the leading loan shark in the USA.[574] He was also, according to Hinckle, a Mossad contact-man: "He wasn't a Mossad, but they'd bring him in for deals. Assassinating was a major activity, that was because he was a big Israeli, but he spent most of his time loan sharking and in major mob stuff and collecting debts."[575]

Hinckle explained how he rationalized his position on Israel to Kayo, having just lost *Ramparts'* key investors over the Israel issue:

"Okay," he says, "How much you want?" I said, "We need a million bucks, a million bucks for the magazine." He said, "Well, where are you on Israel?" I said, "Hey, we just had some guys who took out their dough because it wasn't Israel enough, and I told him to be good for the Jews, you've got to be a little independent, you can't sound Israeli." He says, "Well, what did you say?" "I said these lefties were crazy, that Israel had a right to exist, and we had to defend their right to exist, and the Arabs couldn't invade them again and take them over again." "That's fine, that's all you got to say, I'm with you." All right, okay, I said, "Good, so a million bucks okay. Tell him he'll work it out."[576]

---

[572] Ibid.
[573] Ibid.
[574] Ibid., 44.
[575] Hinckle, interview, 270.
[576] Ibid.

The deal between Kayo and *Ramparts* was to be completed through D. De Jersey Grut (incorrectly rendered in the Hinckle interview as Jersey Dugrut), a member of the Bankers Club of New York and on the board of *Ramparts*. The plan was to publicly announce Kayo's investment at the Bankers Club.[577] Hinckle stated that the attitude of Grut was that "this guy's a big Wall Street guy, but he just thought it was fabulous. 'Why not? It's business.'"[578]

The investment did not eventuate because Hinckle rejected what he regarded as Kayo's mentally deranged literary input.[579]

Vietnam and the Establishment Line

Given the willingness of *Ramparts* under Hinckle to accept money from a hitman and leading *usurer*, to what extent was *Ramparts'* exposé of CIA connections to the embryonic left-wing student movement motivated by sincere moral rectitude? To what extent was it an advertising gimmick, or was it perhaps reflective of factionalism and powerplays? Harold Weisberg, OSS veteran, State Department intelligence analyst, senatorial aide, investigative reporter, and expert on the Kennedy and MLK assassinations, even opined in 1974 that *Ramparts* could have been manipulated by the CIA. He regarded Hinckle as "a common crook, with money," with *Ramparts* acting as a "Department of Misinformation." He wrote:

> If we ignore intent and consider what ends were or could have been served, deal with fact only then on this and what I am really writing about, I think many other stories a different *Ramparts* emerges.
> My question boils down to this: can you recall any major *Ramparts* operation that you can honestly say did not serve some spook or

---

[577] Hinckle, interview, 271. The Bankers Club was an elite reserve that closed in 1979. From Salpukis, "Era Closes with Bankers Club": "When Presidents' needs were financial (and each President has had such needs), they met with Wall Street's elite."
[578] Hinckle, interview, 271.
[579] "From Behind Bars," 50.

spook faction interest—at the time it appeared? Even exposures of the CIA itself?[580]

Regarding the *Ramparts* exposé of the CIA funding of the National Student Association, Weisberg suggested that the story could have been seeded by a CIA faction. Further:

> By the time they were exposing Vietnam, CIA policy and attitude had changed, as the Pentagon papers established. No big deal there and doing what was done through *Ramparts* was effective and least likely to be suspected as of spook inspiration.[581]

Weisberg alluded to the role played by *Ramparts* in opposing US involvement in Vietnam as being in accord with the CIA attitude. The riotous, violent behavior of the New Left, with their slogan "bring the war home," scared Middle America into accepting the American scuttle from the Vietnam imbroglio. As with the other primary issues of the New Left, such as Black integration, the position on Vietnam was not fundamentally different from, let alone in opposition to, the position of the establishment.

Thomas L. Ahern Jr., author of the CIA's history of its role in Vietnam, wrote that "Defense Secretary McNamara had already concluded that military victory was impossible, and in early 1966 he was privately urging a political settlement and a coalition government."[582] The South Vietnamese did not trust the US, especially the CIA. President Nguyen Van Thieu's

> [M]istrust of the US focused increasingly on the CIA, which he saw as an ubiquitous power either beyond Washington's control or being used by the US Government to thwart Saigon's desires. He told one visitor that 'between the infiltrating Communists and the American CIA, the government is stuck.'[583]

---

[580] Harold Weisberg to JDW, December 21, 1974. The recipient, "JDW," was James D. White, a journalist with an interest in the Kennedy assassination.
[581] Ibid.
[582] Ahern, *CIA and the Generals*, 48. Originally classified as "secret" before being authorized for release in 2009, many names, passages, and some whole pages were nonetheless redacted.
[583] Ibid., 87.

Veteran journalist James White replied to Weisberg that he would not challenge the opinion that *Ramparts* served "some spook interest," such as the CIA. White opined that such an expensively produced magazine on the fringe of the left could only survive "by getting solid amounts of dough from some source." White stated that he once visited the *Ramparts* office, which was a "shambles."

> Such disorganization and confusion as to make it certain that they could never survive on their own abilities. As you know, the top staff has changed several times, always mysteriously picking up after being publicly prostrate. They may know what their editorial policy is, but nobody else does, and this has always been the case since it ceased to be an unpretentious Catholic liberal magazine just starting up. They have a way of evading some issues which I don't understand and can only assume there is some reason besides eccentricity. Nothing I can think of contradicts your assumption.[584]

As odd as Weisberg's theory on a *Ramparts*/CIA connection seems (given the public spat between the two), among Hinkle's many friends and associates with intriguing backgrounds was Clay Felker. "My friend Clay Felker" was what Hinkle said in referring to the founder of *New York* magazine and editor of *Village Voice* and *Esquire*. Hinckle stated that he assisted Felker in raising funds to get *New York* magazine started.[585] As we have seen, Felker was one the CIA's Cold Warriors at the Helsinki Youth Festival in 1962, working with future feminist icon Gloria Steinem in the CIA front, the Independent Research Service, editing *Youth News*. In 1972 Felker, *Newsweek*, and *The Washington Post* publisher Katherine Graham, and Warner Communications enabled Steinem to launch the feminist flagship magazine, *Ms.*[586] Felker's name seems to have been absent from *Ramparts'* exposés on the CIA. Perhaps this was an example of *Ramparts* having a "way of evading some issues"?

---

[584] White to Harold Weisberg, December 30, 1974.
[585] Hinckle, interview, 375.
[586] Borman, "Inside the CIA."

JDW: Hinckle/Ramparts   12/21/74   HW

I'm hoping you'll have a brief period like I'm having, not long enough to do work requiring continuity of time, for a few minutes of recollection of the past. It is a subject that long has fascinated me that I'll come to while I'm catching my breath still and cooling off from carrying up a load of long limbs for cutting. By the time I finish this it will be mail time, and when I go out for it, back with another load. How's that for efficiency?

For such moments I accumulate unread clips, etc. I have just finished Geismar's review of Hinckle's book in UR 1/75. Geismar avoids what interests me most, and I think the reason is lack of comprehension. He also treats just plain dishonesties that approach if in fact they were not fraud as no more than principled "madness." Even the attempt to flimflam an emotionally ill patient through Fromm is "hilarious." This is to say that while what can be called Ramparts' accomplishments he reports faithfully, he also avoids some of the sinister, whether from ignorance of not I can't say.

My own documentation of the unprincipled and unethical you know. It is not new and it is as persisting a characteristic as muckraking. Brilliant Hinckle is. Also a common crook, with money and with the work of others.

Geismar finds WRamparts' investigation of President Kennedy's assassination" to be fascinating; some "Hinckle has written only now."

Well, I know something about that, Hinckle's part in it, his deviousness and outright lying in recounting it, and it was a disaster that regardless of its intent could not have been a more perfect working of the Department of Disinformation, beginning with the most brilliant spoof I can remember.

If we ignore intent and consider what ends were or could have been served, deal with fact only, then on this and what I am really writing about, I think many other stories, a different Ramparts emerges.

My question boils down to this: can you recall any make Ramparts operation that you can honestly say did not serve some spook or spook faction interest - at the time it appeared? Even exposures of the CIA itself?

I believe it is possible to theorize that a faction of the CIA - perhaps even its top - wanted to end the dangerous NSA situation. The story then was that they didn't ever want to do it and did it only because nobody else was. This can be credible. And nobody was really hurt by it except a couple of reporters perhaps.

By the time they were exposing Vietnam, CIA policy and attitude had changed, as the Pentagon papers established. No big deal there and doing what was done through Ramparts was effective and least likely to be suspected as of spook inspiration.

Illustrations of this kind tend to make more conspicuous what Ramparts did where spook interest lay in the opposite direction. They were the major single drain on Garrison's funds, the major single misdirector of effort, such as he was capable of (and why then knew?), and without possibility of doubt conned him into a spook trap. They refused to print solid information and to the best of my recollection never once did, the closest I can recall being Lifton's rewrite job, carefully filtered and angled as it was.

So, reminded of this continuing doubt I have entertained since 1965 or 1966 and more than I could add, if you have time to think it through I'd appreciate your thoughts. I never did see it regularly and thus also there can be much of which I'm not aware.

Harold Weisberg's memo theorizing
on the manipulation of *Ramparts*

Funding

Howard Gossage, the *Ramparts* board member who had urged a New Left direction, was the dean of advertising men, and his innovations have had a lasting impact. Hinckle related that Gossage taught him that "if you're selling something, as long as you can do something interesting, you're probably going to get people involved."[587] Among the donors that Gossage gained to pay the printing bills for *Ramparts* when on the verge of bankruptcy was Irving Laucks,[588] plywood and oils manufacturer, who was also a sponsor of the CSDI, IPS, and the New Left School. Bill Honig, an advertising executive in San Francisco, invested $100,000 and sat on the board of directors of *Ramparts*.[589]

When *Ramparts* was going bankrupt, Hinckle was introduced by Peretz to Abby Rockefeller,[590] daughter of David Rockefeller, who enabled her to spend her trust money on New Left causes. Hinckle stated of his introduction to Abby:

> She's one of the Rockefellers, maybe she could help. She says, "Gee, *let's see if I could get my father*, they only let us—" Then you find out about trust funds and how much these kids have access to, it's fun. Abby was like an early green, and she was a good person. I spent a lot of time with her. She was helpful.[591]

The strongly pro-Israel Peretz, being one of the larger donors, presented a problem when in 1967 *Ramparts* ran a feature on the Arab–Israeli war. Hinckle stated that Peretz and Richard Russell were "where the real money came from." "Then with Marty Peretz and Dick Russell, you're going to get into the Israeli politics. It gets very sticky. All the complicated financial vehicles they created."[592]

---

587 Hinckle, interview, 106.
588 Ibid., 185.
589 Ibid., 188.
590 Ibid., 202.
591 Ibid. Emphasis added.
592 Ibid., 191.

Note the last comment: "All the complicated financial vehicles they created." Hinckle mentioned that Peretz's money was from his wife, jazz musician Anne Farnsworth, an heir to Singer sewing machine money:

> And Marty's money was Anne Farnsworth, Singer sewing machine money, right? And they were stalwart proponents of Israel, and gave a lot of money to Israel. So it's impossible to discuss that, because that was the stabilizing investment in *Ramparts*.[593]

Russell and Peretz provided the "stabilizing financing."[594] Hinckle described Russell as "an Israeli advocate, a genius businessman out of Connecticut and an artist." Hinckle stated that Russell advised Peretz on investing his wife's money in left-wing causes. Russell and Peretz had "met over Israeli issues because they both were big Israel partisans."[595] Peretz and Richard Russell broke with *Ramparts* over an article critical of Israel, because, according to Russell, the article was "not one hundred percent" in favor of Israel.[596]

Peretz left *Ramparts* to buy the influential *New Republic*. Hinckle said of Peretz, "his ego was bigger than his loyalty to the ideological political positions he propounded."[597]

Adam Hochschild was approached, "because he's rich as shit because his father was an ambassador, or whatever they call it; had diamond mines in South Africa, right?" Hinckle thought that apart from Hochschild being a good writer, "maybe we'll get some money out of the fucking diamonds."[598] Hochschild was a staff writer for *Ramparts*. Hochschild cofounded the left-wing magazine *Mother Jones* in 1976.

Starting out with only a few thousand subscribers and one small-scale distributor, after a year:

---

593 Ibid.
594 Ibid.
595 Ibid., 203.
596 Ibid., 209.
597 Ibid., 203.
598 Ibid., 196. Hinckle's memory errs. The Hochschild Group was founded on South American copper and tin mining.

> [Hinckle] was able to get *Ramparts*, through a lot of hook and crook and times at conventions with guys who owned these big distributing companies, and dealing with some of the big owners directly, and a little bit with the Mafia, because they had a big hand in this, managed to get *Ramparts* a major national distribution, and it became one of the main sellers on the newsstands for the next three, four years.[599]

When questioned on the Mafia connection, Hinckle replied that the Mafia in certain cities could determine what magazines were acceptable for distributors.[600]

Ramparts hemorrhaged money on staff expense accounts. Nicholas von Hoffman, a left-wing journalist who had from 1953 to 1963 worked with radical icon Saul Alinsky, and subsequently written for *The Washington Post* and CBS, wrote of the "dozens of stories" of Hinckle's "money orgies," "including the time during the airplane strike that he flew to New York via Paris on the grounds that it was the only way to get there."

> Wherever he went, it was first class, even at the 1968 Democratic convention where the magazine's left-radical staff had to suffer their boss and his friends drinking it up in a suite in the city's most expensive hotel while they swallowed tear gas down on the streets.[601]

Sol Stern, the *Ramparts* staff writer who had broken the story on the CIA funding of the NSA, and who like other *Ramparts* eminences (such as David Horowitz) became a "neoconservative," wrote of the heroic portrayals that *Ramparts* editors received from *The New York Times*: "But responsibility and restraint were alien words in the *Ramparts* offices. There were too many Algonquin Hotel junkets, flights around the world chasing stories that never panned out, and three-hour, booze-filled lunches at the priciest restaurants in our San Francisco neighborhood."[602]

---

[599] Hinckle, interview, 170.
[600] Ibid.
[601] Hoffman, "Magazine Experimenting."
[602] Ibid.

Scanlan's

While the court allowed the bankrupt *Ramparts* to continue publishing until 1975, Hinckle founded another magazine, *Scanlan's*, where Schawartzberg resumed his role as the people's ombudsman. Sol Stern remarked:

> I never understood why Hinckle was so reckless with the magazine's future. What I do know is that the miracle of the capitalist system's bankruptcy laws insulated the editors from the consequences of that recklessness. Hinckle went off with [Sidney] Zion to start another muckraking magazine called *Scanlan's*. The new monthly raised $1 million and published nine issues.[603]

Scanlan's was described by Hinckle as "in some ways more left than *Ramparts*."[604] The money for *Scanlan's* was put up by Charles Plohn.[605] This was arranged by lawyer and boxing promoter Bob Arum,[606] who was Plohn's legal representative. Arum suggested that funding could be raised by making *Scanlan's* a public corporation. The amount was $675,000.[607] Charles J. Plohn Sr. was "senior partner of Charles Plohn & Company, a prominent Wall Street underwriting concern" and at the time "the nation's biggest investment banker in terms of the number of his company's underwritings."[608] Plohn, although having a reputation as the issuer of initial public stocks of dubious quality, sat on the boards of the New York Stock Exchange, the American Stock Exchange, and the Pittsburgh Stock Exchange. "In 1968, the Securities and Exchange Commission suspended the Plohn company, Mr. Plohn and other senior officers for three weeks for violations of securities laws."[609] In typically flamboyant style, the cover

---

[603] Stern, "*Ramparts* I Watched."
[604] Hinckle, interview, 276.
[605] Ibid., 275.
[606] Bob Arum has been accused of fight fixing and bribery. See Langford, "Bob Arum."
[607] Hinckle, *If You Have a Lemon*, 362.
[608] Ennis, "Charles T. Plohn Snr. Partner."
[609] Ibid.

of the first *Scanlan's* carried a picture of the check received from Plohn, and the magazine was advertised on newsstands with signs reading "Plohn's folly."[610]

While *Scanlan's* hemorrhaged money like *Ramparts*, the "jailhouse lawyer," Israel Schawartzberg, the people's ombudsman, "office manager," and resident Mafia expert, who "kind of terrorized the girls who were the secretaries," ran petty criminal enterprises out of the office.[611]

[610] Farley, "On July 18, 1969," in *Gonzo Wall Street*.
[611] Hinckle, interview, 337, 361.

19

RACE, RIOTS, AND OLIGARCHS

Ramparts was a zealous promoter of the Black Panthers. Sol Stern, contrite forty years later for his role in *Ramparts*, said of the magazine's promotion of the Black Panthers:

> I also felt partly responsible for creating the myth of the Black Panthers as righteous rebels fighting off brutal police oppression. In 1967, I wrote a hagiographic profile for *Ramparts* of Huey Newton, the Panthers' "minister of defense," and then published basically the same article in the *New York Times Magazine*—yet another indication of the changes in the mainstream media. It soon become clear to anyone who cared to look, however, that Newton and the Panthers were clever street thugs who used revolutionary slogans to avoid accountability for their crimes. As one of the New Left's favorite black criminals, Soledad Prison inmate George Jackson, once put it, "Marxism is my hustle." After my Newton article, *Ramparts* ran three more celebratory cover stories on Panther leaders—Eldridge Cleaver, Bobby Seale, and (again) Newton.[612]

Ramparts published Black Panther minister of information Eldridge Cleaver's *Soul on Ice*, in 1968. Cleaver was a senior editor with *Ramparts*.

---

[612] Stern, "*Ramparts* I Watched."

Black nationalism (separatism) was not what the establishment wanted, but the violence and threatening rhetoric of groups such as the Black Panthers was useful in scaring Middle America into supporting the demands of the NAACP, the Urban League, and MLK, who were extolled as the "moderate" option. The aim was desegregation in the South, racial integration, and what is today called an "inclusive economy." *Ramparts* served this dialectic in promoting both the armed threats of the Black Panthers and the much-heralded "moderation" of MLK and the Southern Christian Leadership Conference. It was a photo feature in *Ramparts*, "The Children of Vietnam," that prompted King to join the anti-war movement in 1967. *Ramparts* soon after published King's "Declaration of Independence from the War in Vietnam," the transcript of a speech at Riverside Church in New York City on April 4th, 1967.[613]

Agitating for Military Occupation of the South

Two years previously, *Ramparts* sought to evoke images of a new Civil War between a new "Union" and a new "Confederacy." Now the "armies of the Union" were, according to *Ramparts*, the Student Nonviolent Coordinating Committee (SNCC) and King's SCLC. The twentieth-century "Confederacy," according to the *Ramparts* scenario, was led by Governor George Wallace of Alabama, colorfully described as this latter-day Confederacy's "titular president." *Ramparts* for its part intoned the zealous rhetoric of the abolitionists who had sought the physical annihilation of the Southern Whites a century before:

> So grotesque is the national situation that the true capital of the Union forces is now in Atlanta, Georgia, which contains the headquarters of the two main armies of the Union, the Southern Christian Leadership Conference and the Student Nonviolent Coordinating Committee. The President of this Union is Dr. Martin Luther

---

[613] King, "Declaration of Independence."

King. The capital of the Confederacy continues to be Montgomery, Alabama, and its President is George C. Wallace.[614]

Like the SDS in the Port Huron Statement, *Ramparts* was calling for another federal military occupation, a Second Reconstruction, of the South, while simultaneously condemning the United States' half-hearted presence in Vietnam as tantamount to genocide.[615]

Three years after the invasion of Mississippi by federal troops to impose school desegregation at bayonet point, *Ramparts* heralded the invasion of Alabama as the battleground against Southern dissent. The new invasion comprised thousands of White and Jewish students, theological students from various denominations, and Blacks coming down from the North, linking with the SCLC and SNCC. While *Ramparts* condemned the "police state activity" of Alabama authorities in maintaining order, they sought the federal military occupation of Alabama. These doves on Vietnam became hawks in agitation against the South, referring to "casualties of war," "war heroes," and "Confederate forces massing outside city limits."

Selma March

If white people realize what the alternative is, perhaps they'll be more willing to hear Dr. King.

– Malcom X

Despite the necessity for *Ramparts* and the New Left to posture about the inadequacy of the Federal Government's response, President Johnson brought the 1,863 Alabama national guardsmen under federal control, sending "them—along with 1,000 U.S. Army troops, 100 FBI men and 100 federal marshals . . . to guard the Great March to Montgomery, finally made by the Union forces," as *Ramparts* colorfully put it.[616] The "Great March" was the march from Selma to

---

[614] Keating, "South at War," 18.
[615] In the *Ramparts* special issue on Selma, the situation is compared with Auschwitz, "the parallel being obvious, even to the insensitive." Ibid., 36.
[616] Ibid., 32.

Montgomery, starting on March 21st, led by Martin Luther King in alliance with SNCC. The march started with about 2,900 participants, under the protection of federal troops, to the outskirts of Selma, and proceeded to Montgomery under the "protective control of the federalized units of the Alabama National Guard."[617] FBI reports described how groups of participants were under federal protection, from wherever in the US they were departing, to converge on the beleaguered Southern state, with the chartering of buses, planes, and trains. While encamped, marchers were guarded by the federalized guardsmen.

Despite the drama evoked by *Ramparts*, there was no violence during the march, and protest was confined to approximately 240 Klansmen, under FBI surveillance, holding a rally at Montgomery, "without incident," prior to the arrival of the marchers.[618]

The Evening Star reported:

> While the weary freedom fighters slept . . . standing among the Alabama pines and underbrush were hundreds of guardsmen to protect the marchers from any hostile whites who might infiltrate the area. The main military force was bivouacked in several locations in the area, their transport trucks and radio-equipped jeeps lining the side of the road. Other military vehicles with motors running were parked along Highway 20 and alongside roads leading to the pasture where the campers spelt.[619]

A UPI report referred to four jet fighters circling the encampment, plus "several other reconnaissance planes," as three hundred marchers led by MLK prepared to set off to Montgomery. "U.S. Army troops and National Guardsmen, most of them armed with carbines, were stationed in fields, along the roadway, on the parameter of the encampment. Troops in jeeps also patrolled the area. . . . King praised the use of Federal troops."[620] The three hundred marchers were met by over twenty-nine thousand at the State Capitol, gathering in the athletic auditorium of the City of Saint Jude Catholic complex.

---

[617] FBI, "March from Selma."
[618] FBI, "March from Selma," 3.
[619] Hunter, "Huge Tents Shelter."
[620] FBI, "March from Selma."

An FBI report cited *Time* reporting that New York Governor Nelson Rockefeller "was sending Alexander Aldrich [Rockefeller's cousin], chairman of the New York State Special Cabinet Committee on Civil Rights, and George Fowler, Chairman of the State Commission on Civil Rights to participate in this march."[621] Also arriving would be the celebrated Black intellectual Dr. Ralph Bunche, United Nations Under Secretary for Special Political Affairs.

Malcolm X, among the most extreme Black nationalists, commented at the time of the Selma March:

> I want Dr. King to know that I didn't come to Selma to make his job difficult. I really did come thinking that I could make it easier. If white people realize what the alternative is, perhaps they'll be more willing to hear Dr. King.[622]

Such is the nature of the establishment dialectic.

NAACP Conceived on Wall Street

Oligarchic patronage of the Negro had been of long duration. The oldest of the primary Black civil rights organizations, the National Association for the Advancement of Colored People (NAACP), had been conceived in 1909 by a leading Wall Street financier, Jacob Schiff, senior partner of Kuhn, Loeb & Co., who had from 1905 funded the revolutionary movement in Russia.[623] Another Wall Street eminence with the NAACP was Herbert Lehman, head of Lehman Bros. and future New York senator and governor, who decades later played a prominent role in the censure of Joseph McCarthy. Other patrons sustaining the NAACP were William Rosenwald, Samuel Fels, Felix Warburg, and Edsel Ford.[624]

---

[621] *Time*, March 20, 1965, 1, 12.
[622] Haines, Black Radicals, 76.
[623] "Kennan Retells History." See Bolton, *Revolutions from Above*, 57–60.
[624] Lau, "Democracy Rising," 73–4.

Another Cold War Issue

The Black issue was important to the establishment for both domestic and international reasons: 1) Segregation, like apartheid in
South Africa, was a hindrance to the development of an expanding
economy. Blacks could be better exploited as fully integrated producers and consumers in an "inclusive economy" than as marginal-
ized and rural peasants. The exploitation could be maintained behind the facade of "civil rights"; and 2) The foreign policy establishment and its oligarchic partners vied with the USSR to fill the vac-
uum created by decolonization, offering American liberalism as the
ideal alternative to Soviet communism. The US needed to be paraded
before the colored world as the paragon of liberty and equality.

Hence the CIA was involved in funding desegregation and racial
integration programs as part of a Cold War agenda, for reasons that
converged with its founding of youth and student projects. The
emergence of the New Left was largely the result of both.

Although the CIA was supposed to only deal with overseas issues,
it gave $6,000 to the Southern Regional Council in 1962 via the Aaron
E. Norman Fund,[625] and $2,000 to the Georgia Council on Humans
Relations. In 1963 $60,000 went to the Southern Regional Council via
the New World Foundation. These funded Black voter registration
drives to break the White South. The National Student Association
was encouraged in its work with Southern Blacks by the CIA on the
basis of presenting the America's image overseas as the leader of decolonization.[626] The Aaron E. Norman Fund was also a contributor
to CORE and the League for Industrial Democracy, the parent body
of the SDS.[627] Andrew Norman, while vice-president of the Norman
Fund, was also a board member of the League for Industrial Democracy. Norman was among several officers of the League for Industrial
Democracy who sought conciliation when LID and SDS relations
were strained.[628]

---

[625] The Norman Fund was established in 1936 to fund Black integration.
[626] Anderson and Pearson, "Those CIA 'Watchdogs.'"
[627] Ibid.
[628] Sale, *SDS*, 43.

From Black Power to Black Capitalism

Professor Joan Roelofs writes of the time:

> The "black power" slogan which emerged from the SNCC, was per-
> ceived as both enormously threatening and capable of deflection
> into harmless channels. Under the leadership of the Ford and Rock-
> efeller foundations the National Urban Coalition was created in
> 1967 to transform "black power" into black capitalism. . . . CORE,
> an organization with strength in the northern ghettos, was the
> most radical group to receive significant funding. They endorsed
> the "black power" slogan; however, CORE leaders were amenable
> to interpretations that were not threatening to the elite. . . . "Black
> power" was becoming increasingly acceptable to major American
> corporations, which financed black power conferences in Newark
> in 1967[629] and Philadelphia in 1968.[630]

Even the Black Panther Party (BPP) succumbed to the aim of Black
capitalism. In analyzing an article by BPP minister of defense Huey
P. Newton on the factionalizing of the BPP between Newton and
Cleaver, Henry Winston, the Black chairman of the (Old Left) Communist Party USA commented:

> That the uneasiness created by this article is well-founded is con-
> firmed by Newton's subsequent writings and speeches, and partic-
> ularly by his May 29 article in the *Black Panther*. Here he announces
> that the party is ready to open, in San Francisco, a shoe factory and
> one to make clothing and golf bags—the first of many factories to
> be operated by the Black Panthers in ghettos across the nation.
>   That these are enterprises of "Black capitalism," Newton does
> not deny. In fact, he states: "I am doing an article now called 'To
> Reanalyze Black Capitalism,' . . . I think this is the kind of thing

---

[629] The Newark Black Power Conference was organized in the aftermath of five days
of rioting, which had resulted in twenty-six deaths and 750 injuries. Delegates came
from Bermuda and Nigeria. This inspired other such conferences throughout the
US.
[630] Roelofs, *Foundations and Public Policy*, 131.

we're involved in and we'll judge how successful we are by whether we can take the community with us."

It will undoubtedly appear to some that there is a head-on contradiction between Newton's "new" direction and his previous "revolutionary" period. The opposite is true. *There is no contradiction between his previous ultra-Leftist role and his present position. In essence, both positions represent accommodations to the status quo—even though the earlier one was more effectively camouflaged with the rhetoric of revolution.* The link between both positions is the fact that neither "Black capitalism" nor ultra-revolutionary rhetoric offers the people the path of struggle. That is why the new form of opportunism (like the old form, still pursued by Eldridge Cleaver) presents no perspective for the Black liberation movement.[631]

Note that Winston alluded to the ultraleft, which is to say the New Left, as being an "accommodation to the status quo," as its revolutionary rhetoric eventually became a dead end. Hence, the ultraleft is co-opted by the establishment. Winston alluded also to how the establishment media promoted a caricature of communism, and he specifically referred to New Left ideologues such as Hayden, Rennie Davis, Marcuse, Newton, and Cleaver, along with the influence of Mao and Trotsky on the New Left:

As part of the ruling class efforts to divert the radicalization process, the mass media have popularized the caricature of Marxism-Leninism, appearing in the writings of Mao, Trotsky, Marcuse, Debray, Cleaver, Newton, Tom Hayden, Stokely Carmichael, Rennie Davis and others. At the same time, they have promoted a "revolutionary" image for many of the new radicals.[632]

Winston considered this promotion of the most extreme factions of the New Left to have served the establishment. (So much for "far-right conspiracy theories.") Winston observed that the elements that the New Left appealed to as a new revolutionary vanguard were those whom Marx and the old-line communists disdained as the

---

[631] Winston, *Crisis of the Black Panther Party*, "Introduction."
[632] Winston, *Crisis of the Black Panther Party*, "The Image Makers and Revolution."

lumpenproletariat, a degenerated class that were readily manipulated by the establishment. Winston regarded the New Left, citing Newton, Cleaver, Hyden, and Yippie leaders Jerry Rubin and Abbie Hoffman, as recruiting the lumpen elements. A particularly useful method by which lumpen elements were created was through the "barbaric promotion of drugs—in the armed forces (particularly in Vietnam), in the ghettos, among the workers, and among the youth on and off the campuses." This drug culture, an offshoot of the New Left, was rapidly hollowing out America's middle class.

> The *lumpenproletariat*, as Engels noted, includes "elements of all classes." This is particularly evident today as large numbers of students, demoralized by drugs, turn away from struggle and become part of the *lumpen* sector for the first time in history.
>
> Together with its mass promotion of drugs, the ruling class is promoting anti-working class ideology on a mass scale in new ways. This is why the media have popularized the writings of such individuals as Regis Debray and Herbert Marcuse, whose views have greatly influenced Cleaver, Newton, Hayden, Hoffman, Rubin and other radicals who foster the idea that workers have "a stake in the system." From this starting point Cleaver and Newton have developed the concept that the *lumpen* sectors, who will resort to anything but work, and not the working class, comprise the vanguard of revolution.[633]

Winston proceeds to consider Newton's development of his program for "Black capitalism," including what Winston saw as "ghetto sweat shops," among a Black *lumpenproletariat*, quoting Newton's article from the *Black Panther*:

> Announcing that the Panthers will now operate factories in ghettos, he [Newton] went on to say: "We will have no overhead because our collective—we'll exploit our collective by making them work free. We'll do this not just to justify ourselves, like philanthropists, to save someone from going without shoes, even though this is part of the cause of our problems. People make the revolution; we will give the process a forward thrust. If we suffer from genocide, we

---

[633] Ibid.

won't be around to change things. So in this way our survival program is very practical."[634]

Seeing Newton's dialectics as "backward," Winston quoted Newton's
rationalization that the system could be adjusted rather than replaced:

> "We can jump too far ahead and say that the system absolutely can-
> not give us anything, which is not true, the system can correct itself
> to a certain extent. What we are interested in is for it to correct
> itself as much as it can do and after that if it doesn't do everything
> that the people think is necessary then we'll think about reorganiz-
> ing things."[635]

Winston remarked:

> Newton offers the people mini-enclaves of Black capitalism in the
> form of ghetto sweatshops across the country.... After "hurling"
> super-revolutionary rhetoric for six years, it appears that Newton
> will now "retire into small passive satisfaction" while Black people
> are given the prospect of working in the ghetto under racist sweat-
> shop conditions.[636]

Winston regarded the BPP's latest course as an accommodation with
the establishment via Black capitalism. He cited Newton as alluding
to the funding that the Black power movement had already received
and how that might be developed.

> In the June 5 *Black Panther*, Huey P. Newton reveals the full nature
> of his projected Black capitalist course. "In the past," writes New-
> ton, "the Black Panther Party took a counter-revolutionary position
> with our blanket condemnation of Black capitalism." Now, how-
> ever, Newton sees a revolutionary role for Black capitalism.
>   He outlines a program in which Black Panther clothing and
> shoe factories and medical programs will be assisted by "contribu-
> tions" from Black capitalists. In exchange, the Panthers will call

---

[634] Winston, *Crisis of the Black Panther Party*, "Incredible Thrust Backward."
[635] Ibid., quoting Newton.
[636] Winston, *Crisis of the Black Panther Party*, "Incredible Thrust Backward."

upon the community to patronize the businesses of these Black capitalists.

"Black capitalists," states Newton, will have "the potential to contribute to the building of the *machine* which will serve the true interests of the people and end all oppression." (Emphasis added— H.W.) One can get an idea of the kind of "machine" Newton intends to build from the following admission: In the past, he writes, "we received money for our survival programs from the big, white capitalists."

Perhaps this admission also casts light on some of the reasons why Newton complained, in his April 17 article, that "our hook-up with white radicals did not give us access to the white community because they did not guide the white community." It now becomes clear that he prefers instead to have "access" to white capitalists— whom he identifies not as the exploiters of Black and white workers, but as the "guides" of the "white community."

Newton cannot, however, camouflage the fact that his "access" to white corporate capital means that he is continuing to serve the monopolists at the expense of Black Americans and all working people. One need not hesitate to predict that his new form of accommodation to the white capitalist "guides" will be exposed far more rapidly than his previous super-revolutionary services to the same forces.[637]

Winston reiterated that both the "super-revolutionary" and the accommodationist courses of the BPP "served the same forces." His party's own commitment to the course of Martin Luther King, however, was hardly less accommodating to the establishment. Winston, analyzing the BPP doctrine on behalf of the Communist Party USA, nonetheless saw that the New Left, White and Black, both in its ultraleft and accommodationist forms, served the system that it purported to be fighting. If a White conservative had said the same, there would be (and indeed now are, more than ever) jeers about "far-right conspiracy theories."

---

[637] Winston, *Crisis of the Black Panther Party*, "The Building of the Machine."

Ralph Hoagland and the Fund for Urban Negro Development

In 1968 Ralph Hoagland, whom we previously encountered as a financial patron of the SDS via a dummy corporation, formed another grant-making entity, the Fund for Urban Negro Development (FUND), with a donor list of over three hundred of Boston's wealthy elite. The purpose of the FUND was to subsidize the newly formed Boston Black United Front. In the wake of Martin Luther King's death, the Black United Front demanded that $100 million be disbursed to the Black community in Boston, the transfer of complete political and financial power to Boston Blacks, the closure of all White businesses while their transfer to Blacks was negotiated, and the Black control of education and of housing programs.

Members of the FUND included Senator Edward Kennedy, United Fruit Company president Harvey Cox, and executives from Honeywell and Polaroid. It becomes evident that the aim was not the transfer of financial and political power to the Black community, but the cultivation of Black capitalism by investment and business "coaching" and "mentorship." Despite their radical rhetoric, the FUND's aim was no different from that of the Ford Foundation and the myriad other donors to Black causes: to subdue Black unrest by creating what these foundations and corporations today call an "inclusive economy." Hoagland's guidance came from Harvard Business School, not from Stokely Carmichael; FUND donors would retain control over their investments. When the Black radicals were not sufficiently compliant, FUND became defunct.[638]

The involvement of Hoagland in trying to encourage capitalism among militant Blacks raises the question as to his motives in funding the SDS. While we might suppose that there are genuine idealists among the wealthy who want to use their money to assist others via political causes, including even wealthy backers of the Communist Party USA such as Corliss Lamont, we should also consider Machiavellian motives.

---

[638] For a summary of research into Hoagland and FUND see Harris, "When White Philanthropy."

Dialectics of Black Power

Massive injections of governmental, business and Foundation aid seemingly opened the way for continued corporate domination of black communities by means of a new black elite.

– Robert L. Allen

This development of Black capitalism, and in particular the assumption even of extremists such as the BPP to new positions of leadership within re-organized Black communities, happened to coincide with the new direction of the establishment. Again, turning to a Black leftist for a cogent explanation on the dialectics at work, Robert L. Allen, in a pamphlet for *The Guardian*,[639] referred to several streams of "Black nationalism," including that embraced by the establishment, when presidential candidate Richard M. Nixon "proclaimed a new political alignment which includes Republicans, the 'new South,' 'new liberals' and black militants."[640]

"Black power as black control of black communities" was called by Allen "the political center of the black power spectrum and the most widely accepted formulation."

> It is what SNCC, in part, originally meant by the term and how the Congress of Racial Equality (CORE) views black power today. It implies a group effort to seize total control of black communities from the white governing structure and business interests.[641]

One would surely assume that this radical strand in the Black nationalist movement would be the most resisted by the establishment. To the contrary, Allen explains:

---

[639] Originally *The National Guardian*, it was founded in 1948 to continue the New Deal doctrine of Roosevelt, backing the presidential candidacy of Franklin Roosevelt's former secretary of agriculture Henry A. Wallace and pursuing a pro-Soviet line. Intriguingly, an inordinate amount of its advertising came from New York Jewish insurance brokers. In 1968 the newspaper changed its editorial team, and its name to *The Guardian*, adopting a Maoist, New Left orientation.
[640] Allen, *Dialectics of Black Power*, 11.
[641] Ibid., 4.

The difficulty with this program is that it overlooks conflicting interests within the black community. It doesn't specify who is to control or in whose interest. Thus, it is open to co-optation by the power structure or may degenerate into black capitalism.[642]

Allen stated that the establishment had changed tactics in its co-optation of Black nationalism, and the way that the inner cities could be controlled by a new Black elite:

The power structure has apparently concluded that direct white rule of the ghettos, at least in some instances, is no longer operating satisfactorily. It is instead seeking out appropriate black groups to administer the colonies. Traditional Negro leaders are not acceptable, having been discredited both within and without the black communities and obviously exercising no real control.[643]

Those who would form this "new Black elite" administering the inner cities on behalf of the establishment would include militant ghetto organizers:

Therefore it is the new black elite, which ironically was created by both the successes and failures of the civil rights movement, to which the power structure must now turn. Some of the members of this group are militant nationalists, even separatists. They tend to be drawn from the traditional black petty-bourgeois class or to be upwardly mobile members of the working class whose mobility in some measure was made possible by early civil rights victories.

But they share a common frustration with the failures of the civil rights movement and often exhibit a genuine desire to improve the lot of black people. Because they are committed militants they also enjoy a certain credibility and acceptance in the ghetto.[644]

This seems to have been the course sought by the Black Panthers under the leadership of Huey Newton several years later. Other militant factions eventually followed them, including those who

---

[642] Ibid., 12.
[643] Ibid.
[644] Ibid.

received federal and foundation funding and imposed what amounted to gangland protection rackets over the communities in which they were empowered.

Allen saw this as part of a bogus "bourgeois-democratic revolution" manipulated by the establishment:

> It is these factors which make this group ideal administrators of the ghetto. They seek improvement, not revolution. Having moved up on the social ladder they do not share the nihilism of the youthful ghetto resident. Because they are accepted, they also have the potential to restore ghetto peace and tranquility. Even the more opportunistic members of this group have their use since they will work for "law and order" in return for the right to control and exploit the ghetto.
>
> In short, black control of the black community is slowly being transformed into black elite control of the black community, and the bourgeois-democratic revolution is being completed, but in a manner designed to buttress the power of the white establishment over the black ghettos.[645]

The second part of Allen's pamphlet specifies the way the Ford Foundation was manipulating Black power. Allen opened, remarking that "one of the most important though least publicized organizations in the civil rights movement today is the multi-million dollar Ford Foundation." Allen stated that "the Foundation plays a key part in financing and influencing almost all major civil rights groups, including the Congress of Racial Equality, Southern Christian Leadership Conference, National Urban League and National Association for the Advancement of Colored People."[646]

> Working directly or indirectly through these organizations, as well as other national and local groups, the Foundation hopes to channel and control the black liberation movement in an effort to forestall future urban rebellions.[647]

---

[645] Ibid., 13.
[646] Ibid., 22.
[647] Ibid.

Allen traced the reorientation of the Ford Foundation's programs in funding Blacks to 1966, under the direction of former US National Security Advisor McGeorge Bundy:

> Prior to that time the Foundation had limited its activities among black Americans to traditional educational efforts and research projects designed to bring more blacks into the middle-class mainstream. The 1966 decision was a direct response to urban revolts, which were growing, both in size and frequency.[648]

Allen said of Bundy, with a specific allusion to the dialectical approach involved:

> From his years of serving the U.S. power structure, Bundy had developed a keen appreciation of the complexities involved in political manipulation and *the seemingly contradictory policies which often must be pursued simultaneously in order to obtain a given end.*[649]

Allen cited an article by Bundy in *Foreign Affairs* where he clearly expounded dialectics as the premise of US foreign and domestic policy.[650] Allen explained in a nutshell that "Bundy learned that it is necessary to work both sides of the street in order to secure and expand the American empire."[651]

In 1967 the Ford Foundation gave grants of over $1 million to the NAACP, the NAACP Legal Defense Fund, and the Urban League in the hope of isolating the increasingly extreme SNCC, which had repudiated "non-violence" and had expelled its White members:

> But for the Foundation's purposes, these groups were less than satisfactory since there was serious doubt as to how much control they exercised over the young militants and frustrated ghetto blacks who were likely to be heaving Molotov cocktails during the summer. If its efforts to keep the lid on the cities were to succeed, the

---

[648] Ibid.

[649] Ibid., 24. Emphasis added. Pursuing contradictory policies for a given end is, in a word, *dialectics*, in the title of Allen's pamphlet. It is the basis of most of what we have been considering throughout.

[650] Ibid.

[651] Ibid., 25.

Foundation must somehow attempt to penetrate militant organizations which were believed to wield some influence over the angry
young blacks of the ghettos.[652]

The Ford Foundation started in May 1967 to cultivate the more militant groups, the first being $500,000 to Kenneth B. Clark's newly
formed Metropolitan Applied Research Center (MARC). The purpose was to organize Blacks in Northern cities. MARC provided fellowships to organizers, the first being Roy Innis, whom Allen described as "chairman of the militant Harlem chapter of the Congress
of Racial Equality (CORE)." Innis soon after became national director
of CORE. MLK and his aide, Andrew Young, supported the program.[653] Clark also discussed fellowships with Floyd McKissick, national director of CORE; Stokely Carmichael, then chairman of
SNCC; Whitney Young of the Urban League; and Roy Wilkins of the
NAACP.[654]

In May and June, Clark held "secret meetings" with leaders from
numerous Black groups with the purpose of calming down unrest in
Cleveland.

> Clark did not mention that the Ford Foundation had been trying to
> "calm" Cleveland since 1961 by financing various local research and
> action projects. But Cleveland blew up in 1966 and further rum-
> blings were heard in the early spring of 1967. Clearly, a new ap-
> proach was needed in Cleveland, and the stage was set for the Foun-
> dation's first direct grant to a militant group—the Cleveland chap-
> ter of CORE.[655]

In July, Ford gave $175,000 to the Special Purposes Fund of CORE to
fund the training of Black organizers in Cleveland.[656]

Allen cogently explained the dialectics at work in the federal and
corporate backing of CORE and other bogus "revolutionaries," as
well as how the Black power movement could be co-opted and

---

[652] Ibid., 26.
[653] Ibid., 26.
[654] Ibid., 27.
[655] Ibid., 28.
[656] Ibid.

manipulated. His analysis accorded with that of Henry Winston regarding the Black Panthers. Allen wrote:

> It must be said that CORE was vulnerable to such corporate penetration. In the first place, they needed money. Floyd McKissick in 1966 had become national director of an organization which was several hundred thousand dollars in debt, and his espousal of black power scared away potential financial supporters.
>
> Secondly, CORE's militant rhetoric but reformist definition of black power as simply *black control of black communities appealed to foundation officials who were seeking just those qualities in a black organization which hopefully could tame the ghettos.* From the Foundation's point of view, old-style moderate leaders no longer exercised any real control while genuine black radicals were too dangerous. CORE fit the bill because its *talk about black revolution was believed to appeal to discontented blacks, while its program of achieving black power through massive injections of governmental, business and Foundation aid seemingly opened the way for continued corporate domination of black communities by means of a new black elite.*[657]

According to Allen, "the Ford Foundation could apparently view its grant to Cleveland CORE as a success. There was no rebellion in Cleveland, and, as the Jan. 6 issue of *Business Week* suggested, *money given to a black militant group helped to elect a Negro moderate* as mayor."[658]

The next move was on Harlem, where the common agenda of the New Left, Black nationalists, and Ford oligarchs was to reform the education system. Allen writes:

> Having proved successful in Cleveland, the Ford Foundation began exploring other ways of ensuring urban tranquility. In March 1967, following a year of demonstrations and boycotts centering around community control of schools, the Harlem chapter of CORE proposed that an independent school board be established for Harlem. According to the proposal, integration had failed and the only way to achieve quality education for Harlem's youth was through

---

[657] Ibid., 28. Emphasis added.
[658] Ibid., 29. Emphasis added.

community control of its schools. Harlem CORE set up a Committee for Autonomous Harlem School District and began organizing support for its proposal.[659]

Having aimed to destroy the South through integration, especially in education, Black power extremists, the Uncle Toms of CORE, NAACP, Urban League, and SCLC, and their patrons from the oligarchy aimed to seize control of local communities behind a façade of independent school board control. The planning came from the Ford Foundation. Bundy, Ford's president, had been given by the state of New York control for reorganizing education:

> The following November, Bundy recommended that New York's school system be decentralized into 30 to 60 semi-autonomous local districts. Bundy had been named head of a special committee on decentralization at the end of April after the state legislature directed Mayor John Lindsay to submit a decentralization plan by Dec. 1 if the city was to qualify for more state aid. Lindsay insisted that decentralization was "not merely an administrative or budgetary device, but a means to advance the quality of education for all our children and a method of insuring community participation in achieving that goal."[660]

While integration was deemed to be a failure in Northern cities, at that very time integration was being imposed at local levels on Southern school boards.

> Starting in 1968, a series of three U.S. Supreme Court decisions increased the pace of school desegregation even more. The first case, *Charles C. Green et al. v. County School Board of New Kent County, Virginia, et al.* resulted in the end of so-called "freedom of choice" plans that shifted the burden of integration from African American students *directly onto school boards.* In 1969, a follow-up ruling based on a desegregation case in Mississippi increased pressure on the South to integrate its schools. Finally, in 1971, the U.S. Supreme Court handed down *Swann v. Charlotte-Mecklenburg, North*

---

[659] Ibid., 29.
[660] Ibid.

Carolina, which legitimized busing as a means of integrating schools and mandated that *southern school districts immediately move to comply with the court's mandates* starting with *Brown* in 1954.[661]

Allen perceptively saw these maneuvers as a means of establishment control, writing that the goal of the Bundy plan was "maintaining the overall balance of power."

Allen wrote that Ford attempted a similar tactic in Detroit, where the Federation for Self-Determination (FSD), a radical Black group, asked the New Detroit Committee (NDC), of which Henry Ford II was a member, for funding. Ford offered $100,000 to the militants, as well as to a more moderate group. The funding was rejected by the FSD because of Ford's insistence on financial oversight by an appointee of the NDC, perhaps a not unreasonable demand given the corrupt and inept manner by which such funding tended to disappear. It is notable that Ford intended to fund both radicals and moderates; here again is the dialectic of encouraging extremes to give an impression of "moderation" and "compromise" for establishment agendas that would otherwise by regarded with apprehension by Middle America.

Allen writes that Ford was "more successful in its efforts to aid Martin Luther King's Southern Christian Leadership Conference (SCLC) and quite possibly partially underwrite King's plans for massive demonstrations in Washington in the spring of 1968."[662] According to Allen, the SCLC had been in dire financial straits ever since King announced his opposition to the Vietnam War the year prior. It is notable that Allen considered it likely that the massive disruption caused in 1968 by King, among others, might have been partly funded by Ford.

Allen concluded by stating that Black militancy had been bought off:

Ford's pioneering efforts in the black movement and the ghettos were quickly followed by America's corporatists. Some 50 white-

---

[661] Daugherity, "Desegregation in Public Schools." Emphasis added.
[662] Allen, *Dialectics of Black Power*, 30.

owned corporations helped finance Newark's Black Power Conference last July [1967]. At the end of that month an Urban Coalition—termed the "Anti-Rioters" by *Business Week*—was organized in Washington. The coalition (*Guardian*, Jan. 13, 1968) includes big-city mayors, labor officials, business figures and Foundation personnel (including Henry Ford II). The coalition is nation-wide in scope and its purpose is to aid private industry's penetration and pacification of the ghettos.[663]

Birmingham—Rockefeller Bail Money

In April 1963, Birmingham, Alabama, became the locus of media attention, as the SNCC and SCLC were agitating there against segregation.[664] Birmingham was a turning point, in terms of worldwide publicity for the Black movement. It was here that King was arrested. Bombs exploded at King's hotel room and the home of a local Black leader. The result was eight hundred demonstrations and fourteen thousand arrests in seventy-five Southern cities. It was the catalyst for the passing of new civil rights legislation in Congress.

Hayden stated that King's bail was arranged through Attorney General Robert Kennedy.[665] What Hayden apparently did not know is that the bail money was put up personally by Nelson Rockefeller. In 2006 Clarence Jones, King's chief adviser from 1960 to 1968, gave an interview to *Vanity Fair* that referred to Jones having "circulated easily among the rich of New York and L.A., [finding] willing donors to fuel King's frenetic activities with the Southern Christian Leadership Conference (S.C.L.C.), which King cofounded. Jones was, in essence, the moneyman of the movement."[666]

Jones stated that entertainer Harry Belafonte had telephoned him stating that he had discussed the Birmingham situation with Nelson Rockefeller's speechwriter, Hugh Morrow. Since 1961, Rockefeller had been regularly donating between $5,000 and $10,000 to the SCLC. Jones traveled to New York City where he met Morrow and

---

[663] Ibid., 31.
[664] Hayden, *Reunion*, 111.
[665] Ibid., 112.
[666] Brinkley, "Man Who Kept King's Secrets."

was told to go to the Chase Manhattan Bank the following day. There he was met by Rockefeller, Morrow, a bank official, and several security guards. A huge vault was opened, and Jones was handed $100,000 in cash. King and the other rioters were bailed out with the Rockefeller money.

> Everybody around Martin knew that I had somehow magically raised bail. I stayed mum all these years about the donor. I didn't tell the story I'm telling you—except to King, who was ecstatic. I had a firm 'Don't Ask' policy.[667]

Despite the cant around King's pacifism and White police brutality against Blacks in Birmingham and elsewhere, King sought to provoke the police to violence for the sake of martyrdom and publicity; his was a "strategy of tension," as he put it. He had been annoyed by the leniency of the police in Birmingham, writing, "Perhaps Mr. Connor and his policemen have been rather nonviolent in public, as was Chief Pritchett in Albany, Georgia, but they have used the moral means of nonviolence to maintain the immoral end of racial injustice.[668]

FBI on King's Funding

Much has been made of the FBI's surveillance of King. This is supposedly proof of King's "anti-establishment" position. The main interest was whether King was a communist, to what extent communists were involved with the SCLC,[669] and King's sexual abuse of women relative to his public moral posturing.[670]

However, the real interest is in King's funding. The FBI reported that in February 1967, the stockbrokerage firm Merrill, Lynch, Pierce, Fenner & Smith contributed $15,000 to the SCLC. In August, the Edward Lamb Foundation contributed stock worth $6,000. In November, the Ford Foundation was slated to give $230,000 for leadership

---

[667] Ibid.
[668] King, "Letter from a Birmingham Jail."
[669] FBI, *Martin Luther King Jr.*
[670] Bostock, "Sealed FBI Audio Tapes."

training for Black ministers. In October 1965, Nelson Rockefeller gave \$25,000 to the Gandhi Society for Human Rights, a fundraising adjunct of the SCLC.[671] With the money that King had received from the Ford Foundation for leadership training, two workshops were held in Miami in February 1968. One attendee was dismayed at the "drinking, fornication and homosexuality" that took place, and an all-night sex orgy with White and Black prostitutes.[672]

The SCLC received federal funding for joint projects with the state. In 1966 the SCLC received a \$4 million loan from the Federal Housing Administration for projects in Chicago, from which it would gain a \$400,000 profit. In November 1967, the Department of Labor contracted the SCLC for \$61,000 to train Blacks in Atlanta.[673]

In February 1968, sixty wealthy individuals were invited to an SCLC fundraising gathering at the home of Harry Belafonte, with tickets sold for \$1,000 per head. Among those invited were Governor and Mrs. Nelson Rockefeller, and Mary and Stephen Rockefeller.[674]

A Close Alliance Between Rockefeller and King

Dr. Kevin M. Burke wrote of what is called a "close alliance" between King and Nelson Rockefeller. Burke stated that Rockefeller aimed to "save capitalism" and to advance Black civil rights. This is why there were expressions of regret by Dr. Burke and other Black commentators that Rockefeller pushed integration but did not support Black "self-determination."

Burke wrote that Nelson Rockefeller was among the first to recognize King's potential in helping to reshape the US in the Cold War.[675] However, Burke, director of research at the Hutchins Center for African and African American Research at Harvard University, did not proceed to place the matter in the further historical context

---

[671] FBI, *Martin Luther King Jr.*, 17.
[672] Ibid.
[673] Ibid.
[674] Ibid., 17–8.
[675] Burke, "Close Alliance."

of the portrayal of the US as the leader of decolonization and the harbinger of a democratic world utopia.

In receiving Nelson Rockefeller's patronage, King was receiving establishment patronage. Drawing on a biography of Nelson Rockefeller by Richard Norton Smith, Burke wrote that in 1961, when King was unknown outside the South, Rockefeller shared a platform with King and hired a film crew to record him. Two years after the Birmingham jailing, Rockefeller sent his cousin Alexander Aldrich on the iconic Selma March in 1965. Referring to the donation of $25,000 to the Gandhi Society for Human Rights, Burke wrote that Rockefeller flew to Atlanta to speak for King at the Ebenezer Baptist Church. Amidst the tumult in the assault on the South, King and his family were entertained at Rockefeller's Fifth Avenue home in New York City. When King was assassinated in 1968, Rockefeller aides organized the funeral. Rockefeller then supplied the plane that enabled Mrs. King to complete her husband's march in Memphis. Rockefeller used King's death and the threat of Black rioting to push through New York's Urban Development Corporation (UDC).

20

HARLEM AND COLUMBIA

I often thought, in the years that followed the great student uprising at Columbia in late April 1968, of the singular political inventiveness that shaped the event. It defined the form student uprisings were to take on campuses all across the country, almost as if a script had been pasted together in the heat of social action that was reenacted, year after year, as a kind of political drama, adaptable to local circumstance but essentially the same.

– Arthur C. Danto, *Artforum*, May 2008

While the Rockefellers held sway over New York, the city became a timebomb awaiting a catalyst for eruption. Black militants and the New Left played a role in creating the pressure from below to reshape New York City and push the ambitions—political and financial—of the Rockefeller dynasty.

Rockefeller's Redevelopment Plans

From 1956 David Rockefeller and other oligarchs had several different plans for redevelopment in New York City. By the late 1960s, the plans had encountered resistance from middle-class residents who opposed the massive public spending required and the wholesale urban redevelopment, which would see the destruction of White

ethnic communities in order to make room for public housing, a euphemism for Black integration. Conversely, ghetto Blacks feared that
they were being sidelined for gentrification. For the New York Urban
Development Corporation (UDC), "redevelopment" meant deliber-
ate racial integration, as implied by the term "mixed incomes":

> In its short period of housing construction, the agency began to in-
> corporate many of the concepts urban renewal's critics had pro-
> moted. Its housing complexes were almost entirely mixed-income,
> including poor, moderate, and sometimes middle class households,
> usually in apartments that were adjacent to one another.[676]

Columbia University Riot

Rockefeller interests had long been prominent in New York real
estate, and so were those of Columbia University. The catalyst for the
Columbia University riots and occupation in 1968 was a plan for the
construction of a university gymnasium on two acres in the Morningside Heights area of East Harlem, an area of vast potential and of
urban decay. David Rockefeller, chief executive of the Chase Manhattan Bank Corporation, was president of Morningside Heights Inc.,
formed in 1947. In conjunction with so-called "community activists"
and Rockefeller money, the rise of Black "self-control" initiatives in
Harlem provided lucrative investments for Rockefeller and other investors. Researching the Rockefeller Foundation archives for a doctoral thesis, Brian Goldstein wrote:

> The role of the Rockefeller family and their associated foundations
> in the postwar urban redevelopment of New York is well-known, in
> such landmarks as the United Nations, Lincoln Center, and the
> World Trade Center. Increasingly, scholars have also come to rec-
> ognize the important support that foundations under the

---

[676] Freemark, "Entrepreneurial State," 17.

Rockefeller umbrella provided to redevelopment's critics, such as Jane Jacobs.[677]

Rockefeller funding was important in the radical planning and design experiments of the postwar era, along with federal support and money from the Ford Foundation, the New York Foundation, and the Vincent Astor Foundation.

In 1946, David Rockefeller hired Wilbur C. Munnecke, a social scientist and vice president of the University of Chicago, to conceive a plan for Morningside Heights' redevelopment.[678] The answer was racial integration to showcase the cosmopolitan and international character of New York City and to break the traditional communities that had kept out Blacks and Jews. The area was envisioned as being nothing less than, in Munnecke's words, "the spiritual, cultural and intellectual center of the world," and, with the United Nations headquarters building going up in Manhattan on land donated by the Rockefellers,[679] "the educational and cultural counterpart of the political Capitol of the World, . . . a community whose facilities can be available without restrictions as to race, color, or creed."[680] This was the origin of Morningside Heights Inc.[681]

However, Governor Rockefeller had to overcome the resistance of the New York legislature in getting the state involved in urban development. *Did the Black, Puerto Rican and New Left student militancy that rocked Harlem and Columbia University create the catalyst to push the Rockefeller plans forward?*

---

[677] Goldstein, *City Within a City*, 3. Jane Jacobs, a radical critic of urban development, had been awarded a Rockefeller Foundation grant in 1958, under the auspices of the foundation's Humanities Division, which sponsored an Urban Design Studies research program. With this grant she wrote the seminal book on urban development, *The Death and Life of Great American Cities*. Here she acknowledged financial support from the Rockefeller Foundation, which made the book possible. For a eulogy on Jacobs by the Rockefeller Foundation, see Rodin, "Legacy of Citizen Jane."

[678] Zipp, *Manhattan Projects*, 167.

[679] Ibid., 38–9.

[680] Ibid.

[681] Ibid., 167.

Between Jane Jacobs, who supported the Columbia University plans for Morningside Heights,[682] and long-time New York City planning czar Robert Moses there was vitriolic rivalry.[683] Moses' long career was finally ended by his being sidelined by Nelson Rockefeller, which involved a secret deal between the governor and his brother David in 1968, exposed in 1974 by Senator Jesse Helms (an opponent of Nelson Rockefeller's appointment to the vice presidency) as a scandalous conflict of interest.[684]

The Urban Development Corporation, created by Governor Rockefeller, was given sweeping powers to circumvent local zoning laws, imposing racial integration on neighborhoods. The UDC sought cooperation from the most radical factions of Harlem, such as the Architects' Renewal Committee of Harlem (ARCH). In 1966 ARCH, "in partnership with some of the leading figures in the Black Power movement in Harlem," formed the Harlem Commonwealth Council (HCC), "a community development corporation that aspired to develop businesses in the neighborhood that would be collectively owned by residents."[685] Funding for HCC came from the Rockefeller Foundation, and from the federal government's Office of Economic Opportunity.

At the 1966 annual conference of the Congress of Racial Equality (CORE) the organization's Harlem leader, Roy Innis, reported that he had helped form HCC with a $50,000 grant from Columbia University. Within ten years HCC was a $32 million corporation that controlled all the real estate on 125th Street. This was the type of Black capitalism that the establishment sought. For example, the Harlem Urban Development Corporation (HUDC), "which had emerged

---

[682] Jacobs, *Death and Life*, 109: "Columbia University in New York is taking a constructive step by planning sports facilities—for both the university and the neighborhood—in Morningside Park, which has been shunned and feared for decade. Adding a few other activities too, like music or shows, could convert a dreadful neighborhood liability into an outstanding neighborhood asset." Jacobs cited as a positive example of inner-city planning the "back-to-the-yards" movement in Chicago, headed by iconic leftist agitator Saul Alinsky, another recipient of Rockefeller money.

[683] Jacobs, *Death and Life*, 131, 361, 367.

[684] Andelman, "'68 Transit Pact Exposed."

[685] Goldstein, *City Within a City*, 15.

from protests against the State Office Building that Governor Nelson Rockefeller planned for Harlem in the late 1960s," ended up being funded by private investors, and "pursued largescale commercial projects like a trade center for 125th Street."[686] HUDC, rather than being a revolt against the New York establishment headed by the Rockefellers, "came into being in order to act as a local subsidiary for the state EDC [Economic Development Corporation] with a mandate to provide planning, feasibility studies, design, financing, construction supervision, and technical assistance to Harlem."[687] Mchunu and Mbatha seem to discern a dialectic at work, writing of "an ambiguous and seemingly contradictory role" for the "community empowerment" organizations that sprouted under federal patronage:

> From the onset, CDCs [Community Development Corporations] like HUDC played an ambiguous and *seemingly contradictory role*. On the one hand, they were attempts to work with and within the pre-existing economic and political structure. On the other hand, they were seen as a sort of permanent opposition, a community's attempt to control its own destiny against "outsiders." Johnson argues that the *HUDC was part of the Harlem political machine and thus proved too useful to city and state politicians in the racial and ethnic political stew of New York state and city.*[688]

While it is supposed that the tumult in Harlem during the late 1960s was directed at a New York establishment headed by Governor Rockefeller, at the same time the Rockefeller Foundation and the Rockefeller Brothers Fund (RBF) were funding this supposed insurrection. So far from defeating the establishment as it existed in New York, the oligarchs profited from this "rebellion." While Goldstein noted that HUDC proved increasingly inept, Rockefeller Foundation records nonetheless highlight the character of the relationship between HUDC and the Rockefeller-led New York City oligarchy:

> The RBF played an important role in helping to reshape HUDC by providing $225,000 over three years to bolster its efforts to attract

---

[686] Ibid., 7.
[687] Mchunu and Mbatha, "Significance of Place," 102.
[688] Ibid., 102–3. Emphasis added.

private financing, especially for housing development. David Rockefeller's New York City Housing Partnership became increasingly
involved in the work of HUDC. RBF staff expressed confidence in
the potential of HUDC's new efforts. "In light of the excellent relationship that has been established between HUDC and the New
York Housing Partnership, prospects are good for expanding
HUDC's outreach to other private-sector organizations," they
wrote.[689]

These liberal and radical schemes were lucrative for the New York
oligarchs.

> In action, the UDC was designed to answer the call for better hous-
> ing opportunities in the state from a technical perspective, but its
> founding was premised on two ideological notions: One, that the
> state government was the heart of the U.S. federal system and that
> it had the right and ability to lead the process of urban redevelop-
> ment; and two, *that private sector growth should be the primary goal
> of state action, and thus that public sector resources should be ori-
> ented to promote profit making in private industry.*[690]

In 1967, the Rockefeller-funded ARCH ostensibly "took a more militantly oppositional stance to urban renewal," in alliance with an increasing Black militancy.[691] In June, Governor Rockefeller took the
controls of the demolition frame and knocked the first blow of the
wrecking ball to clear the reclamation site, where he said a magnifi-
cent State Office Building would be constructed as the basis for urban renewal.[692] In 1968, the city administration along with the Community Association of the East Harlem Triangle commissioned
ARCH to prepare a report on urban renewal. The East Harlem Triangle was an area of great yet untapped commercial potential that was
in decay.

---

[689] Goldstein, *City Within a City*, 15.
[690] Freemark, "Entrepreneurial State," 69. Emphasis added.
[691] Goldstein, *City Within a City*, 5.
[692] Goldstein, *Roots of Urban Renaissance*, 111.

Aftermath of King Assassination

Racial turmoil in the aftermath of Martin Luther King's assassination was a catalyst for imposing new measures on New York to overcome local (which is to say White, and especially White ethnic) opposition to "urban renewal." In 1967, amidst the King and SNCC protests, the president's National Advisory Commission on Civil Disorders (best known as the Kerner Commission) was created, reporting: "Our nation is moving toward two societies, one black, one white. . . . Racial tension—made worse by the discriminatory action by white society—was causing the riots." The establishment had given its endorsement to the Black insurrection. The only possible action, the Kerner Commission suggested, was to pursue integration by improving run-down "ghetto" neighborhoods and "encourag[ing] Negro movement out of central city areas."[693] If White communities did not concede to Black integration they would be faced with violence. Rioting, or even just the threat, was driving the establishment agenda forward.

David Rockefeller intervened with a proposal for Wall Street to fund urban development:

> In early 1967, David Rockefeller, the governor's brother and head of Chase Manhattan Bank, testified before the U.S. Senate Committee on Executive Reorganization. In his speech, he proposed a deal: In exchange for $1 of public sector aid, David Rockefeller and his fellow bankers would invest $4 in new housing capital for low- and middle-income households. "Urban rehabilitation is primarily a task for private enterprise," he said. "Government can lend support and provide incentive . . . but, fundamentally, this is a job of massive financial and human investment that can best be accomplished by the private sector." Effectively, he was asking for a public-private partnership to back a new generation of housing investments.[694]

---

[693] Freemark, "Entrepreneurial State," 34.
[694] Ibid., 90.

Massive urban development would reap huge profits for private developers and lenders:

> The outlines of New York State's future in the housing domain were becoming clearer. Rockefeller's administration would promote an organization explicitly designed to improve the performance of the private sector by providing public sector equity and knowledge upfront. The organization would move toward massive redevelopment of some of the state's most troubled neighborhoods, even as it invested in new cities.[695]

The windfall for private capital was enabled by the UDC being:

> [A]ble to sell off assets to private businesses once those projects were operationally profitable. Effectively, this meant that the UDC was supposed to bring a project as far along as possible until it was making (or expected to make) operating profits; it would then sell off the project, at this point under construction, just completed, or several years in existence, to a willing investor.[696]

Freemark concluded:

> Socializing the risk and privatizing the profit did not seem to be a concern to Rockefeller. Therefore, though the UDC was a comprehensive state-driven development organization, its mission to create more housing for lower-income families concealed a broader drive to induce economic development and bolster the financial and real estate industries. This illustrated in concrete form Nelson Rockefeller's ambition to merge private profits with public mission.[697]

Nelson Rockefeller was blatant, even threatening, in stating that if the program was not supported, more riots would ensue, referring to the Kerner report:

---

[695] Ibid., 92.
[696] Ibid., 98.
[697] Ibid.

On March 6, the Governor finally revealed the actual legislation, stating, "as brought home so forcefully by the recent report of the President's Commission on Civil Disorder—the time for action is growing short." In a speech, he suggested that the problems in the slums "are conditions of concern to every citizen—not only to the victims of these conditions." Rockefeller emphasized the possibility that without actions, more riots would follow; this was more than a simple housing program.[698]

There remained opponents who could foresee exactly what would happen, and indeed what has transpired:

Jane Benedict, chairman of the Metropolitan Council on Housing, which argued in favor of tenants' rights, ridiculed the proposal. *The Times* editorialized that the program would "bulldoze home rule" by "shoulder[ing] the cities out of any role in their own reconstruction" and warned that a revolt against "runaway actions by state authority" was possible. Charlotte Natale, the president of the Greenwich Village Association, adopted the position that the UDC would reinforce existing problems, writing "slums are converted into superslums by the thoughtless stamping out of so-called 'blight' without regard to community needs." The UDC, she argued, would not be able to get rid of slums through "expediency" or "drastic measures in contempt of the public interest." In an age of increasing concern about advancing small-scale democratic involvement, her comments were particularly relevant considering the power of the UDC.[699]

New York Mayor John Lindsay was particularly opposed, wanting the increase of local decision-making. But then came the death of Martin Luther King, and Lindsay capitulated:

The assassination of Martin Luther King, Jr. on April 4th changed the situation entirely. That night, riots in New York City were averted even as other cities like Washington, D.C. erupted into flames; Mayor Lindsay walked through Harlem with black leaders to reassure residents that they were not being ignored, and their

---

[698] Ibid., 102.
[699] Ibid., 103.

fears were apparently subdued. Even so, the death of America's most prominent civil rights leader was a wake-up call even more powerful in New York than had been riots of previous years. Perhaps more than at any time since the passage of the Civil Rights Act in 1964, the country's attention was directed toward the needs of its poor minorities. *Governor Rockefeller saw the death as the political opportunity he had been waiting for—and he immediately began building upon the connections he had made with black legislators.*[700]

Integration and the destruction of local White ethnic communities, long pushed by Governor Rockefeller, proceeded, with the federal government passing laws that ensured that resistance by local zoning, for example, would be eliminated. As some tried to warn, positive results were not long-term:

The UDC built an impressive number of housing units during its short development period, but it was not able to address the broader problems affecting the state. Even as it added more than 15,000 apartments to New York City's streets, landlords were abandoning that many apartments every year during the early 1970s. While the UDC made important investments in Upstate cities, helping to revitalize Buffalo's waterfront and Syracuse's downtown, it could not prevent the continued population losses in those cities that continue there today. Its complexes, such as those at Coney Island and Twin Parks, often suffered from delinquency and violence. The UDC worked to encourage whites to stay in the Bronx and to bring blacks and Puerto Ricans into the suburbs, but if it accomplished either of those things, it was in such minute quantities as to have little effect on the overall situation in those environments. Even as the agency worked to improve the suburban aesthetic in its new towns, its suburban projects increased sprawl.

Nor did the agency's approach necessarily result in better apartment management. Several UDC projects have suffered from problems similar to those of traditional public housing. The physical quality of buildings has been put into question, with certain structures suffering from cheap, thin walls and leaks. For instance, at Harlem River Park Towers, one of the UDC's marquee developments, tenants have suffered from crime, delinquency, and poor

---

[700] Ibid., 106. Emphasis added.

supervision of public spaces. Broken elevators have been the bane of residents' lives. Yet the private manager of the building has done little to improve conditions. The fact that a state development entity built the project did not prevent such difficulties from occurring.[701]

In 1968, city administrator Edward Logue was appointed by Governor Rockefeller to head the New York State Urban Development Corporation, an office he held until 1975. Logue was vested with authority to override local zoning laws and building codes. The aim was to integrate White suburbs with ghetto Blacks:

> Only months into the job in fall 1968, he [Logue] delivered a characteristically blunt message to a national audience of housing and redevelopment officials, provocatively targeting by name—for impact—one of the most elite communities in greater New York. "In the enlightened state of New York," he promised, "New York City is going to be able to count on the services of the state development corporation in rehousing some of its low-income families in Scarsdale."[702]

The UDC plans failed in the face of strong community opposition to integration, but Logue acknowledged that Governor Rockefeller always supported his efforts to circumvent local resistance. Although in 1973 opposition obliged Rockefeller to sign a law returning to local authorities the right to maintain their own zoning and building codes, he increased funding for the UDC to continue its city projects from $1.5 million to $2 billion. Logue commented, "Rockefeller was the last guy to leave that sinking ship, the last guy. And he saw that I got bailed out." On the rejection of UDC redevelopment by one community, "Logue fumed, 'and the goddamn white bigots killed it.'"[703]

Governor Rockefeller spent more than any other governor of the time. His projects resulted in New York being the biggest debtor state in the US. Lynn A. Weikart wrote in a scholarly study that

---

[701] Ibid., 313–14.
[702] Cohen, "Doomed 1970s Plan."
[703] Ibid.

between Nelson as governor and David as chairman of the Chase Manhattan Bank, New York was transformed from a manufacturing economy to the financial capital of the world. The newly constructed buildings included the United Nations headquarters, the World Trade Center, and the World Financial Center. Nelson created 230 public authorities which could bypass the legislature and borrow through "moral obligation bonds." UDC was only the most notable of these. The UDC defaulted in 1974. By that time, Nelson was vice president of the nation, serving alongside Gerald Ford. Neither had been elected by their countrymen for high office. As governor, he had left behind "a mountain of debt," but his brother David loaned enough money to postpone the crisis until Nelson had secured the vice presidency.[704]

Nelson Rockefeller Announces Candidacy

Coincidentally, at the time of the Black and New Left tumult at Columbia University, Governor Nelson Rockefeller announced his bid for the Republican nomination as presidential candidate against Richard Nixon.[705] On the same page that Pennsylvania State University's *Daily Collegian* reported SDS and Black riots on Columbia's campus, and the arrest of demonstrators at the request of the university's beleaguered president Grayson L. Kirk, Nelson Rockefeller was quoted as saying that the reason for his decision to contend the nomination was because "the country has changed. Never in history has so much changed in five weeks. Now I am giving the people an option." He referred to "the gravity of the crisis," to "growing anxiety and unrest at home, and the signs of disintegration abroad."[706] Half a year later, his brother John D. Rockefeller III praised this "unrest at home" as a hopeful sign of youthful idealism that could be co-opted to reshape the US,[707] while niece Abby was helping to fund the New Left from her trust fund.

---

[704] Weikart, *Follow the Money*, 32–4.
[705] Healy, "Columbia," 1.
[706] "Rockefeller Gets into GOP Race."
[707] Rockefeller, "In Praise," 18.

Among those on the Draft Rockefeller for President Committee was Thomas Hoving, who, as New York City recreation and cultural director, had recommended that the Columbia University and Harlem community gymnasium for Morningside Heights *not* proceed. In a eulogistic letter to Hoving's widow, state senator Bill Perkins applauded Hoving for having joined the SDS/Black power tumult on Columbia's campus:

> Dear Mrs. Hoving,
> Many will have much to say in respect to the long and illustrious career of your husband, feeling it all but impossible to single out just one incident which suitably encapsulates his achievement. Not I. How well I recollect the stand he took on behalf of the people of my community, against the greed and insolence of Columbia University.
> Those were great days of protest against the whims of the powerful. In Harlem the people protested the University's plan for a segregated gymnasium in Morningside Park, and students and faculty protested as well. What was so unusual, was to have the City Parks Commissioner, Tom Hoving join us, a man born to privilege, a member of the upper-echelons of the establishment, fighting for the rights of the masses. The basic fairness he supported remains a struggle today. As he said so long ago, "it is hard to imagine the city confiscating parkland where it would disturb the interests of people living on 72nd Street."[708]

While Perkins' standard allusions to the "insolence and greed" of Columbia wanting to establish a "segregated gymnasium" against the wishes of the community, faculty, and students are debatable, what interests us here is that Tom Hoving, as a member of the upper echelons of the establishment, joined the New Left and Black power rioters in what was a defining moment for the New Left. In 1969, Hoving, as director of the Metropolitan Museum of Art, inaugurated the *Harlem on My Mind: Cultural Capital of Black America 1900–1968* exhibition. Although criticized by some for the *lack* of input from Harlem's Black artists, it was nonetheless intended as a propaganda exercise in Black power on establishment terms. To Hoving, the exhibition was

---

[708] Adams, "Thomas Hoving, Wendy Burden."

intended as a "confrontation" at the expense of "White people," despite the lack of Black artists:

> To me *Harlem on My Mind* is a discussion. It is a confrontation. It is
> education. It is a dialogue. And today we better have these things.
> Today there is a growing gap between people, and particularly be-
> tween black people and white people. And this despite the efforts to
> do otherwise. There is little communication. *Harlem on My Mind*
> will change that.[709]

Bridget R. Cooks wrote that the exhibition was held at a time when radical chic, to use the term coined by Tom Wolfe, was in vogue among the New York City elite, who were holding fundraising parties for the most extreme of Black militants and other left-wing extremists. She quoted Bayard Rustin (also co-opted by the establishment) saying of these *soirees* where ghetto Blacks mingled with the likes of Otto Preminger and Leonard Bernstein:

> The phenomenon of Radical Chic created a highly orchestrated ar-
> rangement for the wealthy to protect their social status while being
> moved by (but not enough to actual change) the struggles of the un-
> derclass. Civil rights leader Bayard Rustin was one of many Black
> Americans critical of Radical Chic saying, "These people [the party
> hosts] are really saying 'You sic 'em, nigger Panthers. You bring
> about a revolution for us while we go on living our nice little jolly
> lives. You niggers do it. We'll be right behind you—at a considerable
> distance.'" Dozens of these fundraising parties, which offered the
> wealthy an opportunity to live vicariously through the other, took
> place in New York just minutes away from the Metropolitan Mu-
> seum of Art. The museum's plan to mount *Harlem on My Mind* fol-
> lowed this social trend by extending the tantalizingly transgressive
> interracial event from Park Avenue to its own galleries at the top of
> the art world. Although the Metropolitan is situated in Manhattan's
> Upper East Side at Fifth Avenue and 82nd Street, less than two miles
> from the southern perimeter of Harlem, it is light years away from
> the socio-economic reality of Harlem.[710]

---

[709] Cooks, "Black Artists and Activism," 5.
[710] Ibid.

There seems something highly dubious, or at least ambiguous, about the multifaceted events that took place in Harlem and around Columbia University in 1968, where much of the character of the New Left was formed. The battle lines for urban redevelopment were not clear-cut, and Rockefeller interests were funding elements that were widely regarded as radical. The threat of turmoil was used by Rockefeller to announce his candidacy for the Republican presidential nomination as the "moderate" who could reconcile all sides, while the Rockefeller dynasty's aim had long been to rebuild New York City at the expense of White neighborhoods in order to showcase New York as a world capital. The assassination of Martin Luther King in April 1968 came at a fortuitous moment, adding fuel to the rioting that enabled the establishment to stampede Middle America into the supposed "moderate" direction—which just so happened to tend always leftward and always against the interests of Whites.

21

In Some Mysterious Way

Tom Hayden recalled that the assassinations of Martin Luther King and, two months later, Robert Kennedy:

> [L]ed to a meltdown of the system's core. The breakdown happened not only in Chicago, not only in America; in some mysterious way, it was a global phenomenon. Perhaps history is random and the search for logical meaning a fruitless illusion. But why did so many forces flow toward a climax in this one particular year, the watershed year for a generation? Surely there has been no other quite like it in American history?[711]

The death of King in 1968 instigated the "Days of Rage" in New York City, Chicago, and other cities, where the SDS rampaged, "trashing store windows in Times Square."[712] This was a prelude to chaotic eruptions at the Democratic Party National Convention in Chicago in August 1968, and in Chicago in October 1969.

More civil rights laws were passed in Congress because of the 1968 riots. At Columbia University Mark Rudd of the SDS staged a protest. It was the beginning of the New Left riots of '68 that spread to Europe in May, almost toppling President Charles de Gaulle, and bleeding over into the Soviet bloc.

---

[711] Hayden, *Reunion*, 254–5.
[712] Ibid., 269.

Hayden was puzzled by the seemingly spontaneous outbursts that rocked the world in 1968. He had a hint of that "mysterious way" when referring to the CIA connections with the NSA, and through that organization with both the Black civil rights movement and the New Left.

The riots on campus and among students were undertaken at a time when the Rockefeller Foundation sought to subvert educational and cultural institutions, focusing on the colleges, universities, and the arts.

The 1971 Rockefeller Foundation ten-year report described the foundation's aims against a background of increasing turbulence:

> When The Rockefeller Foundation began its program of Equal Op-
> portunity in September, 1963, the equal rights movement, though
> massive, was still basically nonviolent and substantially middle
> class. The series of shocks to American society—the demonstra-
> tions, riots, and general upheaval that characterized the middle six-
> ties—had not yet taken place (nor indeed were they foreseen). The
> Foundation, therefore, at first viewed the equal opportunity move-
> ment as one in which tried and true measures might be, by and
> large, effective.[713]

The sudden rise of Black violence and separatism might have presented problems for the establishment's aims of neighborhood and
school integration—unless they were co-opted. Integration the
NAACP way had been a slow process, and an eruption of Black violence created a new urgency. As we have seen, Black riots were used
by Governor Rockefeller to push through his integrationist re-devel-
opment for New York City, where state planners were given the authority to usurp local authorities.

The Sixties: Violent, Angry, Revolutionary—and Exuberant

Did the establishment encourage Black militancy to accelerate
their agendas "in some mysterious way"? At any rate, for the

---

[713] Rockefeller Foundation, *President's Ten-Year Review,* 56.

Rockefeller Foundation there was a positive message to be gained from the riots and violence: "The sixties were violent, angry, revolutionary—and exuberant. As the decade wore on, Foundation staff learned what the nation learned to its sorrow: there are no easy answers."[714] The 1971 Rockefeller report continued:

> For America's ethnic minorities the way out of the ghetto had traditionally been through education—why could this principle not apply to America's racial minorities as well?
>
> The earliest objective of those in the Equal Opportunity Program was to open the doors of good universities to minority-group students. Much of America still needed to be convinced of the competence and intelligence of blacks and other minorities. Proof positive for whites, and valuable encouragement for blacks and others, would be numbers of highly visible professional people—minority-group doctors, lawyers, engineers. The Foundation began scholarship programs in a number of first-rank colleges; it also supported academic reinforcement (such as summer school programs and transitional year programs) for students with inadequate high-school training. Finally, the Foundation believed that predominantly Negro colleges would continue to be crucial to black education for some time to come, and it strongly supported those institutions.[715]

It was in the atmosphere of violence that the Foundation trustees met and changed the hitherto gradual tactics, using turmoil to justify co-opting radicals:

> When the Trustees met in December, 1967, this was the most urgent question put before them. The consensus was that the Foundation should respond to new voices and new urgencies by shifting its emphasis from the college campus to the ghetto streets. The Trustees and Program Officers agreed to concentrate mainly on: Improving elementary and secondary schools in urban areas, particularly the inner cities; Training concerned and competent community leaders; Studying the origin and nature of urban ghettos, as

---

[714] Ibid., 66.
[715] Ibid., 58.

a beginning step toward eliminating old slums and preventing new ones.[716]

"Training concerned and competent community leaders" was often a euphemism for Black power and leftist agitators, in some cases even Black gang lords. This explains why funds were given to professional revolutionist organizer Saul Alinsky, for example. It is here that Alinksy was specifically mentioned, should there be any doubt as to the nature of those receiving Rockefeller largesse, with the report stating: "In Chicago, Saul Alinsky's Industrial Areas Foundation trains competent and realistic community organizers—particularly for inner-city slums."[717]

Radicalizing the Arts

The 1968 Rockefeller Foundation five-year report, in referring to its arts agenda, used the rhetoric of the New Left. Shall we be so naive as to think that it is the Rockefeller Foundation that was responding to supposedly spontaneous demands for "change" among a small fraction of students? Rockefeller and other foundations were established to use their grant-making power to change society; to lead, not to follow. The report referred to the nihilistic doctrines of the New Left as being applicable to the arts. This doctrine was to be promoted by Rockefeller's Cultural Development Program:

> The past five years have seen an almost unprecedented interest in American culture. While much of the turmoil of thinking, talking, and doing has taken place in the political and social realms, comparable vigor has been shown in the arts, which are emphasized in the Foundation's Cultural Development Program.[718]

As in the social and political spheres, the arts were being radically revised: "New dimensions and concepts are being formulated, tested,

---

[716] Ibid.
[717] Ibid., 59.
[718] Rockefeller Foundation, *President's Five-Year Review*, 92.

and tried in the arts. Previous assumptions and positions are being radically challenged, if not, in fact, overthrown." The slogan words of the New Left were described as "positive" youthful idealism: "relevance," "participation," "involvement," and "creativity . . . their increasing use by young people is a way of thinking that is both critical about the status quo and wishful and positive about the future."[719]

The status quo of which the New Left was critical was that of *tradition*; the predicate for actual art, without which there is formlessness, nihilism, and debasement. That the Rockefeller dynasty founded the Museum of Modern Art, which played a major role in the CIA's cultural Cold War programs, should be noted. The establishment aims to portray America as *avant-garde*, as the citadel of "freedom" and "equality" against all authority and tradition. This remains its perceived revolutionary mission. It explains how and why there can be such a nexus between the US establishment and its supposed enemies on the left, including the most nihilistic.

The Rockefeller report explained that the arts are a political tool, a means of social change, and a reflection of the forces of production. The new art is cosmopolitan, rootless, and technocratic. The new art would be concomitant with a revolution that would be economic, political, and cultural, and partly driven by the Black revolt:

> The new viewpoint looks at "culture" not as a commodity but as a condition, that is, a situation where changing needs indicate social and artistic changes. In this sense, participatory democracy is related to participatory theatre and visual art; technology influences art forms, interculturalization affects arts and philosophy; and the civil rights movement leads to new political, economic, and artistic positions. The politicization of the arts represents a conviction of more and more people that the arts play a vital role in the establishment and debate of the most essential values of our society.[720]

It can be noted here that:

1. The Rockefeller Foundation's definition of art as a reflection of the forces of social production is a core premise of Marxism,

---

[719] Ibid.
[720] Ibid.

which sees cultural output as a superstructure determined by and built upon the economic base. In other words, art and culture are secondary and tied to the mode of production. In this reductionist doctrine, production determines society, history, religion, and culture.

2. The arts run together with politics and economics, and the progressive trend is toward "participatory democracy." This was also the central demand of the New Left, in particular the SDS. One might cynically wonder why plutocrats are recommending "participatory democracy," if not as a façade to extend their own control.

3. "Politicization of the arts" is seen as progressive. Art hence becomes a social control mechanism and a means of social engineering.

The cultural, economic, and political doctrine of the establishment luminaries who ran the Rockefeller Foundation was the same as that of the New Left.

How the arts had been "politicized" and *weaponized* by the establishment again had its origins in America's Cold War response to the USSR. The Congress for Cultural Freedom, sponsored by the CIA and funded by the tax-exempt foundations, politicized the arts for the purpose of recruiting mainly leftist intelligentsia and artists into the struggle against the Soviet Union. "Abstract expressionism" was in particular portrayed as representative of the ideals of American-style liberal democracy and freedom of artistic expression, in contrast to the totalitarianism of the USSR. Jackson Pollock's large canvases of drunken paint splatter were presented to the world as an example of the artistic greatness that can be created under liberalism, against the static socialist realism of the USSR.

The 1968 Rockefeller Foundation report expounded the need for greater experimentation in "forms, styles and techniques." The report referred to the part played by the Foundation in helping to establish that year the Business Committee for the Arts, "for the express purpose of rallying the business community to the realization that economic development goes hand in hand with cultural development."[721] Here we might see the crux of the matter: the "Cultural Development" chapter of the report opened by stating that culture is "not a commodity," and then alluded to the business opportunities that might be had by investing in the arts. The new "experimentation" in the arts meant new ways to satisfy the profit motive.

Mobilization for Youth

One of the new avenues for investment named in the Rockefeller Foundation's 1968 report was the Mobilization for Youth (MFY) in New York City, "for its cultural arts program during the period April 15 through August 31; $18,000."[722]

The MFY was an example of the politicization taking place at the neighborhood level among ghetto Blacks. Mobilization for Youth was criticized by city officials for its political agitation among young Blacks, yet still received the endorsement of John F. Kennedy and Lyndon Johnson, and like other leftist organizations operated within the context of the federal government's War on Poverty. Mobilization for Youth, working with CORE, has been credited with pioneering the "new social work" of the 1960s. From 1963 MFY reoriented its role from being an advocacy project for slum tenants to being a revolutionary movement. Its director, Ezra Birnbaum, stated that MFY workers would "no longer work with individual tenants unless the tenant is prepared to help organize his building. Only emergencies will be exceptions to this."[723] Ghetto dwellers, mainly Black and Latino, would become revolutionary cannon fodder. Although dissolved in 1970, MFY was a major factor in the formation of the New Left and a training institution for New Left cadres:

> Participation in MFY's community organizing proved to be a radicalizing experience for both residents and staff members, many of whom went on to become lifelong activists. MFY organizer Marilyn Bibb Gore reflected that "one of the greatest things that MFY did

---

[721] Ibid.
[722] Ibid., 11.
[723] Quoted in Carroll, "'To Help People Learn.'"

was help people learn to fight." It fostered several social movements that changed the city's political and social landscape and inspired other activists across the nation.[724]

Like other radical leftist projects, MFY emerged in 1957 from the Henry Street Settlement House, where Wall Street had a looming presence. The conception of MFY was raised among the Henry Street board of directors by board member Jacob Kaplan, founder of the J. M. Kaplan Fund, a conduit for sending CIA money to the National Student Association.

Olivier Zunz stated in a history of philanthropy in the US that Helen Hall, director of Henry Street Settlement House, initiated MFY with money from J. M. Kaplan and the Vincent Astor Foundation. MFY was primarily sustained by money from the Ford Foundation, the National Institute of Mental Health, and the President's Committee on Juvenile Delinquency.[725]

A history of the MFY legal project states:

> In 1961, Mobilization for Youth's 617-page proposal was submitted to Washington and approved. The following year, at a ceremony in the White House Rose Garden in June, President Kennedy presented the organization with a $2.1 million delinquency grant to help pay for its programs. Another $11 million came from the National Institute of Mental Health, the Ford Foundation, the City of New York, and the Columbia School of Social Work. In a front-page spread on June 1, 1962, *The New York Times* described Mobilization for Youth as a project that will "enlist the actionist and the researcher in a joint program of social engineering organized to improve opportunities for youth and guide young people into pursuing them."[726]

The New York Times' allusion to "social engineering" is an interesting choice of words.

Despite attempted whitewashes of the MFY, an investigation of the organization by a New York Senate committee in 1964 was

---

[724] Ibid.

[725] Zunz, *Philanthropy in America*, 212.

[726] Holder and Rodriguez, *MFY Legal Services Inc.*, 4.

undertaken in response to concern by school and other city officials referring to "full-time paid agitators and organizers for extremist groups," with the allegation "that some personnel paid by MFY and some facilities owned or rented by MFY were being used for improper or illegal activities."[727] School principals and superintendents expressed concern, as well:

> The trouble between Mobilization and the school principals began last summer when it suddenly became painfully apparent that massive attacks were being launched against the schools and school personnel by groups organized and led by some staff members of Mobilization For Youth. The destructive, vicious, false charges were different from the city-wide attacks, in that the leaders, supposedly our friends, were professionals engaged in a program supported by public funds. The past major accomplishments of the schools were either unrecognized or ignored. Suddenly the schools—not only the school system but also the local schools, their principals and teachers as individuals—were singled out as the enemy of the community, the reason for all the ills of minority groups. And this has been the discouraging theme for many bitter months.[728]

The school principals regarded the MFY as aiming for a "social revolution," submitting to the Senate committee that:

> Workers paid with public funds—whether school principals or MFY workers—have no right during their official working hours to misuse public funds by secretly proselyting to their own private beliefs and affiliations the innocents who do not realize that they are being used to further someone's desire for a social revolution.
>
> It is not our province as school principals to challenge the desirability of such social revolution.

---

[727] Marchi, *Preliminary Data Report*, 11.
[728] Ibid., 49. Florence Becker had introduced the MFY programs to the school districts. She was placed on the MFY board of directors. Her repudiation of the MFY was in response to the concern expressed by principals on the destructiveness of the organization on teacher morale and school functions.

It is our responsibility as school principals to call to the attention of our superiors the need for investigating a seeming misuse of
public funds.[729]

As with other federal agencies and programs employing Black and
New Left agitators in the name of the Great Society, one of the primary concerns for local authorities was fiscal waste. The investigation cited a report into MFY financial management:

The allegation that public funds had been wasted appears to be
borne out by the inquiry into the expenditure of James E. McCarthy
as Administrative Director of Mobilization For Youth Inc. He spent
an inordinate amount of money for a variety of expenses not seemingly directly connected with the functions of Mobilization For
Youth Inc. Investigation of other allegations of waste is continuing.[730]

Much of the expenditure of this movement in defense of the ghetto
poor was expended on out-of-state travel, hotel accommodation, and
extravagant dining. Despite the scrutiny into the functioning and
ideology of the MFY in 1964, in 1965 the Ford Foundation gave a grant
of $651,000, noting that while MFY had been mainly funded by the
federal government, its initial funding had come from Ford.[731]

Youth Revolt Sponsored by Federal Government

In 1968 the Office of Juvenile Delinquency and Youth Development, a division of the Department of Health, Education, and Welfare, issued a report on its work among six youth organizations,
among which was MFY.[732] The report lauded the federal role in preparing ghetto youth, particularly in Harlem, for the New Left and
Black power tumult. Like Saul Alinsky's Rockefeller-funded projects,

---

[729] Ibid., 69–70.
[730] Ibid., 72.
[731] Ford Foundation, *Annual Report 1965*, 27.
[732] Grosser, *Helping Youth*.

the focus was on reorganizing neighborhoods. The report's author, Professor Grosser, wrote:

> To meet the demand for social change required by such an environ-mental approach, the projects engaged in a variety of strategies. In the forefront was the attempt to engage neighborhood residents in self-determining community organization activities, to involve them in shaping the umbrella of services raised in their behalf.[733]

If this "social change" that motivated the SDS, Alinsky, Rockefeller, Ford, and the federal government was an agent for *genuine* change, and not a part of a dialectical program for the restructuring of the US according to establishment interests, then one must offer other reasons as to why that establishment sponsored the supposed opposition. Disaffected ghetto youth and others were seen as being easily co-opted through buying off their ostensible leaders with money, lucrative jobs, and appeals to power and ego. Grosser described how this was done through "community organization programs," initiated and funded by federal agencies and tax-exempt foundations.[734] The impact of such projects on the agitation of school children and the undermining of authority has been described above. In this instance Grosser stated that the aim was to benefit delinquent youth not by addressing individual needs but by "targeting" institutions with social theories, whereby " through the effective action of the organization (participants) vis-a-vis the school system (target) . . . the juvenile delinquent (client) is benefitted."[735] The primary aims, as we have seen from Nelson Rockefeller's attempts at enforced integration through centralized "urban renewal" in New York City, were the breaking up of White ethnic neighborhoods, the imposition of racial integration, and the "community control" of reconstructed neighborhoods, referred to by Grosser as "the actions of the poor as community representatives on local poverty boards,"[736] but in reality beholden to federal and oligarchic funding.

---

733 Ibid., 2.
734 Ibid., 3.
735 Ibid., 4.
736 Ibid., 5.

The first organization detailed by Grosser was the MFY, which served as a "prototype" for subsequent federal projects.[737] Like MFY director Ezra Birnbaum, Grosser stated that the MFY was focused on institutional change. Grosser alluded to the "MFY youngsters who participated in the August 1963 Civil Rights March on Washington" as "a good example of this theory in action."[738] Hence, it was the priority of the MFY to organize youth into a revolutionary cadre in the service of establishment causes.

The MFY was used to initiate and fund "neighborhood councils" in contract with the Lower East Side Neighborhood Association (LENA). Such neighborhood councils sent representatives to the major civil rights marches and protests, both on the local and national level. LENA also initiated actions on school desegregation and other issues.[739] Just how any of this is supposed to represent an anti-establishment revolt when its cadres, organizations, and leaders were sponsored by that Establishment needs explaining with something other than quips about "conspiracy theories."

MFY also coalesced and sustained several hundred community groups in the inner city.

> The MFY Community development program undertook to work with these existing informal organizational entities with the aim of having them acquire characteristics which would enable them to participate successfully in the organizational life of the community.[740]

The inner-city communities were thus brought under federal patronage. Far from offering dissent, they became grass roots appendages of the system.

> Several strategies were employed. MFY staff workers, professional and indigenous, were assigned to work full time with these informal organizations. To provide the groups with resources whereby they could maintain headquarters, telephone service, and make

---

[737] Ibid., 7.
[738] Ibid., 9.
[739] Ibid., 10.
[740] Ibid., 12.

mailings, funds were made available, first administered through MFY and, subsequently, as grants administered by the organizations themselves.[741]

Grosser referred to what was "as might be expected" rivalry among the various organizations, comprised mainly of Blacks and Puerto Ricans, vying "both for staff and material resources, prestige and influence; organizational strength and self-sufficiency."[742] A term for the process might be *inner-city turf wars*. Grosser even refers to an entrenched "Oligarchy" among the "community organizations" (i.e., *gangs*) when resources (money) began to mount, whereby "leadership tends toward greater control."[743] What the federal agencies and the tax-exempt foundations achieved in empowering inner-city New York was a network of Black and Puerto Rican gangs operating in the name of "community development."

Young Adult Action Group

The Young Adult Action Group (YAAG) was an avowed revolutionist organization that recruited via MFY from the Lower East Side. Grosser states of YAAG:

A Young Adult Action Group (YAAG) comprised of Lower East Side youth was organized in an attempt to direct the anger, frustration, and hurt often expressed in crime, violence, and drug addiction, toward meaningful activity and social change. This organization recruited members from MFY's various programs and the general youth population.[744]

Note that YAAG was intended to "direct" the "anger" of ghetto youth into politics. YAAG, according to Grosser, "participated in a number of direct actions."[745] From what Grosser stated, YAAG did not achieve

---

[741] Ibid.
[742] Ibid.
[743] Ibid., 13.
[744] Ibid.
[745] Ibid.

any tangible results for the ghettos, but channeled the anger into acceptable establishment avenues, "demonstrating to some YAAG members the viability of conventional community life."[746] One should keep in mind that this was a "revolution" directed from above against Middle America, with the intention of channeling volatile ghetto Blacks, the *lumpenproletariat*, and the disaffected elites of the intelligentsia into the left-wing of the system. However, YAAG, as one might expect, experienced blowback and divided into "aggressive and passive subgroups," as did the New Left generally (e.g., the Weathermen against SDS).[747] Like SNCC, there were elements in YAAG that resented White participation, and opted for Black nationalist separatism that was adverse to the integrationist aims of the establishment. The divisions brought YAAG to an impasse.

Harlem Youth Opportunities Unlimited

Among the most radical Black organizations to receive federal and New York City patronage was the Harlem Youth Opportunities Unlimited—Associated Community Team (HARYOU-ACT). Grosser wrote that "planning grants by the President's Committee on Juvenile Delinquency and New York City, eventually led to the formation of Harlem Youth Opportunities Unlimited—Associated Community Teams."[748]

Again, the focus was not on solving specific problems among communities, but on "restructuring" them through "social action."[749] "HARYOU-ACT decided on three vehicles to carry out this community social action program; Harlem Youth Unlimited; the Community Action Institute; and local neighborhood boards."[750] Harlem Youth Unlimited (HYU), intended as a means for organizing ghetto youth in social activism, was, like other ghetto programs, wracked by internal dissension. Grosser alludes to youth feeling being "used and abused"

---

[746] Ibid.
[747] Ibid.
[748] Ibid., 44.
[749] Ibid., 45–46.
[750] Ibid., 46.

by those who ran the program, and HYU was subordinated to the leadership of HARYOU-ACT.[751] Under the latter's direction, intensive training programs were undertaken on what Grosser referred to as "social action techniques."[752] The Community Action Institute was intended to continue HARYOU-ACT training. The neighborhood boards were established to reorganize at local levels, with Harlem divided into five neighborhood board areas. This effort also failed because of power rivalries.[753] Grosser alludes to financial corruption:

> Matters were further complicated by unfavorable publicity spotlighting charges of fiscal mismanagement. Allocation of additional funds was temporarily suspended by Federal and city authorities. Residents questioned neighborhood workers about what was going on.[754]

Shadow Boxing with Nelson Rockefeller

Among those who eulogized Nelson Rockefeller when he died in 1979 was James Farmer, a cofounder of the Congress of Racial Equality (CORE). Farmer called Rockefeller "a man of compassion for all people."[755] Yet it was Farmer who organized the CORE sit-ins at the New York office of Governor Rockefeller in 1963.[756] When the Brooklyn chapter of CORE announced they would disrupt the 1964 World's Fair, during which Governor Rockefeller's New York would be showcased, Farmer attempted to scuttle the protest by suspending the branch. Brooklyn CORE was also condemned by Roy Wilkins of the NAACP,[757] whose organization had always been a well-endowed

---

[751] Ibid.
[752] Ibid., 47.
[753] Ibid., 50.
[754] Ibid., 51.
[755] Gupta, "Family and Friends Mourn."
[756] Severo, "James Farmer, Civil Rights Giant."
[757] Tirella, "Gun to the Heart."

association for establishment house niggers.[758]

CORE made *opposition* to environmental issues a major concern related to Black issues, with CORE director Roy Innis stating: "We believe that the civil rights challenge of our time is to stop extreme environmental policies that drive up the cost of energy and disproportionately hurt low-income Americans and the working poor."[759] It just so happens that ExxonMobil became a large donor to CORE.[760] It is a tangible example of how radicals are bought.

CORE had been discerned from the beginning as part of the controlled opposition. Dean E. Robinson states that, of the various Black power organizations, CORE benefited most from oligarchic patronage. In 1967 the Cleveland chapter of CORE received a $150,000 grant from Ford through the Targets City Project, and then a further $300,000.[761] Of such patronage, Robert L. Allen, the previously cited professor of African-American and Ethnic Studies at Berkley, returning to a theme he had analyzed in 1968,[762] explained:

> From the Foundations' point of view, old-style moderate leaders no longer exercised any real control, while genuine black radicals were too dangerous. CORE fit the bill because its talk about black revolution was believed to appeal to discounted blacks, while its program of achieving black power through massive injections of governmental, business, and Foundation aid seemingly opened the way for continued corporate domination of black communities by means of a new black elite.[763]

---

[758] Roy Innis stated at a CORE national convention: "In America today there are two kinds of black people: the field-hand blacks and the house niggers. We of CORE—the nationalists—are the field-hand blacks. The integrationists of the National Association for the Advancement of Colored People are house niggers." Quoted in McFadden, "Roy Innis, Black Activist."

[759] Innis, "Remarks."

[760] CORE received from the ExxonMobil Foundation $325,000 between 1998 and 2017. ExxonMobil, "ExxonMobil Foundation & Corporate Giving."

[761] Robinson, *Black Nationalism in American Politics and Thought*, 101.

[762] Allen, *Dialectics of Black Power*.

[763] Allen, *Black Awakening in Capitalist America*, 147.

This was the method we have considered with organizations such as MFY, where federal and foundation largesse created a new Black oligarchy, as Grosser observed.

Black Internationalism

As we have seen, the establishment preferred integrationist "house niggers" such as the NAACP, National Urban League, and Martin Luther King, all of whom were funded lavishly. The establishment played a gamble when it backed Black power (and Brown power) when violence was needed to force an issue to conclusion. Nonetheless, it is not Black separatism that is the aim, but an "inclusive economy," where everyone, regardless of gender, race, or creed, becomes part of the economic process in the name of "freedom," "equality," and "human rights."[764] Black separatism is at most only a tool for the destruction of White identities, whether in Southern Africa or the Southern US, so that in the long term both Blacks and Whites can be merged into an integrated economy. What has been called "Black internationalism" was created by the oligarchy and has served both the domestic and foreign policy interests of the US and the global managers.

Bayard Rustin: Cold War House Nigger

Bayard Rustin, cofounder of CORE and architect of the "Freedom Rides" that invaded the Southern states with Northern Blacks and White Liberals, had a "personal relationship" with Tom Kahn, the Shachtmanite labor organizer, and founder of the National Endowment for Democracy (NED). Rustin was the co-organizer (with Kahn) of the 1963 March on Washington, where Martin Luther King delivered his famous "I have a dream" speech.

Rustin was eulogized by the long-time president of NED, Carl Gershman, as "perhaps the archetypal democratic activist of the last

---

[764] See Bolton, *Tyranny of Human Rights*.

century," "the leader of the most ardent anti-Communist tendency within the American Left"—that is to say the Cold War, post-Trotskyite tendency that fixated on the destruction of the Soviet bloc and heralded American liberal internationalism as the doctrine of the world revolution.[765] Of the latter, Gershman referred to Rustin's

> [I]deological anticommunism that was prepared to make moral and political distinctions between the democratic West, with all its flaws, and Soviet totalitarianism. . . . In fact, the world had changed, and the cutting edge of the struggle to expand human freedom—which was always where Rustin wanted to be—had moved from the streets of Birmingham to the shipyards of Gdansk and other distant locales where people were either fleeing oppression or working to open closed systems.[766]

Referring to a film about Rustin, *Lost Prophet* by John D'Emilio, Gershman stated more about Rustin's association with the establishment:

> D'Emilio does briefly mention the various global missions Rustin undertook with Freedom House and the International Rescue Committee. But he omits entirely his chairmanship of Social Democrats, USA—which was his ideological base—as well as his founding of Project South Africa, an initiative to promote the peaceful dismantling of apartheid to which Rustin devoted a good part of his last years before his death in 1987. Finally, noting Rustin's outspoken support for Israel and his formation of the Black Americans to Support Israel Committee (BASIC), D'Emilio cannot help reminding us that here, too, Rustin's stance "troubled many of his old associates in the peace movement."[767]

"And while he spent decades at the cutting edge of the racial-protest movement, often as its most radical tactician, he ended as the most

---

[765] Gershman, having been a Chairman of the Young People's Socialist League, was executive director of the Shachtmanite Social Democrats USA (1975–1980). His Zionist background includes serving on the governing council of the American Jewish Committee.

[766] Gershman, "Lost Prophet."

[767] Ibid.

unyielding adversary within the civil-rights movement of black militancy and separatism."[768] That is to say, Rustin joined the "house nigger" faction of the Black movement. Rustin was posthumously awarded the Medal of Freedom by President Obama for services to US globalism. Rustin's former aide, writing for Freedom House, eulogized: "In his later career, Bayard devoted much of his energy to the struggle for global democracy through campaigns that he led on behalf of Freedom House."[769]As such, he was an important part of the globalist offensive against both the Soviet bloc, particularly via the Solidarity movement in Poland, and against White South Africa and Rhodesia.

Rustin was chairman of the executive committee of Freedom House. Freedom House was founded in 1941, at the behest of President Franklin Roosevelt, to push for US intervention in Europe, when most Americans were opposed. After the war, "Freedom House embraced as its mission the expansion of freedom around the world and the strengthening of human rights and civil liberties here at home," and "strongly endorsed the post-war Atlantic Alliance, as well as such key policies and institutions as the Marshall Plan and NATO."[770]

Like other globalist think tanks, during the Cold War they opposed the USSR abroad ostensibly in the name of fighting communism, while domestically they opposed Joseph McCarthy's investigation of communism within the US, because the establishment feared that McCarthyism might lead to a populist movement:

> Since its founding, Freedom House has helped shaped [sic] the debate on the most pressing issues of its time. It was an aggressive foe of McCarthyism in the 1950s. It was also an early and strong supporter of the movement for racial equality. Throughout its history, Freedom House has included among its leadership prominent civil rights leaders, most notably Roy Wilkins, the director of the NAACP, and Bayard Rustin, a leading adviser to Dr. Martin Luther King, Jr.[771]

---

[768] Ibid.
[769] Freedom House, "Bayard Rustin, A Hero of the Freedom Movement."
[770] From their website's "Our History" page.
[771] Ibid.

Note that Freedom House credits itself with "helping to shape" the direction of US policy, which it has done in conjunction with the CFR, NED, the Ford Foundation, the Rockefeller Foundation, and myriad others. Freedom House makes it plain that racial integrationists such as Rustin, Wilkins, and King served the establishment, while Senator Joseph McCarthy was anathema to that establishment. Hence, it seems reasonable to conclude that US anti-communism was for export only, as part of a geopolitical strategy against the Soviet bloc, not as part of an American ideology at home.

Africa-America Institute and American Neo-Colonialism

Rustin and other "house niggers" played important roles in the US's Cold War geopolitical strategy, alongside the youth and student bodies sponsored by the CIA and tax-exempt foundations. As the "winds of change" blew Africa out of the colonialism of the European settler and toward the neo-colonialism of the international banker, the Black civil rights movement was co-opted to form links with Africa in the name of Black solidarity.

The Africa-America Institute was formed in Washington D.C. in 1953, and was originally called the African-American Institute. The aim was to train Africa's postcolonial leaders and seed the ground for the inclusion of Africa into the global economy. Toward this end, the first AAI African-American dialogue was opened in Kenya in 1968 by President Jomo Kenyatta.[772] The purpose of the meeting was said by AAI to have been to bring together leaders from the "private sector" from Africa and the US to discuss issues of common concern. In 1976 the AAI established a training program in Lesotho for South African and Rhodesian Blacks opposing the remnants of White rule in Africa. The significance became apparent in 1996 when the AAI hosted a conference in Namibia to examine investment opportunities for foreign capital. Again, in 2008 the purpose of African decolonization/recolonization became apparent when the AAI partnered with Goldman Sachs for an economic training program for African

---

[772] See their website's "History" page.

women. The current board of trustees is representative of global capitalism.[773]

Jake Hodder wrote in a paper on Rustin and "Black internationalism":

> Over the past fifteen years, increasing attention has been paid to placing African American history within an international and transnational framework. These approaches have dislodged narrow, nationalistic accounts of the civil rights movement by demonstrating how domestic claims for black citizenship were often *framed in terms explicitly conversant with U.S. foreign policy objectives. This had strength in the context of rising African and Asian nationhood in the 1950s and 1960s when the United States was consolidating its role as a global, moral leader.*[774]

"Black internationalism" was an aspect of the liberal internationalism being promoted by the US establishment, and intersecting with feminism and leftism. "Throughout the twentieth century, generations of African American women built politically dynamic forms of black, feminist internationalism," Hodder wrote. He stated that "recent scholarship has examined the complex interplay among race, sexuality, and mobility," emphasizing the ways by which "queerness challenges not just the nation's familial metaphor of belonging, but disrupts national coherence itself. . . . Queer subjectivity is always already extra-national."[775] Scholarship, stated Hodder, is examining how feminism, Black civil rights, and "queerness" all disrupt the cohesion of the social organism, cutting across traditional boundaries. Inauthentic identities have been fostered by the establishment to break the primary ties described by Eric Fromm and other Freudo-Marxian theorists as repressive. There is a "Black international," a "feminist international," a "queer international," used to deconstruct traditional societies and reconstruct a new world order, based on what the global corporations call an "inclusive economy."

---

[773] See their website's "Board of Trustees" page.
[774] Hodder, "Toward a Geography of Black Internationalism," 1362. Emphasis added.
[775] Ibid., 1363.

Hodder realized that this "identity politics," as it is called, serves economic goals, but whether Hodder realizes that these economic goals are determined by the globalization of capital is unclear:

> There has been a sustained effort to rethink the civil rights movement; for example, by examining how racial injustice was coupled to wider structural transformations of the U.S. economy. Moreover, the ways in which African American political consciousness connected to anticolonial struggles abroad reflects a wide range of geographical imaginations, as much as historical ones. This case has been astutely made in relation to the geographical thought of Martin Luther King, Jr.[776]
>
> In the early 1950s, similar nonviolent campaigns against apartheid in South Africa attracted widespread attention from pacifists and civil rights groups alike. Rustin and Houser helped found Americans for South African Resistance in 1952.[777]

The Black civil rights experience in the US was intended as a model for the entirety of sub-Saharan Africa, which could look to the US as the leader of decolonization rather than the USSR. This would allow Africa to be opened up to international capital. In 1952 Rustin went to West Africa, meeting Kwame Nkrumah, who would become prime minister of Ghana, and Nnamdi Azikiwe, a leading Nigerian nationalist and later president of his country, then undertook a four-month speaking tour of the US to explain the "African revolution."[778]

Rustin was a conscious agent of US neocolonialism. Hodder stated that Rustin "saw the continent as an increasingly important sphere of U.S. political, social, and cultural influence."[779] Despite what he claimed to have seen as Africa's glorious cultural legacy, he wanted to reshape Africa in the image of the US.

---

[776] Ibid., 1364.
[777] Ibid., 1365.
[778] Ibid., 1365.
[779] Ibid., 1373.

22

SAUL ALINSKY

Barack Obama and Hillary Clinton got their "rebel" inspiration from Saul Alinsky, the iconic organizer of "community revolts."

Alinsky began his career as a radical "community organizer" in Chicago in 1938. His specialty was to go into communities to organize the have-nots. Alinsky wrote of revolution and of revolutionary amorality.

In reviewing a biography of Alinsky, Nelson Lichtenstein, a historian at the University of Virginia, made some perceptive observations:

> By the end of World War II Alinsky had won a measure of national renown. His *Reveille for Radicals* (1945) hit the best-seller list, and he secured the fervent support of important liberals like Agnes E. Meyer of *The Washington Post* and the retail magnate Marshall Field 3rd. Though it undercuts his larger portrait, Mr. Horwitt shows that much of Alinsky's acclaim rested upon his promise that social reform and a democratic revival could take place through what Meyer called an "orderly revolution," which would bypass the new power of the unions and reject the growth of an intrusive New Deal state. Thus *Reveille for Radicals*, which ostensibly celebrated social conflict, was panned by most of the left but acclaimed by

Time, The New York Times and other mass circulation publications.[780]

What Professor Lichtenstein alludes to is the celebrity status a self-
declared revolutionary was able to achieve through establishment
channels, particularly the establishment house organs *Time, The
New York Times,* and *The Washington Post*. As the above quoted passage makes clear, Alinsky's "revolution" was the type acceptable to
the establishment. Lichtenstein continues:

> Mr. Horwitt concludes that Alinsky's ideas are still "alive and well,"
> but a more sober assessment would surely reveal that his resolutely
> hard-boiled focus on getting the dispossessed a piece of the action
> *ignored . . . the real structures of political power, which lie far beyond
> city hall.*[781]

That is why Alinsky, Dany Cohn-Bendit, Jerry Rubin, and Occupy
Wall Street have been looked on at least with indulgence if not patronage: the real power structures are ignored. Those who attempt to
draw attention to the real power structures are ridiculed, demonized,
and dismissed as far-right conspiracy theorists, as much by the left
as by the establishment.[782]

The Washington Post eulogized Alinsky, citing Agnes Meyer:

> Thanks to Obama's background as a community organizer in Chi-
> cago, he was able to draw comparisons between his work and
> Alinsky's. Hillary Clinton wrote her college thesis on the man.
>
> Incidentally, Gingrich's comments also contrast with the favor-
> able 1946 review of a book by Alinsky, the first mention of him in
> *Washington Post* archives. In her review of *Reveille for Radicals,* Ag-
> nes E. Meyer, wife of former publisher Eugene Meyer and great-
> grandmother of current publisher Katharine Weymouth, intro-
> duces the emerging Midwestern community activist to her Eastern
> Seaboard audience thusly:

---

[780] Lichtenstein, "It Never Hurts."
[781] Ibid. Emphasis added.
[782] See for example the well-funded Institute for Strategic Dialogue.

"A native of Chicago, he first helped the inhabitants of that city's packing-house district, called Back of the Yards, to seek health, happiness and security through the democratic methods of a People's Organization and a People's Council.

""We the people, will work out our own destiny' is the slogan of this *orderly revolution*.[783] Make no mistake. This people's movement is as orderly as all genuine democracy. Its history and the by-laws appended to this volume prove it. But it is also as revolutionary as all genuine democracy from the days of Tom Paine to Saul Alinsky."

She later continued:

"What is the 'destiny' for which the People's Organizations are fighting? They are fighting in serried ranks for better homes, better health and better education for their children, for religious and racial tolerance, and greater economic security. Above all, they want a voice in the government of neighborhood, the city, the Nation, the world. Their program as Alinsky says 'is limited only by the horizon of humanity itself.'"[784]

The husband of Agnes, Eugene Meyer, was not only the publisher of *The Washington Post*, but also president of the Federal Reserve Board, had a seat on the New York Stock Exchange, was a member of the CFR (from 1930), was a cofounder of the Allied Chemical Corporation, and first chairman of the World Bank Group. When the Marxist journal *The New Leader* was in financial trouble during the mid-1950s, Eugene's son-in-law Philip Graham was among those who donated to keep it going, others being the US Information Agency, the Ford Foundation, H. J. Heinz (CFR), Time Inc., and the CIA.[785] After Graham's suicide in 1963, his widow, Eugene's daughter Katherine Graham, assumed the role of publisher. Under Agnes' direction *The Washington Post* promoted CIA asset Gloria Steinem as the voice of feminism. Would Alinsky (or Steinem) have achieved celebrity status as a radical had it not been for promotional pieces from *The Washington Post*, and other establishment media?

---

[783] Emphasis added.
[784] Bank, "Saul Alinsky."
[785] Saunders, *Cultural Cold War*, 339–40.

The CFR, once a semi-secret society, insofar as the original membership was not published, is now publicly acknowledged as "the nearest thing we have to a ruling establishment in the United States." Moreover, a *Washington Post* journalist lauds the role played by the media in the CFR, and none more so than *The Washington Post:*

> What is distinctively modern about the council these days is the considerable involvement of journalists and other media figures, who account for more than 10 percent of the membership. . . . The editorial page editor, deputy editorial page editor, executive editor, managing editor, foreign editor, national affairs editor, business and financial editor and various writers as well as Katharine Graham, the paper's principal owner, represent *The Washington Post* in the council's membership. . . . The membership of these journalists in the council, however they may think of themselves, is an acknowledgment of their active and important role in public affairs and of their *ascension into the American ruling class. They do not merely analyze and interpret foreign policy for the United States; they help make it. . . . They are part of that establishment whether they like it or not, sharing most of its values and world views.*[786]

Subsidizing Alinsky

RF Illustrated, published by the Rockefeller Foundation, carried a fulsome obituary for Alinsky. The Rockefeller cabal apparently had an esteem for the career revolutionist as high as their CFR colleagues from *The Washington Post:*

> Radical as this sounds, it was really in the best American tradition. Alinsky, for all his baiting of the establishment, was an old-fashioned believer in hard work, cooperation and the value of the individual.
>
> At home, his Chicago-based organization, The Industrial Areas Foundation, operates a training school where organizers are involved for twelve to fifteen months in classroom and community

---

[786] Harwood, "Ruling Class Journalists." Emphasis added. Should this be regarded as a "far-right conspiracy theory"?

work—the institute was funded in part by a $225,000 grant from The Rockefeller Foundation.[787]

Alinsky was quoted by the Rockefeller Foundation writer as stating: "That there are no permanent solutions—that today's revolutionary becomes tomorrow's chairman of the board." The obituary commented on Alinsky's tactic, shortly before his death, of buying up shares to use proxy votes at shareholder meeting to embarrass the megacorporations.[788] This did not seem to perturb the Rockefellers, or impede their funding of the Alinsky organization. Next to the obituary there was a list of the Trustees of the Rockefeller Foundation in 1972, including chairman of the board C. Douglas Dillon (investment banker, treasury secretary under Kennedy and Johnson, and director of the CFR), W. Michael Blumenthal (CFR, chief operating officer of the Bendix Corporation, and Kennedy administration adviser), John D. Rockefeller IV (CFR), Robert V. Roosa (partner in Brown Brothers Harriman investment bank, former vice president of the Federal Reserve Bank at Wall Street, CFR Board), Frank Stanton (CFR life member, RAND Corporation trustee, vice president of CBS), and Cyrus Vance (CFR vice chairman, partner in the Wall Street law firm of Simpson, Thacher and Bartlett, Deputy Secretary of Defense).[789]

The 1968 Rockefeller Foundation report stated: "The Industrial Areas Foundation in Chicago under the leadership of Saul Alinsky, has received partial support for its new Training Institution, which will develop community organizers in both ghetto and middle-class communities."[790] The amount was $225,000 through 1972.[791] The reference to "community organizers" being trained for "middle class areas" was a euphemism for integrating White ethnic neighborhoods.

The 1970 report stated that it was funding community organization programs, including that of Alinsky. This was when the Rockefeller Foundation was still chaired by Dillon. While the RF was

---

[787] "Saul David Alinsky," 3.
[788] Ibid.
[789] Ibid.
[790] Rockefeller Foundation. *President's Five-Year Review*, 131.
[791] Ibid., 140.

backing the NAACP and the National Urban League, it was also aiding other projects:

> At the same time the Foundation is supporting a number of unusual and exceptionally promising projects for demonstrating successful ways to discover, train, and develop leadership in minority groups and indigenous neighborhoods. These projects represent a variety of approaches: formal training institutes for community leaders under the guidance of successful veterans in community leadership (Saul Alinsky's Training Institute in Chicago); programs of sensitivity training for staff members of agencies that work in inner cities and expect to provide similar training for leaders , in these neighborhoods (the YMCA project in Chicago); student internship programs in government offices and under minority-group officials (the Urban Affairs Foundation program in Los Angeles); and classroom training plus supervised participation in neighborhood development programs (the projects of the Ecumenical Institute and the Community Renewal Society in Chicago).[792]

In its 1971 report the Rockefeller Foundation commented: "In Chicago, Saul Alinsky's Industrial Areas Foundation trains competent and realistic community organizers—particularly for inner-city slums."[793]

Another patron of Alinsky was the Midas International Foundation, headed by Gordon B. Sherman. Sherman was also a founder of Chicago Business Executives for Peace in Vietnam. The corporate sponsor gave $200,000 in January 1969 for Alinsky to organize a training school, the Alinsky Institute, for agitators in Chicago. The institute also trained representatives from foundations, corporations, and labor unions. "For several years Alinsky . . . has conducted seminars for corporations who want to know what they can do to keep society free and open," stated the *Chicago Daily News*.[794] The institute was announced by Alinsky at a press conference held in the offices of the Midas International Corporation.[795]

---

[792] Rockefeller Foundation. *President's Review & Annual Report 1970*, 110.
[793] Rockefeller Foundation, *President's Ten-Year Review*, 59.
[794] Willie, "Alinksy Plans Militant Tactics School."
[795] Janson, "Alinksy to Train White Militants."

The relationship between the "revolutionary organizer" and corporate America was symbiotic. Working with such organizations for an "orderly revolution" enabled changes to take place within the inner cities in the direction desired by the oligarchs who provided the funds and paid off those who might threaten actual revolt in ways not conducive to the power elite's aims.

It is apparent that Rockefeller and other oligarchs had no problem funding those who agitated for riots and other violence. Alinsky stated at a press conference, when he had gone to Buffalo to agitate in 1966, that "preventing violence is not in our mind. This is what is in the mind of the white agencies with a zoo keeper mentality—keep the animals quiet in the zoo."[796] Alinsky came to New York preaching riot when Nelson Rockefeller was governor. Several years later, the family foundation was funding Alinsky.

Alinsky also traversed the US speaking at colleges, imbuing students with what became the ideology of the New Left. We might ask why Rockefeller, C. Douglas Dillon, and a cabal of other oligarchs sponsored Alinsky, who wrote the rules for New Left revolt, if not with the aim of advancing the dialectal strategy that was described by conservative commentator Alan Stang, when he called the New Left a "great con,"[797] as part of a "pincer movement" of "pressure from above" (represented by Rockefeller) and "pressure from below" (represented by Alinsky).

In 1968, Alinsky founded the Gamiliel Foundation, which continues to operate.[798] One of those who was trained in Alinsky's methods at Gamiliel was Barack Obama, who became an organizer for the foundation in 1985. Gamiliel has been the beneficiary of money from the Democracy Alliance (wealthy donors of the Democratic Party, including George Soros),[799] Ford, the Charles Stewart Mott Foundation, the Marguerite Casey Foundation, the Open Society Institute

---

[796] *Buffalo Courier Express*, 25.
[797] Stang, *Great Con*.
[798] The Gamiliel Foundation changed its name to Gamiliel Network in 1986, and no longer officially acknowledges its origins with Alinsky.
[799] Markay, "Democracy Alliance Network Revealed."

(Soros), the Tides Foundation, the Bauman Family Foundation, the General Motors Foundation, and Kresge Foundation.[800]

New Left Revolt Becomes "Well Rooted and Good"

In 1971 the Rockefeller Foundation report referred to its own 1968 report, cited above, quoting the "politicization of the arts" and the student revolt that was wracking campuses and streets. The 1960s "were years of cultural sloganeering, of demands for relevance, dialogue, confrontation, and involvement with great social and moral issues of the period." Now the foundation could report: "With the beginning of the seventies, much of the furor seems to have spent itself, leaving behind concepts, movements, and institutions which are well rooted and good, and much that while still in embryo gives promise of a healthy future." The student revolt had been channeled in the desired directions, creating a shift leftward, that was deemed "well rooted," "good," and "healthy."[801]

G. William Domhoff, a sociologist at the University of California at Santa Cruz, indicated the manner by which such "radical" organizations as Alinsky's were integrated into the establishment. The Woodlawn Organization (TWO), founded by Alinsky in 1961:

> [H]ad to settle for becoming a very successful service provider by the early 1970s through grants from the Ford Foundation (for housing development), a major industrial corporation (for job training), and the federal government (for a Head-Start program and other social services). In addition, it also received $750,000 in 1969 from the Ford-funded Center for Community Change.[802]

Ultimately the street level agitation that had busted the ethnic communities had paved the way for urban redevelopment in the name of social housing. Domhoff wondered:

---

[800] See the entry for "Gamiliel Foundation" on Influence Watch.
[801] Rockefeller Foundation, *President's Ten-Year Review*, 68.
[802] Domhoff, "Power at the Local Level."

[W]hether an independent grassroots movement can be developed when it is dependent to at least some degree on the corporate funding that flows to it not only from foundations, but from the United Way and church-related groups, which are heavily dependent upon corporate largesse as well.[803]

In 1978 a report in *The New York Times* indicated the extent to which TWO, like other grassroots organizations, no matter how "radical," had succumbed to corporate and federal money:

> TWO was put together about 15 years ago by Saul D. Alinsky, the late social activist, and led by the [Black] Rev. Arthur M. Brazier. . . . The Ford Foundation's threatened action [over financial irregularities, plus a possible FBI investigation] comes at a time when The Wood-lawn Organization, which long ago abandoned its early militancy in favor of social and economic projects within its community, has recently been named the recipient of two Federal grants. . . . Since 1970 . . . the [Ford] Foundation had put $1 million into redevelopment projects sponsored by the organization, which operates two housing projects, a shopping center, a theater and other enterprises. In addition . . . the foundation has given it $2.5 million in grants and has contributed $250,000 for technical assistance.[804]

Not only did the Ford Foundation not discontinue its funding of TWO for financial mismanagement, but it provided $400,000 to "help TWO retire a $1.8 million debt accumulated when the organization was undergoing financial and management difficulties." The amount was matched by money "from the Chicago business community."[805]

Alinsky's Establishment Publishers

Alinsky wrote: "All societies discourage and penalize ideas and writings that threaten the ruling status quo. It is understandable, therefore, that the literature of a Have society is a veritable desert

---

[803] Ibid.
[804] Kneeland, "Chicago Group Faces Foundation Cutoff."
[805] Ford Foundation, *Annual Report 1979*, 10.

whenever we look for writings on social change."[806] Yet his seminal book on community organizing, *Rules for Radicals*, was published by a major establishment institution, Random House, in 1971.[807]

The year before, Jerry Rubin was published by Simon and Schuster.[808] Conversely, according to Alinsky's perception:

> From the Haves, on the other hand, there has come an unceasing flood of literature justifying the status quo. Religious, economic, social, political, and legal tracts endlessly attack all revolutionary ideas and action for change as immoral, fallacious and against God, country, and mother.[809]

The myth of the establishment suppression of left-wing dissent had to be maintained despite being patently false.

Something was askew with Alinsky's observation. What was this "unceasing flood of literature justifying the status quo" from the "Haves"? Herbert Marcuse was, like Alinsky, sponsored by Rockefeller; Alfred Kinsey's controversial studies on sexology were funded by Rockefeller; Gunnar Myrdal's seminal book on American Blacks was sponsored by the Carnegie Corporation; Erich Fromm's repudiation of the "primary ties" of family, faith, and homeland, *Escape from Freedom*, was published by Farrar and Rinehart;[810] Theodor Adorno's study, *The Authoritarian Personality*, ascribing latent "fascism" intrinsically to "God, country, and mother," was published by Harper & Row;[811] Abbie Hoffman's *Woodstock Nation: A Talk-Rock Album*, was published by Random House in 1969. The same year, Dell

---

[806] Alinsky, *Rules for Radicals*, 23.

[807] Ibid.

[808] Rubin, *Do It!*

[809] Alinsky, *Rules for Radicals*, 24.

[810] See Saunders, *Cultural Cold War*, 242 for John Farrar's role in the CIA's Congress for Cultural Freedom

[811] Harper & Row was at the time headed by Cass Canfield, who was a trustee of the Farfield Foundation, the purpose of which was to channel funds to CIA projects such as the Congress for Cultural Freedom. Canfield had been a fundraiser for the United World Federalists when it was run by Cord Meyer, who later joined the CIA and recruited leftists to the Congress for Cultural Freedom.

published *The Conspiracy: The Chicago Eight Speak Out,*[812] an account by the defendant tried for instigating the riot at the 1968 Democratic National Convention in Chicago.

In 1970, executives of major publishing houses combined against the Vietnam War, forming the Action Committee of Publishers for Peace. These "Haves" were no custodians of "God, country, and mother," to paraphrase Alinsky. Within a few months the committee had reached representation from 120 publishers. The extent to which there were sufficient publishers to maintain an "unceasing flood" of conservative-oriented literature is difficult to imagine.

---

[812] The Chicago Eight became the Chicago Seven when Bobby Seale, leader of the Black Panther Party, was tried separately due to his outbursts in court, that had caused him to be bound and gagged. He, and all other defendants, were acquitted on appeal. They were subsequently eulogized by the establishment media. In 1987, HBO produced a television movie, *Conspiracy: The Trial of the Chicago 8.*

23

Ford Eulogizes the '68ers

As we have seen, the "youthful idealism" of the New Left received fulsome praise from John D. Rockefeller III, while his niece, Abby, organized and funded the most radical of them, courtesy of her family trust. McGeorge Bundy of the Ford Foundation also provided an example of how the establishment viewed with optimism the tumult on streets and campuses that they believed to be a harbinger of "social change." Indeed, "a year of social change" by-lined the annual reports of the Ford Foundation.

While C. Douglas Dillon, investment banker and treasury secretary under Kennedy and Johnson, held the chairmanship of the Rockefeller Foundation, McGeorge Bundy, who had served as National Security Advisor to these same presidents, was president of the Ford Foundation. As National Security Advisor, Bundy oversaw the CIA[813] when it was funding leftist students and intelligentsia through the National Student Association and the Congress for Cultural Freedom. Indeed, funding for CIA operations was channeled through the Rockefeller and Ford foundations.[814] Bundy went straight from his

---

[813] Saunders, *Cultural Cold War*, 142.
[814] The Church committee, a Senate committee investigating the CIA in 1976, stated that of the seven hundred grants given from 1963 to 1966 by 164 foundations, nearly half were given to the CIA. Saunders, *Cultural Cold War*, 134–5: "'Bona fide' Foundations such as Ford, Rockefeller and Carnegie were considered 'the best and most plausible kind of funding cover' for the CIA."

position with the Johnson administration to the presidency of the Ford Foundation in 1966.

It can hardly be said that the left, in its march through the institutions, cunningly took over the oligarchic foundations and directed money to leftists causes, and that the oligarchy was powerless to prevent them. We have previously seen how the Rockefeller Foundation praised the "vigor and politicization" of the arts during the 1960s and looked forward to this heralding a new outlook in the 1970s. The Rockefeller Foundation, while under the leadership of C. Douglas Dillon and sundry other oligarchs, sponsored the leftward shift in US culture and education. They were ideologically committed to it.

The Student Malaise

Bundy, in his preface to the 1969 annual report, which could have been by-lined "a year of chaos" in looking over 1968, rather than a "year of social change," referred to the tax-exempt foundations as entering a "new era." The summary of the foundation's year implicitly endorsed the outlook of the New Left, which it referred to as the "student malaise." The report referred to a conference sponsored by the Ford and Danforth foundations on "the school and the democratic environment," in which the role of ideology in education was discussed with representatives from foundations, government, education, and civic organizations. "The Foundation also sought to address aspects of the student malaise."[815]

The aim of democratizing the education system was the *cause célèbre* of the New Left. The Ford Foundation was endorsing a primary element of New Left ideology, with a commitment to sponsor its implementation. Ford in its program for "academic reform" sponsored universities in a "hard look" at the social role of universities and how they should be administered. Questions to be resolved would be the role of students in university government.[816] Many of the programs sounded harmless or praiseworthy, with studies on

---

[815] Ford Foundation, *Annual Report 1969*, 4.
[816] Ibid., 6.

pollution, for example. Other projects, such as the Leadership Development Program, could mold student attitudes behind the guise of "democratization." The aim was to introduce new ideas through fellowships and internships that would "wrest school systems out of ruts."[817] Among the innovations in overcoming the "traditional" curricula, Ford sponsored "the broadening and deepening" of programs for African-American studies in White and Black colleges. Princeton, Rutgers, Stanford, and Yale were among the universities receiving Ford funds to expand or introduce Black studies. Summer programs were also funded to teach college faculty Black history and culture.[818]

Mitchell Sviridoff, who had been recruited from the AFL–CIO labor movement as the director of research for Ford, opined that the 1960s had "started with high hopes and idealism" and had ended "deep in discontent."[819]

Sviridoff stated that while the Great Depression of the 1930s resulted in Franklin D. Roosevelt's New Deal Federal spending, the Vietnam War had the reverse impact, with federal resources having to be restricted. Sviridoff called the war "tedious and unpopular."[820] Ironically, he was working with the Ford Foundation and writing this report when Ford was being run by Bundy and McNamara, who were largely responsible for the lack of a coherent Vietnam policy. In this regard, it is very strange that even the Council on Foreign Relations, which included Bundy and McNamara as senior members, did not formulate a coherent position on Vietnam either, despite the Council's self-description as the "East Coast foreign policy establishment." The CFR's response was to begin a study in 1971, which was published as an anthology of opinions in 1976. The introduction to the anthology, "The Vietnam Legacy," warned that the "Vietnam experience" might trigger a "nationalistic reaction" among Americans.[821] That was the lesson to be learned from Vietnam by the globalist intelligentsia and oligarchy: that Americans might react nationalistically

---

[817] Ibid., 7.
[818] Ibid., 16.
[819] Ibid., 17.
[820] Ibid.
[821] Grose, *Continuing the Inquiry*, 51–3.

and reject liberal internationalism. It was a replay of the previous fear of Joe McCarthy's anti-communism becoming a nationalist revolt.

Sviridoff concluded that the lesson for the new era was not for federal empowerment, but empowerment on the local community level. Unlike the 1930s, during the 1960s "traditional political and economic responses" were insufficient. Moreover, the issues were not just economic, but were now concerned with local power-sharing, "racial, class, and generational issues."[822] This "local power sharing" became a preoccupation for Rockefeller and Ford, and might be explained by the concept being more readily amenable to oligarchic control through funding. As we have seen, the foundations sought to manipulate this supposed "local community control," this grassroots "democratization," by lavishing grants on "community leaders," no matter how corrupt, inept, or even thuggish.

Despite much rhetoric about "national reconciliation" and an end to divisiveness, the Ford Foundation continued its sponsorship of Black and Brown militants. While the compliant Black organizations, the A. Philip Randolph Education Fund ($155,156) NAACP ($178,000) and National Urban League ($1,255,000) received Ford largesse, so did the more bellicose Congress of Racial Equality ($225,000), the newly formed Southwest Council of La Raza ($545,717), and the Mexican-American Legal Defense and Education Fund ($2069,707). Congressman Henry B. Gonzalez, the first Hispanic representative for Texas, stated his concern at the time Ford was providing the money:

> There are some groups who demand brown power, some who display a curious chauvinism, and some who affect the other extreme. There is furious debate about what one should be and what one should do. . . . I understand all this, but I am profoundly distressed by what I see happening today. . . . Mr. Speaker, the issue at hand in this minority group today is hate, and my purpose in addressing the House is to state where I stand: I am against hate and against the spreaders of hate; I am for justice, and for honest tactics in obtaining justice. . . .

---

[822] Ford Foundation, *Annual Report 1969*, 18.

Not long after the Southwest Council of La Raza opened for business, it gave $110,000 to the Mexican-American Unity Council of San Antonio; this group was apparently invented for the purpose of receiving the grant. Whatever the purposes of this group may be, thus far it has not given any assistance that I know of to bring anybody together; rather it has freely dispensed funds to people who promote the rather odd and I might say generally unaccepted and unpopular views of its directors. The Mexican-American Unity Council appears to specialize in creating still other organizations and equipping them with quarters, mimeograph machines and other essentials of life. Thus, the "unity council" has created a parents' association in a poor school district, a neighborhood council, a group known as the *barrios Unidos*—or roughly, united neighborhoods—a committee on voter registration and has given funds to the militant Mexican-American Youth Organization-MAYO; it has also created a vague entity known as the "Universidad de los Barrios" which is a local gang operation. Now assuredly all these efforts may be well intended; however it is questionable to my mind that a very young and inexperienced man can prescribe the social and political organizations of a complex and troubled community; there is no reason whatever to believe that for all the money this group has spent, there is any understanding of what it is actually being spent for, except to employ friends of the director and advance his preconceived notions. The people who are to be united apparently don't get much say in what the "unity council" is up to. . . .

Militant groups like MAYO regularly distribute literature that I can only describe as hate sheets, designed to inflame passions and reinforce old wounds or open new ones; these sheets spew forth racism and hatred designed to do no man good. The practice is defended as one that will build race pride, but I never heard of pride being built on spleen.[823]

What precisely was the agenda of the oligarchy in funding such organizations, from passive Uncle Toms to gang-aiding radicals? Here we have the Ford advisers alluding to the tumult of the 1960s and offering their solutions for peace and resolution and healing in the 1970s, yet it was foundation and federal agency money that funded

---

[823] Gonzalez, *Congressional Record.*

the tumult. For example, the Mexican-American Youth Organization ("Brown Berets") referred to by Congressman Gonzalez, founded in 1967, was part of the New Left's street confrontation. An article on MAYO stated:

> Like many other Mexican-American organizations in the state, MAYO sought social justice. But unlike older and more established groups, such as the League of United Latin American Citizens, the American G.I. Forum, or the Political Association of Spanish Speaking Organizations, it stressed Chicano cultural nationalism and preferred the techniques of direct political confrontation and mass demonstration to accomplish its goals.[824]

---

[824] Acosta, "Mexican American Youth Organization."

24

A Deep Continuity

The Scranton Report on New Left Riots

The Presidential Commission on Campus Unrest sought to rationalize the New Left tumult. Its chairman, Republican William Scranton, supported President John F. Kennedy's social policies, including the formation of the Peace Corps, being dubbed by the news media a "Kennedy Republican." As we have seen, he had sought the presidential nomination for the Republican Party as the establishment's choice, when Nelson Rockefeller failed to generate sufficient support against Barry Goldwater.[825]

The Presidential Commission on Campus Unrest was established in the wake of the Kent State University riots in May 1970, when the National Guard fired on rioting students, killing four (including two bystanders) and injuring nine, when rioters attacked and threw missiles at the National Guard and firefighters after the ROTC building had been set ablaze. This had followed a night of rioting and the setting of fires in downtown Ohio. The New Left had sought to "bring the war home," organizing riots across the US in reaction to Nixon's invasion of Cambodia. Several days later, two rioters were shot dead and twelve injured at Jackson State College in Mississippi.

The tenor of the Scranton Report was that the deaths at Jackson and Kent State had occurred due to the National Guard being ill-

---

[825] O'Malley, "Gentleman from Pennsylvania."

prepared to deal with rioting. In considering the New Left and student upheaval generally, the Scranton Report portrayed New Left doctrine as reflecting American liberalism, out of which a consensus for change could be reached.

In a letter to President Nixon on the commission's report, stated in summary, Scranton wrote:

> Campus unrest is a fact of life. It is not peculiar to America. It is not new and it will go on. Exaggerations of its scope and seriousness and hysterical reactions to it will not make it disappear. They will only aggravate it.
>
> When campus unrest takes the form of violent and disruptive protest, it must be met with firm and just responses. We make recommendations on what those responses should be. Much campus unrest is neither violent nor disruptive. It is found on any lively college or university campus. It is an expression of intellectual restlessness, and intellectual restlessness prompts the search for truth. We should resist the efforts of some young people to achieve their goals through force and violence, but we should encourage all young people to seek the truth and participate responsibly in the democratic process.
>
> Our colleges and universities cannot survive as combat zones, but they cannot thrive unless they are receptive to new ideas. They must be prepared to institute needed reforms in their administrative procedures and instructional programs.[826]

The Scranton Report surveyed a history of campus riots starting with the rise of the Free Speech Movement at Berkeley in 1964. This is portrayed as "the high spirits and defiance to authority that had characterized the traditional school riot . . . joined at Berkeley [with] youthful idealism" and "social objectives of the highest importance." The onus for campus tumult was placed on "state or university officials reactions and overreactions that promised to keep the whole movement alive," and were seen as "provocation."[827]

The report was critical of television news coverage of campus riots for its "emotional" and "visually exciting" depictions, instead of

---

[826] Scranton, *Report of the President's Commission.*
[827] Ibid., 28.

exploring "the causes and complexity of campus protests."[828] That is to say, the Scranton Report opined that television should have done a better job in presenting the New Left ideology to viewers, rather than the drama of the events.

Campus rioting escalated from 1964 to 1965, during which protests became more politicized, particularly around the Vietnam War and Black civil rights, which was becoming ever more militant and nationalistic, and the democratization of campus functioning.[829] The Scranton Report put the blame for the increasing radicalization of students on the police and National Guard, whom the establishment (in this instance represented by the Scranton Commission) placed, like their counterparts in Vietnam, in a no-win situation. The Scranton Report commented on this:

> The charge that the American system is basically "repressive" originated with radicals. But moderates began to give it credence as student protest encountered official force. Many students were "radicalized" by excessive police reactions to disorderly demonstrations. *Although major property damage in campus disruptions between 1960 and 1970 was almost entirely perpetrated by students, and although injuries to students occurred largely during confrontations which they themselves had provoked, students suffered more deaths than their adversaries.* A growing number of students came to see themselves as "victimized" by law enforcement officials.[830]

It would be overly charitable to say that the Scranton Commission was being naive rather than deliberately obstructive in placing the responsibility for student radicalization on law enforcement officials when they responded to what the Scranton Commission conceded to be a decade of vandalism and confrontation that the New Left had provoked. The Scranton Commission commented on the professional agitators who often descended on campuses from without, that their increasingly stated purpose "was the transformation of the university into a political weapon" in pursuit of their noble aims: to

---

[828] Ibid.
[829] Ibid., 29.
[830] Ibid., 34. Emphasis added.

put an end to "war and racism." Alluding to another official whitewash of New Left violence, the Scranton Commission referred to the New Left mayhem at the DNC in Chicago: "Events at the Democratic National Convention in 1968 had a particularly strong impact. Student protest at the convention was often disruptive, provocative, and violent, and it was met by a police reaction so brutal that the *Walker Report* called it a 'police riot.'"[831] Again the establishment—including the news media—had come down on the side of New Left violence and against local authorities, and police who had sought to maintain order. In particular, the aims of the New Left were regarded as worthy, even if the methods were at times overdone.

Police Are "Criminals"

During the New Left riots at Columbia University in 1968, it was the police whom the Scranton Commission condemned for "excessive force and violence," despite the report's comment that "violence by students was greater at Columbia [with] considerable property damage . . . and some students forcibly resisted arrest." This had escalated into outright terrorism, the report stating:

> Threats against university officials. In April 1968, black students at Trinity College in Hartford, Connecticut, held the school's trustees captive until their demands were accepted. In November 1968, students at San Fernando Valley State College in Los Angeles held officials at knife point. Anonymous threats against university officials and faculty members critical of student activities became more frequent.
>
> Acts of terrorism. In February 1969, a secretary at Pomona College in California was severely injured by a bomb. In March 1969, a student at San Francisco State College was critically injured while attempting to place a bomb in a classroom building. On another occasion, a bomb was placed near the office of a liberal faculty member who opposed the "Third World" strike there. Later that year, a custodian at the University of California at Santa Barbara was killed by

---

[831] Ibid., 34.

a bomb in the faculty club. The underground press proclaimed that the bombing in Madison, Wisconsin, on August 24, 1970, was part of a terrorist strategy. Earlier this summer, Assistant Secretary of the Treasury Eugene T. Rossides reported that, between January 1, 1969, and April 15, 1970, almost 41,000 bombings, attempted bombings, and bomb threats were recorded in the nation as a whole. Most could not be attributed to any specific cause. Of those that could be attributed to some cause, more than half—over 8,200—were attributable to "campus disturbances and student unrest."[832]

While the commission evoked images of an America where indeed the New Left had "brought the war home," the response was to target authorities as the culprits in seeking to maintain order, and to recommend the repeal of legislation such as the Higher Education Act (1968) that denied financial aid to students involved in campus "disruption."[833]

The Scranton Commission was fully aware that the SDS had provoked the rioting as part of a political strategy, citing SDS leader Mark Rudd stating that "issues were simply pretexts for protest; if they had not existed, he implied, others would have been substituted."[834] After having alluded to the "destruction of property, papers, and records," and especially the bombing of ROTC buildings on campuses across the US, it was the police and National Guard who were castigated: "Counterviolence against protesting students by law enforcement officers. There were charges of police brutality at Columbia, and many of them had a basis in fact. Both before and after Columbia, every police bust gave rise to brutality charges. Far too often, they were true."[835] The Scranton Commission regarded as unfortunate the sentiments of many Americans that actually supported the police in maintaining order, claiming that "Such public attitudes clearly encouraged violent responses by civil authorities."[836]

---

[832] Ibid., 38.
[833] Ibid., 40.
[834] Ibid., 36.
[835] Ibid., 37.
[836] Ibid., 44.

In the commission's view, the police and the national guardsmen who shot or assaulted students at Kent State University were "criminals."[837]

High Ideals of Rioters

After an inane condemnation of violence from whatever side it arises to give the appearance of objectivity and balance, the premise of the Scranton Report was given: that the New Left rioters were correct in their assessment of society, if not always in their tactics, and changes must be made according to New Left doctrine.

> Campus protest has been focused on three major questions: racial injustice, war, and the university itself. The first issue is the unfulfilled promise of full justice and dignity for Blacks and other minorities. . . .
>
> A great majority of students and a majority of their elders oppose the Indochina war. Many believe it entirely immoral. And if the war is wrong, students insist, then so are all policies and practices that support it, from the draft to military research, from ROTC to recruiting for defense industry. This opposition has led to an ever-widening wave of student protests.
>
> The shortcomings of the American university are the third target of student protest. The goals, values, administration, and curriculum of the modern university have been sharply criticized by many students. Students complain that their studies are irrelevant to the social problems that concern them. They want to shape their own personal and common lives, but find the university restrictive. They seek a community of companions and scholars, but find an impersonal multiversity. And they denounce the university's relationship to the war and to discriminatory racial practices.
>
> A "new" culture is emerging primarily among students. Membership is often manifested by differences in dress and lifestyle. Most of its members have high ideals and great fears. They stress the need for humanity, equality, and the sacredness of life. They fear that nuclear war will make them the last generation in history. They see their elders as entrapped by materialism and competition,

---

[837] Ibid., 2.

and as prisoners of outdated social forms. They believe their own country has lost its sense of human purpose. They see the Indochina war as an onslaught by a technological giant upon the peasant people of a small, harmless, and backward nation. The war is seen as draining resources from the urgent needs of social and racial justice. They argue that we are the first nation with sufficient resources to create not only decent lives for some, but a decent society for all, and that we are failing to do so. They feel they must remake America in its own image.[838]

Powerful Values of the New Left

The report stated that conciliation is possible because there is an underlying commonality of outlook between the establishment and the New Left, which the report claims to be the premises upon which the US was founded:

There is a deep continuity between all Americans, young and old, a continuity that is being obscured in our growing polarization. Most dissenting youth are striving toward the ultimate values and dreams of their elders and their forefathers. In all Americans there has always been latent respect for the idealism of the young. The whole object of a free government is to allow the nation to redefine its purposes in the light of new needs without sacrificing the accumulated wisdom of its living traditions. We cannot do this without each other.

Despite the differences among us, powerful values and sympathies unite us. The very motto of our nation calls for both unity and diversity: from many, one. Out of our divisions, we must now recreate understanding and respect for those different from ourselves.[839]

What the Government report was signaling to Americans was that those with conservative values were the one's out of kilter with what the US really is. These were the Birchers, the McCarthyites, what Hillary Clinton in recent times called the Deplorables.

---

[838] Ibid., 3–4.
[839] Ibid., 6.

While the report regretted the bombings and other violence of the most extreme elements of the New Left, they were counselled that their "impatience" was shared by those in the establishment who sought the same changes.

> We share the impatience of those who call for change. We believe there is still time and opportunity to achieve change. We believe we can still fulfill our shared national commitment to peace, justice, decency, equality, and the celebration of human life. We must start. All of us. Our recommendations are directed toward this end.[840]

In their "recommendations," the government report sought to conciliate by placing blame on extreme actions by both parties. The morale of police and local authorities attempting to deal with violent nihilism on the ground could only have been undermined by such comments. The New Left, having been assured that their ideological values were not different from the establishment, were also assured that the establishment held police and local authorities complicit in the tumult. The establishment was handing the New Left a moral victory. In particular:

> Actions and inactions of government at all levels have contributed to campus unrest. The words of some political leaders have helped to inflame it. Law enforcement officers have too often reacted ineptly or overreacted. At times, their response has degenerated into uncontrolled violence.
>
> The nation has been slow to resolve the issues of war and race, which exacerbate divisions within American society and which have contributed to the escalation of student protest and disorder.[841]

The report's recommendations to resolve the "crisis" were ultimately founded on a gradual change of the US in accord with the New Left, albeit in an orderly manner: "We support the positions that many students and other citizens now urge." These "positions" are phrased as

---

[840] Ibid.
[841] Ibid., 8.

moralistic slogans: racial equality, social justice, an end to war and to hunger. "National priorities must be reassessed."[842]

Ultimatum to Middle America

The correct course for dealing with the New Left violence on campus was for the colleges and universities to incorporate the left into the system. If the demands of the New Left were met, then the "extremists" would be defused. Middle America was given a choice: accept the demands of the New Left, which were after all just a more excitable version of the best of American liberalism, or provoke the extremists to further violence:

> The main reason for the general nonviolence is again to be found in the paradox of tactics: the massive number of moderates who had joined the protest, partly because of violent acts against students, then guaranteed by their involvement that the protests would be largely nonviolent. In part, moderates were able to do this because they outnumbered extremists. But more important were their decisions: on campus after campus, students, faculty, and administrators set up programs of action designed to provide politically viable alternatives to violent action.[843]

The Scranton Report approvingly referred to the universities where the students could take time off to campaign for New Left candidates, euphemistically dubbed "anti-war candidates":

> Princeton University, for example, decided to reschedule its fall classes to allow students to work in political campaigns for the two weeks before election day. The Movement for a New Congress, an effort to elect anti-war candidates, spread from Princeton to other campuses. ACT scores of colleges, academic requirements were changed to give students time for political activities. These students

---

[842] Ibid., 213–14.
[843] Ibid., 45.

canvassed homes, churches, and service clubs to present their views and gather signatures on antiwar petitions.[844]

Yet the Scranton Report referred also to the sixty thousand students who marched on Washington in an anti-war rally as a victory for the radicals, insofar as they had succeeded in their campaign to politicize universities. The Scranton Commission enthused that the Washington march, although a success for the extremists, had been peaceful, and that the university administration and faculty had joined in union with the New Left in turning their attention off-campus:

> Students, faculty members, and administrators united to turn their attention away from scholarship to what seemed to them the far more urgent demands of politics and of keeping protest activities nonviolent. In May 1970, students did not strike against their universities; they succeeded in making their universities strike against national policy.[845]

This section of the report concluded that "in countless individual instances, what began as an idealistic and hopeful commitment to social change has disintegrated. This is a bleak picture, but an accurate one."[846] The mixed messages of the Scranton Report therefore conclude with an ominous threat: violence will return and escalate unless New Left demands continue to be met. The threat was aimed at Middle America, to whom the report referred as being "confused and indignant over student unrest [concluding] that only harsh and punitive measures could control students."[847] The real threat, at least as perceived by the establishment, was that Middle America—not the New Left, students, youth, Blacks—would arise in a *populist* revolt, associated with names such as Robert Taft, Joe McCarthy, Barry Goldwater, George Wallace, and perhaps most nightmarish, the prosect of resistance led by military figures such as General Edwin Walker, or Douglas MacArthur. The New Left revolt, often seemingly a "generational war," was the means by which Middle America could be

---

[844] Ibid.
[845] Ibid., 46.
[846] Ibid., 49.
[847] Ibid., 44.

subdued into accepting the establishment's subversive program as a moderate compromise that was nothing more extreme than traditional American Liberalism.

The report urged that federal funding of those involved in New Left disruption should not be withdrawn. As we have seen, federal agencies employed New Leftists and Black power militants and outsourced work to them. The report recommended in particular: "New laws requiring termination of federally funded financial aid to those involved in campus disruption should not be enacted; similar provisions in existing federal law should be repealed or allowed to expire."[848]

The Scranton Commission saw the best outcome being that students, including both radicals and liberals, would eschew violence in pursuing their demands; "to press for change which they insisted must come through peaceful, nonviolent means."[849]

That the "change" demanded by the students might itself be flawed or undesirable was not something that the Scranton Commission questioned. That the New Left's doctrine—whether called liberal (as even the SDS was self-described) or radical—might be just plain wrong was not something the report considered. According to the Scranton Report, New Left thinking was a product of American Liberalism at its best. The student protests were the culmination of students being "less and less tolerant of war, of racism, and of the things these entail."[850]

Ford Foundation

The Ford Foundation, stepping in as the voice of reason and moderation, fundamentally supported New Left demands on "education reform." Ford's approach followed the same line as the Scranton Report.

An article by F. C. Ward in the foundation's 1968 annual report referred to "responsible dissidents." The Ford Foundation funded the New College in Florida in implementing the New Left program.

---

[848] Ibid., 222.
[849] Ibid., 44.
[850] Ibid., 61.

Ward regurgitated what the SDS and others had been demanding: the sharing of academic responsibilities with students. Ward referred to grants made by the Foundation to the NSA to establish a "special section" devoted to the "student democratization" that the New Left had been demanding. A Ford grant was made to Teachers College at Columbia University, the center of the New Left, "to enable it to conduct a colloquium on the governance of the contemporary university and to assist a group of Columbia's students to articulate the role of students in their own university."[851]

Ford also provided funds for legal studies on how traditional ways of teaching could be changed according, again, to what had from the start been the demands of the New Left in education reform, and to study the "strengths and limitations of 'student power.'"[852]

The Ford report elaborated on what Ward had written, referring to the foundation's 1968 activity being centered on "helping universities respond" to "broad currents of change." At UC–Berkeley, $500,000 was given to a new University Office of Educational Development "that enlists both students and faculty in the planning and conduct of educational experiments."[853] $315,000 was given to the NSA which would enable NSA staff to become "advisers in university reform efforts" across the US.[854]

> At Columbia University which was severely disrupted by student demonstrations in the spring, grants were made to three groups studying and redefining the roles of faculty, students, administrators, and trustees. They included a faculty committee and a student organization that was active in the demonstrations but is dedicated to restructuring, not overturning, the university.[855]

The Ford Foundation had given grants to at least two New Left organizations to facilitate "education reforms" and "democratization."

---

[851] Ward, "Fabric of Universities," in Ford Foundation, *Annual Report 1968*, 19. Ward was chancellor of the New School for Social Research (1980–83).
[852] Ibid., 19b.
[853] Ibid., 20.
[854] Ibid.
[855] Ibid.

The NSA was given primary responsibility for advising on education reconstruction nationwide. The organization referred to as having been involved in riots at Columbia University was the Students for a Reconstructed University (SRU), which the Ford Foundation was able to portray as an acceptable alternative to the SDS, despite the reference to being involved in the rioting. It is interesting that Ford does not specify the name of this organization. SRU seems to have received $50,000, which is listed under "Studies and experiment in university governance and innovation: Columbia University."[856]

However, apart from the most psychopathic elements of the left that were centered on the Weather Underground, when the war was brought home and promptly dealt with by volleys of shot from the Ohio National Guard, the New Left romance with violence was largely ended. The violence that had been initiated by the New Left and confronted by local and state authorities had culminated in the Kent State deaths, which proved too traumatic for Middle America. The Scranton Report assured Americans that the student rioters were really idealists with the best of intentions, boys and girls who wanted no more than peace and social justice, and whose aims accorded with the best tradition of American liberalism.

Social critic Peter Doggett remarked of the time:

> What happened at Kent State might have triggered an outburst that would have left the events of 1968 in the shade. Instead, just at the moment when armed rebellion seemed inevitable, the movement stepped back from the brink. Radical chic took the place of revolution, as rock stars and activists became increasingly intoxicated by each other's cultural power.[857]

"Rock stars and activists" converged especially in the Yippie movement, with the flamboyant duo of Jerry Rubin and Abbie Hoffman seeking rock star fame in the name of "the revolution." The news media and entertainment industry were most obliging in bringing them stardom, albeit a stardom as fleeting as the other commodities produced according to planned obsolescence.

---

[856] Ibid., 94.
[857] Doggett, *There's a Riot Going On*, 318.

25

SEX, DRUGS, ROCK 'N' ROLL

Jerry Rubin, founder of the Yippies (Youth International Party), described his manic outfit as a combination of hippies and the New Left. The aim was a generation too busy getting high, copulating, and listening to puerile lyrics to provide any real challenge to the establishment. Their purpose was to shock Middle America enough to make the leftward changes desired by the establishment look moderate, even conservative. Rubin stated in his revolutionary bible, *Do It!*: "We see sex, rock 'n' roll and dope as part of a Communist plot to take over Amerika."[858] He saw the Yippies as the ultimate expression of communism.

Rubin on self-reflection acknowledged that he and his kindred spirits were products of "Amerika," not repudiations of it, let alone a movement of transcendence toward authenticity:

> Kids who grew up in the post-1950's live in a world of supermarkets, color TV commercials, guerrilla war, international media, psychedelics, rock 'n' roll and moon walks. For us nothing is impossible. We can do anything.[859]

Rubin entitled the first chapter of *Do It!* "Child of Amerika." He explained:

---

[858] Rubin, *Do It!*, 85.
[859] Ibid., 90–91.

I am a child of Amerika. If I'm ever sent to Death Row for my revolutionary "crimes," I'll order as my last meal: a hamburger, french fries and a Coke. I dig big cities. I love to read the sports pages and gossip columns, listen to the radio and watch color TV. I dig department stores, huge supermarkets and airports. I feel secure (though not necessarily hungry) when I see Howard Johnson's on the expressway. I groove on Hollywood movies—even bad ones. I speak only one language—English. I love rock 'n' roll.[860]

So much for the revolution. Rubin was a happy consumer. It came as no surprise that he would end his days as a Wall Street stockbroker.

"Commercial for the Revolution"

Rubin saw a dialectic at work between the New Left and the establishment but thought it would work in his favor. It might be remembered that Saul Alinsky thought the same; that he could work within the system and change it without being co-opted. Perhaps it was the soma-like effect of marijuana and LSD on the critical faculties that enabled Rubin and the '68ers to be so naive. Rubin recognized television as an agent of the revolt, writing in the chapter entitled "Every Revolutionary Needs a Color TV":

Walter Cronkite is SDS's best organizer. Uncle Walter brings out the map of the U. S. with circles around the campuses that blew up today. The battle reports.

Every kid out there is thinking, "Wow! I wanna see my campus on that map!"

Television proves the domino theory: one campus falls and they all fall.

The first "student demonstration" flashed across the TV tubes of the nation as a myth in 1964. That year the first generation being raised from birth on TV was 9, 10 and 11 years old. "First chance I get," they thought, "I wanna do that too."

The first chance they got was when they got to junior high and high school five years later—1969! And that was the year Amerika's

---

[860] Ibid., 12.

junior high and high schools exploded! A government survey shows that three out of every five high schools in the country had "some form of active protest" in 1969.

TV is raising generations of kids who want to grow up and become demonstrators.

Have you ever seen a boring demonstration on TV? Just being on TV makes it exciting. Even picket lines look breathtaking. Television creates myths bigger than reality.

Demonstrations last hours, and most of that time nothing happens. After the demonstration we rush home for the six o'clock news. The drama review. TV packs all the action into two minutes—a commercial for the revolution.

The mere idea of a "story" is revolutionary because a "story" implies disruption of normal life. Every reporter is a dramatist, creating a theater out of life.

Crime in the streets is news; law and order is not. A revolution is news; the status quo ain't.

The media does not report "news," it creates it. An event happens when it goes on TV and becomes myth.

The media is not "neutral." The presence of a camera transforms a demonstration, turning us into heroes. We take more chances when the press is there because we know whatever happens will be known to the entire world within hours.

Television keeps us escalating our tactics; a tactic becomes ineffective when it stops generating gossip or interest—"news."[861]

Moderate/Radical Dialectic

Rubin explained the role of the establishment media, epitomized by CBS, in presenting the anti-war narrative to the mainstream, and likewise with the Black extremists who stood behind Martin Luther King's relative "moderation":

The Peace Movement was trying to put on a respectable front to convince straight people that you don't have to have long hair to be against the war. The Peace Movement was still using pictures of napalmed babies to shame the public, despite the fact that CBS-TV

---

[861] Ibid., 106–107.

was already doing it better—in color!—on Cronkite. The Peace Movement was too fucking polite. Martin Luther King was only as powerful as the black man standing behind him with a Molotov cocktail. "If you don't listen to me, you're going to have to deal with some mighty mean niggers." Antiwar pacifists are only as strong as crazy revolutionaries who are ready to burn the whole mother-fucker down.[862]

Rubin stated that the histrionic antics of the New Left enabled the core demands to become acceptable to the mainstream by seeming to be a compromise. It was the familiar negotiating tactic of demanding more than what one actually wants.

> Referring to a plan to *threaten* to occupy the Pentagon, Rubin stated: Our scenario: We threaten to close the motherfucker down. This triggers the paranoia of the Amerikan government: The Man then organizes our troops for us by denying us a place to rally and march. Thus just-another-demonstration becomes a dramatic confrontation between Freedom and Repression, and the stage is the world. After our people are organized, we soften our rhetoric and our massive numbers force the government to back down. We end up seizing the Pentagon![863]

Again, the establishment media was the key; extravagant threats were the premise, and a leftward shift is achieved by seeming to moderate. The agenda was written for Rubin and his ilk by the establishment and openly presented in the annual reports and position papers of the oligarchic foundations and think tanks. Martin Luther King was only as powerful as the funds he was given by Nelson Rockefeller and the federal government. Jerry Rubin was only as powerful, by his own description, as the image presented of him to the public, courtesy of CBS and Simon & Schuster.

The Black revolt provided a special degree of unleashed jungle savagery. The New Left street theater, with the Pentagon providing a backdrop, included a cast of both deranged nihilists, such as Rubin and Abbie Hoffman, and respectable-looking types from academia,

---

[862] Ibid., 66–67.
[863] Ibid., 68.

suburbia, and the clerisy. The news media provided the imagery to the masses. The choices shown were the moderate wing and the extremist wing, the latter headed up by H. Rap Brown (evoking nightmares of the Mau Mau coming to suburbia), but they were nonetheless two aspects of the same beast. Rubin explained:

> We needed a spectacular press conference to grab the imagination of the world and play on appropriate paranoias. For that we needed the help of Amerika's baddest, meanest, most violent nigger—then H. Rap Brown. Rap's presence at the press conference, whether or not he even showed up at the Pentagon, would create visions of FIRE. Rap agreed to come.
>
> We needed to fill out the script with the other right character actors—a Vietnam veteran, a priest, a housewife from Women Strike for Peace, a professor, an SDS leader and then such folks as Dick Gregory. Dave Dellinger was Leading Man, combining stirring guerrilla-war rhetoric with a kindly, benign appearance; he could be your Uncle Dave. Bob Greenblatt, national coordinator of the MOB[864] and then a Cornell professor, lent the prestige of the academy. And my wild hair and handlebar mustache suggested the anarchist bomb-thrower, capable of anything.[865]

Using the specter of Black insurrection, Rubin stated that, "We began the press conference by identifying the Peace Movement with the Detroit and Newark riots." The obliging press asked H. Rap Brown whether he would take a gun to the Pentagon, to which he quipped that it would more likely be a bomb.[866]

Rubin remarked that "the press was great."

> They picked up an offhand remark by Dave [Dellinger]—"There will be no government building left unattacked"—and made pacifist Dave sound like a terrorist. AP reported, "When asked if his followers would practice nonviolence in Washington, Rap Brown turned away without answering."[867]

---

[864] National Mobilization Committee to End the War in Vietnam.
[865] Rubin, *Do It!*, 69.
[866] Ibid.
[867] Ibid., 70.

The authorities negotiated an agreement with Dellinger as to what routes the New Left national mobilization on the Pentagon could take, which Rubin described as "scheduled law-breaking":

> Dellinger signed an agreement for us—scheduled lawbreaking! A demonstration with a beginning, middle and an end. Peace Movement people were coming from all over Amerika with round-trip bus tickets! A riot for middle-class commuters?[868]

The housewives, ministers, and teachers would provide the "moderate" face of the New Left to Middle American television viewers, in comparison to the crazy Yippies, Black nationalists, and SDS, who threatened the US with urban warfare.

Revolution is Profitable

Rubin knew that something was going on; that the "revolution" was being co-opted. He wrote a chapter dedicated to the phenomenon, insisting that Yippie nihilism was too extreme to be co-opted: "We cannot be co-opted because we want everything."

> Revolution is profitable.
> So the capitalists try to sell it.
> The money pimps take the best things our hearts and minds produce, turn them into consumer products with a price tag and then sell them back to us as merchandise. They take our symbols, drenched with blood from the streets, and make them chic.
> They own our music—the music produced by our suffering, our pain, the collective unconscious of our community! They put our music on records and in dance halls priced so high that we can't even afford to hear it.
> Paisley rock promoters create fenced-in rock festivals, and pigs use tear gas and Mace to keep us out.
> Beware the psychedelic businessman who talks love on his way to Chase Manhattan. He grows his hair long and puts on a brightly-

---

[868] Ibid., 74.

colored shirt because "that's where it's at"—the money, that is. He has a big pile of cash and a short soul.

A hip capitalist is a pig capitalist.

The hip capitalists have some allies within the revolutionary community: longhairs who work as intermediaries between the kids on the street and the millionaire businessmen.

Beware the longhair who says he's more "revolutionary than thou" because he's "beyond politics." Beware the guru who thinks that his thing—be it scientology, astrology, meditation, vegetarianism, rock music or pacifism will make the revolution all by itself.

Beware the longhair who lets himself get ripped off day after day rather than get bad vibrations. Beware the longhair who defends the longhair businessman.[869]

This was quite perceptive of Rubin, referring cryptically to "intermediaries between the kids on the street and the millionaire businessmen." He saw that the youth revolt was being co-opted by the establishment, but thought that he could be different. Yet he became the epitome of the "hip capitalist," a stockbroker, and allowed his own manifesto to be published by Simon & Schuster, one of the great publishing monopolies. One would rightly suspect that *he* was one of the "intermediaries between the kids on the street and the millionaire businessmen."

The "future Yippieland" would arrive when "millions of young people will surge into the streets of every city, dancing, singing, smoking pot, fucking in the streets, tripping, burning draft cards, stopping traffic."[870] "At community meetings all over the land, Bob Dylan will replace The National Anthem.... The Pentagon will be replaced by an LSD experimental farm."[871] The utopian vision of Yippieland was one of atavistic resurgence, appealing to the most primal layer of the unconscious. Civilization was felt to be a burden, and this unease was rationalized as an ideology of revolt.

---

[869] Ibid., 235
[870] Ibid., 253.
[871] Ibid., 256.

Hoffman's "Suppressed" Best-Seller

While Rubin's *Do It!* was published by Simon & Schuster in 1970, at the same time Yippie cofounder Abbie Hoffman released *Steal This Book*. In keeping with Alinsky's claim that establishment publishers were suppressing dissent, it was alleged that Hoffman's *Steal This Book* was rejected by "at least thirty publishers."[872] Although published by Hoffman under his own imprint, Pirate Editions, it was distributed by Grove Press, and sold 250,000 copies in 1971. The book's alleged "suppression" by the establishment would have given it the notoriety needed for sales and publicity.

Hoffman had no problem getting the establishment to publish and market his other books. Random House had published Hoffman's *Woodstock Nation: A Talk-Rock Album* (1969), the iconic Woodstock Festival having become an event that defined a generation, as we are still told, despite being little more than a massive promotional gimmick for the music industry. *Revolution for the Hell of It* had been published by Da Capo Press in 1968 and The Dial Press in 1969. Da Capo Press continues to publish *Revolution for the Hell of It*, stating in its marketing blurb that "Abbie Hoffman's voice is more essential than ever."

While Hoffman was supposedly being suppressed by the "Haves," to use Saul Alinsky's term, playwright and novelist Dotson Rader was given generous space by the establishment house organ, *The New York Times*, to enthusiastically review *Steal This Book*, describing Hoffman in cult-like reverence:

> It also tells you something remarkable about Abbie Hoffman, something about the gentleness and affection for his people that lies hidden under his public rage. It reads as if Hoffman decided it was time to sit down and advise his children on what to avoid and what was worth having in America.[873]

---

[872] See the Art & Popular Culture Encyclopedia for "Steal this Book."
[873] Rader, "Steal this Book."

Despite the pontificating about "suppression," the actual reason why there were problems getting *Steal This Book* published was not its supposedly radical content, which was no more so than Hoffman's previous books, or those of Jerry Rubin, but because of the problematic character of the title. A study guide for the book explains:

> Hoffman had trouble finding a publisher for *Steal This Book*. He insisted the three-word phrase which had appeared in small print on the back jacket of his earlier book, *Woodstock Nation*, must be the title, even though some publishers would have been glad to print it in spite of its advice for illegal activity, if only it did not tell consumers to steal from *them*.[874]

Other books included *To America With Love: Letters from the Underground*, a collection of letters between Hoffman and his wife Anita, published by Stonehill Publishers in 1976 and distributed by George Braziller, a New York publisher. His autobiography, *Soon to be a Major Motion Picture* (1980), was published by Putnam Publishing Group, at the time owned by MCA. *Steal This Urine Test* (1987) was published by Penguin. Most of Hoffman's publishers were establishment corporations.

Tune In and Drop Out: Establishment Origins of the Psychedelic Revolution

Carl Oglesby, former national president of Students for a Democratic Society, opined years later:

> What we have to contemplate nevertheless is the possibility that the great American acid trip, no matter how distinctive of the rebellion of the 1960s it came to appear, was in fact the result of a despicable government conspiracy.... If U.S. intelligence bodies collaborated in an effort to drug an entire generation of Americans, then the reason they did so was to disorient it, sedate it and depoliticize it.[875]

---

[874] Galens, *Study Guide*, 7.
[875] Oglesby, "Acid Test and How It Failed," 10.

As indicted by Rubin and Oglesby, some leaders of the '68 generation knew that something odd was going on, but they were not sufficiently perceptive to see that the New Left was serving agendas.

In 1975, the Rockefeller Commission reported that the CIA had been testing LSD as part of a wider program since 1953, although there had been experiments since the 1940s.[876] The report, referring to LSD, stated of CIA experiments:

> The drug program was part of a much larger CIA program to study possible means for controlling human behavior. Other studies explored the effects of radiation, electric-shock, psychology, psychiatry, sociology and harassment, substances. . . . Unfortunately, only limited records of the testing conducted in these drug programs are now available. All the records concerning the program were ordered destroyed in 1973, including a total of 152 separate files.[877]

The report concluded on its cursory look at CIA human behavior modification experiments:

> As a result of the Inspector General's study of this drug program in 1963, the Agency devised new criteria for testing substances on human subjects. All further testing of potentially dangerous substances on unsuspecting subjects was prohibited. Between 1963 and 1967 some testing of drugs continued, but only on voluntary subjects, primarily inmate volunteers at various correctional institutions. In 1967 all projects involving behavior-influencing drugs were terminated.[878]

---

[876] Set up by President Gerald Ford to investigate CIA operations within the US, the commission was chaired by Vice President Nelson Rockefeller. The finding on the CIA's activities regarding "American dissidents" during the 1960s and 1970s was that the CIA's interest was whether any of these were receiving funding from foreign sources regarding the anti-war protest movement. The CIA did not find any influence over the New Left from the USSR, China, or Cuba. Had constitutional boundaries not prevented them from investigating domestic sources, they might, ironically, have identified influences from the Rockefeller family, and other oligarchs, as well as programs originating within their own departments in support of the left. As for attitudes on the Vietnam War, the CIA itself did not develop a unified or consistent outlook, and influential quarters within the agency did not support the war effort.

[877] Rockefeller, *Report to the President*, 228.

[878] Ibid.

The obfuscating nature of the Rockefeller report is not surprising given the intimate connections between the Rockefeller dynasty and the CIA. The commission included C. Douglas Dillon, an investment banker who served as chairman of the Rockefeller Foundation from 1971 to 1975. Another member was Lane Kirkland, who became president of the AFL–CIO (1979–1995), received the Democracy Service Medal in 1999 from the National Endowment for Democracy, and was a member of the Brookings Institution and a trustee of the Rockefeller Foundation—all in all, a prime example of the historical nexus between organized labor and the oligarchy. Kirkland, with the CIA, NED, and an array of other US government agencies and oligarchic NGOs, assisted the Solidarity movement in undermining Communist Poland.[879] Nelson Rockefeller, chairman of the commission investigating the CIA, had in the early 1950s received briefings on covert activities from Allen Dulles and Tom Braden of the CIA. Braden later stated that "I assumed Nelson knew pretty much everything about what we were doing."[880]

The Rockefeller Foundation was a primary conduit of funds for CIA projects. Frances Stonor Saunders, referring to a 1976 select committee report on US intelligence, stated that by the mid-1960s, of the seven hundred grants of over $10,000 given by 164 foundations, at least 108 involved CIA funding. There is an allusion to the CIA funding that was being given to leftist groups, a CIA study in 1966 arguing that funding for "democratically elected" leftist organizations through tax-exempt foundations was a means of assuring that members and critics alike would not be aware of the CIA connection.[881] However, the oligarchy, and Rockefeller money especially, had its own agenda for globalization that concurred with the world federalism of the CIA.

While the Rockefeller report stated that the LSD program ended in 1967, it should be noted that the report alludes, without further comment, to the LSD program working in conjunction with studies on "the effects of radiation, electric-shock, psychology, psychiatry, sociology and harassment, substances." Were the '68 generation

---

[879] Bernstein, "Holy Alliance."
[880] Saunders, *Cultural Cold War*, 260–1.
[881] Ibid., 134–5.

both the guinea pigs and the cannon fodder of a vast strategy of human behavior modification? It was the Rockefeller Foundation that subsidized these studies, to which we can include the effects of sound and music.

John Lennon, in a 1980 interview, had the following to say about the origins of LSD as a mind control device and its impact on society:

> You don't hear about it anymore, but people are still visiting the cosmos. We must always remember to thank the CIA and the Army for LSD. That's what people forget. Everything is the opposite of what it is, isn't it, Harry? So get out the bottle, boy . . . and relax. They invented LSD to control people and what they did was give us freedom. Sometimes it works in mysterious ways its wonders to perform.[882]

Lennon knew that LSD was being used as a social control mechanism by the establishment but, like Jerry Rubin, was too much part of the system to critically consider such matters. What is relevant is that he states: "Everything is the opposite of what it is, isn't it, Harry?" He could only see LSD as a means to "freedom." It gave the '68ers the "freedom" of the soft tyranny described by Aldous Huxley in his dystopian novel *Brave New World*, where soma is distributed by the state to keep the masses happy and docile. The Russian philosopher Alexander Dugin has interrogated liberalism's much-vaunted centering of freedom: the "freedom to do what?" Writing of the liberal ideology that motivated the '68ers and that has now been exported across the world by the US, Dugin remarks:

> The individual is the cornerstone of liberalism as an ideology— namely an individual stripped of any collective identity (be it class, national, communal or religious) . . . which seeks to liberate the individual from all forms of collective identity: state, class morality, race, religion, authority, and so on. Then there is "freedom for"— freedom to do something. But in liberal terms this is non-freedom. The liberals say: "We only fight for 'freedom from' (liberty), not 'freedom for.'"[883]

---

[882] Lennon and Ono, interview.
[883] Dugin, *Putin vs. Putin*, 57–8.

This liberal ideology described by Dugin was embraced as much by John Lennon, Jerry Rubin, and Abbie Hoffman, and by the oligarchs who desire freedom for the sake of liberating markets and production from any restraints whatsoever. The restraints of collective identity were the traditional "primary ties" condemned as fascistic by the State Department–funded Critical Theorists. These ties are the collective, organic identities that give meaning to the individual, without which there is hedonism. Yet hedonism is precisely the premise of the mass consumption society: insatiable needs, and the wholesale creation of new desires, in order to ensure that the rate of profit does not decline. These primary ties are that against which oligarchs such as Rockefeller and Soros have expended fortunes to destroy.

There was something else *almost* perceptive that John Lennon said in his 1980 interview, when answering a question about his friend Abbie Hoffman turning himself into the police and reviving his fame on television: "Nixon, Hoffman, it's the same. They are all from the same period."[884] But so was Lennon: Nixon, Hoffman, Lennon. Hence, he did not have the detachment to see that his music, promoting negative liberty rather than positive freedom, was a mirror image of the same period, the same zeitgeist.

Revolting Sounds

In 1937, Paul Lazarsfeld and Theodor Adorno established the Radio Research Project at Princeton University with Rockefeller funding. This was an experiment in mass mind manipulation through music. At first, atonal music was promoted, but afterward it was found that repetition of the type that became the basis for pop, rock, and sundry other mass-market junk genres was more effective in its impact upon the mass unconscious.[885] From the 1930s on, the Rockefeller Foundation began to subsidize experiments in the use of sound as a mass mind-shaping method behind the guise of entertainment. David H. Stevens, a board member of the Rockefeller

---

[884] Lennon and Ono, interview.
[885] Whitcombe, "Adorno as Critic."

Foundation's education and humanities divisions, stated in a 1936 memorandum:

> Both radio and motion pictures are recognized as instrumentalities potentially of great importance alike for formal education and for the general diffusion of culture. But they have so far been exploited for the most part for purposes of entertainment.[886]

Teresa Iacobelli, writing for the Rockefeller Foundation, states:

> Among the most important projects that the RF undertook in the field of communications was the Radio Research Project, housed initially at Princeton University's School of Public and International Affairs and after 1939 at Columbia University. Directed by sociologist Paul Lazarsfeld, the project used the tools of social psychology to study radio.[887]

Note that this was an experiment in "social psychology." During World War II the focus became the study of propaganda methods, in which the New School for Social Research was "particularly important."[888] The New School (like the London School of Economics) had been, since its establishment in 1919, an institution that combined socialism with oligarchic sponsorship.[889]

Jerry Rubin and Dany Cohn-Bendit are agreed on the importance of folk and rock music in shaping the attitudes of the '68ers. Cohn-Bendit related:

> I saw Bob Dylan at the Newport Folk Festival in 1965 and have been a fan of folk music ever since. I was a Stones fan, too—though I also listened to the Beatles. And of course I liked the great French *chansonniers*: Georges Brassens, Jacques Brel, and Hugues Aufray, who covered Dylan in French. In 1968 Joan Baez came to Paris for a discussion with students; it took place in a theater with over two thousand attending.[890]

---

886 Iacobelli, "Rockefeller Foundation Support."
887 Ibid.
888 Ibid.
889 Bolton, *Revolution from Above*, 106–9.
890 "1968: Power to the Imagination."

Cohn-Bendit today seems oblivious as to how easily the collective mind of the '68ers was shaped. Puerile lyrics and atavistic beats molded his generation of "rebels," who were revolting against the remnants of tradition—"the primary ties"—that were encumbrances to market expansion. Like the books of Herbert Marcuse, Theodor Adorno, and Erich Fromm that undermined traditional morals and family bonds for their latent tendency toward "fascism," the music provided to the '68 generation was promoted by the establishment, and the LSD that was lauded as the gateway to a new perception of "reality" was pitched with religious zeal by the CIA asset and '68 generation guru Timothy Leary. It was a package deal, which also included the feminism of CIA asset Gloria Steinem, the Uncle Tom revolt of Rockefeller house nigger Martin Luther King, and the sexology of Rockefeller-funded Alfred Kinsey.[891]

Counterculture: A Profitable Enterprise

The counterculture served as a technique for mass marketing. Analogous to the manner by which Edward Bernays' promotion of cigarettes as a symbol of the "liberated woman" had expanded the market for tobacco, the undermining of tradition by lavishly funded psychologists and sociologists opened the way for new directions in marketing in the name of "freedom." Ryan Moore, in a paper on the sociology of youth culture, made some pertinent comments about the co-optation of the youth counterculture for commercial gain:

> The youth culture of the 1960s was profoundly shaped by these movements for social change, while in turn the New Left's political radicalism incorporated much of the style and sensibility of the counterculture. Keniston (1968) and Roszak (1969) argued that youthful radicalism and the counterculture were shaped by their opposition to a totally administered society or "technocracy" where capital, the state, and mass consumption were fundamentally

---

[891] For Kinsey's "sexological studies," which subverted traditional morals—an important component of New Left ideology—see Bolton, *Perversion of* Normality, 265-2.

intertwined. College students quickly discovered that higher education served as a crucial link in this chain of institutions. In response, young people upheld the pursuit of freedom and pleasure against the systemic demands for conformity, instrumental rationality, and deferred gratification. The affluence and security enjoyed by the middle class presented many young people with the opportunity to "drop out" and experiment with the process of developing an identity and searching for authenticity.[892]

In searching for the authenticity that their professors assured them could be had by acts of rebellion, the '68 generation imagined they were building a new world; in reality, they were simply following the pied pipers who had been provided to them by the establishment. "Innovation," reaching "beyond boundaries" in the arts, and "democratizing" culture for the masses helped to integrate even more consumers into the market—what Bernays had achieved for the tobacco industry was now being achieved on a much larger scale. Ryan Moore continues:

> Advertisers and media sought to profit from the enormous value of young consumers by incorporating some of the imagery, music, and rebellious attitude of the counterculture; appeals to freedom and nonconformity were thus steered toward consumerism.
>
> The vanguard of youth culture in the 1960s was the hippie movement, infamous for its collective pursuit of sex, drugs, and rock 'n' roll but otherwise consistent with some enduring American values of individualism (Miller, 1991). The liberalization of sexuality picked up where the 1920s left off, enabled by innovations in control but also by the continuing transformation toward a culture of consumption and individual choice. By the end of the 1960s, the mixture of New Left militancy and countercultural open-mindedness had helped spark the women's and gay rights movements. The hippie counterculture used drugs as tools for the expansion of consciousness and perception, not simply among individuals but as a kind of religious sacrament in the practice of communal joy. Most influential of all was the music scene, which evolved from folk to electrified rock yet continued to be a powerful vehicle of protest and the basis for youthful identities. Rock music appropriated not

---

[892] Moore, "Sociology of Youth Culture."

only the sounds of rhythm and blues but also the defiantly "cool" bravado of urban African Americans. Rock music soon proved to be ripe for commercial co-optation, and in becoming big business its symbolic acts of rebellion were increasingly severed from movements for social change.[893]

This Imperative of Endless Difference

Thomas Frank lamented in his 1997 book on the youth revolt that, having its origins with the Beat generation of the 1950s, the new hedonism had been co-opted for marketing purposes. Frank precisely articulated the factors at work:

The countercultural idea has become capitalist orthodoxy, its hunger for transgression upon transgression now perfectly suited to an economic-cultural regime that runs on ever-faster cyclings of the new; its taste for self-fulfillment and its intolerance for the confines of tradition now permitting vast latitude in consuming practices and lifestyle experimentation.

Consumerism is no longer about "conformity" but about "difference." Advertising teaches us not in the ways of puritanical self-denial (a bizarre notion on the face of it), but in orgiastic, never-ending self-fulfillment. It counsels not rigid adherence to the tastes of the herd but vigilant and constantly updated individualism. We consume not to fit in, but to prove, on the surface at least, that we are rock 'n' roll rebels, each one of us as rule-breaking and hierarchy-defying as our heroes of the 60s, who now pitch cars, shoes, and beer. This imperative of endless difference is today the genius at the heart of American capitalism, an eternal fleeing from "sameness" that satiates our thirst for the New with such achievements of civilization as the infinite brands of identical cola, the myriad colors and irrepressible variety of the cigarette rack at 7-Eleven. . . .

Capitalism, at least as it is envisioned by the best-selling management handbooks, is no longer about enforcing Order, but destroying it. *"Revolution," once the totemic catchphrase of the*

---

[893] Ibid.

counterculture, has become the totemic catchphrase of boomer-as-capitalist.[894]

Ultimately, this generation in revolt were products of the establishment they imagined themselves to be resisting. As Jerry Rubin admitted, the new revolutionaries were molded by the system, especially the mass entertainment industry, and were aspiring consumers of American junk. The most extreme and enduring of the movements, the Weather Underground, which continued an urban terrorism campaign long after the SDS had expired, was nonetheless just as much a product of the system and succumbed to its origins. Kirkpatrick Sale, writing on the final years of the SDS and the Weather Underground, stated of the New Left: "More emphasis came to be placed on relating to the existing youth culture rather than denouncing it as somehow 'bourgeois': Weathermen came to see it."[895]

Sale quoted Bernardine Dohrn, leader of the Weather Underground and the most extreme of the New Left diehards, on "the forces which produced us, a culture that we are a part of, a young and unformed society (nation)."[896]

"Those groups," continued Sale, "which had chosen to emphasize personal development, trust, love, and communality came to be taken as models over the more militaristic and disciplined ones, and the growing role of liberated women in these 'families' helped to emphasize the search for new styles of sexuality, intimacy, and openness."[897] The '68ers melded chameleon-like into the quagmire of modern liberal-capitalism: the Age of Aquarius had dawned, as heralded by one of the songs of that epoch, in one of the productions (*Hair*). The bliss of the brave, new, drug-fueled world had triumphed, and the '68ers had shown themselves to be the heralds of it, rather than the resistance to it.

---

[894] Frank and Weiland, *Commodify Your Dissent*, "Why Johnny Can't Dissent." Emphasis added.
[895] Sale, *SDS*, "Epilogue 1970–1972."
[896] Dohrn, Weather Underground communique, cited by ibid.
[897] Ibid.

Sound and Fury, Signifying Nothing

I have very little faith in rock 'n' roll entertainers as being anything in this society but bourgeois sell-out people. It's the ability society has to incorporate anything into it and turn it into a commercial item.
— San Francisco KSAN DJ Roland Young.[898]

Rock critic Ed Leimbacker observed in 1969:

> What's most in trouble is the so-long-supposed "revolutionary spirit" of rock—that schizophrenic dream of wishful thinking and self-hype. Take a closer look at the Establishment. See, it's made of rubber—it co-opts by expanding, by stretching a little bit further and absorbing all the freaky excesses and aberrations.... Big Brother moves over just enough; and as soon as he gets a piece of the action, the Angry Young Man settles for a lip-service revolution full of sound and fury and signifying nothing.[899]

"Sound and fury and signifying nothing" sums up the whole of the New Left—the establishment's ability to co-opt it, the methodology of the system against which it was supposedly rebelling. Of the latter, John D. Rockefeller III had been zealous in describing how "youthful idealism" could be co-opted, and the establishment provided agencies such as the Peace Corps and VISTA for the purpose.

Columbia's Revolutionaries

Columbia Records was the first corporation to understand the profitable potential of the revolution in music. Doggett wrote that Columbia Records marketed a sampler album in March 1968:

> [F]eaturing its most prestigious underground rock acts, under the faintly ridiculous title *Rock Machine I Love You*. To sell the album,

---

[898] Doggett, *There's a Riot Going On*, 288.
[899] Quoted in Ibid., 289.

Columbia boasted: 'The Revolutionaries are on the Rock Machine'. It was the theme the company would pursue for the next year.[900]

Doggett referred to the "iconographies of rock and revolutionary politics" intertwining "almost overnight."[901] The portraits of Frank Zappa, Jimi Hendrix, and Bob Dylan were marketed along with the image of Che Guevara, who became a poster child of youthful revolutionary sentiment.

Of Che, Doggett discerned the manner by which the establishment was able to commodify the revolution, as Roland Young lamented:

> Like Jim Morrison of the Doors, whose image was mass marketed around the same time, Guevara's portraits boasted matinee idol looks, fashionably dishevelled hair, and a far-away look in his eyes. . . . But while Hollywood directors competed to rush the first Guevara biopic onto the screen, and students lapped up copies of his handbook, *Guerrilla Warfare*, any sense of the revolutionary leader as a political being, complex and sometimes deluded, was forgotten.[902]

In 1968, Columbia produced what Doggett called the "first musical celebration of Che Guevara," "Love Song for the Dead Che," by Joseph Byrd of the avowedly leftist group The United States of America.[903]

In October 1968, "advertising agencies and entertainment conglomerates joined forces . . . to stage a conference about Selling the American Youth Market." In December, Columbia Records "launched a campaign that perfectly illustrated" the theme of the October conference. Having already borrowed the word "revolutionaries" for its March 1968 compilation, they extended the conceit. All of Columbia's rock releases over January to March 1969 were issued on a compilation in April, a Columbia press release declaring "Victory

---

[900] Ibid., 142–4.
[901] Ibid.
[902] Ibid.
[903] Ibid.

in sight for Columbia's 'Revolutionaries.'"[904] Columbia would supply record retailers with "'Revolutionaries' posters and display racks."[905]

In December 1968 Columbia bought full-page advertising space in the US's most prominent counterculture newspapers for a range of releases. Under the heading "But The Man Can't Bust Our Music":

> [W]ere pictured a motley crowd of long-haired demonstrators, a token African-American among them. Scattered at their feet were their banners, conveying strangely vague, apolitical messages: "Grab Hold," "Music is Love," "Wake Up." The copywriter provided the context: "The Establishment's against adventure. And the arousing experience that comes with listening to today's music. So what? Let them slam doors. And keep it out of the concert halls."

Columbia defiantly assured its consumers that "The Man can't stop you from listening. Especially if you're armed with these." Doggett remarked: "Below were pictures of the records The Man wanted to bust."[906]

Doggett referred to this as "a remarkably crass piece of work. The radicalized gimmick backfired, Columbia Records being widely ridiculed in its efforts to be 'hip.'"[907] Additionally, the FBI leaned on Columbia for its generous advertising purchased in the "underground press," which was essential revenue for newspapers such as the Washington *Free Press* and the *Berkeley Barb*.

Some got frustrated with the establishment having co-opted the music with revolutionary rhetoric. "Up Against the Wall Motherfuckers," (UAW/MF) aligned to the Black Panther Party and the Yippies and regarding themselves as the cutting edge of the revolution, complained that "Bullshit Amerika has been defining what we do and who we are. We have allowed the media, the record companies, the psychedelic merchandisers and the suburban imitators to tell us what the 'Hip Revolution' is all about—NO MORE."[908]

---

[904] Ibid.
[905] Ibid., 220.
[906] Ibid.
[907] Ibid.
[908] Ibid., 222.

Writing for the anarchist review of books *Fifth Estate*, music critic Ralph J. Gleason (a founder of *Rolling Stone* and contributing editor to *Ramparts*) was somewhat cynical about Columbia's role as the vanguard of the counterculture:

LIBERATION News Service—Columbia Records is owned by CBS. It owns the Yankees and God knows what else. Its offices are at 51 West 52 Street in New York in a new skyscraper whose walls are already peeling and crackling.

Right now it is the home of the revolution.

Or almost. It is certainly spending more money promoting the Youth Revolution than one would think possible for a standard American corporate enterprise. Columbia ads divide the world into "we" and "they," with the "we" including the longhairs, the youth and Columbia and "they" including anyone you want to include because you happen to be against him or he against you.

The most recent of the Columbia ads, running in full page spread in college papers and underground papers all over the country, is the one which shows seven guys in a bare room with bars at one end. They are sitting on a bench, standing around.

One is crouched on the floor rolling what I, in a charitable moment, not wishing to infer that Columbia Records Inc. is advocating an illegal act, assume to be a standard cowboy cigarette with Bull Durham and white Zig Zag papers. You think it's something else? Smile, when you say that, Padnuh.

Some of the guys are listening to a phonograph via earphones and the caption on the layout is BUT THE MAN CAN'T BUST OUR MUSIC.

Well, padnuh, I don't know, I just don't know. The name of the game, seen from one point of view, is steal the rhetoric of the revolution like the poverty program stole the organizers.

It is hard to think of revolution being advocated from the architectural prize of 51 West 52 Street, from the record company which withdrew Bob Dylan's John Birch lines. But the times they are a-changin' and this may be part of the change.

On the other hand, I am inclined to think only that there's money in revolution and Columbia is smart. "The only legal trip you can take," it says under the picture of a Terry Riley cover. They gotta be kidding. But no, maybe they aren't kidding, only smart.

Is there that much to be made from revolution? Marx sells in paperback like the *Daily World* never did. Marcuse sells in paperback in quantities sufficient to frighten those fearful of the power of the young.

No, the more I think of it the more I am convinced that it is only that Columbia is smart and smells money. And it only proves what we know already about America, even if we sometimes find it hard to spell out in words.

In this society, if you can make enough money out of it you can go a long way toward making it legal. . . .[909]

Gleason discerned that Western civilization, being in an epoch of decay, would devour itself in the quest for money, and for an establishment organ such as Columbia Records to promote revolutionary rhetoric as a marketing gimmick was a symptom of this terminal decline:

"The man can't bust our music." O.K. That's great and I'll go along with it and even hail it. Thank whoever you thank these days that there is money in revolution and that there continues to be. Hopefully there will continue to be and if there is enough it can be used to bring down the very system which produced it in the first place.

Trojan horse? Man, Trojan horses went out with the rest of the Trojan products, and horse is habit forming. What is going on is the inevitable cannibalism practiced by civilizations in the early but accelerating stages of decay.[910]

Out-revolutionizing Columbia Records, in late 1968 Elektra Records signed MC5. The day after Christmas, wrote Doggett, the Fillmore East, a music hall for the music of the revolution, featured MC5, a proto-punk band. However, UAW/MF instigated a riot, aiming to "liberate the hall" from capitalist exploitation. When MC5 left the stage, hundreds from the audience began to trash their equipment. Those waiting outside, who had not gained entry to the hall:

---

[909] Gleason, "Revolutionaries of Columbia."
[910] Ibid.

[W]hen they saw the MC5 stepping into a plush limousine . . . re-
acted like starving men walking into a banquet. Band members
were pulled from the car; their records were thrown at them, some
of the rioters entering the hall and announcing to the crowd that
they had been "betrayed by phonies."

Ben Morea, cofounder of UAW/MF commented that MC5 had failed
to carry forward the "cultural revolution," and had "ran out, symbol-
ically getting into a limousine going to a restaurant."[911]

MC5 vied with UAW/M for the first place in off-the-wall radicalism. Their core audience was the Yippies. Their manager was John
Sinclair, a founding member of the White Panther Party, a White
support base for the Black Panthers, which MC5 joined. Band members posed for promotional shots with rifles held aloft. The band per-
formed at the New Left demonstration outside the DNC in Chicago
in 1968. An avid proponent of the revolutionary potential of marijuana, Sinclair issued a broadside calling for "Total Assault on the Culture" in March 1968, stating that the three key elements were "rock
and roll, dope, and fucking in the streets," the classic Yippie formula.[912] Sinclair explained that rock 'n' roll was "the great liberating
force of our time and place here in the West." The dictum was "do
what ya wanna."[913]

Elektra Records was already a major player in the industry by the
end of the decade. It was one of the first to sign contracts with psychedelic rock bands, including Love (one of the first multiracial
bands), the Doors, and the Stooges. However, MC5 was dropped by
Elektra in 1969 because of a feud between Hudson's department
store in Detroit and the band, during which Hudson's removed all
Elektra albums.[914] MC5 was within the year signed with Atlantic Records, a subsidiary of Warner Bros. since 1967.

---

[911] Doggett, *There's a Riot Going* On, 224.
[912] Ibid., 226.
[913] Ibid.
[914] Spak, "On this day in 1969." The feud revolved around that enduring revolutionary
slogan, "kick out the jams, motherfuckers," used on the album *Kick Out the Jams*,
which became a rallying cry of the New Left revolt.

Blood, Sweat & Bullshit

The band Chicago, formed in 1967, jumped on the revolutionary bandwagon as part of a youthful trend. Robert Lamm, described by Doggett as the most political member of the band, remarked several decades later: "You argue with the term 'revolution' but for those of us who were sweaty kids in our late teens or early 20s, that sure was a sexy word."[915] Their first album, *Chicago Transit Authority*, included a suite inspired by the riots at the 1968 DNC. Their self-titled second album, from 1970, was dedicated "to the people of the revolution . . . and the revolution in all its forms."[916] Their lyrics include the refrain "we gotta do it right, within the system."

Doggett remarked that "the album remained on the American sales charts for more than two and a half years, which testifies to its musical impact and to the appeal of radical chic." Band member James Pankow later complained of the intensive efforts of "nutcases" such as the SDS and Chicago Seven attempting to recruit them to the barricades, leading the band to shelve its interest in politics.[917] Doggett quoted one underground press reviewer as lamenting "the biggest revolution of all will be in Chicago's bank account."[918]

Blood, Sweat & Tears, described by Doggett as Chicago's closest musical counterpart, went on a tour of Eastern Europe in 1970. This was sponsored by the US State Department. The tour was promoted by the US Information Agency, which had been formed in 1953 by the CIA. Doggett referred to the naivety of the band when the previous year they had been "dumbfounded by the idea that their record company (CBS) was allied to an arms manufacturer."[919]

The Eastern bloc governments were not so naive as to the use of music by the US in its Cold War strategy. Jazz had previously been used to showcase the creativity enabled by American liberal democracy. A *Time* article recently commented on this:

---

[915] Doggett, *There's a Riot Going On*, 224.
[916] Ibid., 362.
[917] Ibid.
[918] Ibid.
[919] Ibid., 363.

The State Department hoped that showcasing popular American music around the globe would not only introduce audiences to American culture, but also win them over as ideological allies in the cold war. The Brubeck Quartet's 12 performances in Poland were some of the first in a long tour that would never stray far from the perimeter of the Soviet Union. They passed through Eastern Europe, the Middle East, central Asia and the Indian subcontinent. Other tours would allow jazz legends like Louis Armstrong and Dizzy Gillespie to trumpet American values in newly decolonized states in Africa and Asia. The idea was always the same: keep communism at bay by whatever means possible.[920]

Presently, a program called hip-hop diplomacy, to showcase American liberal democracy to youth across the world, is sponsored by the State Department.[921]

To their puzzlement, Blood, Sweat & Tears were told by the authorities to depart from Romania, the government having complained to the US embassy that the band should display more reserve in their attire and volume. A riot ensued after they threw a tambourine into the audience, and the police closed the show.[922]

A few weeks later, Blood, Sweat & Tears were picketed by the Yippies in response to what they saw as the band's association with the CIA. In the protest entitled "Blood, Sweat & Bullshit," twenty pounds of manure was dumped outside the venue at Madison Square Garden. A Yippie boycott of the band, albeit ineffectual, was called, and the band continued to enjoy several years of commercial success.[923]

Bill Graham: Father of Rock Festivals

Bill Graham, owner of the Fillmore East venue, ostensibly disillusioned with how the music scene had been co-opted, claimed that the musicians had sold out their principles, while musicians such as UAW/MF blamed the record corporations and promoters such as

---

[920] Perrigo, "How the U.S. Used Jazz."
[921] Katz, *Build*.
[922] Doggett, *There's a Riot Going On*, 363.
[923] Ibid., 363–4.

Graham. "Either way," wrote Doggett, "many of the musicians grew richer; while 'the people' tried to distinguish exactly which sections of the Hip Community meant them well or harm."[924]

Craig Karpel, an adviser to Abbie Hoffman and John Lennon, had some interesting comments to make about Bill Graham:

> Recently, an associate of Bill Graham's wrote the Department of Defense offering the services of his organization in arranging rock concerts for the troops. Graham, he explained, "created the rock scene in San Francisco and New York." This might seem like an arrogant claim, but it isn't. Of course, the rock scene in San Francisco and New York wasn't created by musicians and song writers. It was created by a concert promoter; Bill Graham indeed created the rock scene in San Francisco and New York, and Los Angeles, and Chicago, and Seattle and Kansas City and Billings, Montana, and Bemidji, Minnesota and places he has never heard of.
>
> Graham's act of creation began in Autumn, 1965. He was managing the business affairs of the San Francisco Mime Troupe, the radical theater group. In October, a rock group called the Family Dog had rented a ballroom and staged what would go down as the first San Francisco "community" dance. In November, Graham put on a Mime Troupe Benefit along the same lines, and was overwhelmed by its success.
>
> Then suddenly, Graham got a brilliant idea. Why not run a benefit for . . . me? He found an empty ballroom in the Fillmore ghetto and proceeded to do just that, one benefit after another. As the San Francisco scene became progressively less beautiful, Graham made progressively more money, manufacturing Fillmore oh-wow posters, setting up a management company, leasing a theater on New York's Second Avenue as Fillmore East.
>
> Graham is accused of having snuffed the vibes that made the whole San Francisco music scene well up in the first place—the sense of community among bands and audiences. He is accused of having demonstrated to the record companies in New York and Los Angeles that money was to be made off San Francisco. He made so much money—well into the five figures—weekly net, at least $16,000 a week off the Fillmores alone but he neither dropped prices

---

[924] Ibid., 225.

or gave any tickets away. Now that he made as much as he wanted--
enough to last five lifetimes—he retired.[925]

Hair

Director Tom O'Horgan said at the time that he saw Hair *as a once-in-
a-lifetime opportunity to create "a theatre form whose demeanor, language, clothing, dance, and even its name accurately reflect a social
epoch in full explosion."*

– Scott Miller[926]

The performance of the stage musical *Hair,* debuting in October
1967 and becoming an icon of the era, was initiated by Joseph Papp
through his Public Theater, affiliated with the New York Shakespeare
Festival. The latter received funding from the Rockefeller Foundation as part of a Rockefeller program started in 1966 to subsidize the-
aters that would be available to the "young and non-affluent"—seemingly laudable, assuming that the programs were indeed those of
Shakespeare and other classics. However, we are here dealing with
the "progressive" and "innovative" elements that were a primary element of the New Left counterculture's war on tradition. The Rockefeller Foundation annual report for 1968 stated:

> A healthy theatre requires expanded audiences of all strata of soci-
> ety. In supporting the development of expanded audiences, the
> foundation has placed particular emphasis in involving the young
> and the non-affluent. In 1966 a grant to Theater in the Street, of
> New York, brought theatre into the midst of people who would not
> otherwise be exposed to it. This program and others like it have
> gained favor and subsequently received support from other private
> as well as public sources. Thus Rockefeller Foundation grants to the
> Pittsburgh Playhouse for its Vanguard Projects Division, to the
> Trinity Square Playhouse in Providence for free performances in
> Rhode Island high schools, and to the New York Shakespeare

---

[925] Karpel, "Das Hip Kapital."
[926] Miller, "Inside Hair."

Festival in New York, have had a multiple artistic, financial, and social impact.[927]

The amount of $25,000 was given to the "experimental theater at the New York Shakespeare Festival . . . under the direction of Joseph Papp . . . toward starting a program for new playwrights and directors," should there be any misunderstanding that the money was being used to assist with the production of *Hamlet*.[928]

The following year, Papp's New York Shakespeare Festival received grants of $400,000 for the period 1969–1972, "for use by the Public Theater toward the cost of productions at its experimental theatre and its new theatre for contemporary plays."[929]

The report stated that for 1969 the amount for the Public Theater was $87,500.[930] Other grantees at this time included Saul Alinsky's Industrial Areas Foundation ($75,000); Free Southern Theater, connected to the Student Nonviolent Coordinating Committee; La MaMa Experimental Theatre Club ($4,830), described by notable director Ping Chong, as having "always been a home to rebels and outsiders," but nonetheless sustained by grants from the Rockefellers.[931] Subsidizing the production of *Hair* was therefore part of a program for the radicalization of the arts that was also being pursued by Ford.

Doggett described *Hair* as "a so-called 'ritual rock opera' . . . set against a commune of draft-dodgers . . . ubiquitous in 1969." "Firmly ensconced on Broadway and London's West End," the production won over the initially antagonistic Black Panthers, and the young radicals at a demonstration against the war in San Francisco.[932] Doggett remarked that *Hair* "epitomized the problem" of what top-rated Black San Francisco DJ Roland Young regarded as the inability of rock 'n' roll entertainers to be anything but bourgeois sell-outs.[933]

---

[927] Rockefeller Foundation, *President's Five-Year Review*, 104.
[928] Ibid., 112.
[929] Rockefeller Foundation, *President's Review & Annual Report 1969*, 53.
[930] Ibid., 215.
[931] Ibid.
[932] Doggett, *There's a Riot Going On*, 289.
[933] Ibid., 288.

Woodstock

The Woodstock Arts and Music Festival was a defining moment for the '68ers. Abbie Hoffman wrote a book about his experiences there in 1969, while he was awaiting trial for his role in the 1968 Democratic National Convention. Like Rubin's *Do It*, *Woodstock Nation* was published by Random House.

Woodstock capitalized on the hippie phenomenon, whose most notable manifestation up to this point had been the Human Be-In festival at San Francisco's Golden Gate Park Polo Fields on January 14th, 1967, attended by thirty thousand hippies and New Left activists. Here many iconic figures of the epoch appeared, including Richard Alpert (who soon after transformed himself into New Age guru Ram Dass), LSD prophet and CIA asset Timothy Leary (who here coined the famous slogan of the '68ers, "Turn On, Tune In, Drop Out"), Beat poet Allen Ginsberg, Yippie clown and future Wall Street broker Jerry Rubin, and rock bands such as Jefferson Airplane and the Grateful Dead. The "gathering of the tribes," as it was also called, made the Haight-Ashbury area the center of the emerging counterculture.

The Woodstock Festival was held from August 15th to August 18th, 1969, on land rented to the organizers by a New York farmer. Peter Doggett described the organizers as "a bunch of hippie capitalists with a utopian grasp of the sociological, musical and financial potential of what they were planning."[934]

Investors were solicited when two entrepreneurs formed a corporation, and placed advertisements in the house organs of the establishment. *This Day in Music*, among others, provides a background for the funding:

> The men behind Woodstock were Michael Lang, (who had organised the largest festival on the East Coast at the time, the Miami Pop Festival), John Roberts, Joel Rosenman, and Artie Kornfeld. It was Roberts and Rosenman who had the finances.

---

[934] Ibid., 266.

Roberts and Rosenman placed the following advertisement in *The New York Times* and *The Wall Street Journal* under the name of Challenge International, Ltd: "Young men with unlimited capital looking for interesting, legitimate investment opportunities and business propositions." Lang and Kornfeld answered and the four men got together originally to discuss a retreat-like recording studio in Woodstock, but the idea evolved into an outdoor music and arts festival.[935]

Recording rights for the festival were sold to Atlantic Records, whose president, Ahmet Ertegun, secured the movie rights for Warner Bros. "Even before the festival began, Woodstock had become a corporate symbol," wrote Doggett.[936]

Doggett alluded to the moon walk of that year as being largely forgotten in comparison to Woodstock, its "ephemeral hedonism" having "entered the memory of a generation as the pinnacle of a dream—a fantasy, perhaps, that men and women could share this planet in harmony."[937]

Some on the ultraleft, such as Abbie Hoffman, who was given short shrift from the Who's guitarist Peter Townshend when he tried to make a speech from the stage, considered Woodstock a travesty of the revolution, smacking of capitalism. Although the fences collapsed under a throng of 500,000 attendees, making the festival an unintentionally free event, the organizers could look forward to Woodstock becoming a full-length feature film. Doggett quoted critic and musician Gary Herman as stating that "Woodstock's initial loss of half-a-million dollars was recouped many times over by box-office returns and record sales."[938] Woodstock was always intended as "an exhibition of a new lifestyle," not as a political statement.[939]

Ray Waddell, writing for Reuters forty years later, remarked that while "the Woodstock organizers billed their three-day festival as 'An Aquarian Exposition,' it was conceived as a business proposition."[940]

---

[935] "Woodstock," *This Day in Music.*
[936] Doggett, *There's a Riot Going On*, 266.
[937] Ibid.
[938] Ibid., 268.
[939] Ibid., 269.
[940] Waddell, "40 years later."

And the business has endured. Woodstock Ventures, the firm that oversees the licensing and intellectual property related to the Woodstock festival, is still run by the original producers of the event. And for several decades now, that once ragtag group of hippies has evolved into—if they weren't already—good businessmen with savvy instincts.[941]

Waddell enumerated on the ongoing corporate profits:

> For Woodstock's 40th anniversary—officially August 15–18—the breadth of projects and merchandise is staggering. Rhino and Sony will deliver albums of performances, Warner Bros. will release the original film and the Ang Lee-directed narrative feature "Taking Woodstock," VH1 and the History Channel will air a documentary by Barbara Koppel, several publishers will release books, Target will sell anniversary-themed merchandise, and Sony is launching a social networking/e-commerce site, Woodstock.com.[942]

Dell Furano, CEO of Live Nation Merchandise, working with Target and Woodstock Ventures, expected Woodstock related merchandise in 2009 to reach sales of $50 to $100 million. With Target's exclusive rights of marketing merchandise expiring that year Furano expected department stores like Macy's, JCPenney, and Kohl's, along with specialty stores like Hot Topic, Gap, Spencer's, and Urban Outfitters to add to the Woodstock lines. Sony's Woodstock.com is "dedicated to community as well as commerce." The original Woodstock organizers, who continue to run Woodstock Ventures, insist that they only partner with those who put the Woodstock ideals before money.[943] Woodstock Ventures lists a commitment on their website to "free trade" among the "peace and love" cliches in their "causes," which reads like any other "mission statement" from corporate globalists.

---

[941] Ibid.
[942] Ibid.
[943] Ibid.

Columbia's revolutionary sales pitch

Youthpix—Hollywood

Like the record industry, Hollywood also cashed in on the youth revolution. Aniko Bodroghkozy, professor of media studies at the University of Virginia, wrote of this:

> The Hollywood film industry, in haphazard ways, began trying to win baby-boom viewers to its products with a spate of hippie-oriented films in the mid-1960s. By the end of the decade, the wooing of youth viewers had turned into a full-scale campaign to capture this lucrative but politically and culturally unstable sector of the population. By the late 1960s, Hollywood found itself trying to sell films that represented campus turmoil, the radicalization of young people, and the violence associated with student rebellion. Starting in 1969, a new cycle of film seemed to have been born--one focused on the young revolutionary. Studios such as MGM, which invested heavily in these films, hoped that these productions would finally bring the young people to the box office in large enough numbers to reverse the industry's economic downward spiral.[944]

As with music record sales, revolution became a sales gimmick for the movie industry. The two industries interweaved with the "revolution," with movies such as *Woodstock*. With movies losing family audiences to television during the late 1960s, the new generation of teenagers was seen as a vast new market,[945] analogous to the liberated women preyed upon by Big Tobacco in the 1920s. Like decolonized Blacks, liberated women, and today's endless number of transient genders, the '68ers could be manipulated by corporate public relations and advertising experts into becoming consumers, zombified by puerile slogans masquerading as "ideals." Masses of conformists could be created to follow contrived trends in the name of "non-conformity."

Louis F. Polk came over as an executive from the food industry to MGM in 1968 to provide a more youthful focus for the studio's productions. Polk was candid in his linking MGM profits to youthful

---

[944] Bodroghkozy, "Reel Revolutionaries," 38.
[945] Ibid., 39.

idealism: "The opportunity is to meet what the younger people of our society are demanding from the filmmaker by introducing stimulating and challenging as well as entertaining productions at a profit commensurate with the stockholders' expectation." This was not simply a matter of the studio being driven to provide what the young wanted, however. Rather, Polk saw movies as the best means of *creating* demands, rather than responding to demands. He stated that "no medium has the power to move its audience so immediately and so completely as film."[946] *The "power" rests not with the people the consumers, but with the corporations, think tanks, and funders, who create demands, fashions, and trends in politics and morals, as much as in clothing, fast-food, and entertainment.*

MGM created the genre of "youthpix" in 1970, starting with *Zabriskie Point* and the adaptation of James Kunen's *Strawberry Statement*,[947] both set amidst New Left campus turmoil. Despite the box office failure of both, Universal, Paramount, and Columbia were all interested "in films dealing with student rebellion and campus upheavals."

> Universal obtained an independently produced film titled *The Activist* (1970); Paramount came forward with *Medium Cool* (1969), which contained footage of the riots at the 1968 Democratic Party Convention in Chicago; and Columbia heralded both its Elliott Gould vehicle, *Getting Straight* (1970), which was set on a strike-and riot-prone college campus, and *RPM* (obviously standing for "revolutions per minute," 1970), . . . about a staunchly liberal college president trying to come to grips with his riot-torn campus.[948]

Although there were those who feared negative reactions and boycotts, and while some advertising downplayed or obscured political implications, "Universal's promotion of *The Activist* went to great lengths to emphasize that the film was produced with the cooperation of the Berkeley activist community." The film starred several Berkeley "activists." *Zabriskie Point* included Kathleen Cleaver of the Black

---

[946] Ibid.
[947] Ibid.
[948] Ibid., 40.

Panthers. *The Strawberry Statement* featured the real James Kunen. *Medium Cool* included film footage of the 1968 Democratic National Convention riots in Chicago. All of the films depicted campus protests and uprisings.

Reactions among the New Left were divided. Some critics saw the films as not sufficiently ideological. Given that it was Hollywood showbiz, one might wonder how anything else could be expected. Others were positive. James Lichtenberg, reviewing *Zabriskie Point* for New York's *East Village Other* considered that the fantasy bombing scenes at the end of the film "resonated with prophesy" at a time when the Weather Underground was undertaking a bombing campaign.[949] Emanuel Goldman, writing for Boston's *Phoenix* (an "alternative" magazine founded in 1966 and heavily subsidized by advertising from Boston's commercial sector), rationalized the violent imagery by stating that the bombing scenes only destroyed "American symbols," and that creativity comes from destruction: "And that's what the young are doing: planting new thoughts, raising new children, 'together' children. Yes, there is violence going on, and man, that's part of the scene, too. If you push someone against a wall, he's going to fight."[950] Bodroghkozy pointed out that while *Zabriskie Point* "was in national distribution, four Weathermen accidentally blew themselves up along with the exclusive Greenwich Village townhouse they were using as a bomb factory."[951]

Of *The Strawberry Statement*, Bodroghkozy wrote:

> Perhaps surprisingly, considering the film is all but forgotten today, it generated more copy in the pages of the underground press than almost any other Hollywood offering, including such sixties "youth classics" as *Bonnie and Clyde*, *Easy Rider* (1969), and *The Graduate*. Only *Woodstock* (1970) elicited more attention.[952]

Apparently, this MGM production was a masterpiece of mind-manipulation on audiences. Bodroghkozy cites a writer for *The Great*

---

[949] Ibid., 45.
[950] Ibid., 46.
[951] Ibid., 45.
[952] Ibid., 46.

Speckled Bird, a radical weekly founded in Atlanta in 1968 by students at Emory, who:

> [I]n an effusive review, proclaimed the film "the most effective propaganda statement I've ever seen." The reviewer argued that, in its first hour or so of "bullshit liberal" representations of college life, the film managed to involve the largest number of viewers: "You look around the theater and you see about two hundred nicely dressed, expensively hip college and high school students. All of whom identify madly with the sexist jokes. With the way the hero sympathizes with his radical fellow students, but takes part in their actions only for kicks." The reviewer argued that this liberalism was a mere ploy to break down the defenses of these nonradical students. The film had other purposes—political ones—that manifested themselves during the climactic riot scene:
>
> "Like the film's last fifteen minutes, the effect is incredible. All of a sudden those same people who an hour ago were laughing at the way the hero used those 'just too radical' people for kicks (or sex in the case of the radical women he pursued) . . . all of a sudden those same people who had been identifying for an hour with a bullshit liberal hero . . . all of a sudden those expensively hip kids are sincerely screaming for pigs' blood. Are applauding when the bullshit hero knocks a pig on his ass. . . . I came away from The Strawberry Statement mad . . . radically mad. So did a lot of people like me. We didn't just 'agree' with somebody's analysis of our political situation: our heads were changed."[953]

Scott Griffith, writing for the radical paper *Distant Drummer*, described the film as a:

> [M]asterful piece of propaganda for the Movement. In the final scenes, you can feel your muscles tighten and you want to break your knuckles in some cop's face. It doesn't even try to be objective: it's the story of how one student becomes radicalized, and it's important for that reason alone.[954]

---

[953] Ibid., 47.
[954] Ibid.

There were however others, such as Scott Gitlin (SDS), who saw the "intellectualism" of the film as encouraging a violent trend in the New Left.[955]

The corporate entertainment industry was glamorizing the most violent direction of the New Left at a time when the Weather Underground was undertaking a nationwide terrorism campaign. In a major piece in the *Los Angeles Free Press* (a major New Left journal), Sam Blazer, a pioneer in radical theater, argued: "*The Strawberry Statement* is trying to reach out to the inert—the dazed of the nation whom the radical movement has not yet been gifted or patient or systematic enough to nurture." He went on to point out that the film "is an attempt to reclaim the young before their submission becomes a style, before their detachment takes hold, becomes habitual, ritualized, overwhelming-like the blankness of their elders."[956]

Ironically, it was the book *The Strawberry Statement*, which inspired the movie, where Kunen had referred to oligarchic money being offered to the New Left in order to make a stir. Now MGM and Columbia were promoting this left-wing commotion and getting a visceral reaction from young audiences. The purpose of *The Strawberry Statement* film was frankly stated by its scriptwriter, Israel Horovitz, in an interview with Blazer. Horovitz referred to "the magic of MGM" in radicalizing "kids who are still formative."[957] Bodroghkozy referred to the film as serving "as an organizing tool, perhaps replacing the base-building work that New Left groups increasingly neglected as they found themselves caught up in the urgency of preparing for the imminent revolution."[958]

While many on the New Left applauded MGM's depiction of their "movement," the reviewer of the film for *The New York Times*, author and playwright Dotson Radar, considered it a vapid "slander against those young Americans committed to ending injustice in the United States and the war in Indochina," concluding that "*The Strawberry Statement* is a palpably counterrevolutionary film, and everyone

---

[955] Ibid.
[956] Ibid., 48.
[957] Ibid.
[958] Ibid., 49.

connected with it, including the young Mr. Kunen, ought to be deeply ashamed."[959]

Woodstock was a three-hour Warner Bros. documentary on the "peace and music festival." Warner prepared a "massive advertising campaign . . . that included saturation use of radio spots, large ads, and inserts in newspapers (both mainstream and underground) as well as ads in magazines that the studio had not targeted much in recent years."[960] A show was enacted that pitted the young radical producers of the movie with Warner. "Hagman and Horovitz of *The Strawberry Statement* had tried to construct a similar antagonistic relationship to their studio in the pages of the underground press."[961] The "us versus them" dichotomy between the young radical movie producers and the movie moguls suggests the same charade that was being enacted elsewhere between the establishment and the New Left, reminiscent of the contrived commotion to which Kunen had referred. Bodroghkozy aptly commented: "The agony was in finding one's political stance of negation and opposition hopelessly enmeshed within a system one wished to dismantle."[962] The Yippies organized pickets and threats against movie viewings, the high price of the tickets being a particular grievance of many, but the New Left press was unable to resist Warner's advertising revenue:

> The underground press found itself in the contradictory position of being unable to refuse to accept the much-needed revenue that came with carrying ads for the film in its pages but not wanting to support the studio's profit mongering at the youth movement's expense. *The Los Angeles Free Press's* April 17, 1970, issue carried a lavish eight-page pull-out Woodstock insert supplied by Warner Bros.[963]

As Oswald Spengler pointed out in *The Decline of The West* a century ago, the revolution was always for sale, no matter how radical its posturing, and always moves in the direction indicated by money.

---

959 Rader, "Razzberry for 'Strawberry.'"
960 Bodroghkozy, "Reel Revolutionaries," 49.
961 Ibid., 50.
962 Ibid.
963 Ibid., 52.

Hip Capitalism

The marketing of the counterculture, from movies and music to clothing, became known as "hip capitalism." Bernays had pioneered it with the "torches for freedom" for the liberated woman, and it continues today with commercialization of the transgender fad. Certain leftists condemned the co-opting of the counterculture by the corporations, while many rationalized their working within the system by becoming hip capitalists.

Devon Powers, in his history of rock criticism, wrote of the symbiotic relationship between the music industry and its critics:

> Critics were not the lone rock fans or hip community members growing more at ease with business. As the music industry sought to forge organic connections with the counterculture, some members turned to it for job opportunities, while others joined different industries or started companies that catered to alternative markets. By the late '60s and early '70s, these dynamics acquired the name "hip capitalism," a term applied to a wide range of companies with a "counterculture business philosophy"—from head shop owners to camping goods retailers, vegetarian restaurateurs to rock radio DJs. "The enemy is the machine-like Corporate State," explained Marilyn Bender, who devoted a *New York Times* article to the trend in 1971. Rather than rejecting commercialism outright, hip capitalists wanted to humanize the commercial relationship.

The rationalizations for this apparent sell-out were at times questioned:

> Detractors of hip capitalism stridently questioned its motives. Craig Karpel's 1970 *Esquire* article "Das Hip Kapital" identified hip capitalists as those "who coin their gold from a system their customers would like to destroy" and reserved particularly harsh criticism for anyone who used music to do so. "The bedrock value of hip capitalism is black ink on the bottom line," Karpel opined. "Long hair, dope and rock music have become means to that end. The hair is a way of identifying the market. Smoking dope sensitized the consumer to the product. And rock music is what is sold. . . ."

Karpel was equally skeptical of anyone who wished to challenge the music business from the inside. "The hip capitalist who attempts to work from within soon finds himself within a metaphorical recording studio," Karpel noted. "The men in the booth—the straight executives—dote on him and humor him and send coffee and sandwiches in to him, as much as he wants and more. But they are not about to change the way the board is set up just because he asks them to, let alone invite him to try his hand at the controls."[964]

Powers referred to Woodstock as the "best example of the mutable relationship among capitalism, music, and the 'hip community.'"

Occurring over three days in mid-August 1969, the concert was the joint venture of two "young men with unlimited capital," John Roberts and Joel Rosenman, and two stereotypical "long-hairs," Artie Kornfeld and Mike Lang. Though the men often clashed about their differences of perspective as they planned the event, and would-be participants bristled about the presence of two entrepreneurial "straights," in its aftermath Woodstock was interpreted as a peaceful if somewhat chaotic expression of hippie values.[965]

---

[964] Powers, *Writing the Record*, 82–3.
[965] Ibid., 83.

26

Hippies and Haight-Ashbury

When you're tripping, the idea of race disappears; the idea of sex disappears; you don't even know what species you are sometimes.
 – Ken Kesey, Father of the Counterculture

The hippie flower children that arose as a sub-movement of the counterculture provided many subjects on which to experiment. They were disconnected from any "primary ties" that might protect them. Narcotic-induced schizophrenia was the method most often utilized.

The hippie counterculture went rolling into Haight-Ashbury, a neighborhood of San Francisco, in a psychedelically painted van driven by Ken Kesey and his Merry Band of Pranksters. This had started on a road trip across the US in 1964 to preach the benefits of LSD. Kesey was the father of the hippie movement and of the 1967 Summer of Love. He had been one of the subjects of the CIA's Project MK-Ultra, testing the effects of LSD and other drugs.

In particular, the CIA and the tax-exempt foundations that funded MK-Ultra sought the altering of human behavior in ways that could be observed on thousands of drop-out youths. The ideology provided by Kesey, beat poet Allen Ginsberg, and Timothy Leary, combined with drugs and the subliminal messaging of rock music, formed a new subculture. Kesey, author of *One Flew Over the Cuckoo's Nest*, was, by his own account, operating on what might be called an occult level—"beyond the veil," as he put it. Indeed, his self-description was that of the "Prankster" archetype. Josh Jones comments:

> The acid test parties began after Kesey's experience with mind-altering drugs as a volunteer test subject for Army experiments in 1960 (later revealed to be part of the CIA's mind control experiment, Project MK-Ultra). Kesey stole LSD and invited friends to try it with him. In 1965, after Hunter S. Thompson introduced Kesey to the Hell's Angels, he expanded his test parties to real happenings at larger venues, beginning at his home in La Honda, California. Always present was the music of The Grateful Dead, who debuted under that name at one of Kesey's parties after losing their original name, The Warlocks. The cast of characters also included Jack Kerouac's traveling buddy Neal Cassady, Allen Ginsberg, and Dr. Timothy Leary. Out of what Hunter Thompson called "the world capital of madness," the psychedelic counter-culture of Haight-Ashbury was born.[966]

Kesey had volunteered to undergo the CIA experiments with LSD at the Veterans Hospital in Menlo Park, California, to earn some money while attending Stanford University. Was it only coincidental that the CIA's program was set up so close to the bohemian community at Perry Lane? Before long, LSD was being brought into Perry Lane.[967]

As noted previously, in 1967 the Human Be-In, brought 30,000 youths to Haight-Ashbury along with Timothy Leary, Jerry Rubin, and Allen Ginsberg. The hippies of Haight-Ashbury reached 100,000. According to a *Time* estimate, hippies nationwide numbered 300,000.[968]

Haight-Ashbury Free Medical Clinic

David E. Smith established the Haight-Ashbury Free Medical Clinic in San Francisco in 1967. The purpose was to provide free help

---

[966] Jones, "Ken Kesey Talks."
[967] Brown, "Trip of a Lifetime."
[968] "Youth: The Hippies."

for the hordes of sexually diseased and overdosed young people who exemplified what the utopian future could be. Contributing to a symposium published in 1974 on drug analysis, Smith wrote of the Haight-Ashbury clinic and its participation in drug analysis studies that the work was undertaken as a joint venture between the counterculture and state and university facilities. Smith described the Haight-Ashbury clinic as part of a program analyzing the effects of drugs on the counterculture:

> In general the counter-culture street drug analysis programs had access to a large number of samples and had great credibility with the consumer population with respect to their dissemination of street drug analysis information; however, the technical and scientific aspects of these programs were, for the most part, quite inadequate, and Dr. Hart and his staff noted many weaknesses in the programs. Dr. Hart concluded that the university-based street drug analysis programs were superior to the purely counter-culture analysis programs in terms of technical accuracy. He felt that the best system in many cases was a partnership between counter-culture agencies and the university-based facilities.[969]

The "consumers," in return for their partnership with the establishment as guinea pigs, were able to utilize the findings of the study on the availability of the best drugs. Agencies provided the hippies with the university analysis.

> The agencies, accepted by the consumer population, collected the samples; the university analyzed them and released the information back to the agencies. For example the Do It Now Foundation's counter-culture street drug analysis programs deliver good quality technical analyses of street drugs and also disseminate street drug analysis information in a fashion that is extremely valuable to consumers, helping the agency, and the community at large. In contrast to PharmChem which has its own technical analysis resources, the Do It Now Foundation depends on an excellent university-based street drug analysis program entitled the "Pacific Information Service on Street Drugs," a liberal but certainly not

---

[969] Smith, "Evolution of Culture-Culture," 5.

counter-culture agency. Another excellent example of this type of cooperation is the University of Maryland's street drug analysis program, under the direction of Dr. David Blake.[970]

Some of the drug programs were placed in the hands of hippies, who worked with the establishment agencies:

It is interesting to note, however, that some university-based street drug analysis programs are themselves student-controlled and counter-culture in nature. An example is the University of Oregon program which is affiliated with the Whitebird Free Clinic. Their street samples are analyzed by counter-culture analytic agencies such as PharmChem. The information is then disseminated in objective and acceptable fashion to community, helping agencies and consumers alike. Some university-based and highly qualified street drug analysis programs disseminate their information primarily to physicians and other agencies and do not focus on the community at large or on the consumer. Of a more counter-culture nature, the Berkeley Free Clinic regularly reports via K.S.A.N., the most popular underground FM station in San Francisco, the results of their sample analyses in an attempt to upgrade the quality of drug education in the community through the use of such a mass media street drug information delivery system.[971]

According to the appendices for Dr. Smith's chapter:

The Do It Now Foundation has offices in Los Angeles and Phoenix. Although they collect samples from all over the country, they do not have their own analytical services and utilize established facilities at the University of Southern California and the University of the Pacific. The major emphasis of their program is the rapid dissemination of relevant, objective information through fellow alternative agencies, underground newspapers such as the *Los Angeles Free Press*, underground (FM) radio and mass mailings.[972]

---

[970] Ibid.
[971] Ibid.
[972] Ibid, Appendix A.

Smith alluded to the mind-altering purposes of the drugs and re-garded this as an innate drive:

> Unfortunately, it appears that a large segment of the dominant cul-ture still feels that by withholding accurate information about street drugs, young people will stop using such substances to alter their consciousness. I strongly disagree with this and support Dr. Andy Weil's hypothesis that the desire to alter human conscious-ness is a basic human desire. Many persons will seek psychoactive chemicals as a vehicle for altering their consciousness depending on their philosophy, their psychological make-up, the surrounding socio-cultural circumstances and drug availability. The drugs they use will vary. However, just as the dominant culture demands to know what it is ingesting to alter its consciousness, the counter-culture also has a right to the same information.[973]

Smith wanted the hippie guinea pigs to understand what was being done to them as an experiment in mind manipulation, sold as "con-sciousness raising." However, the establishment preferred a covert approach, as per the CIA experiments from which the gurus of psy-chedelia had emerged. Furthermore, the notion that this was moti-vated by youthful idealism is hard to sell if it is realized that the es-tablishment was its sponsor. A *Time* article on the hippies made a perceptive comment:

> Despite such dire predictions, perhaps the most striking thing about the hippie phenomenon is the way it has touched the imagi-nation of the "straight" society that gave it birth. Hippie slang has already entered common usage and spiced American humor. De-partment stores and boutiques have blossomed out in "psyche-delic" colors and designs that resemble animated art nouveau. The bangle shops in any hippie neighborhood cater mostly to tourists, who on summer weekends often outnumber the local flora and fauna. Uptown discotheques feature hippie bands. From jukeboxes and transistors across the nation pulses the turned-on sound of acid-rock groups: the Jefferson Airplane, the Doors, Dow Jones and the Industrials, Moby Grape (there is also a combo called Time).[974]

[973] Ibid.
[974] "Youth: The Hippies."

The squirming mass of disease, filth, and drugs, with its aborted fetuses epitomizing the character of what was a death cult masquerading as "peace and love," received sympathetic responses from the establishment press. *Time* stated in its feature:

> From this promise, possibly more exciting—and more dangerous—than any adventure offered by travel agents, was born the cult of hippiedom. Its disciples, who have little use for definitions, are mostly young and generally thoughtful Americans who are unable to reconcile themselves to the stated values and implicit contradictions of contemporary Western society, and have become internal emigres, seeking individual liberation through means as various as drug use, total withdrawal from the economy and the quest for individual identity.[975]

Reminiscing thirty years later, Kesey remarked that LSD "lets you in on something. When you're tripping, the idea of race disappears; the idea of sex disappears; you don't even know what species you are sometimes."[976] To Kesey, and other apostles of psychedelia, this is nirvana. No race, no gender, no definitive identity; an amorphous mass without attachments. It accords closely with the corporate globalist vision of the world consumer, producer, technocrat, and manager, who is unattached, rootless, "liberated" from the "primary ties" subverted by the Critical Theorists who provided the philosophical foundation of the New Left.

Haight-Ashbury and MK-Ultra

In 1943, Ewan Cameron had been commissioned by the CIA to establish a mental institution in Montreal, the Allan Memorial Institute for Psychiatry, with a $40,000 grant from the Rockefeller Foundation.[977] Here, patients could be subjected to mind control experiments. So far from being "cured," the patients were relegated to a

---

975 Ibid.
976 Brown, "Trip of a Lifetime."
977 Thomas, *Journey into Madness*, 192.

vegetative state. Cameron's institute was part of the CIA's Project MK-Ultra, whose brief was "to investigate how it was possible to modify individual behavior by covert means."[978]

Mrs. Velma Orlikow (wife of David Orlikow, a Member of Parliament) had sought Cameron for psychiatric help. She was reduced to a zombie-like state by large doses of desoyn and sodium amytal, electro-shock, the repetitive playback of taped "confessions,"[979] and LSD. While Mrs. Orlikow was being rendered helpless through chemicals, "Cameron repeatedly insisted that she must challenge her former values, such as her relationship with her mother and her love for her husband, and their daughter."[980] It is notable that *the bond of family is the primary target of mind-manipulators.* While psychiatrists such as Cameron practiced this process on individuals, the New Left provided the means for manipulating individuals *en masse* in the name of peace, love, and freedom.

Mrs. Orlikow was Cameron's first patient in MK-Ultra Sub-Project 68. He had chosen the subjects most susceptible to feelings of guilt: "Cameron intended his treatment to strip his patients of their selfhood and introduce into their minds what he wanted them to believe."[981]

Human Guinea Pig Farm

Is there more to our hunch that flower power was an experiment in mind-control?

Haight-Ashbury became a center for Cameron's experiments. David Talbot, the notable liberal author, journalist, and founder of *Salon*, cites a CIA agent as referring to Haight-Ashbury as a "human guinea pig farm."[982]

In 1967, at the start of the Summer of Love, CIA-sponsored psychiatrist Louis Jolyon "Jolly" West established himself in a house at

---

978 Ibid., 194.
979 Called "psychic driving," Cameron had promoted this "therapy" at an annual conference of the American Psychiatric Association as "beneficial brainwashing." Ibid., 253.
980 Ibid., 257.
981 Ibid., 263.
982 Talbot, *Season of the Witch*, 128-9.

Haight-Ashbury to observe the neighborhood drifters and their drug intake. During the 1960s and 1970s, West was the head of the University of Oklahoma's department of psychiatry, where he established a CIA-backed program of LSD and brainwashing experimentation. West turned the house in Haight-Ashbury into a hippie pad, where youths could hang out and indulge in various chemicals. Suitably adorned with posters and flowers, for six months an intensive study was carried out on the hippie lifestyle. West wrote that Haight-Ashbury "proved to be an interesting laboratory for observations concerning a wide variety of phenomena." He foresaw, rather obviously, that the hippie movement would self-destruct through the enervation of being doped up. Talbot referred to the "hollowed-out zombies walking the streets, the violent psychotics."[983]

By 1969 Haight-Ashbury had been reduced to a slum, with boarded up shops, the streets haunted by starving junkies (the streets were said to be devoid of cats as a result), and a wave of drug murders. The district of "peace and love" had more weapons than any other part of San Francisco. There were shootouts between Black youths and hippies. Life meant nothing.[984]

The CIA established safe houses in Greenwich Village and San Francisco, where unsuspecting clients were plied with LSD, marijuana, and other drugs. These safe houses were set up by Col. George H. White, who went by the pseudonym Morgan Hall, a colorful federal narcotics agent and CIA consultant.[985] The project was called "Operation Midnight Climax," and was part of MK-Ultra. According to White's diaries, he discussed drugs and safe houses with "such CIA luminaries as Dr. Sidney Gottlieb, head of the Chemical Division of the Technical Services Division and the man who ran MK-ULTRA, and Dr. Robert V. Lashbrook, a CIA chemist who worked with LSD."[986]

---

[983] Ibid.
[984] Ibid.
[985] Ibid.
[986] Jacobs, "Diaries of a CIA Operative."

LSD Soirees

LSD was used among the establishment elite, just as much as among the counterculture, as a means to achieving altered states of consciousness. Prisoners, prostitutes, psychiatric patients, hippies, and cash-strapped university students were not the only subjects of LSD experimentation. With the assistance of Timothy Leary, Mary Meyer (ex-wife of World Federalist eminence and CIA officer Cord Meyer) held LSD parties with an elite Washington circle, which included her lover, President John F. Kennedy.[987] LSD spread out from the research institutions into the streets of Haight-Ashbury and the apartments of the elite. Steven J. Novak stated in a research paper that by 1959:

> One disturbing trend was that researchers were growing lax in controlling the drug. They began to share LSD in their homes with friends. A 1958 article on experiments at the nearby Long Beach VA Hospital let slip that researchers were having "LSD25 social parties." Sessions were held at Huxley's house in the Hollywood Hills and that of the Hollywood producer Ivan Tors. Ditman recalled that "LSD became for us an intellectual fun drug." By the late 1950s such socializing spread to the East Coast. On Long Island, Abramson began holding Friday-night LSD soirees in his home and was "besieged by people who wanted to take the drug."[988]

Novak stated that at the time when the supposed therapeutic benefits of LSD were starting to be questioned, it was entering the campuses.

> Unfortunately, just as the safety of LSD was becoming an issue, the drug was spreading into the undergraduate population. On 20 March 1959 Los Angeles newspapers carried a front-page story about the drug death of a freshman at the University of Redlands, eighty miles east of Los Angeles. The police investigation showed

---

[987] Talbot, *Season of the Witch*, 127.
[988] Novak, "LSD Before Leary," 99.

that he and five classmates had been experimenting with drugs, among them mescaline and LSD, in his dorm room. . . . .[989]

Talbot wrote that, before Allen Ginsberg and Timothy Leary:

LSD's leading apostle in the 1950s and early 1960s was, in fact, a former OSS [Office of Strategic Services, predecessor of the CIA] officer with strong ties to the espionage establishment: Captain Alfred M. Hubbard. He travelled the world, introducing acid to an elite spectrum of statesmen, corporate chieftains, church leaders, and writers, including Aldous Huxley, who became another influential advocate for the drug. "They all thought it was the most marvelous thing," said Hubbard about his acid evangelism among the elite. "And I never saw a psychosis among any one of these cases."[990]

Aldous Huxley, one of the most influential writers of the twentieth century, was introduced to LSD by the CIA. Yet Huxley had published his dystopian novel *Brave New World* in the 1930s, in which he prophetically and skillfully described how "world controllers" maintain a world state, not through overt repression but through pleasure. In his commentary on *Brave New World* several decades later, Huxley explained how the process of what we now call "globalization," aided by technology, would proceed to a communistic centralization, run not by proletarian commissars but by plutocrats. The best way to maintain control is to keep the masses contented, through "sexual freedom" and the abolition of the family, including the use of public orgies accompanied by mind-altering music. In this dystopia, "the systematic drugging of individuals for the benefit of the state . . . was a main plank in the policy of the world controllers."[991] He stated that the nearest substance to this fictional soma was LSD.

Jolyon West, commenting on Huxley, stated that social control could be maintained by the control of drug distribution; that "a government could also supply drugs to help control a population. This method . . . has the governing element employing drugs selectively

---

[989] Ibid., 105.
[990] Talbot, *Season of the Witch*, 127.
[991] Huxley, *Brave New World Revisited*, 34–5.

to manipulate the governed in various ways."[992] Of the hippie communes West said: "the communards with their hallucinogenic drugs are probably less bothersome—and less expensive—if they are living apart, than if they are engaging in alternative modes of expressing their alienation, such as active, organized, vigorous political protest and dissent."[993]

By 1953 Huxley was experimenting with mescaline, and by 1955 with LSD. Although he died in 1963, Huxley's book evangelizing for psychedelic drugs, *The Doors of Perception*, helped lay the ground for the counterculture. In 1958, Huxley explained on *The Mike Wallace Interview* that such a social control drug as soma did not exist, but there were drugs that could be taken "which do no harm," while nonetheless warning that drugs could be used in the way soma was described in *Brave New World*.[994] Huxley knew from his experiences how the CIA was using LSD and other drugs.

Magic Mushrooms

You can draw a woozy but vivid line from the sedate offices of J.P. Morgan and Time Inc. in the '50s to Haight-Ashbury in the '60s to a zillion drug-rehab centers in the '70s. Long, strange trip indeed.

– John Cloud, *Time*, 2007

The properties of the magic mushroom were discovered by Gordon Wasson, chairman of the Council on Foreign Relations, and a vice president of J.P. Morgan & Co. Wasson was the first to describe the effects of the magic mushroom to the public in a *Life* magazine article in 1957.[995] *Life* was very much part of the establishment, as was its publisher Henry Luce. Mr. and Mrs. Luce were among the establishment luminaries who sought to open their "doors of perception" with LSD. *Time* magazine featured an article with an apt title, "When the Elites Loved LSD":

---

[992] Siegel and West, *Hallucinations*, 298.
[993] Ibid.
[994] Huxley, interview.
[995] Wasson, "Seeking the Magic Mushroom."

After Wasson's article was published, many people sought out mushrooms and the other big hallucinogen of the day, LSD. (In 1958, Time Inc. cofounder Henry Luce and his wife Clare Booth Luce dropped acid with a psychiatrist. Henry Luce conducted an imaginary symphony during his trip, according to *Storming Heaven*.) The most important person to discover drugs through the *Life* piece was Timothy Leary himself. Leary had never used drugs, but a friend recommended the article to him, and Leary eventually traveled to Mexico to take mushrooms. Within a few years, he had launched his crusade for America to "turn on, tune in, drop out." In other words, you can draw a woozy but vivid line from the sedate offices of J.P. Morgan and Time Inc. in the '50s to Haight-Ashbury in the '60s to a zillion drug-rehab centers in the '70s. Long, strange trip indeed.

It's difficult to recall now, but there was a period 50 years ago when psychedelics were not only part of the mainstream but of the Establishment. Many academics and wealthy experimental types believed that the way psychedelics work—by expanding sensory awareness even as they disrupt control over the way you normally process information—would lead people to great insights.[996]

At the same time, as if part of a coordinated publicity campaign, the twelve million subscriber *This Week* magazine published another account of Wasson's mushroom experiences, by Wasson's wife Valentina, who had partaken of the mushroom with her husband in Mexico. She described her experience as a "self-induced bout of schizophrenia" inducing a feeling of "supreme happiness and well-being," "enchantingly beautiful . . . a thrilling feeling of total happiness."[997] She referred to mountain mushrooms that would produce even better results than the mescaline described by Huxley in *The Doors of Perception*.

Coincidentally, Gordon Wasson, a journalist who started his Wall Street career as head of public relations for J. P. Morgan, was a friend of Edward Bernays. Now Wasson, with the help of Henry Luce's publishing empire, promoted hallucinogens as "liberating."

---

[996] Cloud, "When the Elites Loved LSD."
[997] Wasson, "I Ate the Sacred Mushroom."

New Left leader Abbie Hoffman considered Henry Luce to have done more to promote LSD than Timothy Leary, and Luce's wife agreed. Hoffman wrote:

> I've always maintained that Henry Luce did more to popularize acid than Timothy Leary. Years later I met Clare Booth Luce at the Republican convention in Miami. She did not disagree with this opinion. America's version of the Dragon Lady caressed my arm, fluttered her eyes and cooed, "We wouldn't want everyone doing too much of a good thing."[998]

Luce also happened to be an important part of the cultural Cold War. He was a member of the American committee that formed the Congress for Cultural Freedom. He provided funds to keep the *Partisan Review* going as a primary organ of the CCF in its recruitment of anti-Stalinist Leftists.

The Wassons had been funded by the CIA to collect mushroom samples in Mexico. CIA director Allen Dulles was personally involved and knew Wasson well. They were influential in the CFR and the Century Association.[999] A memo from MK-Ultra Subproject 58 stated that Wasson's expenses to Mexico would be covered.[1000] Given Wasson's friendship with Allen Dulles, the CIA memo mentioning that Wasson was not aware of the CIA funds seems unlikely.

Charles Manson:
Establishment Guinea Pig and New Left Superstar

Charles Manson was among the more notable denizens of Haight-Ashbury. Manson arrived there in 1967. He did so at the urging of Roger Smith. Roger Smith was, in addition to being a federal parole officer, a student of criminology at Berkeley. Roger Smith assigned Manson to the San Francisco Project, "an experimental parole

---

[998] Hoffman, *Soon to be a Major Motion Picture*, 73.
[999] Dulles, Memo to the Membership Committee.
[1000] CIA, "MKULTRA Subproject 58."

program funded by the National Institute of Mental Health."[1001] Roger Smith stated to Tom O'Neil in an interview that he had sent Manson to live in Haight-Ashbury to "soak up" some of the "vibes . . . of the peace and love movement exploding in the district that summer. Maybe it would allay some of Manson's hostility."[1002]

Once Manson arrived at Haight-Ashbury he became a daily user of LSD, and "seemingly overnight transformed himself into an archetypal hippie."[1003] The National Institute of Mental Health, a conduit for CIA funds, funded a study, the Amphetamine Research Project, on the effects of amphetamines on hippie behavior in Haight-Ashbury, and how this might be controlled. Roger Smith was chosen to head this study. He ran ARP out of David Smith's Haight-Ashbury Free Medical Clinic.[1004] Manson became a mainstay at the clinic, where he and his entourage of women could be treated for their regular bouts of venereal disease.[1005]

Roger Smith and his colleagues closely studied the daily routines of the hippie communes in Haight-Ashbury, which involved the immersion of the researchers into the lifestyle.[1006]

It is widely said that the 1969 murders orchestrated by Charles Manson and undertaken by his "Manson Family" cult ended the flower power mystique of the 1960s in a bloodbath among Hollywood's elite, in which names such as Roman Polanski and Dennis Wilson (drummer for the Beach Boys) crop up, yet others intimately connected with Manson, such as Columbia's Terry Melcher, were protected from scrutiny.[1007]

Manson, a parolee, received a mostly "hands-off" attitude from the police, although his crimes, while under police surveillance at the Spahn Ranch, included rape, contributing to the delinquency of a minor, drug dealing, and grand theft auto. ARP participants such as Manson had what amounted to immunity from police investigation. Tom O'Neil suspected that the transformation of Manson and his

---

[1001] O'Neil, *Chaos*, 287.
[1002] Ibid., 289.
[1003] Ibid., 290.
[1004] Ibid., 302.
[1005] Ibid.
[1006] Ibid., 300–1.
[1007] Ibid., 129–34.

cult from carrying flowers to daggers was facilitated by Roger Smith and the Free Clinic.[1008]

According to Manson acolyte Tex Watson, Mason "had a special hatred for women as mothers . . . this probably had something to do with feelings about his own mother, although he never talked about her."[1009] Manson "loathed the influence of parents." One of the Manson Family associates, Greg Jacobson, was esteemed as "an angel" because he had been "parentless."[1010]

When "kill your parents" became a widely touted slogan of the New Left, it emanated from the same sources as Manson's psychosis. Bill Ayers, cofounder of the Weather Underground, summed up the doctrine in 1970: "Bring the revolution home, kill your parents, that's where it's really at."[1011] For Jerry Rubin there was a life-long search for escape from his mother. He stated at a group therapy session in which participants sought liberation from "childhood deprivation":

> I started shouting at my mother for the specific messages she gave me. 'Thanks, mommy. You white-skinned no-good sexless asshole . . . who destroyed me at birth. . . .' Oh, it is so liberating for me to tell the truth. Mommy, I am glad that you died. If you had not died of cancer, I would have had to kill you.[1012]

Substitute "families" emerged, based around runaway kids, especially underage girls, who were preyed on by males acting spontaneously and creatively in acts of universal love for humanity. Bill Ayers wrote of this time as being one of feverish experimentation, where instincts were "anarchistic, vigorous, and unrestrained."[1013] Violent street rampages would be followed by large orgies under "a huge Vietcong flag."[1014]

The murder of Sharon Tate and others by the Manson Family brought Manson superstar status among the New Left. At a "war

---

1008 Ibid., 303.
1009 Ibid., 28–9.
1010 Ibid., 136.
1011 "More on Ayers."
1012 Rubin, *Growing (Up) at 37*, 140–2.
1013 Ayers, *Fugitive Days*, 147.
1014 Ibid.

council" held at Flint, Michigan, in 1969 by the Weather Underground, Bernadine Dohrn praised the murders as a revolutionary act. She introduced the Weathermen's three-fingered "fork salute," symbolizing the fork used to split open the stomach of the pregnant Sharon Tate. She jocularly referred to the victims as the Tate Eight. "The Weathermen dig Charles Manson," she stated.[1015] Yippies Jerry Rubin and Phil Ochs visited Mansion in prison. Manson said he hoped to perform in court like the Chicago Seven.[1016] The underground newspaper *Tuesday's Child*, predecessor of the *Los Angeles Free Press*, featured on its cover a crucified Manson during his trial. Another issue proclaimed Manson "man of the year."[1017]

Manson also entered the repertoire of "hip capitalism," with Sophie Gilbert commenting in *The Atlantic*:

> Manson's real power, it turned out, was over popular culture. He inspired books and songs and operas and TV series and Diane Sawyer specials and clothing lines and the name of an American band that itself became synonymous with fears of societal breakdown. He's the subject of Quentin Tarantino's next film. He inspired one of the breakout literary hits of 2016, a novel that won its unknown 25-year-old author a $2 million advance.[1018]

[1015] Hayden, *Reunion*, 379.
[1016] Ibid.
[1017] Ayers, *Fugitive Days*, 149.
[1018] Gilbert, "Real Cult of Charles Manson."

27

EUGENE MCCARTHY, WALL STREET, AND VIETNAM

With the assassination of Robert Kennedy in June 1968, the New Left placed its hopes for the presidency on Senator Eugene McCarthy. He was also Wall Street's choice. A similar situation during Obama's 2008 campaign. Eugene McCarthy and Obama distilled the hopes of the generation that thinks itself "rebellious," and of Wall Street. Eugene McCarthy was the anti-war candidate.

It is erroneous to assume that Wall Street was avidly backing the Vietnam War and reaping profits for the oligarchy. Wall Street's position was dramatized in 1969 when stockbrokers joined with the New Left to demand an end to the war. *The Guardian* reported:

> Wall Street stopped today, filled from end to end and bank to bank with thousands of protesters chanting "peace now" in a cavernous cry which echoed off the skyscrapers. In front of the barred doors of the US Treasury, the protesters heard business leaders, lawyers, and bankers join with hippies and folk singers to roar: "We shall overcome." They heard the Wall Street attorney, who organized it all, shout: "Wall Street is not afraid of peace."[1019]

Marching up Wall Street to Trinity Church was ex-White House Press Secretary Bill Moyers, who gave a speech. Others included André Meyer, head of the international investment bank Lazard Frères,

---

[1019] Preston, "From the Archive."

who *The Guardian* called "one of America's top six investment bankers and a man of immense influence."[1020] Meyer also served on the boards of Rockefeller's Chase Manhattan Bank, RCA, and others.[1021]

In an allusion to McCarthy, *The Guardian* commented: "The well-heeled who quietly give funds to Eugene McCarthy are on the public platforms now."[1022]

Vietnam War Distorted U.S. Economy

Despite the fact that the New Left continually referred to the "military–industrial complex," during the Vietnam War, when Wall Street was presumed to be reaping profits, the stock market declined. "The inflationary role of the Vietnam War did not help expectations in the market."[1023] Unlike World War II, which was the main factor in lifting the US out of the Great Depression, the Vietnam War caused one of the greatest slowdowns in US economic growth.

Vietnam was not advantageous to Wall Street, despite the assumptions of the New Left. The oligarchs preferred to extend their influence over the world with economics, not weapons. Generals and oligarchs do not tend to make the most harmonious bedfellows, despite the implication of the term "military–industrial complex." The generals are the last resort. Certainly, one sees what happens when a military man gets awkward—such as General Patton and General Edwin Walker in Occupied Germany, or General Douglas MacArthur in Korea—when they take their oath of loyalty to be concerned with a national loyalty rather than a loyalty to the global elite. The oligarchs would rather establish their plutocracy with the etiolating but profitable enticements of dope and entertainment.

Richard J. Barnet and Robert E. Müller stated in their classic study of the transnational corporations, based on extensive interviews with globalist executives:

[1020] Ibid.
[1021] Smith, "Andre Meyer, N.Y. Investment Banker."
[1022] Preston, "From the Archive."
[1023] IEP, *Economic Consequences of War*, 13.

What, then, is the security role which the United States is expected to play in the Global Shopping Center? What the World Managers want from the American state is a low military profile and a much more aggressive economic policy. "It is time the United States developed an economic foreign policy instead of a political foreign policy," says Fred Borch, former head of General Electric.[1024]

Continentally, that was *exactly* the doctrine articulated in the Port Huron Statement.

Barnet and Müller assert that the "World Managers" aimed for a "belt of capitalism" that would integrate the Eastern Bloc.[1025] They saw Nixon's foreign policy as being "precisely in accord with the global corporations' own political strategy" in opening up trade relations with China and the USSR.[1026] This foreign policy was pursued by Henry Kissinger, a protégé of David Rockefeller from the start of his career. While China became so completely integrated into the world economy that its relationship with global capital was symbiotic, the USSR and the Soviet bloc presented geopolitical problems that could only be resolved by the fall of the Soviet Union via a combination of well-funded color revolutions (which had begun with the "Prague Spring" in 1968), arming the Mujahedeen in Afghanistan against the Soviet military, and the internal treachery of Gorbachev, now feted as a great globalist.[1027] As for Vietnam, the South was scuttled and Kissinger led the way.

Barnet and Müller comment:

> When the executives call themselves "peacemongers," they are being perfectly sincere. It is in their interests that the game of nations be transformed from a military duel which no one can win and which threaten all their dreams. A world in which military power will be dominated by national governments, which for the foreseeable future will continue to have an effective monopoly on such power. But if economic power is dominant, corporations with control over an ever-increasing share of the world's production system,

---

[1024] Barnet and Müller, *Global Reach*, 95.
[1025] Ibid.
[1026] Ibid., 95–6.
[1027] Bolton, *Russia and the Fight*, 139–56.

money markets, and communications resources, will gain increasing political leadership. The more economic issues overshadow military security, the more the global corporation is likely to take power away from the nation-state.[1028]

The Pentagon was pursuing a policy in Vietnam "long after some of the country's corporate elite wanted it ended."[1029] The same can be said for the present saber-rattling between the US and China, which does not accord with the interests of the financial elite.

The January 1968 Tet Offensive, when North Vietnamese forces launched a surprise attack against the Republic of Vietnam, caused a sense of urgency among the oligarchs. European bankers began cashing in their dollars for gold, and in March, Arthur Okun, chairman of the Council of Economic Advisers, referred to the world financial markets as "having a bad case of the shakes."[1030] A world financial crisis loomed. Citibank president Walter Wriston, one of the most influential bankers in the US, said to a group of European bankers in January that the possibility of economic stabilization "would be greater if the Vietnamese war ended."[1031] Roy Reierson, senior vice president and chief economist for the Bankers Trust Company, said in March that the war had caused domestic inflation and burdened the balance of payments deficit. Sidney Homer, a partner and senior researcher at Salomon Brothers, warned that military setbacks would "surely intensify attacks on the dollar."[1032] The war had aggravated economic problems and "in a sense frozen them."[1033] Goldman Sachs reported to investors that reduced spending in Vietnam "could contribute significantly to the solution of many problems currently plaguing the U.S. economy."[1034] Louis B. Lundborg, chairman of the Bank of America, testified before the Senate Foreign Relations

---

[1028] Barnet and Müller, *Global Reach*, 96.
[1029] Ibid., 94.
[1030] Buzzanco, "Ruling-Class Anti-Imperialism," 213.
[1031] Ibid.
[1032] Ibid.
[1033] Ibid.
[1034] Ibid., 215.

Committee in 1970 on the subject, "why peace would be good for America."[1035]

Chairman of the Federal Reserve William McChesney Martin commented to bankers in March that Vietnam and the balance of payments deficit had put the US economy in its worst position since 1931:

> I have been trying for the past two years to make the point on 'guns and butter' and the cost of the Vietnam War, economically, without too much success but I think in due course the chickens will come home to roost.[1036]

The Washington Post noted that when there are rumors of peace negotiations "stock prices go up sharply—and that's about the only time they do go up."[1037] When fighting intensifies there is a "sharp price break."[1038]

Business Executive Moves for Vietnam Peace

The Business Executive Moves for Vietnam Peace and New National Priorities (BEM) was organized in 1967. Their importance in the anti-war movement has been obscured by the flamboyance of the street protests.[1039]

The keynote address at the founding meeting was given by investment banker Marriner Eccles, who had been chairman of the Federal Reserve Board, and who had been at the Dumbarton Oaks conference that established the international banking system after World War II. Eccles warned that the war was causing a serious problem for the US's balance of payments.[1040] The BEM was given favorable publicity by NBC and CBS, becoming an important lobby among politicians and officials in Washington. By 1970, BEM had eleven

---

1035 Smith, "What Would Peace," 211.
1036 Ibid., 198.
1037 Ibid., 199.
1038 Ibid.
1039 Ibid., 198.
1040 Ibid., 205.

thousand members, including Robert Bernstein and Bennett Cerf of Random House, George Weissman of Philip Morris, Max Palevsky of Xerox, and Lawrence Philips of Phillips-Van Heusen.[1041] That year BEM aligned with the Corporate Executive Committee for Peace, which was composed of 350 Wall Street executives.[1042]

In early 1968 the financial brokerage house, Paine, Webber, Jackson & Curtis, ran an advertisement in *The New York Times* asking, "what would peace in Vietnam mean to you?" The PWJ&C analysis stated that the war had "stretched the nation's production facilities to the point where there was virtually no remaining reserve of economic resources."[1043] In April members of BEM testified before the House Committee on Veterans Affairs, referring to the advertisement, with Erwin Salk, a prominent mortgage banker, answering: "Peace in Vietnam would be the most constructive—and the most bullish thing that could happen to the stock market."[1044]

Action Committee of Publishers for Peace

The New York Times ran a story on the founding of the Action Committee of Publishers for Peace. The article is reproduced in full as follows:

> A group of executives and editorial employes *[sic]* of many of the nation's leading publishing houses has started a protest movement against the war in Indochina through a sustained campaign and lobbying in Congress.
>
> Christopher Cerf, an editor at Random House and chairman of the Action Committee of Publishers for Peace, spent Friday and yesterday meeting with colleagues to devise the new strategy.
>
> "Everybody is very anxious to do something," the 26-year-old Mr. Cerf said. "The publishing industry is supposed to represent national discourse, so we intend to use all our resources and skills

---

[1041] Ibid., 206.
[1042] Ibid., 207.
[1043] Ibid., 199.
[1044] Ibid., 199.

to help make the Nixon Administration aware of this new groundswell for peace."

Among the resources, he pointed out, is the wide use of advertising space by publishers to promote their books as well as close personal ties of many editors with members of Congress and officials in Washington who have written books in various fields. Mr. Cerf is the son of Bennett Cerf, chairman of Random House.

The committee was formed by a group of 50 to 60 publishers and editors at a meeting at the American Institute of Graphic Arts on Thursday to co-ordinate the growing demands for antiwar action at numerous publishing houses following the killing of four students at Kent State University last Monday.

150 Sign at Holt

At Holt Rinehart & Winston for example, 150 persons signed a petition to President Nixon protesting the war and the student deaths. The signers included Ross D. Sackett, chairman of the board, Aaron Asher, editorial director, and Tom C. Wallace, editor in chief.

Among those who met at the institute were Chester Kerr, director of the Yale University Press; John Jay Iselin, editorial director of Harper & Row; Arthur Wang, president of Hill & Wang; Sol Stein, president of Stein & Day; Gail Rentsch, publicity director of Atheneum Publishers, Hal Sharlott, editor in chief of E. P. Dutton, and Andre Schiffrin, editorial director of Pantheon.

In an initial step, employes of Random House have raised funds for an advertisement in *The New York Times* and *The Washington Post* urging the public to view a special program, "To End the War," on NBC-TV at 7:30 P.M. Tuesday, featuring Senators George McGovern, Democrat of South Dakota, Mark Hatfield, Republican of Oregon, Charles E. Goodell, Republican of New York, and Frank Church, Democrat of Idaho, who will outline plans for an amendment to curtail military procurement authorization.

"The time for rhetoric is past," said Robert Bernstein, president of Random House. "We must work on practical measures to influence legislation. If we feel there's great danger in the continuance of present policy, it's just not fair to leave it to the young, many of them without a vote, to make these changes."

The next step in the committee's strategy is a resolution seeking industrywide support for the protest. The resolution will be submitted at the opening session of the annual meeting of the

American Book Publishers Council, a trade association, at a Po-
conos resort in Pennsylvania Monday after noon.

Another move planned by the committee is to use next month's
annual meeting of the American Booksellers Association in Washington to send delegations to Congress to lobby against the war.[1045]

Within several weeks the Action Committee of Publishers for
Peace had organized a rally "by employes of 70 publishing houses
at Dag Ham Hammarskjold Plaza on 47th Street, near the United Nations."[1046]

The National Layman's Digest, citing the conservative magazine *Human Events* on a book auction to finance congressional
"peace candidates" sponsored by the Action Committee of Publishers for Peace, aptly stated that "these were the chief executives, not some down-the-line employees in the publishing
firms. The houses named were Random House, McGraw-Hill,
Yale University Press, Alfred A. Knopf, Farrar, Straus and
Giroux, W. W. Norton and Simon and Schuster."[1047]

Robert Kennedy and Eugene McCarthy:
Wall Street/New Left Candidates

Robert Kennedy had the family investments handled by Lazard
Frères. When Kennedy was looking for investors for federal projects
he went first to Andre Meyer. Meyer agreed to chair the Bedford-
Stuyvesant Corporation (named after a giant ghetto in New York
City) if Kennedy would commit to a stronger stand against the Vi-
etnam War.[1048]

With the assassination of Robert Kennedy in 1968, the New Left
turned to Senator Eugene McCarthy. James Kunen related in *The*

[1045] Raymont, "Book Publishers Act Against War," 26.
[1046] Raymont, "Kazin Delivers Lecture on Flag." The article centered on author Alfred
Kazin's condemnation of the use of the American flag by construction workers as a
symbol of patriotism.
[1047] "Another Volume of Subversion."
[1048] Thomas, *Robert Kennedy*, 325.

Strawberry Statement that business interests sought to use the New Left dialectically to gain support for Eugene McCarthy:

> The only way McCarthy could win is if the crazies and young radicals act up and make Gene look more reasonable. They offered to finance our demonstrations in Chicago. . . . We were also offered Esso (Rockefeller) money. They want us to make a lot of radical commotion so they can look more in the center as they move to the left.[1049]

The anecdote by Kunen is supported by the character of McCarthy's campaign funding. Jon Wiener, a columnist for the left-liberal newspaper *The Nation*, wrote:

> The 1968 McCarthy campaign . . . was not a grassroots, shoestring volunteer effort. In fact, it was the most expensive and best-financed campaign in the history of Democratic primaries until that time. McCarthy's money came primarily not from small donations but rather from big contributors—especially from Wall Street.[1050]

Wiener noted that the news media was entirely positive toward the McCarthy campaign. The finance manager of the campaign was Howard Stein, head of the Dreyfus Corporation, one of the US's major investment funds.[1051]

Stein, one of the most important investors on Wall Street, is portrayed as an idealist. However, the conversations that took place in 1971 between Richard Nixon, Henry Kissinger, and other Nixon aides show that Stein met with Kissinger to discuss support for Eugene McCarthy as part of a strategy. Kissinger commented that he would tell Stein over lunch that McCarthy should be encouraged to form a third party, and urged Stein to fund McCarthy.[1052] Nixon's White House Chief of Staff, H. R. Haldeman, commented to Nixon that Stein was "working on" persuading McCarthy to form a fourth

---

[1049] Kunen, *Strawberry Statement*, 64.
[1050] Wiener, "Eugene McCarthy."
[1051] Ellis and Vertin, *Wall Street People*, vol. II, 71.
[1052] Kutler, *Abuse of Power*, 26–7.

party.[1053] In September 1971 Kissinger met "with a group of Howard Stein's friends"—that is, Wall Street operatives—to discuss support for McCarthy. Kissinger commented that he'd "been building up McCarthy like crazy on the West Coast," and that Stein would do the same on Wall Street.[1054] That Stein is often claimed to have been on President Nixon's "enemy list" is a red herring, and one which was maintained by Stein himself when interviewed by *Bloomberg* in 1993.[1055] Some accounts refer to Stein being an idealist in his backing of Eugene McCarthy and his invitations for Gloria Steinem to speak about feminism to Dreyfus directors.[1056] However, Stein's support for Eugene McCarthy's opposition to the Vietnam War, itself quite sudden in the senator's career, was based on what was "best for the U.S. economy and stock market."[1057]

The '68ers mobilized to riot and adopted the slogan "bring the war home." However, Robert Buzzanco, a leading American scholar on the Vietnam War, opined that it was not the New Left that was the critical factor; rather it was the opposition of Wall Street that led to de-escalation in Vietnam.[1058] Eric R. Smith similarly states that "what finally threatened the Cold War endeavor in Vietnam was business-as-usual, but not necessarily the business of war."[1059] Congress responded not to New Left riots "but to businessmen concerned about the American economy."[1060]

[1053] Ibid., 33.
[1054] Ibid., 34.
[1055] Bruno, "Howard Stein."
[1056] Ibid.
[1057] Ibid.
[1058] Buzzanco, "Ruling Class," 217.
[1059] Smith, "What Would Peace," 215.
[1060] Ibid.

28

The Chicago Seven (Eight):

In 1969, Dell published *The Conspiracy: The Chicago Eight Speak Out*, an anthology of essays by the defendants tried for instigating the riot at the 1968 Democratic National Convention in Chicago.

Attorney General Ramsey Clark discouraged a prosecution, but the decision rested with local government.[1061] Sentiment from influential quarters was against the police and Mayor Richard Daley rather than against the exuberant hijinks of those well-meaning kids from the New Left and Black Panthers. The defense even attempted to call Clark as a witness, but this was rejected by Judge Julius Hoffman. Prior to the riots, Clark had arranged a meeting between Mayor Daley and Assistant Attorney General Roger Wilkins. The latter had found Daley's attitude toward the various elements of the New Left in Chicago "not very satisfactory," although he was "favorably impressed" with SDS organizer Rennie Davis, who coordinated the riots.[1062]

The testimony was heard in private before Judge Hoffman. Eight policemen were also under indictment. Rioters and police were eventually acquitted.

[1061] Ramsey Clark, however, seems a genuine idealist who never sold out or acted as anyone's lackey. For example, he sought to defend Milosevic and Saddam Hussein, and consistently condemned American interventionism.
[1062] Lukas, "Chicago 7 Judge Bars Ramsey Clark as Defense Witness."

The Chicago Eight became the Chicago Seven when Bobby Seale, a leader of the Black Panther Party, was tried separately for contempt of court due to his continuous outbursts, which resulted in Judge Hoffman ordering him to be bound and gagged. They were subsequently eulogized as heroes by establishment media: In 1987 HBO produced a television movie, "Conspiracy: The Trial of the Chicago 8."

Jerry Rubin

Jerry Rubin, one of the Chicago Seven, became a Wall Street stockbroker in 1980. *The Washington Post* featured Rubin in his new persona, describing himself as one of the most famous stockbrokers in the US. After taking a position as securities analyst with John Muir & Co., he described himself as a "venture banker," he is quoted from the Op-Ed page of *The New York Times*, declaring: "'Welcome, Wall Street, here I come!"[1063] The former radical had finally decided that power lay in the boardrooms, not the streets. "Let's make millions of dollars together. . . . Let's make capitalism work for everyone," he exhorted.[1064] *The Post* continued: "He sees himself in the future as a lecturer on venture capital, economics, the stock market. Rubin likes to characterize himself as an 'entrepreneur.' In a half-hour interview he used that word a dozen times."[1065]

Rationalizing his career in terms of social capitalism, Rubin stated: "What I am now is a businessman who wants to make a big impact in the financial world in the '80s and '90s. We're going to do an advertising campaign to make this the most famous brokerage firm in the country." Comparing his time as a Yippie protest leader to his life as a venture banker, he stated: "Then, I saw myself as an outsider. Today, I see myself as an insider. That's the difference."[1066]

Shortly after the interview, Rubin left Muir & Co. to form his own company, which included Muir & Co. as a partner. *The New York Times* reported:

[1063] Ross, "On Wall Street."
[1064] Ibid.
[1065] Ibid.
[1066] Ibid.

Mr. Rubin, 42, said he left his post because "I'm into total money management, not only stock brokerage." The firm, yet to be named and still being formed, will offer such financial services as tax shelters, financial planning, real estate and venture capital investments, said Mr. Rubin. . . .

His decision to join Muir last July was greeted with much media fanfare. "Money is power," Mr. Rubin said in explaining his decision. Last January, Mr. Rubin further cemented his relationship with Wall Street when he passed the National Association of Securities Dealers' examination, to qualify as a registered securities salesman.

More recently, Mr. Rubin has been holding a series of "salons" in his Upper East Side apartment, in which he invites people he would like to meet and asks them to bring their friends. It is, in part, from these "networking social events" that the idea grew to form a private money management firm, he said. As a consultant, Mr. Rubin said he will bring to Muir private investors and private companies that are candidates for new issues.[1067]

The Rubin and Hoffman Traveling Roadshow

Yippie cofounder Paul Krassner wrote of Rubin and Abbie Hoffman:

Indeed, Rubin and Hoffman went on tour with a debate, "The Yippies Versus the Yuppies." At a San Francisco nightclub, I moderated their performance and mentioned, "If Abbie Hoffman were to throw money in the Stock Exchange today,[1068] this time, Jerry Rubin would invest it."[1069]

This was surely the perfect characterization of the capitalist–New Left dichotomy: a sideshow debate between two phony "adversaries" acting out before the public. In a report on the Hoffman/Rubin traveling roadshow, Rubin was quoted as stating in the debate:

[1067] Sloane, "Business People; Jerry Rubin."
[1068] An allusion to Hoffman's stunt in 1967 at the Wall Street Stock Exchange, when he threw money onto the floor from the visitor's gallery.
[1069] Krassner, "Hippies, radicals, pranksters."

We are living in a transformation from industrial to an informational society. We are in an entrepreneurial transformation. Business is changing, and that gives people the chance to be successful.[1070]

Krassner's report continued:

Although Rubin said he remains proud of his past, he contended that the best way to change society is through capitalism rather than radicalism. Both men denied suggestions that their nationwide tour is a calculated attempt to make money, saying the debates are designed to stimulate discussion among people with different political beliefs.[1071]

Yippies and Yuppies

Rubin explained the evolution from Yippie to Yuppie in a lengthy article. It was a natural development for a movement that was based on the primacy of the individual without restraint; the anarchism of the left morphing into the anarchism of the free market. Now the formerly riotous Yippie co-leader and other '68ers were enacting a quieter rebellion, "so, today, I never leave home without my American Express card."[1072]

Today I am one of the leaders of a new movement—one that will have as much impact on the 1980s and 1990s as the long-haired Yippies had on the 1960s. From the ranks of yesterday's rebels has come a new breed of ambitious, fast-track young urban professionals. The insurgents have become the insiders. The Yippies have become the yuppies.

To the Yippies of the '60s, you were square if you didn't smoke marijuana. To the yuppies, you're out of touch if you don't have an answering machine. The Yippie home was filled with posters, macrame and Indian bedspreads. The yuppie home features a

---

[1070] "Hoffman vs. Rubin."
[1071] Ibid.
[1072] Rubin, "Yuppie America's Economic Savior."

computer, a VCR and a personal gym. Yippies camped out on other people's real estate. Yuppies are the ones who now own that real estate.[1073]

Rubin identified the crass materialism of the new generation as having emerged from the New Left to become the epitome of the good consumer. Recall that even Abbie Hoffman had stated in *Steal This Book* that he was a typically American consumer. There was never transcendence for the '68ers, never the depth of repudiation of the system that Evola advised for rightist youth in *Ride the Tiger*. The Yuppie outlook described by Rubin is the same as that used by the system to rationalize the virtues of the free market: we can all be successful if we run fast enough on the economic treadmill; we can all find self-realization via shopping; the quality of life can be enhanced via the marketplace:

> Yuppies believe in meritocracy: If you work and plan to get ahead, you will. Yuppies respect technology: The easier machines make our work, the more we can achieve. Yuppies practice self-reliance: Life is tough? Then do something about it. The yuppie lifestyle of individual entrepreneurship, self-responsibility, personal growth and enjoyment of life is changing the world by example.
>
> At first, it looks as if the only yuppie goals are to make money and pursue pleasures. But that is untrue: Yuppies know there's only one way to make money—by creating products and services other people will want and pay for. You grow rich by improving the quality of life and winning in the marketplace.[1074]

Rubin credited Yuppieism for destroying the traditional family. There is no institution more hated by the left and more demanding of elimination by the oligarchy than the traditional patriarchal family. One of the major laments of Trotsky was that Stalin had reinstated and strengthened the family and motherhood, reversing the early work of the Bolsheviks, who had started replacing the role of parents with the factory crèche and the family hearth with communal factory canteens, so that women had been "liberated" from

---

[1073] Ibid.
[1074] Ibid.

hearth and home and fully integrated into the production process. Trotsky had stated that "the revolution had made a heroic effort to destroy the so-called 'family hearth'—that archaic, stuffy, stagnant institution in which the women of the toiling classes perform galley labour from childhood to death."[1075] The family would be replaced by "the complete absorption of the housekeeping functions of the family by institutions of the socialist society."[1076] This has been precisely the aim of the oligarchy, to replace the family by crèches, to integrate women into the production process, and it explains why the oligarchs, through their tax-exempt foundations, have funded the ironically named women's liberation movement. It was the ideology given social scientific credence by the Critical Theorists, describing the patriarchal family and parenthood as innately fascistic and repressive, and it is why Ford, Soros, and Rockefeller lavish grants on the social sciences.

For Rubin, Yuppieism fulfilled the revolution, and the result was capitalism: "In just a handful of years, then, yuppies have changed the economic, social and familial face of America."[1077]

Rennie Davis

Rennie Davis, SDS organizer, became a venture capitalist. An article on Davis in 2005 stated: "He has consulted and developed business strategies for Fortune 500 companies and is the founder of Ventures for Humanity, a technology development and venture capital company providing resources to commercialize breakthrough technologies."[1078] A *Forbes* article about him commented: "He has appeared on numerous television programs, including the 'Legends' series produced by CBS, Larry King Live, Barbara Walters' and Phil

---

[1075] Trotsky, *Revolution Betrayed*, "Family, Youth and Culture." On the differences between Trotsky and Stalin regarding the family see Bolton, *Stalin*, 13–20.
[1076] Ibid.
[1077] Rubin, "Yuppie America's Economic Savior."
[1078] Moore, "Rennie Davis."

Donahue's shows and on CNN. He has also been financial adviser to various CEOs and senior executives from major companies."[1079]

Davis sought his nirvana via a questionable Hindu guru, an obituary stating:

> As the energy leached out of leftist politics, Mr. Davis's promotional instincts took a surprising turn when he accepted a free plane ticket to India to learn about Guru Maharaj Ji. He later said that the experience had filled him "from head to toe with light." He became a convert and spokesman for Maharaj Ji (who was born Prem Pal Singh Rawat), saying the guru's teachings would provide "a practical way to fulfill all the dreams" of the 1960s, "a practical method to end poverty, racism, sexism, imperialism."
>
> At 32, he proclaimed, "I would cross the planet on my hands and knees to touch his toe."
>
> That movement peaked with an underwhelming turnout at an event called Millennium 73, held at the Astrodome in Houston in November 1973, where Guru Maharaj Ji appeared in a glittering silver suit on a blue plexiglass throne. Mr. Davis had billed it as "the most important gathering of humanity in the history of the world" and said he expected 100,000 people to show up. The police estimated the turnout at 10,000, and even some of the guru's followers began to question the young man's lavish lifestyle, complete with a Rolls-Royce. His celebrity soon waned.[1080]

Rennie Davis had gone from being a dupe of one bogus, world-saving ideal to another. Behind the utopianism of each stood vast amounts of money.

Lee Weiner

Lee Weiner became a marketing data analyst, working with the Anti-Defamation League in New York, an omnipresent Zionist organization specializing in smearing critics of Israel. Of his ADL activities, he stated:

[1079] Hoffman, "Hippie."
[1080] Applebome, "Rennie Davis."

Designed and led ADL's national mail and telemarketing campaigns for fundraising and constituency development with an internal staff of 5; expended donor base from fewer than 75,000 to 250,000, raising almost $7 million dollars annually in contributions; participated in ADL strategic planning as member of senior staff; helped specify and select CRM database software; helped initiate online fundraising'.[1081]

Tom Hayden

Tom Hayden wrote in his autobiography:

> After the Chicago trial experience, I had to acknowledge that the system was beginning to work. It had gone to the brink of breakdown, to the preliminary stages of civil strife, but now there were signs that working within the fabric of society was producing change. Now it was time, I thought, to make an adjustment to reality. But were those who went through trauma and trial capable of returning to reform? The difference that bewitched my "religious conversion" and Rennie's [Davis] was that I was a "born again" Middle American, emotionally charged by my reacceptance in the political mainstream. . . .
>
> Millions of Americans had been changed by the decade, and I felt energized by the new possibilities of the mainstream.[1082]

Hayden was elected to the California State Assembly and later the California Senate. As he said in *Reunion* several decades later, the New Left revolt had spread across the world, suddenly, in some mysterious way. Hayden had from the start seen how the CIA operated among students, and that it had kickstarted the career of Gloria Steinem. He saw that the system was working in the direction of the left. Did he not ponder that perhaps bringing society to the brink of breakdown might have been something stage-managed to push Middle America in a leftward direction that seemed "mainstream" by comparison to the most radical elements of the counterculture? He

---

[1081] From Weiner's LinkedIn profile.
[1082] Hayden, *Reunion*, 465.

had gone through the process, becoming part of that new mainstream he had helped to create.

The New Yorker reported on the marriage of Hayden and Jane Fonda's son, actor Troy Garity, to Black actress Simone Bent in 2007:

> Speaking off the cuff, Garity's father, the political activist and politician Tom Hayden, who was Fonda's second husband (neither parent wanted Troy to bear the weight of a famous last name), said that he was especially happy about his son's union with Bent, who is black, because, among other things, it was "another step in a long-term goal of mine: the peaceful, nonviolent disappearance of the white race."[1083]

Few statements could be clearer or more explicit. Here is evident the psychosis of the '68ers, starkly unencumbered by rationalizations. *The final goal: the disappearance of the White race.*

Eulogizing Hayden on his death in 2016, Bill Clinton wrote: "Hillary and I knew him for more than thirty years and valued both his words of support and his criticism."[1084] For his part, Hayden supported the presidential campaigns of Obama and Hillary Clinton, both the choices of Wall Street.[1085] A Bernie Sanders supporter, Norman Solomon, made some perceptive comments regarding Hayden's backing of Hillary Clinton: "And Tom Hayden, who we just heard — who has really saddened me and many other people because he's thrown his lot in with the war hawk and corporatist Hillary Clinton."[1086] Hayden was challenged:

> I think probably for people who are familiar with your work, this would probably be the biggest area of surprise hearing that you're

---

[1083] Als, "Queen Jane, Approximately."

[1084] Clinton, "Statement from President Clinton."

[1085] Obama raised $45 million for his presidential campaign, three times more than his Republican opponent, John McCain. Funding for the Obama campaign came from Lazard Freres, Goldman Sachs, Coca-Cola, Pepsi, Dow Chemical, Salomon Bros., Rand Corp., Merrill Lynch, and Citigroup. See Bolton, "Obama." Hillary Clinton received $9 million from George Soros in her presidential campaign. There were many others, largely under the auspices of the Democratic Alliance, a cabal of wealthy patrons of the left.

[1086] Solomon, "With Great Respect."

intending to cast your vote for Hillary Clinton. By many measures she is the most hawkish major party candidate left in the race, even when compared to Donald Trump. She supported the invasion of Afghanistan, she supported the invasion of Iraq, she beat the drums of war around Iran and Libya. Even Donald Trump at this point is coming across as more of an isolationist than she is. How do you square supporting her with your principles?[1087]

Hayden responded with puerility: "Well, Trump is for the revival of torture to the extreme, let's not forget what Trump stands for. And he's a belligerent, irrational candidate, potentially with a nuclear capability."[1088] It was a replay of the smears that had been vented against Barry Goldwater, invoking the specter of a global nuclear holocaust and the establishment of a Nazi regime. But the uncomfortable truth that Norman Solomon was unlikely to accept was that it was historically the American right that eschewed America's involvement in foreign wars, founded on the isolationist doctrine of George Washington himself.

[1087] Ibid.
[1088] Ibid.

29

The Explosive Issue of Student Restlessness

Paris '68

Dany Cohn-Bendit recalled that the worldwide '68 revolt was more "American" than the European New Left cared to admit. He was in the US from 1965 to 1966 and met Mark Rudd, organizer of the SDS at Columbia University. Cohn-Bendit stated "But essentially the revolt was spurred by the idea of a counterculture, which was mainly carried via rock music. 'Woodstock Nation': that was the myth of a new America, and we were all for it."[1089]

The puerility of Cohn-Bendit's "Woodstock Nation" ideology was transplanted to France, where the adolescent preoccupation with sex metamorphosized into a revolutionary ideology and became the *cause célèbre* that ignited the Paris revolt: Cohn-Bendit occupied the girl's dormitory at the University of Nanterre, with the demand that the dormitories should be assessable to male students. Rumors that he would be expelled led to a student revolt resulting in the upheavals of May 1968 that brought the De Gaulle government to the brink of collapse. The month previously, Cohn-Bendit's American colleague, Mark Rudd, became the leader of the student revolt at Columbia.

Although mostly remembered for his leadership of the 1968 riots in France, Cohn-Bendit was a German citizen residing in France. Like

---

[1089] Cohn-Bendit and Leggewie, "1968: Power to the Imagination."

the German youth of the '68 revolt, including the notorious Red Army Faction, he saw his existence as defined by Hitlerism:

> I do feel that I'm rooted in Judaism, but in a cultural, not a religious sense. At the center of it all is my parents' story of escape: as German Jews and political refugees they had to hide from the Nazis and their collaborators. That's something I cannot shake off.[1090]

De Gaulle Opposes US Hegemony

Suspicions of the CIA backing the '68 revolt in France persist. Charles de Gaulle was the only Western statesman of the time challenging US global hegemony. He withdrew France from NATO military command. In 1967 he put an arms embargo on Israel and cultivated relations with the Arab world.[1091] He worked for a neutral, united Europe. Perhaps most of all, Gaullist France had resisted the domination of the US dollar over the world economy.

Morgan Sportès described de Gaulle as the real rebel in May '68, not Cohn-Bendit. Sportès writes of the time:

> In the USA, an anti-Gaullist press campaign of incredible violence and stupidity was in full swing. . . . The only thing for which the Americans have never forgiven him, Pierre Messmer told me shortly before his death, is not his exit from NATO's integrated defence, nor his famous speech denouncing the war in Vietnam, but it is his questioning of the "exorbitant privilege of the dollar."
>
> The press from across the Atlantic screamed loudly, denouncing "Gaullefinger!" In addition, he was trying to build a Europe "independent of the two blocs," that would include eastern countries. In the same spirit he had developed an "all-round" defence, his nuclear missiles to be turned eastward but also to the west (General Ailleret implemented this policy, and would die opportunely in a plane crash in March 68, on the eve of the famous month of May).[1092]

[1090] Ibid.
[1091] "See French Embargo."
[1092] Sportès, "LE MAI 1968."

The journalist Vincent Nouzille, who spent five years researching CIA archives for the period from 1958 to 1981, found that five French embassies in Latin America were instructed to "fend off U.S. policy in the Dominican Republic."[1093] This was relayed to the US in May 1965 by Jean de La Grandville, head of France's Atomic and Space Affairs Department, who was working for the CIA. Nouzille revealed that Washington encouraged opponents of de Gaulle, welcomed France's destabilization in May 1968, and even prepared a secret plan for military intervention. The US backed the Socialist leader Francois Mitterrand, who aimed to unite the left and attain the presidency.

US and Soviet Responses to May '68

In June 1968, Cohn-Bendit said to eminent journalist Hervé Bourges, who later became France's ambassador to UNESCO:

> It seems that the CIA has been interested in us lately: some news-papers and American associations, subsidiaries and intermediaries of the CIA, have offered us significant sums. . . . The feelings of the CIA with regard to de Gaulle, we know through a report by Richard Helms to President Johnson on May 30, 1968 denouncing the general as a dictator who will stay in power by pouring rivers of blood.[1094]

While Cohn-Bendit berated Herbert Marcuse on suspicions of being a CIA agent,[1095] he was consciously willing to pursue a primarily CIA agenda in trying to topple de Gaulle, one of the few real obstacles to US global hegemony.

[1093] Nouzille, *Des secrets si bien gardés.*

[1094] Farkas, *La Pavé.*

[1095] A Jewish source commented on the antagonism between the two Jewish New Left eminences at the time, regarding Marcuse's wartime employment as an analyst by the OSS (predecessor of the CIA): "When Herbert Marcuse, one of the leading lights of the Frankfurt School, held a talk in Rome in 1968, he was interrupted constantly by Daniel Cohn-Bendit. The German-French student leader, who today is a Green Party politician, demanded that Marcuse give an accounting of his 'scandalous past' as a CIA operative during the Second World War." Sattler, "Philosophers Beat Hitler."

A feature in *The Irish Times* is worth citing in full. Referring to the examination of CIA and Soviet archives by French journalist Vincent Jauvert, it was shown that the CIA regarded de Gaulle as an enemy of US foreign policy, while the USSR, which de Gaulle naively assumed to be behind the leftist revolt as part of a communist plot, appealed to the French Communist Party to try and stymie the chaos:

> In mid-Cold War, the US and Soviet intelligence agencies watched the May 1968 events in France with alarm. The French journalist Vincent Jauvert of the *Nouvel Observateur* went to archives in Texas and Moscow to search out the CIA and KGB reports of the time. The documents he found are startling.
>
> Far from supporting Gen. Charles de Gaulle's right-wing regime, the US blamed him for the anarchy in France and apparently hoped the Socialist patriarch, Pierre Mendes France, would take power. On May 30th, 1968, the head of the CIA, Richard Helms, sent a five-page secret memorandum to President Lyndon Johnson. De Gaulle had just returned from Germany, dissolved the National Assembly and vowed on television to save France from the threat of "totalitarian Communism."
>
> Helms was merciless in his criticism of the General who had two years earlier expelled NATO headquarters from Paris. "The Gaullists have repeatedly violated and perverted their own constitution," he reported to President Johnson. "They have treated even the moderate opposition with disdain and indifference."
>
> France was "on the knife-edge of disaster," Helms said. "By refusing to resign, de Gaulle has taken on the workers and students frontally. He has reverted to type, the powerful, challenging autocrat. He has come out of his corner swinging defiantly at opponents who thought that they had him on the ropes."
>
> The General had divided France into those who were with him and his enemies—all considered Communist dupes. "When, how and if a head-on collision between right and left will occur is not yet clear, but a spark could set it off," the CIA chief reported.
>
> To force de Gaulle to resign, 10 million striking workers might cut gas and electricity supplies and sabotage the factories they were occupying. If they did so, de Gaulle would have to call in the army—which Helms expected to obey orders. The CIA chief said de Gaulle could break the back of the rebellion if the labourers returned to work. "If not, civil conflict of major proportions will almost

certainly ensue." In the short term, he thought the government could restore order and essential public services "but only at the cost of poisoning political life for the indefinite future. Whatever the short-term outcome," Helms concluded, "France faces a period of unrest and, eventually, even civil war."

French officials believed the French Communist Party (PCF) and their Soviet backers were fomenting revolution. Nothing could have been further from the truth, as shown by secret telegrams sent in May 1968 by the Soviet ambassador to Paris, Valerian Zorine. In the words of the French historian, Jean Lacouture, Zorine had "the face of a starving alligator." The USSR's former ambassador to the UN Security Council, Zorine was also a member of the central committee of the Communist Party of the Soviet Union.

After a lengthy meeting at the embassy with the treasurer of the PCF, Gaston Plissonier, Zorine addressed the memo recently unearthed by Vincent Jauvert to only two people: the Foreign Minister, Andrei Gromyko and Boris Ponomarev, the head of the international department of the Soviet Communist Party.

Together, Plissonier and Zorine concluded that May 1968 must not be a new Bolshevik revolution. "The student movement has no serious prospects since the French students are mainly from the lower and middle bourgeoisie," Zorine wrote. "Those from the working class represent only 10 per cent, and what is more, the students are in the grip of leftist and Trotskyist elements."

The French government had failed to understand how much the Communists disliked their left-wing cousins. Ironically, Moscow wanted to keep the right-wing de Gaulle—the bug-bear of Washington—in power. Throughout the secret telegrams, ambassador Zorine railed against "leftists." A few days earlier, the student leader Daniel Cohn-Bendit had pushed his way in front of Communist demonstrators in a march, saying he was happy to be ahead of "the Stalinist toad."

The strategy of the PCF, related by Plissonier to Zorine, was "on the one hand to support the students against police repression and on the other hand to isolate the leftists who are trying to provoke further clashes with the police."

The PCF and its Soviet backers wanted to maintain control of the French working classes. Despite its revolutionary heritage, the PCF hoped to break out of its "internal exile" by consolidating ties with the Socialists and sharing power with them in government. The French Communists were deeply alarmed that de Gaulle named them as the enemy in his May 30th address. The last thing they wanted was to lose their "respectability" by provoking the intervention of the army, so Plissonier promised Zorine that gas and electricity workers would follow orders from the Communist trade union, the CGT, not to interrupt supplies. "In the absence of a revolutionary situation," Zorine concluded, "if the PCF had taken the path which the leftist elements wanted to drag them into, the Party would have doomed itself to destruction."[1096]

US Visas for the New Left

One might wonder about the danger that leading New Left agitators actually posed to the establishment when they could travel to the US on State Department visas in the aftermath of the Paris revolt, and when the streets and campuses of the US were being convulsed.

In 1968 a US State Department memorandum was leaked to the conservative publication *Human Events*, "approving entrance of foreign student revolutionaries into the United States."[1097] The memorandum appeared just prior to the famous riots at the DNC in Chicago. The proposals had been drafted by Deputy Under Secretary of State Charles Bohlen, and approved on August 1st by Under Secretary Nicholas Katzenbach.

The Bohlen-Katzenbach memo stated that if radical leaders such as Rudi Dutschke or Daniel Cohn-Bendit were invited by New Left leaders to the US they should be permitted entry. The memo referred to "the general encouragement of our government for informal contacts between U.S. and foreign youth leaders," and that the likes of Dutschke and Cohn-Bendit should be no exception.[1098] Evidently, the longstanding policy of encouraging dialogue between leftist student and youth leaders throughout the world had not changed, despite of the turmoil that was taking place on US streets and campuses.

Human Events gave the example of Jean Dube, a leader of the Trotskyite Revolutionary Communist Youth (JCR) who had started a

---

[1096] Marlowe, "Paris Provoked CIA and KGB Alarm."
[1097] "Importing Student Subversives."
[1098] Ibid.

three-week tour of the US and Canada on August 8th. He was seeking support for jailed leaders of the riots in France, in which he had played a role.

The US State Department granted a visa in 1969 to Karl Dietrich Wolff, one of the most prominent German revolutionists, to lecture on US campuses. Subpoenaed before the US Senate Internal Security Subcommittee, Wolff obstructed and grandstanded and attempted to make himself appear a martyr, claiming that he had been refused a visa on multiple occasions. Senator Sourwine retorted that Wolff's application for a visa had been referred to the US State Department in Washington and that it had been granted in January 1969.[1099] After one day of testimony, Wolff departed the United States. A memorandum appended to the Senate committee's report stated that in his application for a visa Wolff had been invited to the US by the New School for Social Research in New York City. Wolff had abandoned his application to visit in September, but reapplied and was granted a visa in January 1969 for one year. At the Senate subcommittee hearing, Wolff postured to the public gallery, claiming that he had been harassed and denied visa applications, regardless of being free to travel around the US lecturing at campuses. The memorandum stated:

> It was determined by a competent authority, according to report, that Wolff was not a Communist, did not belong to any class prohibited from entry into the United States or ineligible for a visa, and that he should, therefore, be issued a visa.[1100]

The memorandum stated that Wolff was a former national president of the Socialist German Students Federation, "a militant leftist oriented student organization in West Berlin and the Federal Republic of Germany. He had attended the World Youth Festival at Sofia, "and current travel to the United States and Canada designed to raise funds for legal assistance for individuals arrested during demonstrations in Germany."[1101] The memorandum stated that it was "noted"

[1099] *Testimony of Karl Dietrich Wolff*, 19.
[1100] Ibid.
[1101] Ibid.

that Wolff had accompanied Cohn-Bendit and his lawyer during Cohn-Bendit's trial in Frankfurt in January 1969, and that "Cohn-Bendit is one of the leading student revolutionaries in Europe."[1102] Wolff entered the US in January 1969, and was placed on "parole status," during which he was listed as lecturing students and faculty at at least thirteen separate major US universities.[1103] At some of these meetings, Wolff advocated armed revolt.

When it was determined that Wolff was "not a Communist," presumably what was meant was that he was not an apologist of the USSR. During the meetings he described himself as a Marxist, and advocated violence. This did not disqualify him from entering the United States. The year before, the US State Department had already determined that far-left youth organizers were permitted entry into the US, as part of a program to encourage exchanges between youth organizers. Wolff met the criterion as one such youth organizer.

Soviet Repudiation of New Left

Wolff's reception at the World Youth Festival in Bulgaria, mentioned in the Senate committee's appended memorandum, was far removed from the relative freedom he had in touring US campuses the following year. A CIA intelligence briefing remarked that there had been tensions between the pro-Soviet delegates and the delegations from Czechoslovakia (then attempting to break from the Soviet bloc), Yugoslavia, and Israel. The memo stated that Bulgarian authorities had suppressed a demonstration of delegates—mainly West Europeans—from staging an anti-Vietnam war protest outside the US embassy in Sofia. Notably, "Radical West German student leader Karl Dietrich Wolff declared that the demonstrators were also protesting the lack of wide political discussion at the festival."[1104]

The CIA review concluded by remarking on the World Youth Festival: "Before the festival ends on 6 August, Bulgarian officials may find it necessary to employ even harsher measures to subdue

---

[1102] Ibid.
[1103] Ibid., 27–28.
[1104] CIA, "Youth Festival."

discordant elements in Sofia, especially if the explosive issue of student restlessness is surfaced."[1105]

Barbara W. Bright attended the Ninth World Youth Festival as an observer for the Institute of Current World Affairs (ICWA), and was accredited as a reporter for *Newsweek*. She commented in a report to the ICWA director, Richard H. Nolte, that the delegations from Czechoslovakia and West Germany were regarded with particular suspicion by the Bulgarian authorities.[1106] The German delegation was headed by Wolff.[1107] Bright stated that Wolff, leading a group of delegates from Western Europe, "seized the Vietnam issue as a pretext for protesting the absence of free discussion at the festival." While the delegates led by Wolff were a minority faction, their opponents were labeled Stalinists. However, Wolff was supported by West Germany's national student council, the youth wing of the Social Democratic Party, and a liberal student organization. Ironically, the Bulgarian authorities formed a thick line around the US embassy. The Wolff group formed a sit-in, but the demonstration disintegrated when there was disagreement as to whether the group should sit-in or march. Wolff was pushed aside by the Bulgarian police.[1108] Wolff, disheveled, returned, and the demonstrators, which included Czechs, Americans from the SDS, Yugoslavians, Iranians, Italians, and Argentinians, reassembled and were addressed by Wolff.[1109] It was resolved that a "teach-in" would be held in front of the dormitory of the West German delegation, in what Bright called the "beginning of the snit-festival."[1110]

While the Czechoslovak delegation caused trouble of its own, "the New Left student groups, led by West Germany, stirred the political brew among the delegates from capitalist and 'third world' countries."[1111] At the "teach-in," delegates from Western Europe, the US, and several Latin American countries "heard students protest

---

[1105] Ibid.
[1106] All of her posts and dispatches can be found at Institute of Current World Affairs.
[1107] Bright, "World Youth Festival I," 4.
[1108] Ibid., 7–8.
[1109] Ibid., 9.
[1110] Ibid., 10.
[1111] Ibid.

against the Festival's dogmatic inflexibility."[1112] To a question by Bright on why he bothered attending the Festival, a delegate from the German student league said that the "plan was to make contacts," and to "break the form of the Festival."[1113] The teach-in was the first of several held by "anti-authoritarian" delegations for the rest of the Festival.[1114] The Wolff-led faction of delegations was decidedly pro-Mao, and as a further provocation Wolff paid a "courtesy call" to the Chinese embassy, while other students had procured Maoist literature from the embassy.[1115]

Wolff had succeeded in causing a great deal of disruption at the Festival, and was able to play on the antagonism of Czechoslovakia, Romania, and Yugoslavia toward the Soviet bloc.[1116] Barbara Bright concluded by wondering whether "the anti-authoritarian rebellion of the West European New Left didn't leave its mark on Soviet party-liners . . . and if the totalitarian rigidity of 'such crap' [paraphrasing a comment from a delegate] didn't shed a little light on practical Marxist politics for some idealistic Western students."[1117]

Given the long history of CIA and State Department involvement in subverting the world youth festivals with leftist students, it seems plausible that the US foreign policy establishment (a few conservative politicians notwithstanding) saw Wolff and his ilk as valuable if unwitting assets in the Cold War, regardless of any amount of impotent anti-American and anti-NATO rhetoric. Wolff and those like him had inflicted more harm on the Soviet bloc than any of their words and actions relative to the US. The Bulgarians regarded these New Left students as CIA provocateurs.

[1112] Ibid.
[1113] Bright, "World Youth Festival II," 3.
[1114] Ibid.
[1115] Ibid., 4.
[1116] Ibid., 5.
[1117] Ibid., 6.

Cohn-Bendit "Unwelcome"

Cohn-Bendit had been condemned by Bulgaria as an agent of Zionists and of the CIA the month prior to the World Youth Festival. In the CIA intelligence briefing for June 1968, the Bulgarian response was commented on:

> Danny the Red is getting it from all sides—even the Bulgarians. A 22 June article in the Bulgarian youth paper described Daniel Cohn-Bendit as a "German Jew" in a class with Maoists and Trotskyites, and suggested that he may be taking orders from the Zionists in the employ of the West German Government and the CIA. This exceptionally sharp attack is probably intended to warn Bulgarian youth to stay clear of such rabble rousers and also to serve notice on Cohn-Bendit that he is distinctly unwelcome at the upcoming World Youth Festival at Sofia.[118]

It is notable that the CIA reported that the Bulgarian authorities seemed to be warning Cohn-Bendit to stay away from the World Youth Festival. Yet syndicated columnist Henry J. Taylor, for example, citing FBI reports, was claiming that the student agitation was being run and funded from China, the USSR, and Cuba. Such reports served as a means to distract attention from the actual centers of the New Left. Although the New Left did idolize Mao, Castro and Che, the USSR was not included for praise in their liturgy.

"False Prophet Marcuse and his Vociferous Disciples"

While Marcuse, like other Critical Theorists, had launched his career as an exile from Germany through the sponsorship of the State Department and the Rockefeller Foundation, the USSR had him pegged with precision. In June 1968, at the height of the New Left tumult, *Pravda* ran a lengthy analysis of Marcuse by Yury Zhukov, the newspaper's foreign affairs commentator, entitled "Werewolves

---

[118] "Danny the Red Working for CIA?"

—on the False Prophet Marcuse and His Vociferous Disciples." Zhukov said that the "German-American professor" had "emerged from the darkness of obscurity" to have his name "endlessly repeated in the Western press . . . being publicized as if he were a movie star . . . and his books as if they were the latest brand of tooth paste or razor blades."

Zhukov referred to "the three Ms": Marx, Marcuse, and Mao, whose names were being chanted in unison by students across the world. Now even Mao Zedong was considered worthy of glorification in the bourgeois press, with Zhukov referring to the regurgitation of the "three M formula" as "no accident." Of Mao, he referred to a secret memo from the director of the US Information Service (USIS), exposed in the *Ceylon Tribune* in February 1967, stating that USIS employees across the world "must take advantage of every opportunity to strengthen the position of Mao's supporters," since their activities were aimed against the USSR and Moscow-aligned parties.

At this time *Soviet News* had also reported:

> The *Washington Post* has said that officials in Washington believe that Mao is serving American interests and they are therefore even thinking of cultivating Maoism as a means of bringing pressure to bear on Moscow. The magazine *United States News and World Report* has directly stated in this connection that American officials tend to prefer a victory for Mao Tse-tung in his struggle to destroy more moderate elements [in China], because that would mean more trouble for Soviet Russia.[119]

Returning to Zhukov, he referred to a speech delivered at a UNESCO celebration in France on the 150th anniversary of Marx's birth, where Marcuse talked of what has now become familiarly called identity politics—that the working class had lost its revolutionary potential, which must be assumed by racial minorities and youth. Zhukov regarded Marcuse as encouraging the alienation of youth from the working class in opposing capitalism. In this vein, Zhukov cited *The New York Times* as having referred to this as a process of "decommunizing Marx," *The Times* approvingly referring to Marcuse's Parisian

---

[119] "Anti-Soviet Policy of Mao Tse-tung."

disciples as raising the "black flag of anarchy, not the red flag of communism." Zhukov stated that Marcuse's biography was receiving considerable publicity in the major press, pointing out that he had served with US intelligence and then in the Russian Institute at Harvard as an analyst.

Zhukov identified the basis of Marcuse's ideology as being to replace class conflict with "generational conflict"—young people must struggle against adults "everywhere" was Marcuse's message. Organization is eschewed in favor of "spontaneous rebellion," based around "a small handful of intellectuals." Marcuse claims, stated Zhukov, that industrialization must be rejected in order that those who have stood outside the process—"racial minorities, hardcore unemployed and lawbreakers"—can be mobilized, "and at the top, privileged cultural figures who are able to avoid subjugation." Zhukov had realized the character of Marcuse and the nihilistic ideology of the New Left; what Marx and Engels rejected as the *lumpenproletariat* was co-opted by those uppermost—"privileged"—echelons, those who control the purse strings and fund these movements. Zhukov stated that the working class is thereby excluded, remaining in servitude, while the privileged few use the *lumpenproletariat* of what has now become "identity politics" to extend their control.

Interestingly, Marx and Engels regarded the *lumpenproletariat* as the element of the social strata which can most readily be bought off to serve a ruling class. What Marcuse's "privileged" represents is an oligarchy. The New Left was intended to mobilize this *lumpenproletariat* to serve an oligarchy and squeeze the great majority—condemned as "bourgeois"—between them.

Zhukov saw this as being aligned with Maoism. Although the New Left was verbally abusive toward the "imperialists," wrote Zhukov, "the governments of the capitalist states have very tolerant attitudes toward dissemination of [Maoist] 'ideas,' and at the same time toward the activities of Marcuse and his vociferous disciples as well."

Zhukov saw this "ultraleftist," "anarchistic" doctrine as being useful to the establishment in sowing "discord and confusion," with the aid of Maoism, among "inexperienced young people" to make them "blind tools of provocations."

Zhukov stated that Cohn-Bendit, while living off a stipend from the West German state, organized students violently against the French Communist Party, and attempted to disrupt mass protests, shouting provocative slogans. Zhukov stated that Benoit Franchon, chairman of the General Confederation of Labor, speaking to workers at the Renault Automobile Plant on May 27th, claimed that the CIA was inciting the student riots.

Prague Spring

On July 28th, 1968, the Soviet-sponsored World Youth Festival started in Sofia. Elements of the Italian delegation wanted to hold a "Day of European Youth Revolt," but the organizers vetoed the proposition. This reflected the conservative perspective of the Soviet bloc toward the New Left and the riots that were spreading across the world. The CIA report to Lyndon Johnson referred to this when alluding to the "conservative men in the Kremlin."[1120] In an annex to the daily brief the CIA referred to the concern of the Kremlin at the "ferment brewing for the World Youth Festival."[1121] It reflected a division among the communist parties that eventuated as "Eurocommunism" and set those parties, particularly at first in France and Italy, on a course that was more liberal than Marxist. Eventually even the former communist parties of the Soviet bloc embraced the whole gamut of "political correctness" and the ideology that had been espoused during the 1960s by Marcuse.[1122]

The Kremlin response to the New Left riots in the West was described as "apprehensive." Quoting Party Secretary Demichev, speaking at a social science conference on June 19, the CIA report stated that he described the student revolt as that of "revisionist ideologists" trying to replace class struggle with struggle between

---

[1120] CIA, "Italy: Summary."
[1121] Ibid.
[1122] An indication of this is the affiliation of many former communist parties, renamed "social democratic," with the Progressive Alliance and the Socialist International. See Bolton, "Labour Party's Communist Allies."

generations, proclaiming "young people to be the only true revolutionary force of our time," as the CIA paraphrased it.[1123]

After alluding to the Zhukov condemnation of Marcuse, the CIA report referred to Soviet leaders as regarding Soviet youth as having become "susceptible to the temptations of student radicalism in Europe."[1124] "Youth and teacher conferences throughout the Soviet Union have made the younger generation the focal point of current efforts to shore up ideological defenses against the unorthodox concepts seeping in from the outside."[1125] The CIA report quoted Demichev as stating that the Soviet state's initiatives for youth were intended to instill "a purposeful, ordered system of views."[1126] The CIA's optimistic assessment was that such efforts would lead to the alienation of youth from the regime.[1127]

The most significant incursion of the New Left into the Soviet bloc had been the Prague Spring, beginning in March 1968. Hence the situation at the World Youth Festival soon after had been particularly intense between pro- and anti-Soviet factions. Marcuse was among the first to condemn the Soviet invasion of Czechoslovakia in suppressing the revolt, writing critically of other academics who were tardy in responding:

> My position is a matter of the public record. In fact, I did not wait, and 12 hours after the invasion, I, together with philosophers from Yugoslavia, Hungary, Czechoslovakia and the Western world, signed a statement which unequivocally condemned the invasion. The statement addressed itself to the Warsaw Pact nations, and was published in the European press. Moreover, I myself, as an individual, was interviewed, in the days that followed, by various European journalists, and my statements condemning the invasion were again printed in a number of European papers. I have also stated my view on the Czechoslovak crisis in an interview with *L'Express*, the French weekly, which will appear on September 16.[1128]

[1123] "Moscow Turns Wary Eye of New Left," 5.
[1124] Ibid.
[1125] Ibid.
[1126] Ibid.
[1127] Ibid., 6.
[1128] Kellner, *New Left and the 1960s*, 118.

Marcuse was following the line he had always taken as an anti-Soviet analyst brought to the US by the State Department and the Rockefeller Foundation and employed by the establishment.

The USSR and its allies saw the Prague revolt as having a significant Zionist presence. There had been collusion between Zionist interests and US agencies, according to Soviet allegations. This suggested a repeat of the accusations of US/Zionist subversion of the Communist Party in Czechoslovakia in 1952, when eleven of the fourteen defendants accused of treason, including party general secretary and vice-premier Rudolf Slansky, were Jews. They were condemned for collusion with Zionism and Israel, and most were hanged.[1129]

Caution: Zionism! by Yuri Ivanov was a detailed exposition of these allegations. Ivanov drew alleged connections to the "Main Documentary Center" in Vienna, which was presumably a reference to the Jewish Documentation Centre founded by Simon Wiesenthal. Ivanov alleged that the JDC was a front for "a large espionage organization created by the International Zionist Organization and the CIA, acting in many cases under orders from the Israeli Embassy in Vienna."[1130] Networks of Czechoslovak dissidents were stated to have been set up by Zionist organizations in both Israel and Czechoslovakia.

Although Simon Wiesenthal stated that an inflammatory letter (mentioned by Ivanov) addressed to Czechoslovak Jews and allegedly signed by him on JDC letterhead was a forgery,[1131] there is evidence for other Soviet contentions, and events described by Ivanov, regarding collusion between Zionists and student organizations in Prague in 1968. Paul Lendvai, while repudiating any such allegations about "Zionist plots," seeing these as a symptom of Soviet anti-Semitism, wrote that at student protests held on May Day, youths carried Israeli flags and banners reading "Let Israel Live."[1132] Students and faculty at Prague's Charles University issued a petition calling for the restoration of diplomatic relations with Israel. This was followed by

---

1129 "Communists Aped Hitler," 1.
1130 Ivanov, *Caution: Zionism!*, 128.
1131 "Wiesenthal Says 'Zionist Plot.'"
1132 Lendvai, *Anti-Semitism in Eastern Europe*, 260.

an appeal in the newspaper, *Student*, which announced the formation of a "Union of the Friends of Israel."

The Writer's Union was said by Ivanov and other Soviet commentators to have been a center of Zionist activities against the state. Again, there is confirmation of this from Zionist sources. The *Australian Jewish Times* identified the "key role" played by Eduard Goldstuecker,[1133] in the liberalizing government of Alexander Dubček, while drawing parallels to the Prague trials of 1952, in which Goldstuecker had been a defendant:

> Combatting anti-Semitism was a deliberate policy of the Dubček program. The new Government appointed on April 8 of this year, was given an action program which affirmed "that all manifestations of anti-Semitism and racism will be combatted." This policy was personified in the key role played recently by Professor Eduard Goldstuecker. A victim of the Slansky trials, Goldstuecker became president of the Writers' Union on January 24, 1968.[1134]

It should be noted that Goldstuecker was a vice-chancellor of Charles University, which, as stated above, was the center of both anti-Soviet and pro-Israel agitation.

The *Australian Jewish Times* alluded to a "continuing theme" of the Dubček government being the "rehabilitation" of Jews purged in 1952:

> Another continuing theme was the campaign to rehabilitate Jewish communists liquidated in the Stalinist purges of the early '50s. There were repeated calls for the rehabilitation of Slansky, and the Government agreed to draft a special bill. Slansky, the first secretary of the Communist Party, had been accused of high treason, espionage, sabotage and participating in an alleged Jewish plot to overthrow the Government. Eleven out of the 14 defendants in the main trial and several others in the subsidiary trial were Jews. Eight of the 11 Jews and three non-Jews were executed.[1135]

[1133] Goldstuecker was a member of the interim Czech National Council intended to govern Czechoslovakia until general elections that had been scheduled for 1969. In 1949 he had assumed the position of Czechoslovakia's first Ambassador to Israel.
[1134] "Fears for Czech Jews," 1.
[1135] Ibid.

Ivanov and other Soviet commentators were also correct in stating
that the Writers' Union, headed by Goldstuecker, was at the center
of Zionist agitation, particularly among the youth. Again, Zionist
sources confirm this, and allude to connections between the forces
of "liberalization" and support for Israel:

> Distress was reported growing this week among Czech intellectuals
> and particularly the youth over the Government's acceptance of a
> clause condemning Israeli aggression in the communique issued
> last week at the conference of Eastern European Communist Party
> leaders at Bratislava. Some circles are sharply critical of party leader
> Alexander Dubček whom they believe should have objected to the
> anti-Israel wording. Many of the 6,000 participants in the recent
> Communist Party Congress have expressed such opinions in inter-
> views published in the evening newspaper *Vecerni Praha*. But reli-
> able Government sources told the JTA unofficially that the denun-
> ciation of Israeli aggression was inserted only because Czechoslo-
> vakia is dependent on the Soviet Union in foreign policy matters
> and could not act as freely as it would have liked. The objections
> among supporters of the Dubček regime are attributable to a large
> measure of goodwill toward Israel in many Czech circles despite
> the fact that diplomatic relations with that country were severed
> after the Six-Day War and have not been restored.
>
> But even more evident is the feeling that with the growing in-
> ternal liberalization, Czechoslovakia should have struck out for a
> more independent foreign policy and that the Bratislava conference
> and the earlier talks with Soviet and other Communist chiefs at Ci-
> erna was the time to do it. Many Czechs are still fearful that a deal
> was made with the Soviets at Cierna despite official assurances to
> the contrary, in general, they believe that a foreign policy domi-
> nated by dogmatic Stalinist prejudices such as hostility toward Is-
> rael is not compatible with the liberalization at home.
>
> Meanwhile, a group of prominent Czech writers met here to
> discuss the new political situation. Among them were Ladislav
> Mnacko and Eduard Goldstuecker, a Jew who is chairman of the
> Czech writers union. It was learned that many in this group believe
> that Czechoslovakia should not have agreed to the anti-Israel

phraseology. Mnacko, a non-Jew, went into self-exile in Israel when Czechoslovakia broke diplomatic relations with Israel.[136]

Soviet news agency TASS remarked:

> Israel and international Zionism had watched developments in Czechoslovakia closely since January 1968. . . . Israel as well as Zionist organizations in the United States and the West European countries have allocated huge sums to finance internal opposition in Czechoslovakia.[137]

Plastic People and the Legacy of '68 in Czechoslovakia

In January 1968 the First Secretary of the Communist Party had been voted out, in favor of Alexander Dubček, a liberalizing reformist. Dubček eliminated state supervision over the arts. This allowed for the prompt entry of the West's cultural pathogens, which the Soviet bloc had realized would have a devastating impact since 1949, when, in a major article, F. Chernov condemned the infiltration of cosmopolitanism into Soviet arts, sciences, and history.[138]

Chernov began by referring to articles appearing in *Pravda* and *Kultura i Zhizn* ("Culture and Life"), which "unmasked an unpatriotic group of theatre critics, of rootless cosmopolitans, who came out against Soviet patriotism, against the great cultural achievements of the Russian people and of other peoples in our country."[139] Chernov described this coterie as "rootless cosmopolitans" and "propagandists for decadent bourgeois culture," who were "defaming Soviet culture."[140] The culture of the West was described as "emaciated and decayed," a description with which any Spenglerian conservative would concur. The "Soviet culture" referred to by Chernov is the classic "great culture of the Russian people."[141] By 1949, the highest Soviet authority,

---

[136] "Czech Intellectuals Upset over Anti-Israel Statement," 5.
[137] Lendvai, *Anti-Semitism in Eastern Europe*, 291.
[138] Chernov, "Bourgeois Cosmopolitanism."
[139] Ibid.
[140] Ibid.
[141] Ibid.

whose views Chernov must have been conveying, had perceived that the USSR was the target of broad-ranging cultural subversion: "Harmful and corrupting petty ideas of bourgeois cosmopolitanism were also carried over into the realms of Soviet literature, Soviet film, graphic arts, in the area of philosophy, history, economic and juridical law and so forth."[1142]

It was not until 1968 that the cracks in the Soviet bloc's cultural bulwark began to appear through Czechoslovakia and the liberalizing regime of Dubček.

The "rootless cosmopolitanism" directed against Czechoslovakia centered around the importation of rock music and psychedelia. Playwright Václav Havel traveled to New York, where he took part in New Left demonstrations. He wandered around Greenwich Village and bought a lot of psychedelic posters. He returned to Prague with Czechoslovakia's first copy of an album by the Velvet Underground, which was widely copied, and "inspired a generation of underground rock bands."[1143] Among these bands was Plastic People of the Universe. In 1990 Havel recalled: "The whole spirit of the 60s [in the USA], the rebellion against the establishment, affected significantly the spiritual life of my generation and the younger people, and in a very strange way transcended into the present."[1144]

While Soviet tanks succeeded in thwarting Dubček's attempts at liberalization, the grounds had been seeded in 1968 with the cultural pathogens that would help to bring down the Soviet edifice and force much of the former Soviet bloc into the orbit of globalization, debt, consumerism, and degeneration—what the late West called "freedom."

The rot that was eating away within the Warsaw Pact was organizationally focused on groups such as Charter 77 in Czechoslovakia and Solidarity in Poland. The Charter 77 manifesto was drafted, and a movement formed after the imprisonment of fans of Plastic People of the Universe.

These groups were instigated and funded by the network of currency speculator George Soros and an array of subversive, largely US-

---

[1142] Ibid.
[1143] Doggett, *There's a Riot Going On*, 164.
[1144] Ibid.

based and government-connected think tanks. When Charter 77 was cofounded by Havel in 1977, its manifesto was published by the Western media by pre-arrangement in the *Frankfurter Allgemeine Zeitung, Corriere della Sera, The Times* of London, and *Le Monde*.[1145]

Just how significant this culture war in the service of globalization is can be seen in the role the band Plastic People of the Universe (PPU) played in serving as a catalyst for the Velvet Revolution. The band is acknowledged as musically unremarkable, yet its backers ensured that it became *politically* remarkable. Its origins go back to the 1968 revolt.[1146] Its members became the "fathers of the Czech musical underground."[1147]

One commentator stated that "an entire community of Czech dissidents sprung up around the band."[1148] According to bassist and founding member Milan Hlavsa:

> The Plastic People emerged just as dozens and hundreds of other bands—we just loved rock'n'roll and wanted to be famous. We were too young to have a clear artistic ambition. All we did was pure intuition: no political notions or ambitions at all.[1149]

Although the band's professional license was revoked by the government in 1970, they worked around the regulations, and their music was released in the West. Lyrics for the allegedly non-political PPU were written by Czech dissident poet Egon Bondy.[1150] What emerged around PPU was a so-called second culture which played at music festivals. There were arrests, but most were soon released after international condemnation. The official indictment accused the bands of "extreme vulgarity" with "an anti-social impact," extolling "nihilism" and "decadence."[1151]

It was in support of this cultural nihilism and decadence that Charter 77 emerged as a movement, with Havel as its figurehead.

[1145] Prečan, et al., "Charter 77 After 30 Years."
[1146] See the Prog Archives entry for "Plastic People of the Universe."
[1147] Ibid.
[1148] Ibid.
[1149] Unterberger, "Plastic People of the Universe."
[1150] Ibid.
[1151] Ibid.

Havel stated that PPU were defending "life's intrinsic desire to express itself freely, in its own authentic and sovereign way."[152] It was the doctrine of the Critical Theorists and their New Left interpreters. Havel began selecting lyrics for PPU. This supposedly "non-political," innocent, artistic free expression has since been described by *The New York Times* as being "wild, angry, and incendiary," and "darkly subversive."[153] *The Times* enthused that PPU "helped change the future direction of a nation," stating:

> Václav Havel, the music-loving former Czech president and dissident who championed the band's cause when several members were imprisoned in 1976 for disturbing the peace, credits it with inspiring Charter 77, the manifesto demanding human rights that laid the groundwork for the 1989 revolution. "The case against a group of young people who simply wanted to live in their own way," he recalled, "was an attack by the totalitarian system on life itself, on the very essence of human freedom."[154]

Havel's statement, it might be said, had all the banality of a Columbia Records advertising blurb from the late '60s, but for the intelligentsia of the late West it is esteemed as philosophically deep.

It was, according to Bilefsky, "the ultimate rock 'n' roll rebellion."[155]

Paul Wilson, PPU's Canadian manager in Prague, reminisced that it was through music that the puerile ideals of manipulated Western youth were introduced to their Czechoslovak counterparts, beginning in the 1960s.

> One of the things that was very marked in the 1960s was that although intellectuals found it very hard to get a hold of books it was very easy for kids to be right on top of things because records were brought in and the music was broadcast over Voice of America and other radio stations. So, there was a very current music scene here, with a lot of knock-off bands and a lot of fans of different groups

---

[152] Bilefsky, "Czech's Velvet Revolution Paved."
[153] Ibid.
[154] Ibid.
[155] Ibid.

just the way you'd find them in the West. The other thing, too, is that the Prague music scene, very early, attracted the attention of the western press, because for them the existence of rock bands in a communist country was a sign of change.[1156]

Note that the Voice of America and other US agencies were promoting subversion through music. The Voice of America was transferred from the aegis of the State Department to the US Information Agency when the latter was established in 1953. The US originally used jazz and Abstract Expressionism as part of their strategy in the cultural Cold War.[1157] Today the focus is on the use of hip-hop to sell American "freedom" to alienated youth.[1158] The West's youth subculture was the most efficacious way of subverting and weakening a state and remains so. We might recall the program of exporting cultural degeneration, outlined by Ralph Peters, as the most destructive weapon that the US can use against a targeted state.[1159]

It is ironic that the USSR had been accused of backing a plot to subvert Western youth and to create tumult in Western cities and campuses. Even Charles de Gaulle succumbed to the assumption, while conservative columnists in the US alluded to Russian and Chinese money backing New Left organizations, which congressional hearings promptly investigated.

"Let Russia Have It":
An Ominous Sign of Moral Decay

By 1970, youth in the Soviet bloc were succumbing to Western nihilism. *The Chicago Tribune* editorialized that the cultural subversion of youth could be the key to winning the Cold War, writing of a shift in attitudes: "not so long ago youthful Soviet audiences sat in rapt attention at performances of the great Soviet classics. But no

---

[1156] Velinger, "Paul Wilson—The Impact."
[1157] Saunders, *Cultural Cold War*, 256.
[1158] See the "About" page on Next Level's website, an initiative of the US State Department. Its byline is "Building Global Community through Hip Hop culture."
[1159] Peters, "Constant Conflict."

more. At a recent performance of Chekhov's 'Cherry Orchard' in Moscow, the young Russians drunk wine from bottles, yelled obscenities, smooched their girlfriends, and raised such a racket that the actors quit."[1160] Soviet trade union newspaper *Trud* commented that "this was a devilish disregard and immunity to beauty"; *The Chicago Tribune*, paraphrasing *Trud*, noted that this was "an ominous sign of moral decay among Soviet youth."[1161]

> They would rather tune their transistor radios in to non-Russian broadcasts of Western hard rock or buy Beatles records from tourists. Their rapt attention now goes to a Czechoslovakian pop singer who can belt out "The Age of Aquarius," and other songs from the American hard rock musical *Hair*.

The Chicago Tribune opined that the CIA was losing an opportunity and should embark on a strategy of instilling in Soviet youth "America's decadent youth culture." *The Chicago Tribune* concluded:

> Imagine the effect on the Kremlin if the CIA arranged to dump the whole rock musical culture bit, complete with drugs, electronic guitar and long hair, on the Soviet Union. Russia would never be the same. And neither would we. Peace might even return to the United States. Or is our generation gap showing?

In 1970, Yuri Bezmenov, who had held a minor job at the RIA Novosti press agency, defected to Canada with the assistance of the CIA and made a name for himself as a lecturer and author, alleging an immense plot by the USSR to subvert the morals of the West, particularly the youth.[1162] This served as a red herring, whether by coincidence or design, by obscuring the actual origins of this very real subversion of youth throughout the world, that continues to emanate from the USA, in which the CIA had played a leading role. In the last few years Bezmenov's views have been resurrected, as a renewed Cold War against post-Soviet Russia proceeds. Given the mediocrity

---

[1160] "Let Russia Have It."
[1161] Ibid.
[1162] "KGB Defector Blames '60s Activists."

of his books, it is perhaps more an indictment on the state of Western academia than on Russia that his views are now being discussed seriously. Unfortunately, certain elements of the right that have not moved beyond the Cold War see Bezmenov's claims as justification for their own Russophobia.

30

GERMANY—NEW LEFT DEFINED BY NAZI PAST

In Germany those who sought to destroy traditional organic bonds, or the "primary ties" as the Critical Theorists called them, pointed an accusing finger at parents and grandparents who were held responsible for Nazism. The postwar de-Nazification process produced a generation that could be readily alienated from its family, its homeland, and its culture, a generation that could be easily enlisted as shock troops for the culture war that would establish the new international order.

The Socialist German Student Union (SDS) provided inspiration for the creation of the Students for a Democratic Society in the USA. The German SDS had been founded in 1946 as the youth wing of the Social Democratic Party. No political organization could operate in Germany without the sanction of the Allied occupation authorities. The authorities were prompt in banning the Socialist Reich Party which, advocating a neutralist position, rejected Germany's imposed role as the frontline against the Soviet bloc during the Cold War.

Paradoxical as it might seem, it was the New Left that regarded the Soviet bloc with hostility, while much of the German radical right resisted embroiling Germany in another confrontation with the USSR. Prior to that, Mensheviks, Trotskyites, and Social Democrats had flocked to the Congress for Cultural Freedom. The CCF had a major role in cultivating the anti-Soviet Left in Germany and France.

The founding conference was in Berlin in 1950. Anti-Fascism provided the impetus, and Stalin became the new Hitler.

The '68ers in Germany were rebelling against their parents and grandparents. The '68ers were enchained to the era of Hitler, struggling to overcome the legacy, yet defined by it nevertheless.

Bettina Röhl—daughter of Klaus Rainer Röhl, founder of the left-wing student magazine *Konkret*, and of Ulrike Meinhof, founder of the Red Army Faction—has excellent insight into the milieu from which the New Left arose in Germany. Röhl states that the '68ers did not create the post-1945 era, but were the products of it. They worked within a milieu that had triumphed in the name of anti-fascism. Röhl writes:

> The fact that the '68ers had won, was because all doors and gates in this society opened to them. Most of them went into the institutions, abandoned their desire to make a revolution, but they also carried the spirit of their protests into the last corner of West German society. After all, it was not as the 68-story legend would have us believe: there was no fascist society against which the '68ers had to fight. *The society was open and the '68ers made a career in it. And in this process, the former revolutionaries then established themselves. An establishment emerged that glorified its "revolutionary" past. . . .*
>
> *In fact, the '68ers are not the engine of liberalization, but they have benefited from this process, which is already taking place in society anyway. The '68ers are the children of a luxuriant society.* There were jobs and holidays, there was the pill and money. This all came together and shaped the Western societies after the period of reconstruction after the destruction of the Second World War. The '68ers are the first luxury generation of the Federal Republic. They only knew of having more and more. That was the reason for their nonchalance. It was also the first generation to always have the music they wanted to hear. There was a technical revolution. Suddenly everyone had their own record player or tape recorder and radio.
>
> Everything was available. They freaked out. People talk a lot about the feeling of freedom. But perhaps it was even more the feeling that everything came to you, *that only a few old-fashioned obstacles were in the way and one could have had paradise for all.* That

came from the life situation of these spoiled generations. Not unsympathetic, but not very intelligent. The extremism they plunged into was then a step backwards.

The Beatles, the Rolling Stones, Pink Floyd—that was not counterculture. That was the culture of that era. It was the counterculture of the previous time. But in this sense almost every culture is also counterculture. Do you remember Herbert Marcuse's *One-Dimensional Man*? It did not exist at all with us. Everything was colorful in the West. The most varied styles and world views were expressed. Mao's millions of Red Guards, on the other hand, were indeed one-dimensional people with only the red Mao Bible in their hands. And with a lot of blood on the hands. At the time, everyone in the world was talking about the "new man" that had to be created: in the cadre parties, in the underground organizations and alternative projects. He did not show up anywhere. Nobody ever saw him. He was a fixed idea. It was derived from people with no idea of how to transform the whole world. That's all Mao Zedong. That fascinated the '68ers.

Revolution was in vogue. The revolutionary phantasm ruled. How do you make revolution was the question, and so was the issue of violence on the agenda. This is also true in the logic of the revolution: there has not yet been a revolution in which blood did not flow. In truth, revolutions were rarely huge popular uprisings, they were actions less people, which then resulted in civil wars, in which then hundreds of thousands or even millions were involved. The '68ers were of the opinion that whoever wanted the revolution had to enforce it by force. Therefore, *the Red Army Faction was not a foreign body, but an integral part of '68.* "Of course, you can be shot," said Ulrike Meinhof in 1970 in *Der Spiegel*. The publisher *Rudolf Augstein later regretted that he had printed this. But the fact that he did shows how far the 68er Revolutionary paradigm had already penetrated into the middle of society.*[1163]

The supposedly "revolutionary" youth were nothing but pawns. They were spoiled hedonists suckled by the establishment. They easily became parts of the establishment, just like their counterparts in the Anglosphere.

[1163] Widmann, "Mit diesem Personal war." Emphasis added.

Rudolf Augstein, mentioned above, was editor and publisher of Germany's most influential newspaper, *Der Spiegel*. As Bettina Röhl discerns, there was a common outlook between Augstein, paragon of the liberal German establishment, and Ulrike Meinhof, the most extreme of the '68ers. Augstein, editorializing at the time of the Red Army Faction trials in Germany, also saw the "anarchists" as products of the era, offering an apologia:

> The anarchist sprouts from the ground. They promote anarchy, but they are its product, not its originators: Sensitive and psychologically susceptible sensors, certainly as much victims as perpetrators. . . . The anarchists do not create the anarchy; rather anarchy creates anarchists.[1164]

The vilification of older generations created a crisis of conscience among the young that many sought to assuage by showing how far removed they were from their parents and grandparents.

Augstein had a certain sympathy for Meinhof, a successful ex-journalist and socialite. While Meinhof was still a celebrated columnist, she and Augstein had shared an animosity toward the iconic Bavarian conservative politician Franz Josef Strauss. A recent appraisal in *Der Speigel* of the relationship between Augstein and Meinhof stated that, before forming the Red Army Faction, Meinhof had reported on sensitive, controversial issues such as the rearming of the Bundeswehr and silence about the Nazi past. "She quickly learned to moralize forcefully and attacked right-wing politicians with great acuteness."[1165] Again, the specter of another Hitler defined her outlook. Any assertion of German sovereignty—despite the left's stated aim of opposing American imperialism—was condemned as a resurgence of "Nazism" by the Allied authorities, by establishment figures such as Augstein, and by the ultraleft.

In 1962 and 1966 Augstein financially supported Meinhof, who faced prosecution for her defamation of Franz Josef Strauss.[1166] While Augstein could not continue his association with Meinhof after she

---

[1164] Augstein, "Mit den Bomben leben."
[1165] Sontheimer, "RAF Wie sich Rudolf Augstein."
[1166] Ibid.

cut her ties with their mutual liberal friends, he did maintain a relationship with the student leader Rudi Dutschke, head of the German SDS, providing money for Dutschke and his family.[1167]

Return of Critical Theorists

Der Spiegel, in reflecting on Dutschke and the rise of the '68 generation in Germany, noted the influence of the Critical Theorists who had returned to Germany from the US:

> The movement was fuelled in part by the cultural criticism of the Frankfurt School of philosophers including Max Horkheimer and Theodor Adorno and tracts printed by the Suhrkamp Verlag. Local theaters staged productions by Sartre and Brecht and a new kind of thinking started to take shape—one that rejected previous notions about the formation of identity and focused on individualism.[1168]

Der Spiegel noted that conservative attitudes on nation, religion, and tradition were stifled amidst revived anguish over the Nazi past. The new ideal was in the detached individual:

> Dissenting voices from conservative circles who considered nation, religion and tradition more important than modern individualism, died down as a series of trials publicly aired the scope of the elite's participation in the vast crimes committed by Adolf Hitler's Third Reich. And as the Frankfurt "Auschwitz Trials" began in 1963, many young people developed a deep skepticism toward their parents' generation. They saw the generation which preceded them as responsible for National Socialism, and, even worse, responsible for suppressing that terrible history during the first decades after the war—a time characterized by the country's reconstruction and the ensuing "economic miracle."[1169]

[1167] "'Spiegel'-Gründer Augstein."
[1168] "Attack on Rudi Dutschke."
[1169] Ibid.

Joining the Mainstream

In Germany, as in the Anglosphere, the '68 generation ended up being mainstreamed, joining the establishment:

> The RAF [Red Army Faction] was part of an ideological splintering of the 1968 movement that saw Rudi Dutschke famously part ways with more radical elements. Most of the movement would later merge into former Chancellor Willy Brandt's reform-era SPD [Social Democratic Party], but it also sparked a far-reaching cultural revolution. As happened elsewhere in the world, most of the 1968ers ultimately joined the mainstream, with a number of 1960s activists—including Rudi Dutschke—later paving the way to found the Green Party. Dutschke himself was to be a key figure in the party, but he died shortly before its official creation in 1980. Some of them, most famously Joschka Fischer, became ministers in the German government led by Chancellor Gerhard Schröder.[1170]

In their introduction to an academic collection of essays on the '68 revolt across the world, Philipp Glassert and Martin Klimke stated of the research that "the relationship between activists and established political figures, likewise, is increasingly scrutinized. From research on West Germany's student movement, we now know that many politicians were sympathetic to it, even though they quite adamantly criticized violent excesses."[1171] They cited '68er and academic Götz Aly as providing "some remarkable insight into the discussions within the Chancellor's office in Bonn. Chancellor Kiesinger and some of his advisers perceived the students *as helpful in broadening democratic attitudes in Germany.*"[1172] The establishment in Germany, as in the US, saw the New Left as a means of shifting popular attitudes to the left.

Of the long-term effects, Klimke and Glassert concluded of the worldwide '68 charade:

[1170] Ibid.
[1171] Glassert and Klimpke, *1968: Memories and Legacies,* 15.
[1172] Ibid. Emphasis added.

The argument could be made, however, that new academic paradigms and fads coming out of the 1960s, such as ethnic and women's studies, post-colonialism, and the much broader cultural studies, have further *strengthened the cultural influence of the United States abroad.*[1173]

These "new academic paradigms" that are now universally enforced dogmas emanated from the establishment-sponsored Frankfurt School. As for the '68ers, where else would they go except into the establishment that had spawned them? One notable exception was Horst Mahler. An attorney, he had been with the German SDS, and was a founder of the Red Army Faction, spending ten years in jail for left-wing terrorism. In 2000 Mahler came to the realization that *capitalist* globalization is not resisted by *leftist* globalization but by rightist nationalism. In joining the National Democratic Party (NPD), which the establishment has constantly tried to ban, Mahler commented: "The NPD is against globalization. . . . [It] knows that the only power that can stand up against globalization is the nation."[1174] According to the establishment smear-mongering agency, the Southern Poverty Law Center: "The purported goal of the NPD, according to a recent German intelligence report, is to 'build a new Germany out of the rubble of liberal capitalism.'"[1175] Since his conversion to the right, Mahler's life has been one of continual persecution, not for terrorism, but for thought crimes. His treatment at the hands of the establishment is a stark contrast to the positions maintained by former German, British, and American left-wing extremists, who are often lauded for their "idealism."[1176]

[1173] Ibid. Emphasis added.
[1174] Lee, "Former Left-wing German Extremist."
[1175] Ibid.
[1176] See for example Frank, "My Friend Bill Ayers."

31

LEGACY

The '68ers and Globalist Wars

The '68ers entered the establishment and became zealots for globalization and the repression of actual dissent, whether from populist protest movements or "rogue states." The seed was already present in the Port Huron Statement, which called for global industrialization and world government under UN auspices.

Cohn-Bendit became a leader of the Green bloc in the European Parliament. He is a vehement critic of Hungary's Viktor Orbán, one of the few leaders to oppose globalization and the machinations of George Soros. *The Atlantic* laments such "right-wing authoritarianism":

> The billionaire financier and philanthropist survived Nazi-occupied Hungary as a boy, and his foundation has been funding civil-society initiatives in Hungary and across Eastern Europe since before the end of the Cold War, as well as programs in Hungary and across Europe aimed at supporting immigrants. It's the immigration programs that have riled up Orbán. Ever since the migration crisis of 2015, Fidesz has been depicting the nation and Europe as besieged by foreigners. Before the elections, Fidesz spent millions on ad campaigns Open Society called anti-Semitic, including a

doctored image of Soros with his arms around opposition leaders who are taking wire cutters to the border fence.[1177]

Cohn-Bendit condemned Orbán for his opposition to the globalization of labor, which is promoted by the oligarchy via open borders. Damning Orbán seems analogous to Cohn-Bendit's enduring grievance with Charles de Gaulle; both allegedly authoritarian leaders resisted globalization. Open borders is one of the many aims the ultraleft has in common with the globalist oligarchy and the managerial elite.[1178]

Cohn-Bendit, like other '68ers who now circulate in the corridors of power, also supports regime change against the few states that remain hindrances to globalization, whether with military intervention as in Libya and Yugoslavia, or with the color revolutions used to threaten Russia's internal security and undermine its status as a counterweight to global homogenization. With fellow Green Party politician and German foreign minister and vice chancellor Joscha Fischer, also a veteran of the '68 generation, Cohn-Bendit supported the destruction of Yugoslavia in a war that was intended to globalize and privatize the vast mineral wealth of Kosovo.[1179]

Benjamin Schett, writing for *Global Research*, observed of the West European Left, including Cohn-Bendit:

> It is their promotion of the self-contradictory concept of "humanitarian interventionism" (as carried out, for example, against Yugoslavia in 1999 and Libya in 2011) that has come to make the approach of allegedly "progressive" policy-makers so subversive. . . .
>
> In Western Europe, most proponents of militarisation on the mainstream Left are associated with Green or Social Democratic parties. One of the first advocates of militarized "humanitarian intervention" was Daniel Cohn-Bendit, member of the Green Party of France. . . . During the Civil War in the former Yugoslav Republic of Bosnia, Cohn-Bendit demanded that the Serbs had to be bombed, and anyone who didn't agree with that would carry the

---

[1177] Donadio, "How Hungary Ran Soros."
[1178] Bolton, "United Nations Global Compact."
[1179] "Draft Strategy of the Privatization Department."

same burden of guilt as those who turned a blind eye to the Fascist mass murder in World War Two:

"Shame on us! We, the generation that held our parents' generation in such contempt because of its political cowardice, now we watch on seemingly helpless, powerless and yet still holier-than-thou as the Bosnian Muslims are ethnically cleansed."

Indeed, the ploy of drawing parallels with Nazi crimes in order to demonise a rival who stands in the way of Western geostrategic interests was perfected during the Bosnian war. . . .

When the United Nations Security Council proposed Resolution 1973 on the establishment of a no-fly zone over Libya in March 2011, which served as a pretence for attacking the country, Germany abstained from voting, along with Russia, China, India and Brazil. The German conservative-liberal coalition government was heavily criticised by Social Democratic and especially Green circles for not taking a stronger pro-war stance. Former Foreign Minister Joschka Fischer attacked his successor Guido Westerwelle for not having supported the resolution of the warmongers, and added that Germany could now "forget about a constant seat in the UN Security Council."

Therefore, it is not surprising that in the current conflict in Syria (which is significantly orchestrated and financed by the West, as were the civil wars in Yugoslavia and Libya), Western Europe's Green politicians and other liberal leftists are the strongest proponents of a policy of escalation toward the Al Assad government. Claudia Roth, one of the two current German Green Party chairs, recently hosted a TV debate on Syria and shouted down any voice of reason pleading for negotiations with the Al Assad government. . . .

In the cases of both Libya and Syria, Bernard-Henri Lévy, a French "nouveau" philosopher, professional self-promoter and frequent object of media mockery, called upon his government to intervene and prevent the "killing of innocent civilians."[1180]

Cohn-Bendit's colleague, Bernard-Henri Lévy, regarded as France's "foremost intellectual," was in Kiev in 2014, assisting with the color revolution that was being promoted by local and global oligarchs.[1181]

[1180] Schett, "Europe's Pro-War Leftists.'"
[1181] Bolton, "Geopolitics and Oligarchy at Work."

Lévy stated, "I'm not pro-American as much as anti-anti-American. When the French begin to feel a mad visceral hatred toward an imagined America, I know the cauldron is boiling and the filthy genie is about to jump out again."[1182] What he means is that those resisting globalization and Americanization are rightists. Lévy sees fascism as endemic in France. Although Lévy was not with Cohn-Bendit on the streets in '68, he was with Cohn-Bendit as a founder of the lobby group JCall, dedicated to supporting Israel and guiding European foreign policy.

It is notable that Bernard-Henri Lévy and Cohn-Bendit were among eighty-nine people prohibited from entering Russia, while the Russian state prohibited a large number of globalist NGOs.[1183] It is Putin's Russia that is the primary obstacle to globalization. The '68 generation is again doing its best to destabilize the real opposition. Putin is today's de Gaulle.

Frightened of Populist Revolts

The '68 generation has condoned color revolutions orchestrated by US, oligarchic, and globalist agencies against rogue states. Yet when an actual people's revolt—like the "Yellow Vests" in France— did spontaneously arise, Cohn-Bendit and other '68ers became fearful.[1184]

[1182] Buck, "France's Prophet Provocateur."

[1183] Medias-Presse-Info, "Bernard-Henri Lévy."

[1184] The mass mobilizations of truckers and others in Canada, New Zealand, Australia, the US, and Europe, in opposition to compulsory pandemic mandates, also induced fear by those who saw the protests as a resurgence of *populism*, which they cannot control through their phony left-wing movements. In New Zealand, the Labour Government condemned this embryonic people's mobilization as "fascist," "white supremacist," "anti-Semitic," and "a river of filth," vitriol suggesting the ultraleft in its most psychotic forms. A New Zealand Labour Government senior minister, Michael Wood, said of an encampment of protesters on parliament grounds: "We feel for those people. But underneath all of that, there is a river of filth. There is a river of violence and menace. There is a river of anti-Semitism. There is a river of Islamophobia. There is a river of threats to people who work in this place and our staff. Those are things that we should not in any way be condoning." NZ Herald, Covid-19 Omicron Convoy Protest.

In an interview, Cohn-Bendit condemned the movement, show-ing his fear of the people's instinct, an instinct that, once aroused, is not so easy to channel into paths that can be made innocuous or used to further globalist agendas. He disparaged and feared the "ordinary people" as the type "who pushed Trump into power."[1185] Cohn-Bendit stated that he was appalled by the "violence," which he called intrin-sically "right-wing."[1186] Perhaps Cohn-Bendit, in his old age, is suffer-ing from memory loss; the protests he led in the 1960s were anything but peaceful. Did he repudiate his former American comrade, Mark Rudd, cofounder of the terroristic Weather Underground, who was a fugitive for seven years, or any other New Left violence?

Cohn-Bendit's comments are worth quoting at length:

> The last time Paris burned, his was the face of insurrection. Dany le Rouge (Danny the Red—a nickname that partly reflected his pol-itics and partly his hair) was the hero of a generation.
>
> Even when Daniel Cohn-Bendit, leader of the May 1968 student uprising, changed his colours to Danny the Green and *went main-stream*—representing ecology parties in France, Germany and Brussels—he never quite shook off his reputation as a rebel and po-litical trouble-maker.
>
> Half a century on, Paris is burning and barricaded again and the city's cobble stones are being prised up to be hurled at police once more, but Cohn-Bendit sees little comparison with the clashes of 50 years ago. He views the *gilets jaunes* not as revolutionaries but as a movement veering dangerously into authoritarianism. In an interview with the *Observer*, Cohn-Bendit, *now a friend and adviser to President Emmanuel Macron*, said: "This movement is very dif-ferent to May 68. Back then, we wanted to get rid of a general (Charles de Gaulle); today these people want to put a general in power," he said, referring to calls by certain *gilets jaunes* for the former chief of defence staff General Pierre de Villiers, who re-signed after falling out with Macron in July 2017, to be made prime minister.
>
> "And nobody in 68 made death threats against those who want to talk. This is the power of force. *All those on the left thinking this is a leftwing revolution are wrong: it's veering to the right.* To hear

---

[1185] Willsher, "May 1968 was a revolution." Emphasis added.
[1186] Ibid.

that *gilets jaunes* who want to negotiate are receiving death threats is evidence of this authoritarian right.

"I hear people from *la France Insoumise* (hard left), talking about this being a great people's revolt and how the people are speaking, *but these are the same ordinary people who pushed Trump into power. . . .*"

"We saw in Germany in 1933 what 'ordinary' people did. *Not all ordinary people are good . . .* it's not an accident that this movement has proposed General de Villiers as an alternative leader."

Cohn-Bendit speaks from family experience. He was born in France to German-Jewish parents who fled Nazi Germany in 1933. Now 73, he holds dual nationality and splits his time between the two countries. More importantly, he has Macron's ear; the president reportedly offered Cohn-Bendit the environment minister's job, which he turned down.

Although he admitted that torching cars and street violence were "very France," he said there was something "dangerous . . . and frightening" about the current waves of violence. "There have been many great revolts by the working class in French history. And there's the mythology of the French Revolution. It's part of the genetic culture. But we are witnessing the kind of extreme violence never seen before," he said. . . .

When Paris burned in May 1968, and 6,000 students battled 1,500 police, it was a revolution. Today, Cohn-Bendit worries the insurrection risks becoming an "authoritarian danger."[1187]

Neo-Jacobinism vs. Yellow Vests

Bernard-Henri Lévy, a leader of the *nouveaux philosophes* (New Philosophers), feared the Yellow Vests for the same reasons as Cohn-Bendit.

The CIA was encouraged by the emergence of this New Philosophy, which, like the entry of Marxists into the Congress for Cultural Freedom, was the result of an existential crisis among the leftist intelligentsia. In their report on the New Philosophers, the CIA opined:

[1187] Ibid., Emphasis added.

[In the] new climate of intellectual opinion in France, [a] spirit of anti-Sovietism . . . will make it difficult for anyone to mobilize significant intellectual opposition to US policies. . . . It is clearly now the Soviet Union that is on the defensive with New Left intellectuals.[1188]

It is a shift that the CIA saw as having begun "at least since the early 1970s." "Anti-Sovietism has become the touchstone of legitimacy in leftist circles, weakening the traditional anti-Americanism of the leftist intellectuals and allowing American culture—and even political and economic policies—to find new vogue."[1189]

The origin of the "New Philosophers" was identified as "mostly former Communists who left the party after the traumatic events of May 1968."[1190] In a footnote the report alluded to the French Communist Party as having denounced the 1968 riots as the result of "woolly-minded anarchists."[1191]

Bernard-Henri Lévy and André Glucksmann were cited as the two founders of the New Philosophy. Lévy, as editor-in-chief of the Grasset publishing house, one of the largest in France, ensured the New Philosophy an influential readership.[1192] Glucksmann and Lévy are credited with taking the French intelligentsia in an anti-Soviet direction, seeing the USSR as "a monstrous reactionary machine" rather than the utopian "withering away of the state."[1193] A disdain for the USSR had become "newly fashionable" among the New Left, to the point that the primary trait for a leftist intellectual in France was not a concern for Pinochet's destruction of socialism in Chile, the foreign policy of Ronald Reagan, or labor problems, but "a critical attitude toward the USSR."[1194]

The prospect was for a continuing wave of pro-Americanism, "rooted in the vogue for American popular culture," economic vitality, and self-confidence. The New Left had become critical of

---

[1188] CIA, "France: Defection of the Leftist Intellectuals."
[1189] Ibid.
[1190] Ibid.
[1191] Ibid., 4.
[1192] Ibid., 5.
[1193] Ibid., 6.
[1194] Ibid., 11.

"primitive anti-Americanism."[1195] It was now time for Lévy's anti-anti-Americanism.

Like Cohn-Bendit, Lévy saw in the Yellow Vests the specter of "Nazism" haunting Europe, writing:

> I have spent a large part of my life observing, praising, and, whenever I could, supporting movements of popular revolt that aspired to greater quantities of liberty, equality, and fraternity. The case of France's Yellow Vests, however, marks the first time that such a movement has caused me, from the start, to have such strong and persistent doubts, despite my agreement in principle with many of its claims.[1196]

The disquiet was caused by this being a genuine revolt of the people, the "populism" that elites fear, whether they belong to the left-wing intelligentsia or the financial oligarchy. Both Cohn-Bendit and Lévy claim to speak for a united Europe. As they make plain, it is the united Europe of neo-Jacobinism.[1197] It is Lévy's Jacobin commitment to "liberty, equality, and fraternity" that gave France ethnic cleansing in Vendée, Robespierre's Committee on Public Safety, and the Reign of Terror, but what they fear is a new "authoritarianism" reminiscent of Charles de Gaulle, or the success of Marine le Pen, which might amount to an actual revolt of the people against globalization and American cultural imperialism.

Tom Hayden and Establishment Insiders

In 2012, Tom Hayden assessed the Port Huron Statement and the legacy of the '68ers after fifty years. He saw the color revolutions as the hope of the future. Celebrating the fiftieth anniversary of the Port Huron Statement, he saw the New Left's concept of participatory democracy being manifested in the Arab Spring, the election of Barack

---

[1195] Ibid.
[1196] Lévy, "Blinding Rage of the Yellow Vests."
[1197] Bolton, *Occult and Subversive Movements*, 227–30.

Obama, and the protests in Russia, facilitated by a "technological revolution":

> [A]mong the demands of young people in Tunisia, Egypt and other Middle Eastern countries in the Arab Spring of 2011. Spontaneous democratic demonstrations erupted in Russia late last year, organized on Facebook by young people seeking honest elections.
>
> On the other hand, there are sources of hope now that we couldn't imagine in 1962. The technological revolution of the Internet and social media is propelling a global revival of participatory democracy. Facebook and Twitter are credited with a key role in movements from Cairo to the volunteer campaign for Barack Obama. For the next generations, perhaps the most important issue for participatory democracy will be ownership and control of the means of producing and distributing information.[1198]

As in his SDS days, Hayden's doctrine was in accord with the establishment against which he was supposedly rebelling. Perhaps it was intended as a dialectical paradox, an ideological contradiction. He acknowledged that the globalist social media corporations were pivotal in the Arab Spring and in trying to undermine Russia, yet presumably did not question why he was on the same side as the oligarchs in wanting regime change for those states, any more than he questioned why John D. Rockefeller III was so enthused about the "youth idealism" of that era. He presumably did not ask whether the New Left of the 1960s and 1970s had played a role analogous to that played by Movements.org, established by oligarchs in conjunction with the State Department to manipulate youth into revolt through social media. Yet when he was writing in 2012, the role of these oligarchs in fomenting the revolts and color revolutions he was praising was already well-known.

Tony Cartalucci, writing for *Global Research*, remarked on what could be called the "digital New Left":

> In 2008, the Alliance of Youth Movements held its inaugural summit in New York City. Attending this summit was a combination of State

---

[1198] Hayden, "Participatory Democracy."

Department staff, Council on Foreign Relations members, former National Security staff, Department of Homeland Security advisers, and a myriad of representatives from American corporations and mass media organizations including AT&T, Google, Facebook, NBC, ABC, CBS, CNN, MSNBC, and MTV. . . .

Movements.org is officially partnered with the US Department of State and Columbia Law School. Its corporate sponsors include Google, Pepsi, and the Omnicon Group, all listed as members of the globocrat Council on Foreign Relations (CFR). CBS News is a sponsor and listed on the globocrat Chatham House's corporate membership list. Other sponsors include Facebook, YouTube, Meetup, Howcast, National Geographic, MSNBC, GenNext, and the Edelman public relations firm."[1199]

This is an indisputable example of how the establishment can and does manipulate youthful idealism behind the banners of "freedom" and "human rights." Snide quips about "far-right conspiracy theories" cannot take one far.

Hayden then enthused about the prospect of a Black president. Since Obama, like Eugene McCarthy before him, was Wall Street's choice, it was balderdash for Hayden to pretend that this was "the first presidential campaign in our lifetime" where the candidate would take on Wall Street. If a candidate genuinely did revolt against Wall Street, Hayden and the rest of the '68ers would be the first to scream about "fascism." Referring to the Obama campaign and the innocuous Occupy Wall Street phenomenon, Hayden saw the exciting possibilities that could be achieved if this potential new "revolt" would reanimate his Port Huron Statement to provide ideological orientation:

> This year marks the first presidential campaign in our lifetime when the gluttony of Wall Street, the failures of capitalism, the evils of big money in politics and a discussion of fundamental reform will be front and center in election debates. No doubt the crisis that gave rise to Occupy will not be fixed by an election, but that's beside the point. Elections produce popular mandates, and mandates spur popular activism. It's time to organize a progressive majority,

[1199] Cartalucci, "Google's Revolution Factory."

and the vision and strategy of *Port Huron* is worth considering as a guide.[1200]

Writing of the Global Financial Crisis, journalist and constitutional lawyer Glenn Greenwald discerned that the Obama administration both "shielded and feted" Wall Street oligarchs, who "overwhelmingly supported Obama's 2008 presidential campaign."[1201]

Nonetheless, Hayden continued to support Obama, which is perhaps best explained psychologically by his own stated goal of eliminating the White race. Hayden saw White leftist disappointment in Obama as a product of racism, writing in a left-wing Jewish periodical: "When African American voters favor Obama 94–0 and the attacks are coming from the white liberal-left, something needs repair in the foundations of American radicalism."[1202] Hayden further confessed, in a late hour of the day, that the erstwhile "revolutionaries," the supposed "anti-establishment revolt" of a generation, had worked in conjunction with "establishment insiders" for long-term objectives:

> A strategy for social change grew from our direct experience, that of outside (often radical) forces taking direct action to awaken and link with establishment insiders to achieve all that was possible, and to lay the foundations for later movements.[1203]

In his assessment of the Port Huron Statement, Hayden quoted from Kirkpatrick Sale's 1970 book on the SDS:

> [SDS] was set firmly in mainstream politics, seeking the reform of mainstream institutions rather than their abolition, and it had no comprehension of the dynamics of capitalism, of imperialism, of class conflict, certainly no conception of revolution. But none of that mattered.[1204]

[1200] Hayden, "Participatory Democracy."
[1201] Greenwald, "Untouchables."
[1202] Hayden, "Saving Obama, Saving Ourselves."
[1203] Ibid.
[1204] Hayden, "Participatory Democracy."

"None of that mattered" because the New Left was intended as a pseudo-revolt to push the dialectic leftward and reconfigure what was considered acceptable and mainstream. Hayden came close to seeing that establishment dialectic when:

> In 1961 at a National Student Association convention I found a yellow pad with a chart identifying SDS in a box on the left, Young Americans for Freedom on the right and an entity named Control Group in the center-top. Six years later *Ramparts* magazine revealed that the secretive Control Group included CIA agents whose work was to promote a pro–cold war global student movement.[1205]

Hayden had found a reference to the left and right "wings" of a "control group." It is a pity that the discovery did not prompt some introspection, or "self-criticism," as Hayden's leftist peers would say.

Angst emerged when it was realized that the youth and Black civil rights movements had been sponsored as part of a Cold War agenda. Many leftists so hated the way the USSR had developed after the ouster of Trotsky that they were willing to become tools for anti-Soviet Cold War operations. Hayden wrote of this time:

> The importance of this sojourn into left-wing history is that SDS and SNCC (and King, among others) were unaware of the company we were keeping. The unmovable obstacle to the coalition we hoped to build with organized labor was the secret pro–cold war element within liberalism, directly and indirectly tied to the CIA, which was fiercely opposed to our break from cold war thinking. On the one hand, the UAW's[1206] Reuther brothers[1207] helped fund and provide conference quarters at Port Huron; supported the March on Washington and the early UFW organizing effort; and were frustrated by Meany's[1208] archconservative views.
>
> On the other hand, the right-wing AFL–CIO foreign affairs department carried on the anti-communist crusade with its covert operations. The Reuther wing was tied to Johnson's leadership and

---

[1205] Ibid.

[1206] United Auto Workers, one of America's largest and most important unions.

[1207] Victor and Walter Reuther, close to the Kennedy administration.

[1208] George Meany, head of the American Federation of Labor/Central Industrial Organization (AFL–CIO).

unwilling to break from Meany. There was no way, in other words, that the New Left could have joined organized labor in 1964–65 around the Port Huron foreign policy vision, because the AFL–CIO was shackled to the CIA without our knowledge.[1209]

The rejection of an anti-Soviet foreign policy in the Port Huron Statement did not preclude the usefulness of the SDS. The New Left still acted within the establishment's mainstream parameters. If the New Left had been genuinely dissident, Hayden could not have stated that "the '60s movements stumbled to an end largely because we'd won the major reforms that were demanded."[1210] The reforms were "won" only because they were of the type that were wanted by the establishment.

The John Birch Society and those who supported Goldwater did not get even the crumbs from the establishment table, as tame as they were, let alone Southern segregationists, who were crushed by federal troops. Hayden concluded by acknowledging that "we were fully aware of the dangers of being co-opted into the system, the managed cooling of street heat, the predictable countermovements that would rise up."[1211] The predictable countermovements that would rise up were demonized beyond-the-pale, while Hayden was too befogged or ego-drunk to acknowledge that the New Left largely "won the major reforms that were demanded" precisely because the movement was co-opted into the system, started within the system, and reflected the doctrines of the system.

Two years after the Port Huron Statement, President Lyndon Johnson launched the Great Society, a legislative agenda that he saw as the continuation of Roosevelt's New Deal. Labor historian Joshua B. Freeman writes of the time:

> Well into the mid-1960s, programmatically the student movement remained within the parameters of liberalism. The 1962 *Port Huron Statement*, issued by one of the new campus groups, the Students for a Democratic Society (SDS) put out a sweeping indictment of

---

[1209] Hayden, "Participatory Democracy."
[1210] Ibid.
[1211] Ibid.

American society—for racism, inequality complacency, and bureaucracy. But its suggested remedies—federal initiatives in the areas of civil rights, poverty housing and economic development and a realignment for the Democratic Party into a national party of liberalism—went only a bit beyond Fair Deal–New Frontier liberalism.[1212]

While Freeman opines that the New Left started to challenge mainstream liberalism, he also states that, when Johnson inaugurated the Great Society, his speechwriter, Richard Goodwin:

> [L]ater said that one of his influences in writing the Great Society speech had been the SDS's *Port Huron Statement*, whose principal author, Tom Hayden, had adopted some of the cadences and tone that John Kennedy had used in his inaugural address, a measure of how much mainstream liberalism and the movement to its left had penetrated one another by the mid-1960s.[1213]

The New New Left

The "later movements" of a new New Left referred to by Hayden have always been lurking and taking different forms, but one constant remains: their sponsorship by the oligarchy.

Veterans of the SDS, led by Paul Buhle,[1214] established the New SDS in 2006. As ancillary to this, the Movement for a Democratic Society (MDS) was formed, to allow the veterans to support the new generation of activists. Notables on the MDS board included Noam Chomsky, Tom Hayden, Mark Rudd, Al Haber, Howard Zinn, Bill Ayers, and Bernadine Dohrn.[1215]

[1212] Freeman, *American Empire*, 193.
[1213] Ibid.
[1214] Buhle had been editor of the original SDS journal *Radical America*, and was at the time editor of *Democratic Left*, organ of the Democratic Socialists of America (US affiliate of the Socialist International).
[1215] See Key Wiki entry for "Movement for a Democratic Society."

Democracy Matters Institute

If the efforts to re-establish the SDS seemed rather abortive, Democracy Matters is more in evidence. Democracy Matters is a continuation of the New Left.

The stated purpose of Democracy Matters is to take "big private money out of politics." DM states of itself on its "About" page:

> Democracy Matters (DM) empowers students with a voice in politics, skills for life-long civic engagement, and the passion to create a just, fair, and inclusive democracy. Our non-partisan college and high school chapters inspire and mobilize students to take action. DM students fight to expand voting rights, defeat the power of big money in politics, and uplift social justice activism.
>
> Democracy Matters was founded in 2001 by NBA basketball player, poet, and activist Adonal Foyle. With his parents, Joan and Jay Mandle, college professors and life-long organizers, Foyle created a non-partisan organization that built a national network of student chapters engaged in social justice activism.
>
> DM's staff, experienced in grassroots organizing and campus activism, trains student interns and chapter members for effective social change. Our annual Summits bring student activists together to network, share best practices, and plan programming that can build a democracy truly of, by, and for the people.

DM acknowledges the funding they receive from "big private money" to take "big private money out of politics," stating on their page at American University:

> The Democracy Matters Institute is supported in part by grants from the Carnegie Corporation of New York, the Ford Foundation, Z. Smith Reynolds Foundation, Rockefeller Brothers Fund, San Francisco Foundation and others. We would also like to thank Adonal Foyle and our many individual donors for their generous support.

The Board of Directors includes Brandy Bones, expert consultant at ICF International, a global consulting corporation. Among the partners of the corporation are the US Army Research Lab (since 1996) and USAID. ICFI specializes in consultancy work, including security, for the US government and the European Union.

Another DM board director is Daryn Cambridge, who is also Senior Director of Learning and Digital Strategies at the International Center on Nonviolent Conflict (ICNC). The ICNC was founded by Council on Foreign Relations board member, former Freedom House chairman, and managing director of Rockport Capital Incorporated Peter Ackerman.[1216] ICNC is one of a plethora of globalist NGOs that encourage "regime change" and color revolutions for rogue states and other nations who do not toe the Western line. He is also a project manager with the Training Resources Group (TRG), a consultancy firm that works with USAID, US federal departments and agencies, the World Bank, and the International Monetary Fund.

As one should expect by now, while the Rockefeller Brothers Fund and the Rockefeller Foundation wax lyrical on the need to "protect democracy" from being bought out by big money, Rockefeller Philanthropy Advisors exhort "democracy-focused philanthropy" as the means by which oligarchs can throw their money in directions that will promote their version of "democracy," stating:

> As recent elections and societal trends have made all too clear, enabling an effective democracy is an important and much-needed focus of those pursuing social justice, racial equity, and the continuation of a civil society. Philanthropy has a significant role to play in this regard, and the rise in funding over the past decade shows how funders are stepping up. According to *Candid's Foundation Funding for U.S. Democracy* data tool, grant dollars dedicated to campaigns, elections and voting; civic participation; government; and other democracy-related activities in the United States went from a total of $740 million in 2011 to $2.5 billion in 2020. Given the importance of this issue to constitutional democracies, it is critically important that institutions funding democracy employ practices and approaches that make the organization's work as impactful as possible.[1217]

[1216] See the Sourcewatch entry for "Peter Ackerman."
[1217] "Democracy-Focused Philanthropy."

Democracy Matters is one of many heirs to the New Left that continue receiving oligarchic money, in this instance, in the name of keeping money out of politics.

CONCLUSION

Several decades after the frenetic days of the SDS, Tom Hayden undertook some introspection. Writing of an interview with Hayden, Peter Doggett remarks:

> As he scratched around for answers, he slowly unpicked the thread of the counter-culture. What had killed the movement, he suggested, wasn't political repression or FBI harassment, or even (in the classic Marxist equation) a mismatch of economics and social conditions. The culprit was none other than the counter-culture itself, "the sense that the kind of things that were supposed to be naturally ours were getting out of our control." He singled out "the absorption of Yippie-type theatrics into the media": the leaders of the movement had allowed themselves to become distracted by the possibility of stardom and ego gratification. Worse still, however, was "the feeling that people had been ripped off on a widespread basis by the absorption of rock music into the commercial culture." As soon as "The Revolutionaries Are On Columbia Records," they are no longer revolutionaries. When "The Man Can't Bust Our Music," the music is already busted, in every sense of the word.[1218]

Perhaps Hayden was in self-denial. His autobiography *Reunion* had been published by Random House in 1988, and Penguin Books in 1989. This is no different in principle than the marketing of the "music

---

[1218] Doggett, *There's a Riot Going On*, 516.

of the revolution" by Columbia Records and CBS. He had boasted that the Port Huron Statement had influenced the Kennedy administration, and he and other members of the SDS were offered jobs in federal agencies. The SDS actively campaigned for the presidential candidacy of Lyndon Johnson, and later backed Eugene McCarthy, Wall Street's choice for the Democratic presidential nomination.

Sol Stern, having rejected the New Left of his youth, reminisced on Hayden after his passing in 2016, and alluded to the way Hayden was able to work the system. Although Stern ascribed this to the generosity of American democracy, such generosity toward actual dissent has never been accorded to anyone even moderately on the right. Proceeding to Stern's obituary on Hayden:

> With a boost from [Jane] Fonda's movie earnings, Hayden entered electoral politics as a member of the Democratic Party, the same party he had denounced a few years earlier as a "criminal" enterprise. He was elected to the California state assembly and served continuously in the legislature for 18 years. He also attended ten Democratic Party conventions, six times as a delegate from California.
>
> Hayden's life in politics after the 1960s proved that he . . . [was] wrong when [he] claimed that the democratic system was rigged. Hayden collaborated with America's enemy during wartime and was never punished. He conspired to start a riot in Chicago to disrupt the Democratic Party, yet he beat the federal rap. He entered electoral politics and helped push the Democratic Party so far to the left that it would be unrecognizable to the 1968 Chicago protesters. When Hayden died, the mainstream media's obituaries celebrated his achievements in human rights but erased from history his advocacy for violent revolution.[1219]

Much the same could be said about the leniency and even the praise accorded to the most extreme elements of the New Left, such as Weather Underground leaders Bill Ayers and Bernadine Dohrn. Ayers and his wife became prominent university professors. After a decade as a fugitive, Dohrn surrendered herself to the authorities in 1980. Her only punishment was a $1,500 fine and three years' probation. Charges had been dropped against Ayers and other wanted

---

[1219] Stern, "American Turncoat."

Weathermen. In 1997, Ayers received Chicago's "Citizen of the Year" award.

Timothy Noah, writing the "Chatterbox" column in *Slate*, referred to the good fortune of Bill Ayers:

> The astonishing luck of Bill Ayers, unrepentant former Weather Underground revolutionary, continues unabated. Today the state of New York refused to grant parole to Kathy Boudin, another Weather Underground radical, convicted 20 years ago of second-degree murder for participating in a Brink's truck robbery in which two policemen and a security guard were killed. That's bad news for Boudin, who by all accounts has been a model prisoner. But it's great news for Ayers—who, with his wife, Bernardine Dohrn, jointly raised Boudin's son—because it's bound to help Ayers sell his new memoir, *Fugitive Days*.
>
> Chatterbox isn't sure he's ever read a memoir quite so self-indulgent and morally clueless as *Fugitive Days*. (He's certainly never before read one festooned with glowing blurbs from respectable folk like Scott Turow–"a gripping personal account.") "Memory is a motherfucker," begins Ayers, establishing the book's literary tone and unreliability in one compact sentence.[1220]

As we have seen, the establishment intersects with the "revolution." Like many of his peers, Ayers' memoirs were published by a major publishing house. Random House presented Ayers as "a highly respected educator" whose cause remains noble and relevant:

> Bill Ayers was born into privilege and is today a highly respected educator. In the late 1960s he was a young pacifist who helped to found one of the most radical political organizations in U.S. history, the Weather Underground. In a new era of antiwar activism and suppression of protest, his story, *Fugitive Days*, is more poignant and relevant than ever.[1221]

The Weather Underground's terrorist campaign of bombings and shootings was described by Random House as "poignant and

---

[1220] Noah, "Radical Chic Resurgent."
[1221] Ayers, *Fugitive Days*, description.

relevant," and the failed attempts of the FBI and police to prosecute him were deemed a "suppression of protest."

Timothy Noah continues:

> Throughout *Fugitive Days*, Ayers reminds his readers that he's had to omit or change many facts throughout his narrative because they describe actions on his part that are, well, illegal. In the turbulent early 1970s, Ayers helped set off bombs in two dozen places, including the Pentagon and the U.S. Capitol. Supposedly nobody was hurt—the Weatherpeople always issued agitprop-laden bomb threats in advance—though Chatterbox has never seen a scrupulous accounting. (Ayers never did jail time for the bombings because of prosecutorial misbehavior.) Ayers was also a leader of the Days of Rage, a vandalism spree in Chicago in which bystanders were assaulted, though Ayers neglects to mention that. . . .
>
> Much of what Ayers self-interestedly leaves out of his book is more personally embarrassing than illegal. Ayers takes care not to dwell on his own Establishment credentials. (His father was chairman of the energy company Commonwealth Edison, a fact Ayers conveys only by writing, "My dad worked for Edison.") Ayers omits any discussion of his famous 1970 statement, "Kill all the rich people. Break up their cars and apartments. Bring the revolution home, kill your parents, that's where it's really at." He also omits any discussion of his wife Bernardine Dohrn's famous reaction to the Manson killings, as conveyed by journalist Peter Collier: "Dig it. First they killed those pigs, then they ate dinner in the same room with them, then they even shoved a fork into a victim's stomach! Wild!" (In a 1993 *Chicago Magazine* profile, Dohrn claimed, implausibly, that she'd been trying to convey that "Americans love to read about violence.")[1222]

Perhaps Hayden did not so much "work the system" as become a herald of it. The Old Left of several generations before had been funded by the wealthy. Even Karl Marx had seen free-trade capitalism as a necessary part of the movement of history, and in this he was reflecting spirit of his age. Such a fundamental

---

[1222] Noah, "Radical Chic Resurgent."

commonality of outlook between socialists and capitalists was not going to represent a genuine revolt against plutocracy.

Why else were the Rockefellers and other bankers funding the London School of Economics from the start, when it was established by the Fabian Society as a training institution for a future socialist bureaucracy? Were they duped or stupid, or did they have a strategy? The same plutocrats also funded the New School for Social Research. Both institutions continue to receive such funding. The sources are not kept secret. For example, a "Sir Ernest Cassel Chair of Economics" was established at the LSE in 1920.

While it is very simple for mediocre academics to prattle about "far-right conspiracy theories" when such facts are presented, Richard B. Spence, emeritus professor of history at Idaho State University, differentiates between "conspiracy theory" and "conspiracy fact" when documenting the financing of the Russian revolutionary movement—Mensheviks and Bolsheviks—in his *Wall Street and the Russian Revolution*. That Spence's study stops at 1925 is significant. In 1925, Stalin started to move against Trotsky and other Old Bolsheviks, and pursued a new direction which, after the alliance with the US against Germany, would see a post-1945 epochal breach, resulting in the Cold War.

Such was the hatred for Stalin's redirection of Russia that, when it became clear that Russia was on a course far removed from that envisaged by Trotsky, many on the left, from liberals to social democrats, Mensheviks to Old Bolsheviks, regarded this Bonapartism—in Trotsky's parlance—as anathema. They began to align themselves with the US against the Soviet bloc, and even acclaimed American liberalism as the true doctrine of the world revolution. It was from this Cold War milieu that the New Left emerged.

In fundamental outlook there never was disagreement between the establishment and the New Left. The same situation pertains today: the left plead for an "inclusive society," while the oligarchs and managerial elite, in their board rooms and at their think tanks and NGOs, plan the construction of an "inclusive economy." Both see this vision in global terms. Such has been the sales pitch for this common ideology of "inclusiveness," in the name of so-called human rights and "democracy," that the convergence between oligarchy and revolt can be readily observed in the recurrent waves of color revolutions against those peoples (whether Afrikaner, Serb, Syrian, Iranian, or Russian) who cannot be amalgamated into this common vision of a global, inclusive dystopia. The supposed dissent comes from the heirs of the '68ers who, like their predecessors, are in revolt only against the primary ties of family, ethnos, and nation—the same things abhorred as much by the globalist oligarchy and its managerial elite as by the left. Their "revolt" is a false one, their ideology nothing but dogmatic yea-saying to the demands of their economic overlords. From its very beginnings and into the present, the New Left has served as nothing more than a useful idiot for the elite in the struggle between the deracinated archons of the world and those who hold fast to hearth and homeland.

BIBLIOGRAPHY

Books and Dissertations Cited and for Further Reading

Adorno, Theodor W., Else Frenkel-Brunswik, Daniel J. Levinson, and R. Nevitt
  Sanford. *The Authoritarian Personality*. New York: Harper and Brothers, 1950.
Ahern, Thomas L., Jr. *CIA and the Generals: Covert Support to Military Government
  in South Vietnam*. Washington, DC: Center for the Study of Intelligence, 1998.
Alinsky, Saul. *Rules for Radicals*. New York: Vintage/Random House, 1989.
Allen, Robert L. *Black Awakening in Capitalist America*. Trenton, New Jersey:
  Africa World Press, 1992.
Allen, Robert L. *Dialectics of Black Power*. New York: The Guardian, 1968.
Andersen, Joakim. *Rising from the Ruins: The Right of the 21st Century*. London:
  Arktos Media Ltd., 2018.
Armentrout, Anna Jane. "The Politics of Experience: Peace Corps Volunteers,
  Vietnam Veterans, and American Internationalism, 1961–1985." PhD diss.,
  University of California, Berkley, 2012.
Ayers, Bill. *Fugitive Days: Memoirs of an Antiwar Activist*. New York: Penguin
  Random House, 2009.
Barnet, Richard, and Ronald E. Müller. *Global Reach: The Power of the
  Multinational Corporations*. New York: Simon & Schuster, 1974.
Bernays, Edward. *Propaganda*. 1928; New York: Ig Publishing, 2004.
Bolton, K. R. *Babel Inc*. London: Black House Publishing, 2013.
Bolton, K. R. *The Decline and Fall of Civilisations*. London: Black House Publishing,
  2017.
Bolton, K. R. *The Occult and Subversive Movements*. London: Black House
  Publishing, 2017.
Bolton, K. R. *The Perversion of Normality: From the Marquis de Sade to Cyborgs*.
  London: Arktos Media Ltd., 2021.
Bolton, K. R. *Revolution from Above*. London: Arktos Media Ltd., 2011.
Bolton, K. R. *Russia & the Fight Against Globalisation*. London: Black House
  Publishing, 2018.

Bolton, K. R. *Stalin: The Enduring Legacy*. London: Black House Publishing, 2012.

Bolton, K. R. *The Tyranny of Human Rights*. Antelope Hill Publishing, 2022.

Brick, Howard., Robbie Lieberman, and Paula Rabinowitz, eds. *Lineages of the Literary Left: Essays in Honor of Alan M. Wald*. Ann Arbor, MI: Michigan Publishing, University of Michigan Library, 2015.

Burke, Edmund. *Reflections on the Revolution in France*. 1790; Jonathan Bennett, 2017.

Cohen, Robert, and Reginald E. Zelnik, eds. *The Free Speech Movement: Reflections on Berkeley in the 1960s*. University of California Press, 2002.

Conkling, Winifred. *Ms. Gloria Steinem: A Life*. New York: Square Fish, 2020.

Cutlip, Scott M. *The Unseen Power: Public Relations: A History*. Hillside, NJ: Lawrence Elkbaum Associates, 1994.

Doggett, Peter. *There's a Riot Going On: Revolutionaries, Rock Stars and the Rise and Fall of the '60s*. New York: Canongate, 2007.

Doyle, William. *An American Insurrection*. New York: Random House, 2003.

Duberman, Martin. *Left Out: The Politics of Exclusion—Essays 1964–99*. New York: Basic Books, 1999.

Dugin, Alexander. *Putin vs. Putin*. London: Arktos Media Ltd., 2015.

Ellis, Charles D. and James R. Vertin. *Wall Street People*. New York, Wiley, 2001.

Eringer, Robert. *The Global Manipulators*. Bristol: Pentacle Books, 1980.

Farkas, Jean-Pierre. *La Pavé*. Phonurgia nova editions, 1998.

Farley, Richard E. *Gonzo Wall Street*. Regan Arts, 2022.

Frank, Thomas, and Matt Weiland. *Commodify Your Dissent*. New York: W. W. Norton and Co., 1997.

Freeman, Joshua. *American Empire: The Rise of a Global Power, the Democratic Revolution at Home 1945–2000*. Penguin Books, 2013.

Freemark, Yonah. "The Entrepreneurial State: New York's Urban Development Corporation, an Experiment to Take Charge of Affordable Housing Production, 1968–1975." Master's thesis, Massachusetts Institute of Technology, 2013.

Fromm, Erich. *Escape From Freedom*. New York: Rinehart & Co., 1941.

Galens, David, ed. *A Study Guide for Abbie Hoffman's "Steal this Book."* Missouri: Gale Inc., 2003.

Geidel, Molly. *Peace Corps Fantasies: How Development Shaped the Global Sixties*. Minneapolis: University of Minnesota Press, 2015.

Glassert, Phillipp, and Martin Klimpke, eds. *1968: Memories and Legacies of a Global Revolt*, Washington D.C., German Historical Institute, 2009.

Goldstein, Brian. *A City Within a City: Community Development and the Struggle Over Harlem, 1961–2001*. Cambridge, Massachusetts: Harvard University, 2012.

Goldstein, Brian. *The Roots of Urban Renaissance: Gentrification and the Struggle over Harlem*. Cambridge, Massachusetts: Harvard University, 2017.

Goldwater, Barry. *With No Apologies*. New York: William Morrow & Co., 1979.

Gromyko, Andrei. *Memories*. London: Hutchinson, 1989.

Grose, Peter. *Continuing The Inquiry: The Council on Foreign Relations from 1921–1996*. New York: Council on Foreign Relations Press, 2006.

Haines, Herbet. *Black Radicals and the Civil Rights Mainstream, 1954–1970*. Knoxville: University of Tennessee Press, 1995.

Hastings, Max. *Vietnam: An Epic Tragedy 1945–1975*. London: William Collins, 2018.

Heidegger, Martin. *Introduction to Metaphysics*. New Haven: Yale University Press, 2000.

Hertko, Joyce Mary. "The Internationalization of American Higher Education During the 1960s: The Involvement of the Ford Foundation and the Carnegie Corporation in Education and World Affairs." EdD diss., Indiana University, 1996.

Hinckle, Warren. *If You Have a Lemon, Make Lemonade*. New York: G.P. Putnam's Sons, 1974.

Hoffman, Abbie, and Bobby Seale, Rennie Davis, David Dellinger, John Froines, Tom Hayden, Jerry Rubin, Lee Weiner. *The Conspiracy: The Chicago Eight Speak Out*. Chicago: Dell, 1969.

Hoffman, Abbie. *Soon to be a Major Motion Picture*. New York: G.P. Putnam's Sons, 1980.

Holcombe, R.G. *Writing Off Ideas: Taxation, Foundations, and Philanthropy in America*. New York: Routledge, 2017.

Huxley, Aldous. *Brave New World Revisited*. London: Chatto & Windus, 1974.

Ivanov, Yuri. *Caution: Zionism! Essays on the Ideology, Organisation and Practice of Zionism*. Moscow: Progress Publishers, 1970.

Jacobs, Jane. *The Death and Life of Great American Cities*. New York: Random House, 1961.

Johnston, Angus. "The United States National Student Association: Democracy, Activism, and the Idea of the Student, 1947–1978." PhD diss., City University of New York, 2009.

Jonas, G. *One Shining Moment: A Short History of the American Student World Federalist Movement 1942-1953*. iUniverse, 2000.

Kahn, Otto H. *Of Many Things*. New York: Boni & Liveright, 1925.

Katz, Mark. *Build: The Power of Hip Hop Diplomacy in a Divided World*. Oxford University Press, 2019.

Keller, Rosemary Skinner, and Rosemary Radford Ruether, eds. *Encyclopedia of Women and Religion in North America*. Bloomington: Indiana University Press, 2006.

Kellner, Douglas, ed. *The New Left and the 1960s: Collected Papers of Herbert Marcuse, Volume Three*. New York: Routledge, 2005.

Komarovsky, Mirra. *The Unemployed Man and His Family*. New York: 1940.

Kotek, Joel. *Students and the Cold War*. London: Macmillan, 1996.

Kunen, James. *The Strawberry Statement: Notes of a College Revolutionary*. New York: Random House, 1969.

Kutler, Stanley. *Abuse of Power: The New Nixon Tapes*. New York: The Free Press, 1997.

Lau, Peter F. *Democracy Rising: South Carolina and the Fight for Black Equality Since 1865*. Lexington, KY: The University Press of Kentucky, 2006.

Laudani, Raffaele, ed. *Secret Reports on Nazi Germany: The Frankfurt School Contribution to the War Effort: Franz Neumann, Herbert Marcuse and Otto Kirchheimer*. Princeton University Press, 2013.

Lendvai, Paul. *Anti-Semitism in Eastern Europe*. London: Macdonald & Co., 1971.

Marcello, Patricia Cronin. *Gloria Steinem: A Biography*. London: Greenwood Press, 2004.

Marcuse, Herbert. *Eros and Civilization*. Boston: Beacon, 1955.

Marcuse, Herbert. *One-Dimensional Man: Studies in the Ideology of Advanced Industrial Society*. London: Routledge, 1964.

Marx, Karl, and Frederick Engles. *The Communist Manifesto*. Translated by Samuel Moore. 1848. Marxist Internet Archive. https://tinyurl.com/4k8uteje.

Mattson, Kevin. *Intellectuals in Action: The Origins of the New Left and Radical Liberalism*. State College, Pennsylvania State University Press, 2002.

Matz, Mary Jane. *The Many Lives of Otto Kahn*. New York: Macmillan Company, 1963.

McAdam, Doug. *Freedom Summer*. Oxford: Oxford University Press, 1988.

McMeekin, Sean, *History's Greatest Heist*. New Haven: Yale University, 2009.

McMillian, John, and Paul Buhle, eds. *The New Left Revisited*. Philadelphia: Temple University Press, 2003.

Mills, Ami Chen. *CIA Off Campus: Building the Movement Against Agency Recruitment & Research*. Boston: South End Press, 1991.

Mjagkij, Nina, ed. *Organizing Black America: An Encyclopedia of African American Associations*. New York: Garland Publishing, 2001.

Mueller, Brian Scott. "A Think Tank on the Left: The Institute for Policy Studies and Cold War America, 1963–1989." PhD diss., University of Wisconsin-Milwaukee, 2015.

Nouzille, Vincent. *Des secrets si bien gardés: Les dossiers de la Maison-Blanche et de la CIA sur la France et ses présidents 1958-1981 (The Secret So Well Kept: Records of the White House and CIA on France and Its Presidents 1958-1981)*. Paris: Fayard, 2010.

Oglesby, Carl. *The Yankee & Cowboy War: Conspiracies from Dallas to Watergate & Beyond*. Berkley Publishing Corp., 1977.

O'Neil, Tom. *Chaos: Charles Manson, The CIA and the Secret History of the Sixties*. London: Little Brown & Co., 2019.

Parmar, Inderjeet. *Foundations of the American Century: The Ford, Carnegie and Rockefeller Foundations in the Rise of American Power*. New York: Columbia University Press, 2012.

Powers, Devon. *Writing the Record: The Village Voice & the Birth of Rock Criticism*. Boston: University of Massachusetts Press, 2013.

Price, David H. *Cold War Anthropology: The CIA, the Pentagon, and the Growth of Dual Use Anthropology*. Durham, NC: Duke University Press, 2016.

Quigley, Carroll. *Tragedy and Hope: A History of the World in Our Time*. New York: Macmillan 1966.

Rice, Gerard T. *Peace Corps in the 80's*. Washington, DC: Peace Corps, 1986.

Robinson, Dean E. *Black Nationalism in American Politics and Thought*. Cambridge University Press, 2001.

Roelofs, Joan. *Foundations and Public Policy: The Mask of Pluralism*. New York: State University of New York Press, 2003.

Rothman, Stanley, and S. Robert Lichter. *Roots of Radicalism: Jews, Christians and the New Left*. 1996; New York: Routledge, 2017.

Rubin, Jerry. *Do It!* New York: Simon and Schuster, 1970.

Rubin, Jerry. *Growing (Up) at 37*. New York: Warner Books, 1976.

Sale, Kirkpatrick. *SDS: The Rise and Development of the Students for a Democratic Society*. New York: Random House, 1973.

Saunders, Frances Stonor. *The Cultural Cold War: The CIA and the World of Arts and Letters*. New York: The New Press, 1999.

Schlafly, Phyllis. *A Choice, Not an Echo: The Inside Story of how American Presidents are Chosen*. Alton, IL: Pere Marquette Press, 1964.

Schuman, Tomas (AKA Yuri Bezmenov). *Love Letter to America*. Los Angeles: W.I.N. Almanac Panorama, 1984.

Schwartz, Eugene G., ed. *American Students Organize: for the National Student Association After World War II: An Anthology and Sourcebook*. Westport, CT: Praeger Publishers, 2006.

Scott-Smith, Giles, and Hans Krabbendam, eds. *The Cultural Cold War in Western Europe 1945–1960*. London: Frank Cass, 2003.

Siegel, Ronald, and Louis Jolyon West. *Hallucinations: Behavior, Experience, and Theory*. New York: Wiley, 1975.

Snodgrass, Mary Ellen. *Encyclopedia of Feminist Literature*. New York: Facts on File, 2013.

Spence, Richard B. *Wall Street and the Russian Revolution: 1905–1925*. Springfield, OR: Trine Day LLC, 2017.

Spengler, Oswald. *The Decline of the West*. New York: Knopf, 1926.

Stang, Alan. *The Great Con: A Message for Young Radicals*. Belmont, MA: American Opinion, 1970.

Steege, Ted. *Radicals in Professions*. Ann Arbor, MI: Radical Education Project, 1967.

Talbot, David. *Season of the Witch: Enchantment, Terror, and Deliverance in the City of Love*. New York: Free Press, 2012.

Taylor, Harold. *The World and the American Teacher: The Preparation of Teachers in the Field of World Affairs*. Washington DC: American Association of Colleges for Teacher Education, 1968.

Thomas, Evan. *Robert Kennedy: His Life*. New York: Simon & Schuster, 2007.

Thomas, Gordon. *Journey into Madness: Medical Torture & the Mind Controllers*. Corgi Books, 1989.

Trotsky, Leon. *The Revolution Betrayed*. 1936.

Weikart, Lynn A. *Follow the Money: Who Controls New York City Mayors?* New York: State University of New York Press, 2009.

Weinberg, Steve. *Armand Hammer: The Untold Story*. Boston: Little Brown & Co., 1989.

Wells, H. G. *The Open Conspiracy: Blue Prints for a World Revolution*. Garden City, New York: Doubleday, Doran, 1928.

Windmiller, Marshall. *The Peace Corps and Pax Americana*. Washington D.C.: Public Affairs Press, 1970.

Winston, Henry. *The Crisis of the Black Panther Party*. Communist Party USA, 1971.

Zipp, Samuel. *Manhattan Projects: The Rise and Fall of Urban Renewal in Cold War New York*. Oxford University Press, 2010.

Zunz, Olivier. *Philanthropy in America: A History*. New Jersey: Princeton University Press, 2012.

All Other Sources Cited

Acosta, Teresa Palomo. "Mexican American Youth Organization." Texas State Historical Association, 1976. Updated April 8, 2020. https://tshaonline.org/handbook/online/articles/wem01.

Adams, Michael Henry. "Thomas Hoving, Wendy Burden and the End of Elite Privilege?" *Huffpost*, May 21, 2010. https://tinyurl.com/2zz9uyb9.

Additional Procurement of M-16 Rifles, Before the Special M-16 Rifle Subcommittee of the Preparedness Investigating Subcommittee of the Committee on Armed Services United States Senate, 90th Con. (1968). https://tinyurl.com/365xspj5.

Allen, Gary. "Who is Paying for the Student Revolutionary Movement?" *American Opinion*, November 1970.

Als, Hilton. "Queen Jane, Approximately." *The New Yorker*, May 9, 2011. https://tinyurl.com/3ec3f8wc.

Altbach, Philip G. *The Student Internationals: An Analysis of International and Regional Student Organizations*. Madison: University of Wisconsin, October 1970. https://files.eric.ed.gov/fulltext/ED048091.pdf.

Andelman, David A. "'68 Transit Pact Exposed." *The New York Times*, October 24, 1974. https://tinyurl.com/4heyw79c.

Ango, Junald Dawa. "An Un-American Foreign Policy: The Peace Corps Overseas, 1961–71." *Procedia—Social and Behavioral Sciences* 65, (December 2012): 498–504. https://doi.org/10.1016/j.sbspro.2012.11.155.

"Another Volume of Subversion." *The National Layman's Digest* 2, no. 21 (November 1, 1970).

"Anti-Soviet Policy of Mao Tse-tung and His Group, The." *Soviet News*, no. 5370 (February 17, 1967): 93–96. Translated from *Pravda*, February 16, 1967. https://tinyurl.com/yf46m98u.

Applebome, Peter. "Rennie Davis, 'Chicago Seven' Antiwar Activist, Dies at 80." *The New York Times*, February 3, 2021. https://tinyurl.com/2d2y74aa.

"Attack on Rudi Dutschke: The Revolutionary who Shaped a Generation, The." *Spiegel International*, April 11, 2008. https://tinyurl.com/2ayh9mst.

Augstein, Rudolf. "Mit den Bomben leben." *Der Spiegel*, June 2, 1975.

Backman, Jussi. "Radical Conservatism and the Heideggerian Right: Heidegger, de Benoist, Dugin." *Frontiers in Political Science* 4, (September 16, 2022). https://doi.org/10.3389/fpos.2022.941799.

Ball, Molly. "The Secret History of the Shadow Campaign That Saved the 2020 Election." *Time*, February 4, 2021. https://tinyurl.com/yc3cvd7k.

Ballesteros, Carlos. "Trump State Department Accused of Abandoning Global Democracy in New Budget." *Newsweek*, March 5, 2018. https://tinyurl.com/4e6pya5m.

Bank, Justin. "Saul Alinsky: His Political Influence Exhumed." *The Washington Post*, January 24, 2012. https://tinyurl.com/5t4s24xc.

Barnes, Bart. "Philip M. Stern, Dies, 66." *The Washington Post*, June 2, 1992. https://tinyurl.com/z3bwca5n.

Barnes, Bart. "Barry Goldwater, GOP Hero, Dies." *The Washington Post*, May 30, 1998. https://tinyurl.com/4kwdyr8c.

Barnett, Ross. "Governor Barnett's Declaration to the People of Mississippi." Television and radio broadcast, September 13, 1962. https://microsites.jfklibrary.org/olemiss/controversy/doc2.html.

Bekoe, E. Ofori "The United States Peace Corps as a Facet of United States-Ghana Relations." *The Journal of Pan African Studies* 4, no. 10 (January 2012): 227–39. http://jpanafrican.org/docs/vol4no10/4.10UnitedStates.pdf.

Bernstein, Carl. "The Holy Alliance." *Time*, June 24, 2001. http://content.time.com/time/magazine/article/0,9171,159069,00.html.

Bilefsky, Dan. "Czech's Velvet Revolution Paved by Plastic People." *The New York Times*, November 15, 2009. https://tinyurl.com/59ezhdr4.

Bilek, Jennifer. "Transgenderism is Just Big Business Dressed Up in Pretend Civil Rights Clothes." *The Federalist*, July 5, 2018. https://tinyurl.com/4p82yubm.

Blumenthal, Sidney. "The Left Stuff." *The Washington Post*, July 30, 1986. https://tinyurl.com/2u3nrz5h.

Bodroghkozy, Aniko. "Reel Revolutionaries: An Examination of Hollywood's Cycle of 1960s Youth Rebellion Films." *Cinema Journal* 41, no. 3 (Spring 2002): 38–58. https://doi.org/10.1353/cj.2002.0007.

Bolton, K. R. "Don't Blame the Brits." *Foreign Policy Journal*, August 8, 2010. https://www.foreignpolicyjournal.com/2010/08/08/dont-blame-the-brits/.

Bolton, K. R. "Geopolitics and Oligarchy at Work in Ukraine Crisis." *Foreign Policy Journal*, March 5, 2014. https://tinyurl.com/22d2hm4d.

Bolton, K. R. "Joe McCarthy and the Establishment Bolsheviks." *Counter-Currents*, November 6, 2013. https://tinyurl.com/h34x4hrp.

Bolton, K. R. "Joe McCarthy's Real Enemies." *The Occidental Quarterly* 10, no. 4 (Winter 2010–2011): 75–102. https://tinyurl.com/6a9epvur.

Bolton, K. R. "Labour Party's Communist Allies." *The European New Zealander*, October 7, 2020. https://tinyurl.com/4rfm7hft.

Bolton, K. R. "Obama—Catspaw of International Finance." *Rense*, August 28, 2008. https://rense.com/general83/cats.htm.

Bolton, K. R. "Some Factors Behind the Ukraine Crisis." *Geopolitika.ru*, February 28, 2022. https://tinyurl.com/4ek426rh.

Bolton, K. R. "United Nations Global Compact on Immigration: Origins and Aims." *Arktos Journal*, January 7, 2019. https://tinyurl.com/mu99mzx8.

Boon, Maxim. "Vaslav Nijinsky: Still Dancing with his Demons." *Limelight*, Australia, August 25, 2016.

Borman, Nancy. "Inside the CIA with Gloria Steinem." *Village Voice*, May 21, 1979. https://www.mail-archive.com/ctrl@listserv.aol.com/msg02217.html.

Bostock, Bill. "Sealed FBI Audio Tapes Allege Martin Luther King Jr. Had Affairs with 40 Women and Watched While a Friend Raped a Woman, a Report Claims." *Business Insider*, May 29, 2019. https://tinyurl.com/2596azuh.

Bovard, James. "The Forgotten Failures of the Peace Corps." Peace Corps Worldwide, April 1, 2011. https://tinyurl.com/3u969r49.

Brecher, Jeremy. "The Elections—and After." *Students for a Democratic Society Bulletin* 3, no. 3 (November–December 1964). https://tinyurl.com/f8wpv7az.

Bright, Barbara. "World Youth Festival I." Barbara Bright to Richard H. Nolte, September 9, 1968, in Institute of Current World Affairs. http://www.icwa.org/wp-content/uploads/2015/09/BWB-2.pdf.

Bright, Barbara. "World Youth Festival II." Barbara Bright to Richard H. Nolte, September 11, 1968, in Institute of Current World Affairs. http://www.icwa.org/wp-content/uploads/2015/09/BWB-3.pdf.

Brinkley, Douglas S. "The Man Who Kept King's Secrets." *Vanity Fair*, April 2006. https://tinyurl.com/43c47pem.

Brown, Maoz. *Philanthropy and the US Student Movements: Four Cases.* Washington, DC: Urban Institute, April 2019. https://tinyurl.com/5n7y8jkf.

Brown, Mick. "Trip of a Lifetime: Ken Kesey, LSD, The Merry Pranksters and the Birth of Psychedelia." *The Telegraph*, November 2, 2016. https://tinyurl.com/5n6m3hxx.

Bruno, Mark. "Howard Stein, former Dreyfus chairman and CEO, dies at 84." *Investment News*, June 12, 2011. https://tinyurl.com/yckk4ph6.

Buck, Joan Juliet. "France's Prophet Provocateur." *Vanity Fair*, January 2003. https://www.vanityfair.com/news/2003/01/levy200301.

Buffalo Courier Express. New York, October 25, 1966.

Burke, Kevin M. "A Close Alliance between MLK and Nelson Rockefeller Revealed." *The Root*, November 1, 2015. https://tinyurl.com/48bbm8ct.

Burlage, Robb. *Johnson With Eyes Open.* New York: Political Education Project, 1964. https://tinyurl.com/3nemcnkc.

Bush, George H. W. "Out of these Troubled Times a New World Order." *The Washington Post*, September 12, 1990. https://tinyurl.com/4hrzp5zw.

Buzzanco, Robert. "Ruling-Class Anti-Imperialism in the Era of the Vietnam War." In Tyrell, Ian, and Jay Sexton, eds. *Empire's Twin: U.S. Anti-Imperialism from the Founding Era to the Age of Terrorism.* Ithaca: Cornell University Press, 2015. 202–18.

California Legislature. *Fourteenth Report of the Senate Factfinding Subcommittee on Un-American Activities, 1967.* Sacramento: Senate of the State of California, 1967.

Carroll, Tamar W. "'To Help People Learn To Fight': New York City's Mobilization For Youth And The Origins Of The Community Action Programs Of The War On Poverty." The Gotham Center for New York City History, October 8, 2015. https://tinyurl.com/mrxx3zcs.

Cartalucci, Tony. "Google's Revolution Factory—Alliance of Youth Movements: Color Revolution 2.0." *Global Research*, February 19, 2011. https://tinyurl.com/mt9kf8sy.

Chernov, F. "Bourgeois Cosmopolitanism and its Reactionary Role." *Bolshevik: Theoretical and Political Magazine of the Central Committee of the ACP(B)*, no. 5 (March 15, 1949): 30–41. https://tinyurl.com/z3w4fpju.

Church League of America. *The National Laymen's Digest* 2, no. 18 (September 15, 1970).

CIA. "France: Defection of the Leftist Intellectuals: A Research Paper." CIA Directorate of Intelligence, Office of European Analysis, 1985. https://tinyurl.com/5yybza3d.

CIA. "Italy: Summary." President's Daily Brief, Central Intelligence Agency, July 1, 1966. https://tinyurl.com/mvkeejxa.

CIA. "MKULTRA Subproject 58, Invoice #1." CIA Memorandum, March 28, 1956. https://tinyurl.com/4d46e7mn.

CIA. "Youth Festival." *Central Intelligence Bulletin*, July 31, 1968. https://tinyurl.com/czh5kay.

CIA Executive Officer. CIA Executive Officer to Edward Bernays, April 2, 1958. https://tinyurl.com/38mumpcy.

Clinton, Bill. "Statement from President Clinton and Secretary Clinton on the Passing of Tom Hayden." Clinton Foundation, October 24, 2016. https://tinyurl.com/3e4e6z5r.

Cloud, John. "When the Elites Loved LSD." *Time*, April 23, 2007. http://content.time.com/time/nation/article/0,8599,1613675,00.html.

Cohen, Lizabeth. "The Doomed 1970s Plan to Desegregate New York's Suburbs." *Bloomberg*, October 21, 2019. https://tinyurl.com/mrx8k7ms.

Cohn-Bendit, Daniel, and Leggewie, Claus. "1968: Power to the Imagination." *The New York Review*, May 10, 2018. https://tinyurl.com/2rpadupt.

"Communists Aped Hitler in Prague Trials Says World Congress Report." *B'nai B'rith Messenger* (Los Angeles), November 27, 1953.

Connolly, Richard J. "Businessman, Dummy Firm, Fund Boston SDS." *The Boston Globe*, July 12, 1969.

Cooks, Bridget R. "Black Artists and Activism: *Harlem on My Mind* (1969)." *American Studies* 8, no. 1 (Spring 2007): 5–39. https://doi.org/10.1353/ams.0.0137.

Creegan, Jim. "The Left Wing of the Permissible: The Politics of Michael Harrington." *Counter-Punch*, September 7, 2017. https://tinyurl.com/3e599upd.

"Czech Intellectuals Upset over Anti-Israel Statement," *The Sentinel* (Chicago), August 22, 1968.

"Danny the Red Working for CIA?" *Eastern European Intelligencer*, CIA EE
	Division, January 2 to June 28, 1968. CIA archives.
	https://tinyurl.com/47f2ca28.

Danto, Arthur C. "The Student Revolt at Columbia University." *Artforum*, May
	2008. https://tinyurl.com/mbn5ycja.

Daugherity, Brian J. "Desegregation in Public Schools." *Encyclopedia Virginia*,
	Accessed August 13, 2023. https://tinyurl.com/2ynv9j9f.

"Democracy-Focused Philanthropy: Choosing Operating Models for Deeper
	Impact." Rockefeller Philanthropy Advisors, December 2, 2022.
	https://tinyurl.com/9fhv5bv4.

Diamante, John C. "Black Power in Action? The National Conference for New
	Politics." *The Southern Courier* 3, no. 39 (September 1967).

Dickerson, John. "Never Goldwater: The Attempt to Wrest the 1964 GOP
	Nomination form the Arizona Senator and the Birth of the Modern GOP."
	Slate, May 12, 2016. https://tinyurl.com/4a4kdufs.

Domhoff, G. William. "Power at the Local Level: The Ford Foundation in the Inner
	City: Forging an Alliance with Neighborhood Activists." *Who Rules America?*
	September 2005. https://tinyurl.com/ytaajkyf.

Donadio, Rachel. "How Hungary Ran Soros out of Town." *The Atlantic*, May 15,
	2008. https://tinyurl.com/37nfsxmm.

Donnelly, Sue. "Funding the Vision—Henry Hunt Hutchinson and His Will." LSE,
	September 30, 2015. https://tinyurl.com/y89jy3j2.

"Double Standard on Tax Exemption." *The Weekly Crusader* 7, no. 45 (September
	22, 1967).

"Draft Strategy of the Privatization Department of the Kosovo Trust Agency."
	European Stability Initiative, April 2004. https://tinyurl.com/ms6ermef.

Dulles, Allen. Memo to the Membership Committee of The Century Association.
	CIA Archives, April 3, 1957. https://tinyurl.com/5devszy6.

Dvorsky, George, and James Hughes. "Postgenderism: Beyond the Gender Binary."
	Institute for Ethics and Emerging Technologies, March 2008.
	https://ieet.org/wp-content/uploads/2021/05/IEET-03-PostGender.pdf.

Eastland, James O. "National Conference for New Politics." *Congressional Record*,
	September 22, 1967. https://tinyurl.com/58726afc.

Egerman, Howard. "'Students for a Democratic Society' Might be Recruited for
	Peace Corps." *California Aggie* 68, no. 20 (November 23, 1965).

Elliott, Debbie. "Integrating Ole Miss: A Transformative Deadly Riot." NPR,
	October 1, 2012. https://tinyurl.com/yr6zkv4t.

Engburg, Jens. "Royalist Finances During the English Civil War 1642–1646."
	Scandinavian Economic History Review 14, no. 2 (1966): 73–96.
	https://doi.org/10.1080/03585522.1966.10407649.

Ennis, Thomas W. "Charles T. Plohn Snr. Partner in Wall Street Concern in 1960s."
	The New York Times, July 24, 1984. https://tinyurl.com/23hz53td.

"Extent of Subversion in Campus Disorders." Hearings Before the Subcommittee to
	Investigate the Internal Security Act & Other Internal Security Laws of the

Committee on the Judiciary of the U.S. Senate, Ninety-First Congress, First Session, Part 3. June 26, 1969. #1017–1018. https://tinyurl.com/yepkaztv.

ExxonMobil, "ExxonMobil Foundation & Corporate Giving to Climate Change Denier & Obstructionist Organizations." ExxonMobil Worldwide Giving 1998–2017. https://tinyurl.com/5f636tx2.

FBI. "FOIA: FBI Monograph Fund For The Republic, Inc." Federal Bureau of Investigation, November 1955. https://tinyurl.com/hxa5364m.

FBI. "March from Selma to Montgomery, Alabama, Commencing March 21st, 1965." FBI memo to US Attorney General, March 22, 1965. https://tinyurl.com/336e9enh.

FBI. *Martin Luther King Jr.: A Current Analysis*. Federal Bureau of Investigation, March 12, 1968. https://tinyurl.com/4nr7hend.

"Fears for Czech Jews Polish Style Purge." *Australian Jewish Times* 75, no. 45 (August 29, 1968).

Ford Foundation. *Annual Report 1964*. New York: Ford Foundation, 1965. https://tinyurl.com/47hwsp73.

Ford Foundation. *Annual Report 1965*. New York: Ford Foundation, 1966. https://tinyurl.com/2j6whb3x.

Ford Foundation. *Annual Report 1968*. New York: Ford Foundation, 1969. https://tinyurl.com/jfw2ued5.

Ford Foundation. *Annual Report 1969*. New York: Ford Foundation, 1970. https://tinyurl.com/3m2zavsv.

Ford Foundation. *Annual Report 1970*. New York: Ford Foundation, 1971. https://tinyurl.com/3u6sfw7m.

Ford Foundation. *Annual Report 1972*. New York: Ford Foundation, 1973. https://tinyurl.com/322x9vaf.

Ford Foundation. *Annual Report 1974*. New York: Ford Foundation, 1975. https://tinyurl.com/4y5cs637.

Ford Foundation. *Annual Report 1979*. New York: Ford Foundation, 1980. https://tinyurl.com/ypc2r2xs.

Ford Foundation. *Annual Report 2005*. New York: Ford Foundation, 2006. https://tinyurl.com/2hsxmxhn.

Fosdick, Raymond. Raymond Fosdick to John D. Rockefeller, Jr., June 13, 1924, Rockefeller Archive Center (RAC), Rockefeller Family Boards, RG III 2 K, Box 1, Folder 1.

"Foundations, Private Organizations Linked to CIA." *Congressional Quarterly Special Report*, February 24, 1967.

Frank, Thomas. "My Friend Bill Ayers." *The Wall Street Journal*, October 15, 2008. https://www.wsj.com/articles/SB122402888900234543.

Franklin, Bruce. "The Lumpenproletariat and the Revolutionary Youth Movement." Bay Area Revolutionary Union, *Red Papers*, no. 2 (1969). https://tinyurl.com/49svtuwa.

Freedom House. "Bayard Rustin, A Hero of the Freedom Movement." August 12, 2013.

"From Behind Bars Kayo Tried to Buy into a Magazine." *Life* 70, no. 25 (June 25, 1971).

Gentry, Dick. "The Sad Story of the Journalist and the Jukebox Repairman." *Hotty Toddy*, June 18, 2014. https://tinyurl.com/ycyscrx5.

Gershman, Carl. "Lost Prophet: The Life & Times of Bayard Rustin." National Endowment for Democracy, Accessed August 14, 2023. https://www.ned.org/lost-prophet-the-life-and-times-o/.

Gilbert, David, Robert Gottlieb, and Gerry Tenney. "Toward a Theory of Social Change: The 'Port Authority Statement.'" 1967. In Carl Davidson, *Revolutionary Youth & the New Working Class: The Praxis Papers, the Port Authority Statement, the RYM Documents and Other Lost Writings of SDS*. Pittsburg: Changemaker Publications, 2011. https://tinyurl.com/37zn9f3z.

Gilbert, Sophie. "The Real Cult of Charles Manson." *The Atlantic*, November 20, 2017. https://tinyurl.com/vm8eaem9.

Gleason, Ralph J. "The Revolutionaries of Columbia." *Fifth Estate*, no. 79 (May 15–28, 1969). https://tinyurl.com/ye5629pm.

Goldberg, Jonah. "'America first' isn't a Trump creation." *The Baltimore Sun*, January 26, 2017. https://tinyurl.com/ywjkk75e.

Gonzalez, Henry B. *Congressional Record,* 91st Congress, 1st Session. April 22, 1969.

Greenwald, Glenn. "The Untouchables: How the Obama Administration Protected Wall Street from Prosecutions." *The Guardian*, January 23, 2013. https://tinyurl.com/bdfeapmp.

Gregory, Erik M. "Edward Bernays, Uncle Freud, and Betty Crocker: The Plague of Self-Consciousness." *Psychology Today*, April 6, 2016. https://tinyurl.com/4zt2hk5w.

Grose, Peter. "Rogers Seeks Divergent Views; Invites Aid of Young Diplomats." *The New York Times*, January 23, 1969.

Grosser, Charles F. *Helping Youth: A Study of Six Community Organization Programs*. Washington, DC: Office of Juvenile Delinquency and Youth Development, 1968. https://files.eric.ed.gov/fulltext/ED025053.pdf

Gupta, Pranay. "Family and Friends Mourn for Rockefeller." *The New York Times*, January 28, 1979.

Haines, Herbert. "Black Radicalization and the Funding of Civil Rights: 1957–1970." *Social Problems* 32, no. 1 (October 1984).

Harris, Marilyn. "When White Philanthropy Funded Black Power." *Philanthropy New Digest*, August 30, 2019. https://tinyurl.com/4rry2fb8.

Harwood, Richard. "Ruling Class Journalists." *The Washington Post*, October 30, 1993. https://tinyurl.com/yhtwf7sr.

Hayden, Tom. "Bobby and Barack." *Huffpost*, June 5, 2008. https://www.huffpost.com/entry/bobby-and-barack_b_105406.

Hayden, Tom. "The CIA's Student Activism Phase." *The Nation*, November 26, 2014. https://tinyurl.com/jchjpm3j.

Hayden, Tom. *Liberal Analysis and Federal Power*. New York: Students for a Democratic Society, 1964. https://tinyurl.com/bdsb9hbj.

Hayden, Tom. "Participatory Democracy: From the Port Huron Statement to Occupy Wall Street On its Fiftieth anniversary, the Founding Declaration of SDS Echoes Today in Democracy Movements Around the World." *The Nation*, March 27, 2012. https://tinyurl.com/4pschtpr.

Hayden, Tom. "Personal Statement: Fifty Years Later, Still Making a Statement." *The Michigan Daily*, October 25, 2012. https://tinyurl.com/3742hc8y.

Hayden, Tom. *The Port Huron Statement*. New York: Students for a Democratic Society, 1962. https://tinyurl.com/47fpn5ve.

Hayden, Tom. "Saving Obama, Saving Ourselves." *Tikkun*, September 5, 2012. https://tinyurl.com/3eyh3ja4.

Healy, Brian. "Columbia: No Easy Answers." *The Daily Collegian* 68, no. 114 (May 1, 1968). https://www.1968.psu.edu/assets/uploads/collegian/05-01-1968.pdf.

Hitchens, Christopher. "Minority Report." *The Nation*, July 13, 1985.

Hinckle, Warren. "Warren Hinckle: Journalist, Editor, Publisher, Iconoclast." Interview by Lisa Rubens. 2009–2012. Regional Oral History Office, The Bancroft Library, University of California, Berkeley, 2013. https://digicoll.lib.berkeley.edu/record/218768?ln=en.

Hodder, Jake. "Toward a Geography of Black Internationalism: Bayard Rustin, Nonviolence, and the Promise of Africa." *Annals of the American Association of Geographers* 106, no. 6 (2016): 1360–1377. https://doi.org/10.1080/24694452.2016.1203284.

Hoffman, Leah. "The Hippie: Rennie Davis." *Forbes*, February 14, 2006. https://tinyurl.com/5fjy5huw.

Hoffman, Nicholas von. "Magazine Experimenting." *The Washington Post*, September 11, 1970. https://tinyurl.com/2hnxh4d3.

"Hoffman vs. Rubin 'Yuppies vs. Yippie Debate.'" *AP News*, February 2, 1985.

Holder, Akilah, and Josh Rodriguez. *MFY Legal Services Inc., 45th Anniversary 1963–2008*. New York: MFY Legal Services, 2008. https://tinyurl.com/bdexeb2k.

Holland, Steve. "Trump to West Point Grads: 'We are Ending the Eras of Endless Wars.'" *Reuters*, June 14, 2020. https://tinyurl.com/3ym3jmer.

Hunter, Clarence. "Huge Tents Shelter Civil Rights Army." *The Evening Star*, March 22, 1965.

Huxley, Aldous. Interview by Mike Wallace. *The Mike Wallace Interview*, ABC, 1958. Audio, 28:12. https://tinyurl.com/yckazdst.

Iacobelli, Teresa. "Rockefeller Foundation Support for the Communications Media in the 1930s and 1940s." Rockefeller Foundation, January 6, 2022. https://tinyurl.com/a4wjbe4r.

IEP. *Economic Consequences of War on the U.S. Economy*. New York: Institute for Economics and Peace, 2011. https://tinyurl.com/t2p82429.

"Importing Student Subversives." *Human Events*, September 14, 1968.

Innis, Roy. "Remarks by Roy Innis before the 2011 International Conference on Climate Change." *CORELATOR* 43, no. 22 (Summer 2011): 1. https://tinyurl.com/3cj6pjem.

IPS. *Annual Report 2018*. Institute for Policy Studies, 2019. https://ips-dc.org/2018-annual-report/

Jacobs, John. "The Diaries of a CIA Operative." *The Washington Post*, September 5, 1977.

Janson, Donald. "Alinksy to Train White Militants: Institute for Middle Class Reformers Established." *The New York Times*, August 7, 1968.

"Johnson Names Blaustein a Trustee of Eleanor Roosevelt Foundation." Jewish Telegraphic Agency, February 19, 1964. https://tinyurl.com/mthzpevw.

Johnston, Angus. "A Brief History of the United States Student Association." *Student Activism*, July 15, 2010. https://tinyurl.com/37by4nk8.

Jones, Josh. "Ken Kesey Talks About the Meaning of the Acid Tests." *Open Culture*, January 4, 2013. https://tinyurl.com/44u94smk.

Karpel, Craig. "Das Hip Kapital." *Liberation News Service*, no. 358 (July 14, 1971).

Kauffman, Bill. "When the Left was Right." *The American Conservative*, May 19, 2008. https://tinyurl.com/ycy6ht3d.

Keating, Edward M. "The South at War." *Ramparts*, June 1965. https://www.crmvet.org/info/6506_ramparts_selma-r.pdf

Kellner, Douglas. "Marcuse, Herbert." *The American National Biography*, 1999. https://doi.org/10.1093/anb/9780198606697.article.2001202.

"Kennan Retells History: Relates how Jacob H. Schiff Financed Revolution Propaganda in Czar's Army." *The New York Times*, March 24, 1917.

"KGB Defector Blames '60s Activists for Soviet Success." *Redding Record-Searchlight*, March 24, 1986. https://tinyurl.com/2jw3vau7.

King, Martin Luther, Jr. "Letter from a Birmingham Jail." April 16, 1963. http://www.africa.upenn.edu/Articles_Gen/Letter_Birmingham.html.

King, Martin Luther, Jr. "Declaration of Independence from the War in Vietnam." *Ramparts* (May 1967): 33–37. https://tinyurl.com/4ahjf2zv.

"Kinsey Institute Exposed: A Warning to Parents & Governments Throughout the World, The." Stop the Kinsey Institute. https://tinyurl.com/353tn778.

Kneeland, Douglas E. "Chicago Group Faces Foundation Cutoff." *The New York Times*, February 14, 1978. https://tinyurl.com/4t2m28p3.

Korberg, Rachel, and Rob Garris. "Inclusive Economies, Sexual Orientation, and Gender Identity Expression." The Rockefeller Foundation, August 15, 2014. https://tinyurl.com/yc7646hm.

Krassner, Paul. "Hippies, radicals, pranksters: Jerry Rubin has a bio and Paul Krassner has our review." *Los Angeles Times*, August 31, 2017. https://tinyurl.com/mrbw8wne.

Langford, Richard. "Bob Arum: Boxing Must Rid Itself of Shady Promoter." *Bleacher Report*, June 10, 2012. https://tinyurl.com/yrvyrmwu.

Lasch, Christopher. "The Revolt of the Elites: Have they cancelled their allegiance to America?" *Harper's Magazine* (November 1994): 39–49. https://tinyurl.com/2r4f8d4z.

Lee, Jennifer S. "Big Tobacco's Spin on Women's Liberation." *The New York Times*, October 10, 2008. https://tinyurl.com/2s3fry9v.

Lee, Martin A. "Former Left-wing, German Extremist Horst Mahler Switches to Neo-Nazi National Democratic Party." *Southern Poverty Law Center*, August 29, 2001. https://tinyurl.com/bdfm2v6w.

Lennon, John and Yoko Ono. Interview by David Sheff, September 1980, *Playboy*, January 1981. http://www.beatlesinterviews.org/dbjypb.int3.html.

"Let Russia Have It." *Chicago Tribune*, July 22, 1970.

Lévy, Bernard-Henri. "The Blinding Rage of the Yellow Vests." *Tablet*, December 13, 2018. https://tinyurl.com/5n73s8r2.

Lichtenstein, Nelson. "It Never Hurts to Have a Few Enemies." *The New York Times*, November 12, 1989. https://tinyurl.com/t8md983f.

Lofton, J. D. "Ms. Steinem's CIA Connection." *Human Events*, May 10, 1975.

Lubasch, Arnold H. "Goldwater in Book Suit." *The New York Times*, February 4, 1982. https://tinyurl.com/y6zfn2az.

Lukas, J. Anthony. "Chicago 7 Judge Bars Ramsey Clark as Defense Witness." *The New York Times*, January 29, 1970. https://tinyurl.com/2nsuj3er.

Magid, Larry. "Magid: Back to the Future with Education." *East Bay Times*, June 19, 2014. https://tinyurl.com/4kkph34d.

Mair, John. "The Agitators." *The Guardian*, July 10, 2003. https://www.theguardian.com/education/2003/jul/10/students.uk.

Marchi, John J. *Preliminary Data Report of the Senate Committee on Affairs of the City of New York on Mobilization for Youth Inc.,* State of New York, Legislative Document No. 45. Albany, 1964. https://tinyurl.com/mwdze77w.

Marcuse, Herbert. "Marxism and Feminism." *Women's Studies* 2, no. 3 (1974): 279–288. https://doi.org/10.1080/00497878.1974.9978359.

Markay, Lachlan. "Democracy Alliance Network Revealed." *The Washington Free Beacon*, May 19, 2014. https://tinyurl.com/3zvybcvu.

Marlowe, Lara. "Paris Provoked CIA and KGB Alarm." *The Irish Times*, May 9, 1998. https://tinyurl.com/3v6duexa.

Maunders, David. "Controlling Youth for Democracy: The United States Youth Council and the World Assembly of Youth." *Commonwealth Youth and Development* 1, no. 2 (2003). https://hdl.handle.net/10520/EJC30826.

McFadden, Robert D. "Roy Innis, Black Activist with a Right-wing Bent, Dies at 82." *The New York Times*, January 10, 2017. https://tinyurl.com/ypdbsjzy.

Mchunu Koyi, and Sandile Mbatha. "The Significance of Place in Urban Governance: Mart 125 and the Politics of Community Development in Harlem, New York." *Mediterranean Journal of Social Sciences* 9, no. 2 (March 2018): 99–108. https://doi.org/10.2478/mjss-2018-0030.

Medias-Presse-Info. "Bernard-Henri Lévy and Cohn-Bendit Banned from Stay in Russia." *OverBlog*, May 30, 2015. https://tinyurl.com/2szv3pzm.

Mehnert, Klaus. "Moscow & the New Left: From Mao & Marcuse to Marx." *Encounter*, (February 1974): 39–42. https://tinyurl.com/2sras94c.

Miller, Scott. "Inside Hair." In *Rebels with Applause: Broadway's Ground Breaking Musicals.* Heinemann Publishing, 2001. https://tinyurl.com/mptv3k56.

Moore, James. "Rennie Davis: From Chicago 7 to Venture Capitalist to Grand Canyon Visionary." *The Iowa Source*, 2005. https://tinyurl.com/44th4pej.

Moore, Ryan. "Sociology of Youth Culture," in *International Encyclopedia of the Social & Behavioral Sciences* (Second Edition), (2015): 813–818. https://doi.org/10.1016/B978-0-08-097086-8.32173-0.

"More on Ayers." The Thomas B. Fordham Institute, May 19, 2008. https://fordhaminstitute.org/national/commentary/more-ayers.

"Mrs. Lehman Named Foundation Trustee." *The New York Times*, February 16, 1964.

Nation Editors. "Happy Fiftieth Anniversary, IPS!" *The Nation*, September 25, 2013. https://tinyurl.com/3fmdcmyp.

"New Left School of Los Angeles." *Fire and Police Research Association of Los Angeles News*, October 1965.

Noah, Timothy. "Radical Chic Resurgent." Chatterbox, *Slate Magazine*, August 22, 2001. https://tinyurl.com/yyf8apxh.

Novak, Steven J. "LSD Before Leary: Sidney Cohen's Critique of 1950s Psychedelic Drug Research." *Isis* 88, no. 1 (March 1997). https://doi.org/10.1086/383628.

NZ Herald. "Covid-19 Omicron Convoy Protest: Govt in Crisis Meeting Over Protest, MP Michael Wood Speaks out on Dark Undercurrent." *NZ Herald*, February 17, 2022. https://tinyurl.com/2r3z2stf.

O'Flynn, Edward J. "Ramparts Magazine, Inc." Federal Bureau of Investigation, October 3, 1968. https://tinyurl.com/3nmprxha.

O'Malley, Michael. "The Gentleman from Pennsylvania: An Interview with William W. Scranton." *Pennsylvania Heritage* (Winter 2001). https://tinyurl.com/2p9f6rrs.

Oglesby, Carl. "The Acid Test and How It Failed." *The National Reporter*, Fall 1988.

"Opinion from Moscow." *The Student Federalist*, January–February 1946.

Oppenheimer, Harry. "Portrait of a Millionaire: I, Harry Oppenheimer." In *Africa South*. South Africa Foundation, 1960. 7–16. https://tinyurl.com/3s6uszfr.

Peace Corps, *2nd Annual Report to Congress for the Fiscal Year Ended June 30, 1963*. Washington, DC: Peace Corps, 1963. https://eric.ed.gov/?id=ED209548.

Peace Corps Worldwide. "Peru's First Peace Corps Staff." *Peace Corps Worldwide*, October 7, 2018. https://tinyurl.com/ycywwdt7.

Peace Corps Worldwide. "A Small Peace Corps Connection in the Life of Tom Hayden who Passed Away on Sunday at Age 76." *Peace Corps Worldwide*, October 24, 2016. https://tinyurl.com/3jf2jhht.

Perrigo, Billy. "How the U.S. Used Jazz as a Cold War Secret Weapon." *Time*, December 22, 2017. https://time.com/5056351/cold-war-jazz-ambassadors/.

Peters, Ralph. "Constant Conflict." *Parameters* 27, no. 2 (Summer 1997): 4. https://apps.dtic.mil/sti/pdfs/ADA543039.pdf

Plys, Kristin. "Immanuel Wallerstein." Oxford Bibliographies (July 28, 2021). https://doi.org/10.1093/OBO/9780199756384-0183.

Prečan, Vilém, Svetlana Savranskaya, and Thomas Blanton, eds. "Charter 77 After 30 Years." The National Security Archive, January 6, 2007. http://www.gwu.edu/~nsarchiv/NSAEBB/NSAEBB213/index.htm.

"Present Status of SNCC." *Student Voice* 1, no. 1, June 1960. https://www.crmvet.org/docs/sv/sv6006.pdf.

Preston, Peter. "From the Archive, 16 October 1969: The Day Wall Street Stopped." *The Guardian*, October 16, 2012. https://tinyurl.com/27curpfp.

Prins, Nomi. "The Bankers Behind FDR and the Glass-Steagall Act." *Fortune*, March 19, 2014. https://tinyurl.com/2p8sbrpp.

Rader, Dotson. "A Razzberry for 'Strawberry.'" *The New York Times*, July 19, 1970. https://tinyurl.com/bdhhftsk.

Rader, Dotson. "Steal This Book" Review, *The New York Times*, July 18, 1971. https://tinyurl.com/46dt2kdd.

"Ramparts: Gadfly to the Establishment; Ramparts: New Gadfly to the Liberal Establishment." *The New York Times*, February 20, 1967. https://tinyurl.com/yc2b5wy3.

Rarick, John R. "The Institute for Policy Studies." Congressional Record (House) Proceedings and Debates, November 16, 1970. https://tinyurl.com/3exju4zb.

Raymont, Henry. "Book Publishers Act Against War." *The New York Times*, May 10, 1970. https://tinyurl.com/mr48k4r8.

Raymont, Henry. "Kazin Delivers Lecture on Flag." *The New York Times*, May 29, 1970. https://tinyurl.com/mr3uvs7e.

Redmon, Michael. "Center for the Study of Democratic Institutions: Santa Barbara's Prominent Think Tank." *Santa Barbara Independent*, May 28, 2009. https://tinyurl.com/3pafyu7v.

"Redstockings' Statement." Off Our Backs 5, no. 6 (1975): 8–33. http://www.jstor.org/stable/25772264.

Reed, Roy. "Youth Council to Investigate Charge of C.I.A. Link." *The New York Times*, March 6, 1967.

"Return of the National Student Association." *Human Events*, March 21, 1981, 5. https://tinyurl.com/2s3vw8d9.

"Rift on Peace Corps Healing in Nigeria." *The New York Times*, November 7, 1961. https://tinyurl.com/3hntydbm.

Robert, Frédéric. "The Rhetoric of Social Movements: Differential Images of the Recruitment in Students for a Democratic Society (SDS), 1960–1965." *Revue française d'études américaines* 1, no. 99 (2004): 85–102. https://doi.org/10.3917/rfea.099.0085.

Rockefeller, Nelson A. *Report to the President by the Commission on CIA Activities Within the United States.* Washington, D.C.: Superintendent of Documents, U.S. Government Printing Office, 1975. https://tinyurl.com/ykw4wzau.

Rockefeller, John D, III. "In Praise of Young Revolutionaries." *Saturday Review*, December 14, 1968. https://tinyurl.com/3n5eampd.

Rockefeller Foundation. *President's Five-Year Review & Annual Report 1968.* New York: The Rockefeller Foundation. https://tinyurl.com/3e4see4n.

Rockefeller Foundation. *President's Review & Annual Report 1967.* New York: The Rockefeller Foundation. https://tinyurl.com/yc3pz7b9.

Rockefeller Foundation. *President's Review & Annual Report 1969.* New York: The Rockefeller Foundation. https://tinyurl.com/5mwz23a6.

Rockefeller Foundation. *President's Review & Annual Report 1970.* New York: The Rockefeller Foundation. https://tinyurl.com/43pxe6nw.

Rockefeller Foundation. *President's Ten-Year Review & Annual Report 1971.* New York: Rockefeller Foundation. https://tinyurl.com/3dpa4hb5.

Rodin, Judith. "The Legacy of Citizen Jane." Rockefeller Foundation, November 16, 2016. https://www.rockefellerfoundation.org/blog/the-legacy-of-citizen-jane/.

Ross, Nancy L. "On Wall Street, Former Yippie Stages First Financial Hurrah." *The Washington Post*, April 12, 1981. https://tinyurl.com/v6y22wh6.

Rubin, Jerry. "The Yuppie America's Economic Savior . . . Former Anti-War Activist Jerry Rubin Now Preaches the Gospel of Yuppiedom, Claiming that Yuppies are Responsible for America's Good Economy." *Sun Sentinel*, October 19, 1985. https://tinyurl.com/mry2teud.

Russell, Francis H. "Toward a Stronger World Organization." *U.S. Department of State Bulletin*, XXIII, August 7, 1950.

Salpukis, Agis. "Era Closes with Bankers Club." *The New York Times*, February 3, 1979. https://tinyurl.com/t536pkv8.

Sattler, Dieter. "Philosophers Beat Hitler." *Jewish Voice from Germany*, July 4, 2016. https://tinyurl.com/mued5en7.

"Saul David Alinsky." *RF Illustrated* 1, no. 1 (October 1972): 3.

Schett, Benjamin. "Europe's Pro-War Leftists: Selling 'Humanitarian Intervention,'" *Global Research*, September 21, 2012. https://tinyurl.com/y2t6aw34.

Scranton, William W. *The Report of the President's Commission on Campus Unrest.* Washington, DC: US Printing Office, 1970. https://tinyurl.com/38xbd58p.

"See French Embargo on Wart Materiel as Move to Weaken Israel, Win Arab Favor." *Jewish Telegraphic Agency*, January 8, 1969. https://tinyurl.com/4p4uxsmw.

Seidenbaum, Art. "Portrait of a Young Man Being a Revolutionary." *Los Angeles Times*, November 13, 1968. https://tinyurl.com/bdf8mhbh.

Severo, Richard. "James Farmer, Civil Rights Giant in the 50's and 60's, Is Dead at 79." *The New York Times*, July 10, 1999. https://tinyurl.com/ys7ftmps.

Sheehan, Neil. "Foundations Linked to C.I.A. are Found to Subsidize 4 Other Youth Organizations." *The New York Times*, February 16, 1967.

Siaya, Laura, and Fred M. Hayward. *Mapping Internationalization on U.S. Campuses.* Washington DC: American Council on Education, Funded by the Ford Foundation, 2003. https://tinyurl.com/mrx9nrpd.

Sloane, Leonard. "Business People; Jerry Rubin Plans Firm." *The New York Times*, August 3, 1981. https://tinyurl.com/mr2r4khf.

Smiley, Joseph R. *Fifth Annual Report of the U.S. Advisory Commission on International Education and Cultural Affairs.* Washington, DC: US Government Printing Office, 1968. https://tinyurl.com/2pjcaaru.

Smith, David E. "The Evolution of Culture-Culture Street Drug Analysis Program." In Joan A. Marshman, ed. *International Symposium on Alcohol & Drug Addiction.* Toronto: University of Toronto, 1974.

Smith, Eric. "What Would Peace in Vietnam Mean for You as an Investor? Business Executives and the Antiwar Movement 1967–75." In John and Phillips-Fein. *Capital Gains: Business and Politics in Twentieth-Century America.* Philadelphia, University of Pennsylvania Press, 2017.

Smith, J. Y. "Andre Meyer, N.Y. Investment Banker, Philanthropist, Dies." *The Washington Post*, September 11, 1979. https://tinyurl.com/mref8cy9.

Snitow, Ann. "Sex and Socialism." *Monthly Review*, February 1, 2020. https://monthlyreview.org/2020/02/01/sex-and-socialism/.

Snow, Crocker, Jr. "World Image of U.S. at Lowest Ebb." *Globe*, November 2, 1969. https://tinyurl.com/bd5nhcs9.

Solomon, Norman. "With Great Respect for Tom Hayden, I Gotta Say: His Support for Hillary Clinton Makes Less and Less Sense the More He Tries to Explain It." *Huffpost*, June 2, 2016. https://tinyurl.com/2zrcph5n.

Sontheimer, Michael. "RAF Wie sich Rudolf Augstein und Ulrike Meinhof näherkame." *Der Spiegel*, May 15, 2017. https://tinyurl.com/2jz5w3xn.

Spak, Anthony. "On this day in 1969, Elektra Records drops MC5 for attack ad on Hudson's." *Detroit Metro Times*, April 16, 2018. https://tinyurl.com/msn8k9j4.

Sportès, Morgan. "LE MAI 1968 dont les médias n'ont pas voulu parle." Comite Valmy, October 24, 2017. https://tinyurl.com/mr4a7nxy.

"'Spiegel'-Gründer Augstein nterstützte Dutschke finanziell." *Frankfurter Allgemaine*, July 27, 2018. https://tinyurl.com/3b93yh4b.

"Stanford Workshops on Political and Social Issues (SWOPSI)" 1960s, Activism @ Stanford. Accessed August 16, 2023. https://tinyurl.com/yuuf3mhz.

Stern, Sol. "A Short Account of International Student Politics & the Cold War, with Particular Reference to the NSA, CIA etc." *Ramparts*, (March 1967): 29–38. https://www.cambridgeclarion.org/press_cuttings/ramparts_mar1967.html.

Stern, Sol. "American Turncoat: The Meaning of Tom Hayden's Life." *City Journal*, November 4, 2016. https://www.city-journal.org/article/american-turncoat.

Stern, Sol. "The *Ramparts* I Watched." *City Journal*, Winter 2010. https://www.city-journal.org/html/ramparts-i-watched-13251.html.

Subversive Involvement in Disruption of 1968 Democratic Party National Convention Part I, Before the Committee on Un-American Activities House of Representative. 90th Con. (1968). https://tinyurl.com/37r225ys.

Szasz, Thomas S. "The Shame of Medicine: The Case of General Edwin Walker." Foundation for Economic Education, September 23, 2009. https://tinyurl.com/2eu7a7bu.

Tanenbaum, Laura. "Ann Snitow (1943–2019)." *Jacobin*, August 17, 2019. https://jacobinmag.com/2019/08/ann-snitow-obituary.

Tax-Exempt Foundations, Before the Special Committee to Investigate Tax-Exempt Foundations and Comparable Organizations House of Representatives, 83rd Con. 1016–1050 (1954) (statement of H. Rowan Gaither, Jr., President and Trustee, Ford Foundation). https://tinyurl.com/2n87yd2y.

Tax-Exempt Foundations, Report of the Special Committee to Investigate Tax-Exempt Foundations and Comparable Organizations House of Representatives, 83rd Con. 110–114 (1954) (The Fund for the Republic). https://tinyurl.com/2n87yd2y.

Tax Reform 1969, Before the Committee on Ways and Means House of Representatives, 91st Con. 865 (1969) (statement of David R. Jones, Executive Director, Young Americans for Freedom, Inc.). https://tinyurl.com/yuasvzb5.

Testimony of Karl Dietrich Wolff, Before the Subcommittee to Investigate the Administration of the Internal Security Act and Other Internal Security Laws of the Committee on the Judiciary United States Senate. 91st Con. (1969). https://tinyurl.com/jz9dpxzf.

Thurmond, Strom. "Elizabeth Osth's Commentaries on the New Left." *Congressional Record – Senate*, Vol. 113, Part 25, December 4, 1967. https://tinyurl.com/mrx32s9j.

Tirella, Joseph. "A Gun to the Heart of the City." *Slate*, April 22, 2014. https://tinyurl.com/2fy32xk7.

Turner, William W. "Some Disturbing Parallels." *Ramparts*, (January 1968): 33–36. https://tinyurl.com/ycywhwzx.

Unterberger, Richie. "The Plastic People of the Universe." Accessed August 16, 2023. http://www.richieunterberger.com/ppu.html.

Vandenberg, Bill. "Raising New Voices in the 2010 Election." Open Society Foundations, November 1, 2010. https://tinyurl.com/yc74vy4y.

Velinger, Jan. "Paul Wilson—the Impact of the Plastic People on a Communist Universe." *Radio Prague International*, May 31, 2005. https://tinyurl.com/33cndk4h.

Waddell, Ray. "40 years later, Woodstock a thriving business." *Reuters*, August 15, 2009. https://tinyurl.com/2p936msj.

Walker, Darren. "Old Money, New Order: American Philanthropies and the Defense of Liberal Democracy." *Foreign Affairs* 97, no. 6 (November/December 2018): 158–67. https://www.jstor.org/stable/26797941.

Washington, George. "Farewell Address." September 19, 1796.

Wasson, R. Gordon. "Seeking the Magic Mushroom." *Life*, (May 13, 1957): 100–146. https://tinyurl.com/mwr4d3zn.

Wasson, Valentina P. "I Ate the Sacred Mushroom." *This Week*, May 19, 1957. https://tinyurl.com/2fdye96j.

Watts, W. L. "Taylor Fascinates Audience on War, Peace, and Education." *Tech Talk* 21, no. 5 (November 13, 1969): 1. https://tinyurl.com/bdcjd6wj.

Weisberg, Harold. Harold Weisberg to JDW: Hinckle/Ramparts. December 21, 1974. The Weisberg Archive, Beneficial-Hodson Library, Hood College. https://tinyurl.com/4acrvjvz.

Welsh, David, and David Lifton. "The Case for Three Assassins: A Special Report." *Ramparts*, (June 1966): 77–100. https://tinyurl.com/y46eym4r.

Whitcombe, Elizabeth. "Adorno as Critic: Celebrating the Socially Destructive Force of Music." *The Occidental Observer*, August 28, 2009. https://tinyurl.com/5xr5er6x.

Widmann, Arno. "Mit diesem Personal war keine Revolution zu Machen." *Frankfurter Rundschau*, January 5, 2019. https://tinyurl.com/bdshata7.

Wiener, Jon. "Eugene McCarthy: 1916–2005." *The Nation*, April 15, 2004. https://tinyurl.com/yzdtam6u.

"Wiesenthal Says 'Zionist Plot' Alleged by Opponents of Czech Reform in Spring." Jewish Telegraphic Agency, August 28, 1968. https://tinyurl.com/3mha5bf4.

Willie, Lois. "Alinksy Plans Militant Tactics School." *Chicago Daily News*, August 6, 1968.

Willsher, Kim. "May 1968 was a revolution—now the violence is just frightening." *The Guardian*, December 8, 2018. https://tinyurl.com/tf7kuufx.

Wolfe, Tom. "Phil Spector: First Tycoon of Teen." *New York Herald Tribune*, January 3, 1965.

"Woodstock." *This Day in Music*, September 10, 2018. https://www.thisdayinmusic.com/liner-notes/woodstock/

World Assembly of Youth: International Organization of Non-Communist Youth, The. Department of State, Office of Intelligence Research, OIR Report No. 5256, August 10, 1950.

"World Government Visions in U.S." *Newsweek*, October 14, 1946.

Yoder, Jon A. "The United World Federalists: Liberals for Law and Order." *American Studies* 13, no. 1 (Spring 1972): 109–129. http://www.jstor.org/stable/40641065.

"Youth: The Hippies." *Time*, July 7, 1967. https://tinyurl.com/5bmpnkp3.

Zhukov, Yury. "Werewolves—on the False Prophet Marcuse and his Vociferous Disciples." *Pravda*, 30 May 1968.

ABOUT THE AUTHOR

Kerry Bolton has been widely published on a variety of subjects in scholarly and specialized media, and has served as a peer reviewer for several journals. His books include:

Artists of the Right (two volumes)
Revolution from Above
The Parihaka Cult
The Banking Swindle
Opposing the Money Lenders
Peron and Peronism
Stalin: The Enduring Legacy
Geopolitics of the Indo-Pacific
Babel Inc.
The Occult and Subversive Movements
Zionism, Islam and The West
The Decline and Fall of Civilisations
Russia and the Fight Against Globalisation
Yockey: A Fascist Odyssey
The Perversion of Normality
The Tyranny of Human Rights

ENJOYED THIS BOOK?

TO READ MORE, VISIT US AT

ANTELOPEHILLPUBLISHING.COM

www.ingramcontent.com/pod-product-compliance
Lightning Source LLC
Chambersburg PA
CBHW020428130626
46549CB00001B/27